FIROR, RUTH ANITA. Folkways in Thomas
Hardy. 357p $3 Press of the Univ. of Pa. [12s
6d Oxford]

823　Hardy, Thomas.　Folklore—England.
Dorset, England—Social life and customs
31-25191

A study of the folk-lore and folk customs in
Hardy's novels and poems. Contents: Omens,
premonitions, and fatality; Divination; Ghost
and fairy lore; Magic and witchcraft; Folk-
medicine; Weather lore and the language of
country things; Seasonal festivals and customs;
Sports and pastimes; Folk-songs, country-
dances, and folk-drama; Folk wit and wisdom;
Folk-law; Prehistory and survivals of ancient
religions; Medieval legends and Napoleonana;
Hardy's use of folklore and folk-custom. Bibliography. Index.

Booklist 28:142 D '31

"For the most part Miss Firor sticks with
reasonable closeness to her theme of folkways
in Hardy; and her illustrations of each quaint
credulity and grim belief make fascinating reading. . . She has accomplished a book of two-fold
appeal: to all lovers of Thomas Hardy and to
everyone interested in the quaint and curious
customs and credulities, now fast vanishing, of
the immemorial folk."　S. C. Chew
　　+ Books p20 O 4 '31 650w

"Miss Firor, by bringing together all of the
evidence that Hardy was saturated in the popular lore of his native country, not only clarifies
our image of him as an artist but in a sense
builds a new man for criticism henceforth to
deal with. Further studies will be made of
Hardy, but all of them will have to take account of Miss Firor's distinguished contribu-
tion."
　　+ Nation 133:466 O 28 '31 80w

" 'Folkways in Thomas Hardy' is a fascinating exegesis. The author not only brings to
light the rich folk-backgrounds of the novels,
poems, and tales, but she has put together in
an engaging manner a folk-book that may be
read for its own inherent interest without reference to the works from which it springs. But
most readers will wish to keep it close to
Hardy. If this is done, the great Wessex novelist becomes even more profoundly human in
his sympathies and his readings of life, although one would scarcely have thought this
possible."　Percy Hutchison
　　+ N Y Times p18 O 18 '31 900w

Pittsburgh Mo Bul 36:77 N '31

"Regarded simply as a study of Hardy, there
is bound to be a disproportion in a book which
concentrates on this one side of him and is,
hardly less, a study of folk-lore; but Miss Firor
shows a sensitive appreciation of him as a poet
and man whenever she allows herself a general
comment, and she has worked out her own
theme in a way that gives his art a fresh il-
lumination. An accumulation like this of all
Hardy's uses of omens and divination, folk-
medicine and magic, folk-law and custom, is
surprising even now in its rich fertility."
　　+ Times [London] Lit Sup p772 O 8 '31

FOLKWAYS IN THOMAS HARDY

London: Humphrey Milford: Oxford University Press

Folkways
in
THOMAS HARDY

by

Ruth A. Firor

1931

UNIVERSITY OF PENNSYLVANIA PRESS

Philadelphia

Copyright *1931*
UNIVERSITY OF PENNSYLVANIA PRESS
Printed in the United States of America

TO
Cornelius Weygandt

PREFACE

A GREAT deal has been written about Thomas Hardy's philosophy and reading of life. Lionel Johnson has said the last word on Hardy's art as a novelist, and we can only regret that we do not have from his pen a similar study of Hardy's poetry. As I read and reread my Hardy, the thought came to me that Hardy's roots go deep in the soil; that he was influenced, not only by the physiognomy of Wessex and a familiarity with Wessex peasant life in its more evident, external features, but also by a profound spiritual sympathy with the land and the people. Bits of folklore like the telling of the bees and folk-customs like the dreaded Skimmity began to take shape and pattern in my groping thought. At last I realized that, in a very true sense, Hardy had worked with a collaborator—the folk; that a study of the folklore and the folk-custom of his people might throw light on his subtle art and much mooted reading of life. If the present study should prove helpful to the student of Hardy here or there, its aim would be accomplished. It has already rewarded me richly.

It was my good fortune at the University of Pennsylvania to know a man who is as accomplished a folklorist as he is scholar, critic, and essayist. Dr. Cornelius Weygandt shared with me his wide knowledge of Pennsylvania Dutch folklore and folk-custom. His cordial encouragement made the necessary taskwork almost easy; his admirable judgment again and again brought my findings back to their goal— the study of Hardy's use of folklore.

I am also grateful to Dr. Clarence Griffin Child, of the University of Pennsylvania, whose amazing erudition suggested several important lines of research to me, and to Dr. James A. Montgomery, also of the University, who cleared up a vexed question which only a skilled Orientalist could pronounce upon. Mr. T. H. Tilley, the Honorable Stage Manager of the Dorchester Dramatic and Debating Society, generously sent me programs of the Hardy Players' 1923 presentation of the Play of Saint George, *O Jan! O Jan! O Jan!,* and *The Queen of Cornwall,* and wrote me in some detail as to his reminiscences of the performance.

I am indebted to the Macmillan Company for permission to quote from their editions of Hardy's poetical works, *The Collected Poems, The Queen of Cornwall,* and *The Dynasts;* and to Harper and Brothers for their generosity in permitting me to quote, almost without cuts, long passages from the novels and tales.

To my brother, Frederick Leonard Firor, and my colleague, Professor Charles Marston Lee, I am grateful for their patient assistance in the reading of proof.

Ruth A. Firor

CONTENTS

Let Me Enjoy

Let me enjoy the earth no less
Because the all-enacting Might
That fashioned forth its loveliness
Had other aims than my delight.

About my path there flits a Fair,
Who throws me not a word or sign;
I'll charm me with her ignoring air,
And laud the lips not meant for mine.

From manuscripts of moving song
Inspired by scenes and dreams unknown,
I'll pour out raptures that belong
To others, as they were my own.

And some day hence, towards Paradise
And all its blest—if such should be—
I will lift glad, afar-off eyes,
Though it contain no place for me.

I
OMENS, PREMONITIONS, AND FATALITY

~~~~~~

Omens and premonitions play a large part in the fortunes of Hardy's people. Certain times, places, and weather have a fatality of their own. A well marked streak of ill luck follows Elfride, Tess, and Eustacia Vye; Jude Fawley and Sue Bridehead are victims of a predisposition to failure and unhappiness. Certain families have unmistakable death-warnings; Nelson and the Duke of Brunswick foresee the hour of their death. Omens often occur in premonitory dreams, but are more likely to happen as a set of curious accidents or sheer coincidence which, to the mind of the superstitious, have the force of veritable causes. The attitude of Hardy's folk toward the future is sometimes eager and hopeful, or, as with Henchard, a stubborn determination to know the worst the future has in store. The belief that "What will be, will be" runs all through the novels and poems; it is one source of the quiet, undemonstrative courage with which many of Hardy's characters face whatever comes to them. The spectacle of human patience and sweetness invariably moves the poet to pity: and there are moments in *The Dynasts* when man seems most helpless in the tangled web of circumstance that utter Hardy's proud conviction that man must somehow triumph over all the violence and cruel irony of senseless things. There is more radiance in this rare mood of the poet than in volumes of facile optimism. On the whole, however, Hardy's use of omens accentuates the gloomy tinge of his mind, and would sometimes be almost too painful were it not for his abundant sympathy with all that "lives and moves and has its being."

We shall expect to find rather few omens of unmixed good fortune in Hardy. Among a large number of sinister omens, these omens of good luck stand out brightly. There is the swarming of the bees just before Dick Dewy's wedding; the "letter in the candle" seen but not heeded by Miller Loveday; and the luck of the caul and of the last comer, in both of which Christian Cantle places his timid dependence.

A most delightful token of good luck is the swarming of the bees just before Dick Dewy's wedding to Fancy Day. Fancy was on the verge of tears as Dick failed to appear, and both Reuben and Grandfather James plied her with tales of bridegrooms who missed their weddings. Just then Nat Callcome, the best man, burst into the room with his story: the new hive of bees Dick's mother had given him had swarmed just as he was starting out; and Dick, vowing that Fancy wouldn't wish him to lose a stock of bees, had stopped to ting to them and shake them. There were expressions of approval at this news, overheard by Dick, who entered, flustered and full of apologies:

"That my bees should have swarmed just then, of all times and seasons! . . . And 'tis a fine swarm, too: I haven't seen such a fine swarm for these ten years."

"An excellent sign," said Mrs. Penny. . . .

"Well, bees can't be put off," observed grandfather James. "Marrying a woman is a thing you can do at any moment; but a swarm of bees won't come for the asking." [1]

The belief is widespread that a stolen or stray swarm, that is, any swarm not formally purchased, is lucky.[2] Things found, begged, or stolen, are lucky; in finding things, the favor of fortune comes into play; to things begged the

[1] *Under the Greenwood Tree,* Part V, Chap. I.
[2] G. H. Kinahan, *Folk-Lore Record,* IV, 97; Rev. Walter Gregor, *Notes on the Folk-Lore of the North-East of Scotland,* p. 147; John Brand, *Popular Antiquities of Great Britain,* Sir Henry Ellis, ed., II, 300–301.

labor, and to things stolen the risk of acquisition, lends additional value.[3] A contradictory opinion is that a stray swarm alighting on a house, hedge or tree means bad luck—fire, perhaps,[4] a death in the family within the year,[5] or some undefined disaster. Pliny describes the panic in Drusus' camp at this omen.[6] Bees have an elaborate folklore. This is not the place for a study of bees as messengers of the gods and part of the cult of the sacred oak.[7] Folklore, however, notes the uncanny supernatural knowledge of the future which bees possess, and their deep affection for their masters—a fact revealed in the custom of "telling the bees" of the death of the bee-master.[8] Bee culture is shrouded in superstition: some say that bees will not thrive for those who lead an unchaste life, and that they fare best with man and wife;[9] others that partners in bee-keeping should not be married;[10] all agree that one person alone has no success.[11]

There is another possible reason why the swarming of the bees at Dick's wedding was held lucky; a familiar English rhyme runs:

> A swarm of bees in May is worth a load of hay;
> A swarm of bees in June is worth a silver spoon;
> A swarm of bees in July is not worth a fly.[12]

Dick's wedding, as he himself told Maybold, was set for Midsummer; but the season Hardy describes might be May. But let us hope what is more probable and more auspicious, that the wedding came in June; for however lucky "a swarm

[3] J. Grimm, *Deutsche Mythologie,* Stallybrass, trans. III, 1137–1138.
[4] Grimm-Stallybrass, *Deutsche Mythologie,* III, 1136; Lady Camilla Gurdon, *The Folk-Lore of Suffolk,* p. 6.
[5] Elizabeth Mary Wright, *Rustic Speech and Folklore,* p. 216; Gurdon, *op. cit.,* pp. 6–7.
[6] Grimm-Stallybrass, III, 1136.
[7] Rendel Harris: *The Ascent of Olympus,* pp. 1–3; *Picus Who Is Also Zeus,* 52–56; G. L. Gomme, *Ethnology in Folklore,* p. 127, Note 2.
[8] N. Thomas, *Folk-Lore of Northumberland,* p. 12.
[9] Gregor, *op. cit.,* p. 147.
[10] Thomas, *loc. cit.*
[11] *loc. cit.*
[12] C. J. Billson, *Folk-Lore of Leicestershire,* p. 146.

of bees in May," the month has an evil name for everything else from May kittens to May weddings! [13] An old song goes, "May was never the month of Love." [14] And so, remembering the song of the nightingale, and Fancy's resolve to have no secrets from Dick from that day, let us leave them jogging happily down the road in their new spring-cart.[15]

Another omen of good fortune is the "letter in the candle" which appeared to Miller Loveday. A letter from his son John had been lying at the post office for three days; when told about it, the miller exclaimed,

"Ah, now I call to mind that there was a letter in the candle three days ago this very night—a large, red one; but foolish-like I thought nothing o't." [16]

The "letter" is a bright spark visible within the body of the flame, and is caused by the irregular burning of the wick. The person who sees it must thump the table; if the spark disappears immediately, the letter is in the post; if several thumps are necessary, that number of days must elapse before the letter arrives; a very large spark means a parcel! [17]

The most amusing case of a lucky omen occurs in *The Return of the Native*, in the scene where Christian Cantle is almost persuaded to dice for the gown-piece which is being raffled off at the Quiet Woman Inn. The pedlar insinuates,

"I think you might almost be sure . . . now I look in your face . . . I can say that I never saw anything look more like winning in my life."

"You'll anyhow have the same chance as the rest of us," said Sam.

"And the extra luck of being the last comer," said another.

"And I was born wi' a caul, and perhaps can be no more ruined than drowned? . . ." [18]

---

[13] E. M. Wright, *Rustic Speech and Folklore,* p. 218.
[14] Morley's *Ballets,* 1595, in *The Book of English Songs,* p. 16.
[15] *Under the Greenwood Tree,* Part V, Chap. II.
[16] *The Trumpet-Major,* Chap XII.
[17] G. E. Hadow, *Folk-Lore,* XXXV, 351; L. M. Eyre, *Folk-Lore,* XIII, 172.
[18] Book III, Chap. VII.

Hardy refers again to the belief in the lucky caul; Mark Clark, speaking of the discharged bailey in *Far from the Madding Crowd,* says of him that he is a "queer Christian 'like the Devil in a cowl.' " Hardy amends this from the meaningless rustic phrase, "As the Devil said to the Owl." The Devil in a cowl, or caul, would have more than his usual luck at card-play.[19]

The lucky caul is a world superstition; it goes back to Greek and Roman belief, but it is far older, having its roots in savage custom. It is thought to confer on one born with it health, immunity from certain dangers, like death by drowning, and success in a chosen career.[20] It also endows its possessor with the doubtful gift of second sight.[21] The Scotch term it the *sely how,* or *sillyhoo;* that is, the blessed or lucky hood.[22] The Pennsylvania Dutch say that one born with it will be a "notable man";[23] the French say of a lucky man, *Il est né coiffé.*[24]

The life of the real owner depends mysteriously upon the caul; the luck of the latter may, however, be transferred. In Suffolk they hang up the caul, keeping it carefully covered: if illness befalls the one born with it, it will "overgive," or weep; it is dry when he is well, and shrivels up at his death. The "fylgia" is thus part of the soul, or perhaps the guardian spirit.[25] After a physician's explanation of the amnion, Sir Thomas Browne ridicules the lawyers of the day who paid for cauls, thinking they "advantaged their promotion"; he disclaims for it any "magic signalities."[26] It was held to preserve sailors from drowning: *The Times*

[19] Chap. VIII.
[20] Grimm-Stallybrass, II, 874, and Note 1.
[21] W. H. Babcock, *Folk-Lore Journal,* Vol. VI, p. 93.
[22] J. G. Dalyell, *The Darker Superstitions of Scotland,* pp. 199–200.
[23] E. Fogel, *The Beliefs and Superstitions of the Pennsylvania Germans,* Proverbs 70, 141.
[24] T. Pettigrew, *On Superstitions connected with . . . Medicine and Surgery,* p. 86.
[25] John Brand, *Popular Antiquities,* Sir Henry Ellis's ed., III, p. 115; Gregor, *Notes on the Folk-Lore of the North-East of Scotland,* p. 25; N. Thomas, *Folk-Lore of Northumberland,* p. 58; Grace E. Hadow, *Folk-Lore,* XXXV, 349: Grimm-Stallybrass, II, 874 and Note 1.
[26] Sir T. Browne, *Vulgar Errors,* Book V, Chap. XXIII, Sect. 5 and Ed. Note.

contained many advertisements for cauls in the nineteenth century, and during the submarine campaign of the World War, these advertisements appeared in English papers.[27] The custom of hanging the afterbirth of calves over the byre to ensure a cow-calf the next year is identical with the Cherokee custom of hanging the navel-string of a boy baby on a forest tree to make him a great hunter.[28] The Bataks of Sumatra, the Baganda, and others preserve the placenta, believing that in it resides part of the external soul.[29] Altogether the lucky caul is one of the most direct survivals of primitive belief we possess.

As to the "extra luck of being the last comer" which is used as an inducement to Christian Cantle to try his luck with the dice, there are contradictory opinions. There is a Worcestershire proverb, "Last has luck; found a penny in the muck." [30] But the unpopularity of the last bit of edible, "the morsel for manners" left on the dish, which the Chinese call the "poison piece," and the dislike of the last card dealt, all point to a sort of "devil's portion," which may have originated in the old custom of saving the last of the food and drink for the gods.[31]

Omens of general ill luck are as follows: Stumbling; the gift of hair; bad weather on a wedding day, changing the date for a wedding, or being married on a Friday; cockcrow at an unusual hour, especially afternoon cockcrow; the belief, "No moon, no man!"; the appearance of a comet; and other omens which are more commonly interpreted as death omens proper.

At the opening of the final part of *The Dynasts*, Napoleon's horse stumbled and threw him. The Spirit of the Years spoke:

---

[27] T. J. Pettigrew, *On Superstitions connected with Medicine*, p. 86; J. G. Dalyell, *Darker Superstitions of Scotland*, p. 200; *Folk-Lore*, XXVIII, 99–100, quoting *The London Times*, March 5, 1917.

[28] Brand, III, 119; J. Aubrey's *Remaines of Gentilisme and Judaisme*, p. 73; James Frazer, *The Golden Bough*, ed. 1922, p. 40.

[29] Frazer, *loc. cit.*

[30] V. S. Lean, *Collectanea*, Vol. II, Pt. II, p. 41.

[31] V. S. Lean, *op. cit.*, Vol. II, Pt. II, pp. 41, 151; N. B. Dennys, *The Folk-Lore of China*, p. 65.

> *"The portent is an ill one, Emperor;*
> *An ancient Roman would retire thereat!"*

Napoleon demanded:

> "Whose voice was that, jarring upon my thought
> So insolently? . . ."

Haxel and the others replied in haste:

> "Sire, we spoke no word."

And Napoleon's old spirit asserted itself, in the defiant cry:

> "Then, whoso spake, such portents I defy!"[32]

Every incident attending the beginning of a journey was held significant among the Romans, who thought stumbling an appalling omen, and punished severely the augur who stumbled in the performance of his sacred office.[33] Meetings that presage a lucky or unlucky journey or enterprise are included in the Teutonic term of *angang*.[34] Spenser, Milton, Congreve, and Hall refer to the bad luck of stumbling.[35] When a Sumatran chief stumbles, he abandons his journey; if a Pennsylvania Dutch pallbearer stumbles at a funeral, it is held a sign of some one's speedy death.[36] Strange to say, an actor's stumbling is thought lucky![37] There is one case in history when stumbling was lucky— for the stumbler: William the Bastard tripped as he stepped on English soil![38] On the whole, however, the following story shows pretty clearly folk-belief on this score: An old fellow of eighty-six said to a writer in *Folk-Lore*, "I did go a walloper today, an' th' old lady shruk out fit to bring the place down"; and "the old lady" replied, "I don't like

[32] *The Dynasts,* Part Third, Act I, Scene I.
[33] Aubrey's *Remaines,* 20, 26, 32, 56, 60; Ellis's Brand, III, 249; Grimm-Stallybrass, I, 70, Note 4.
[34] Grimm-Stallybrass, III, 1117.
[35] Ellis's Brand, III, 249; Aubrey's *Remaines,* 26.
[36] Frazer, *Folk-Lore,* I, 155–56; Fogel, *The Beliefs and Superstitions of the Pennsylvania Germans,* Proverbs 324, 573.
[37] W. G. Black, *Folk-Lore Record,* II, p. 204.
[38] *Saxo-Grammaticus,* ed. York-Powell, Intro., p. lxxix.

folks to fall about. You can never tell what that mean." [39]
We shall see other cases of "angang" later in the chapter.

The heroine of *Desperate Remedies,* Cytherea Graye, has
unwillingly set the day for her marriage to Manston on
Old Christmas Day; thinking it is a Friday, she hastily
changes it, only to learn that the new date is this unlucky
day, but lets it stand in the belief that to change it will
be more inauspicious than to be married on a Friday. After
a night of broken sleep, she awakes to find Knapwater in the
grip of a sleet storm. The whole household feel the ominous
threat of the savage weather. The marriage, however, is
celebrated, with what gloomy results the reader recalls:
Manston is a bigamist and a madman; only "desperate
remedies" effect Cytherea's release from her terrible situation.[40]

Hardy refers to the prophetic character of wedding-day
weather in the poem, "The Country Wedding"; the weather
was beautiful but changeful:

> Little fogs were gathered in every hollow,
> But the purple hillocks enjoyed fine weather
> As we marched with our fiddles over the heather
> —How it comes back!—to their wedding that day. [41]

The fiddlers insisted on preceding the bridal pair, contrary
to village custom, and made so madly merry that the bride
cried in alarm,

> "Too gay! Clouds may gather, and sorrow come." [41]

A year later the band are burying the wedded pair, on a
day like the first, half hazy, half bright.[41]

The saying, "Blest is the bride the sun shines on," immortalized in the *Hesperides,* is familiar all over Christendom.[42] The Pennsylvania Dutch proverb runs: "Wi der
dak as mer heirt, so di familie. Wann regert brot mern
schtrübliche familie (di fra muss fil heile); wanns schtaermt

[39] Mrs. C. M. Hood, *Folk-Lore,* XXXVII, 370.
[40] Chap. XIII.
[41] *Late Lyrics:* "The Country Wedding."
[42] Brand, II, 152; W. Henderson, *Folklore of the Northern Counties,* p. 34.

fechte die leit fil; is der hie henker los": "As the weather
on the wedding day, so the married life. Rain . . . fore-
shadows trouble and sorrow; storm, quarrel, or the devil
to pay." They do not postpone weddings, either.[43]

Friday is the most famous of "Egyptian days," as unlucky days have been termed all the way down from late
classical through medieval medicine, and as days of witchcraft are still called in Yorkshire.[44] Yet Friday is a day
of good repute in modern folk-medicine, however ill-omened
for all else.[45] On Friday witches and fairies are abroad:
the Pennsylvania Dutch say, "If you talk of witches on
Friday, do it under your own roof and be sure to mention
the day." [46] As spirits dislike iron it is the part of wisdom
to refrain from ploughing and even grave-digging on Friday.[47] Friday is *not* the day on which to visit a sick friend or
begin a journey, especially on sea; [48] to begin any new enterprise or even to cut hay! [49] Its reputation as a wedding day
varies: in the Scottish Lowlands, it is a favorite; in the
Highlands, unlucky; and a Northumbrian and Sussex saying
runs, Let not Friday be your wedding day, or you and your
wife will lead a cat-and-dog life.[50] Thor's day, Tiw's Day,
and Sunday are favorites in Teutonic lore.[51] Friday's ill
repute has been fancifully accounted for as resulting from
the fact that it was the day of the Crucifixion, or the day
when Eve ate the fatal apple! [52]

[43] Fogel, *op. cit.,* Proverbs 220, 234.
[44] J. F. Payne, *English Medicine in Anglo-Saxon Times,* 20–21; Brand, II,
47, 152, 167; Gutch, *The Folk-Lore of Yorkshire,* p. 218.
[45] W. G. Black, *Folk-Medicine,* p. 133.
[46] *Denham Tracts,* II, 84; Fogel, Proverb 1295.
[47] J. G. Campbell, *Witchcraft and Second Sight in the Scottish Highlands,*
p. 298.
[48] Campbell, *op. cit.,* p. 298; C. Latham, *Folk-Lore Record,* Vol. I, p. 13;
Denham Tracts, Vol. II, pp. 342–44.
[49] *Denham Tracts,* II, 342–44; Wm. Henderson, *Folk-Lore of the Northern
Counties,* p. 33; Brand, II, 48; W. Gregor, *Notes on the Folk-Lore of the
North-East of Scotland,* p. 148; N. Thomas, *Folk-Lore of Northumberland,*
p. 60; C. Latham, *Folk-Lore Record,* Vol. I, p. 13; Lady Gurdon, *Folk-Lore
of Suffolk,* p. 129.
[50] Campbell, *Witchcraft and Second Sight* . . . 299; Wm. Henderson, *Folk-
Lore of the Northern Counties,* p. 33; C. Latham, *F. L. Record,* I, 13.
[51] Grimm-Stallybrass, III, 1138–39; IV, 1278.
[52] Wm. Henderson, *Folk-Lore of the Northern Counties,* p. 33.

There is a charming scene in *A Pair of Blue Eyes* where Elfride, debating with herself as to what gift she shall make her fastidious betrothed, rejects the romantic idea of a lock of her hair, for hair is unlucky.[53] None of Elfride's frailties is more captivating than this bit of superstition: we almost see the girl at her mirror, looking absently at her own image, her great blue eyes filled with fine feminine calculation and a shadow of worry lest Knight will not approve her choice. Her utterly impulsive and timid nature makes her Knight's natural victim; these little superstitions throw her tragedy into deeper relief, but sometimes light it with a gleam of ironic humor. To send or accept the gift of a lock of hair is fatal to lovers.[54] The belief has a very primitive origin.

The elaborate rules prescribed by Varro, Pliny, and Petronius as to cutting the hair and beard of the Flamen Dialis, and for the care of the combings of the Vestal Virgins, and the severe dressing of the Roman bride's hair, reveal a powerful taboo—a taboo in which the fear of offending the spirit in the hair is revealed as well as the bit of sympathetic magic which fears black witchcraft, wrought by some enemy who has secured a part of the possessor's external soul![55] At Tubber Quan in Ireland is a holy well, where many sufferers from headache claim to have been cured; the trees nearby are full of hair to which the disease has been transferred.[56] Agnes Sampsoun was a sixteenth-century witch who was shaved to induce confession.[57] From the savages of Polynesia to the Scottish Highlands we find the use of hair to work black magic upon the possessor.[58] Hair was originally substituted for human sacrifice to the gods.[59] The superstition is familiar that if combings or

[53] Chap. XXX.
[54] V. S. Lean, *Collectanea,* Vol. II, Part 1, p. 80.
[55] Browne, *Vulgar Errors,* Book V, Chap. XXIII, Sect. 10; Aubrey's *Remaines,* 196; W. R. Halliday, *Greek and Roman Folklore,* pp. 39, 62–63; Frazer, *Golden Bough,* 231; Wimberly, 68, 72.
[56] Pettigrew, *op. cit.,* pp. 39–40.
[57] Dalyell, *Darker Superstitions,* 638.
[58] C. L. Wimberly, *Folklore in the English and Scottish Ballads,* 71–72.
[59] Dalyell, *op. cit.,* p. 181.

cuttings are built into birds' nests, the owner will suffer from headache.[60] There is an elaborate ritual for combing and cutting hair, beard, and nails, revealing a primitive taboo; [61] and to dream of losing one's hair is a sign of the loss of health or friends.[62]

The afternoon Tess was married, the cock crowed three times; all the dairy folk and Tess herself felt that it boded ill. Crick "hooshed" the cock away, then fell to musing:

"Now, to think of that just to-day! I've not heard him crow of an afternoon all the year afore." [63]

Hours later Kail brought Tess and Clare the word that Retty had tried to drown herself, and Marian had drunk herself into a stupor. The superstitious old fellow was quick to remind them of the sinister afternoon cockcrow.

Introduced from Persia, the cock was sacrificed to Æsculapius, god of medicine; all through the Middle Ages physicians administered drugs by cockcrow.[64] St. Chrysostom rebuked the superstitious man who thought himself "undone by the crowing of a cock." [65] It is likely that the cock acquired his prophetic character from the fact that, as one of the earliest announcers of time, he was expected to be regular. But he plays a rôle in the world of ghosts: his crow at midnight was a sort of "Get ready!" to wandering spirits of the night, and his crow at daybreak was a command to go.[66] The clever early churchmen put the pagan cock on Christian steeples as a symbol that the clergy must be eternally vigilant, and that they, too, had power to drive out

[60] Gregor, *Notes on the Folk-Lore of the North-East of Scotland*, p. 26; C. Latham, *Folk-Lore Record*, I, 44; Fogel, *op. cit.*, Proverbs 1812, 1824, 1825.
[61] G. H. Kinahan, *Folk-Lore Record*, IV, 124; Fogel, Proverbs 1815, 1820, 1826, 1828; J. G. Campbell, *Superstitions of the Scottish Highlands*, pp. 236–37.
[62] J. Harland and T. T. Wilkinson, *Lancashire Folklore* . . . p. 147.
[63] *Tess of the d'Urbervilles*, Chaps. XXXIII, XXXIV.
[64] Dalyell, 420; Aubrey's *Remaines*, 196; R. Harris, *The Ascent of Olympus*, p. 20.
[65] Henderson, *Folk-Lore of the Northern Counties*, p. 5; Homily on Eph. IV, 17.
[66] C. L. Wimberly, *Folklore in the English and Scottish Ballads*, pp. 31, 104, 248 ff.

evil spirits! [67] Who but remembers the prophetic cockcrow
when Peter had thrice denied his Master? Cockcrow at an
unusual time is almost universally held ominous.[68] The
Pennsylvania Dutch have a witty proverb which runs in
English, "One cock crows, it is good to be here; the other,
don't crow, it won't last long." [69] The Scotch have the most
picturesque form of this superstition: they say the cock pre-
sages death only if his legs are cold, and it is coming from
the direction in which he faces. To avert the danger one
must make a martyr of the unfortunate prophet.[70] A
traveler in Wessex a quarter of a century ago heard an
old woman exclaim against the cock who crowed after twelve
o'clock noon, on the grounds that this meant that her man
John was ill again.[71]

In *The Return of the Native* Christian Cantle was lamenting the fact that he was the man no woman would marry,
only the "rames" of a man. He feared this was because he
was born at an ill-omened hour when there was no moon:

". . . Do ye really think it serious, Mister Fairway, that there
was no moon?"

"Yes; 'No moon, no man.' 'Tis one of the truest sayings ever spit
out. . . . A bad job for thee, Christian, that you should have
showed your nose then of all days in the month."

"I suppose the moon was terrible full when you were born?" asked
Christian, with a look of helpless admiration at Fairway.

"Well, 'a was not new,' Mr. Fairway replied . . ." [72]

The belief that the moon affects plant and animal life
is as old as Aristotle and Galen, and much older.[73] The
Scotch preserve eggs laid in the wane, saying that hens come
from them, and vice versa; they call puny children "birds

---

[67] John Brand, II, 56–57, Ellis's ed.
[68] Dennys, *The Folklore of China,* p. 34; *Denham Tracts,* II, p. 271; Gregor,
140; J. G. Campbell, *Superstitions of the Scottish Highlands,* 257.
[69] Fogel, Proverb 310.
[70] Gregor, 140; Campbell, *Superstitions of the Scottish Highlands,* 257.
[71] Wilkinson Sherren, *The Wessex of Romance,* 27.
[72] Book I, Chap. III.
[73] Pettigrew, *On Superstitions connected with Medicine and Surgery,* p. 21.

of the increase." [74] A writer in *Folk-Lore* heard in Washington, D. C., the saying, "A child born at the full of the moon will be a boy." [75] Tusser's *Rules of Husbandry,* followed by generations of English farmers, taught:

> Cut all things or gather, the moon in the wane,
> But sow in encreasing, or give it his bane. [76]

Herbs were formerly gathered at certain set times, because under planetary influence. [77] Because anything done on a waxing moon tends to develop and vice versa, many simple practices have developed. The wane is the time to take pigs from the sow and lambs from the ewe; it is not the time to fatten poultry, or to butcher, for fear the meat will shrink or spoil. It is not, above all, the time to breed. [78] The belief that the moon may make or mar a child is but a part of a larger astrological tenet. Young Banks, in *The Witch of Edmonton,* voiced a familiar belief when he said, "When the moon's in the full, then wit's in the wane." [79] But Clarinna, "anatomizing" Crosby, exclaims scornfully: "Have you ever seen such a monster? He was begot surely in the wane of the moon!" [80] The epithet "moon-calf," that is, "misbegotten," was applied contemptuously alike to an illegitimate child, a monstrosity like Caliban, a credulous fool, and a villain. [81] We are prone to forget how short a time has passed since medical men definitely attributed lunacy and other disorders to the effect of certain phases of the moon. [82] Modern science is still carefully studying the subject.

Rustic superstition seasoned with common sense is seen in Nat Chapman's view of the comet that alarmed Haymoss:

[74] Campbell, *Witchcraft and Second Sight* . . ., p. 306.
[75] W. H. Babcock, *Folk-Lore Journal,* VI, p. 91.
[76] Lady Gurdon, *The Folk-Lore of Suffolk,* 160.
[77] Pettigrew, 21, 23.
[78] Brand, III, 150; *Folk-Lore,* II, 222; Billson, 40; Gregor, 151.
[79] Prof. Samuel C. Chew, *Thomas Hardy, Poet and Novelist,* 120; cf. Ellis's Brand, III, 145.
[80] S. Glapthorne, *The Lady Mother,* Act I, Scene III; Chew, 120.
[81] Ellis's Brand, III, 143; Grimm-Stallybrass, III, 1158–59; *The Tempest,* II, II, 114.
[82] Black, 135.

"And what do this comet mean?" asked Haymoss. "That some
great tumult is going to happen, or that we shall die of a famine?"

"Famine—no!" said Nat Chapman. "That only touches such as
we, and the Lord only consarns himself with gentlemen. It isn't to
be supposed that a strange fiery lantern like that would be lighted up
for folks with ten or a dozen shillings a week and their gristing, and
a load o' thorn faggots when we can get 'em. If 'tis a token that he's
getting hot about the ways of anybody in this parish, 'tis about my
Lady Constantine's, since she is the only one of a figure worth a
hint." [83]

Chapman's is a pagan god, one the old Romans knew:

> When beggars die, there are no comets seen;
> The heavens themselves blaze forth the death of princes . . ." [84]

There are numerous omens of death in Hardy's work.
Most frequent and impressive are the following: "the coffin-
spehl"; the breaking of a key, ring or mirror; the falling
of a portrait; the sight of one magpie; the screech of owl
or raven; a ringing in the left ear; the clock's falling or
striking crazily; a gathering of thirteen persons; the limp
corpse or the corpse that won't keep its eyes closed; the
sound of trotting does in a deserted park; the shadow on a
sundial pointing to one who is next to die; flies or bees
wearing crape scarves; rats deserting a doomed house or
ship; a sudden shiver; the sound of a bell as it "goes
heavy"; the familiar whine or howl of dogs in the presence
of death—an indication that dogs, like horses, are ghost-
seers; and the appearance of wraiths to the living. Many
premonitions are not so unmistakably defined as omens; we
shall consider the premonitory dream along with premonitions in general.

In somber contrast to Miller Loveday's delight in "the
letter in the candle," is the "coffin-spehl," a little column
of tallow left standing after most of the candle has been
consumed, fantastically like a coffin or winding shroud.
Hardy uses the omen with solemn effect in the poem, "Stand-

[83] *Two on a Tower*, Chap. XIII.
[84] *Julius Cæsar*, II, ii, 30.

ing by the Mantelpiece": The lover, estranged and utterly
out of love with life, sees the candle-wax taking the shape
of a shroud, and accepts the omen by moulding it, as he
hopes, to his fate.[85] In "She Hears the Storm," the omen
occurs again.[86] Primitive Germanic tribes called this phenomenon the "wolf in the candle," perhaps a reference to
the myth of Loki, who is some day in the shape of a wolf
to pursue and devour sun and moon.[87] The "coffin-spehl"
has struck terror to many a superstitious heart.[88]

In "Honeymoon Time at an Inn," the joy of the newly
wedded pair is rudely disturbed by the fall of a mirror;
the bride fears "long years of sorrow"; the Spirits Ironic
laugh in glee, but the Spirits of Pity declare that the portent
is one they cannot abide.[89] When Marie Louise was almost
persuaded to marry Napoleon, her portrait fell suddenly
to the floor. The Spirit of the Years questioned, "What
mischief's this? The Will must have its way." The sardonic
answer comes, "Perhaps Earth shivered at the lady's say." [90]

Breaking a mirror is interpreted variously as seven years'
bad luck [91] or the death of friend or relative.[92] Napoleon, it
is said, in alarm at breaking the glass on Josephine's portrait,
could not rest until assured that she was well.[93] Old Aubrey
is full of tales of falling portraits, scepters, and trees—
all portending death for some royal or noble person; finely
ironic is the legend, taken from Prynne's Diary, of the
falling of Laud's portrait the day the Long Parliament first
sat.[94] In 1902, in Achill, Dr. Weygandt frightened two
Irish peasants with his camera. An old Wiltshire woman

---

[85] *Winter Words.*
[86] *Time's Laughingstocks.*
[87] Grimm-Stallybrass I, 245–46.
[88] Henderson, *Folk-Lore of the Northern Counties . . .*, pp. 48–49; Gregor,
204; Sherren, *The Wessex of Romance,* 24; Ellis's Brand, III, 181; Harland
and Wilkinson, *Lancashire Folk-Lore,* p. 18; Gurdon, *The Folk-Lore of
Suffolk,* 30–31; N. Thomas, *The Folk-Lore of Northumberland,* p. 58.
[89] *Moments of Vision.*
[90] *The Dynasts,* Part Second, Act V, Scene IV.
[91] Fogel, Proverbs 480; Billson, 65.
[92] Ellis's Brand, III, 170; Napier, 137; Dennys, 35; C. Latham, *F. L.
Record,* I, 51; Gregor, 203; Gurdon, 30.
[93] Dennys, 35.
[94] Aubrey's *Miscellanies,* Bohn ed., pp. 42, 46.

recently objected to being painted, shouting her defiance
as she fled, "He shawn't take oi!" [95] In the jungle, one need
only bring out his camera to be speedily alone.[96] The broken
mirror is only a small part of a larger primitive fear, and
the same is true of the falling portrait. Shadows, reflections
in shining surfaces like water or mirrors, any image or
likeness, were once thought to hold the soul of their original,
a soul which might too readily be coaxed or driven away
from its body. The mirror plays a rôle in divination and
magic. Poor Narcissus lost his soul to the malicious water
sprites! [97] This is one reason why in the house of death
mirrors are turned to the wall; it is feared that the soul of
the survivor, projected in the mirror, may be seized by the
lurking ghost of the departed, or by one of the spirits who
may be lying in wait for this selfsame ghost. It is a "safety
first" device similar to closing the eyes of the corpse and
mourning garb.[98]

The night Bathsheba slipped away to meet Troy, the
discovery of her absence threw Weatherbury Farm into
extravagant alarm, which was increased by Maryann's tale
of the unlucky omen which came to her that morning.

"I went to unlock the door and dropped the key, and it fell upon
the stone floor and broke into two pieces. Breaking a key is a dreadful
bodement . . ." [99]

The bad luck of breaking a key depends partly upon the
metal of which the key is made; iron, we know, has magic
properties. Horseshoes owe their efficacy, not only to their
shape and to the fact that they have been worn by horses,
the best of all ghost-seers, but also to the fact that they are
made of iron. The remedy for bewitched milk is to plunge a
hot poker into it.[100] Bells owe some of their power to the

[95] *Folk-Lore,* XXVII, 308; *Folk-Lore,* XX, 83.
[96] Frazer, *The Golden Bough,* 192–193.
[97] Frazer, *loc. cit.*
[98] Frazer, *loc. cit.*
[99] *Far from the Madding Crowd,* Chap. XXXIII.
[100] Harland and Wilkinson, 154, 166; E. Fogel, Proverbs, 848–861.

metal in them.[101] Keys are still placed in coffins in England; and it is too poetic an interpretation to say that they are for the use of the dead at the resurrection.[102] They were intended to frighten away evil spirits from the spirit of the dead, which for several days kept to its old haunts. Breaking a wedding ring, a common sign in our ballads, is token of the loss of love.[103]

Closely allied to the belief in the external soul which is revealed in the omens of the broken mirror or falling portrait, is the fear of the limp corpse, or the corpse which will not keep its eyes decently closed. Hardy refers to the ominous limp corpse in the little poem "Signs and Tokens," in which the mourners take the uncanny fact as a token of another death within the house before the year is out.[104] The reader of *The Mayor* will recall Mrs. Henchard's insistence that the great copper pence she had saved be placed upon her eyes and buried with her.[105] The Pennyslvania Dutch say that the corpse who will not keep his eyes shut is "looking for the next one to follow." [106] The use of copper coins on the eyes of the dead, like mourning garb, special roads for funerals, known as "corpse-ways," turning mirrors to the wall, and shutting up the room of death, originated in the fear that the ghost of the deceased might find his way back and annoy the living.[107] The limp corpse is a common omen.[108]

The omen of the falling portrait calls to mind the clock which falls suddenly, or strikes crazily. In the tale of "The Waiting Supper," Christine, thinking herself deserted by

---

[101] Aubrey's *Remaines,* Britten ed. 19, 22, 96; Wm. Henderson, *Folk-Lore of the Northern Counties,* 62; Wimberly, *Folk-Lore in the English and Scottish Ballads,* 37.

[102] E. Hull, *Folk-Lore,* XXXVIII, 208; M. M. Banks, *Folk-Lore,* XXXVIII, 399.

[103] Wimberley, *op. cit.,* 219; Dennys, 15.

[104] *Moments of Vision.*

[105] *The Mayor of Casterbridge,* Chap. XVIII.

[106] Fogel, Proverbs, 550, 582.

[107] Sabine Baring-Gould, *Curiosities of Olden Times,* 8–12; G. L. Gomme, *Ethnology in Folklore,* 120–121; Grimm-Stallybrass, II, 801, 836.

[108] Gregor, 211; G. F. Kinahan, *F. L. Record,* IV, 106; R. Clark, *F. L. Record,* V, 82; C. Latham, *F. L. Record,* I, 51; Mrs. Gutch, *Folk-Lore of Yorkshire,* 301; Gurdon, 29; I. Barclay, *Folk-Lore,* V, 337–38.

her husband, has at last consented to marry her one-time
lover: the table is set for the supper when the news comes
that her husband has been seen on his way home. The
wedding is off, but the house seems waiting for something.
Suddenly the great family clock slowly inclines forward and
falls full length on the floor.

> "What does it mean, Mrs. Wake? . . . Is it ominous?"
> "It is a sign of violent death in the family . . ." [109]

Years pass, but Bellston does not come; the lovers, afraid
to marry, are in the habit of meeting at a waterfall. One
day they find a watch and other belongings of Bellston's:
he had fallen into the water the night of the "waiting
supper."

In the poem, "Premonitions," a crazy old clock which
had not gone for years, suddenly struck twelve in the dead
of the night, making the owner wonder who next was to
die.[110]

In many English counties it is believed that the striking
of a clock during a wedding ceremony portends the death
of bride or groom before the year is out.[111] There is a tale
of a Suffolk eight-day clock, "kidding," that is, telling, the
approaching death of its mistress, and faring "in the biggest
of agony." [112]

The little poem "Premonitions" refers to the heavy sound
of the church bell, usually interpreted as an omen of death.
The listener asks herself moodily who can be meant by the
sinister sound.[113] There are tales of experienced ringers
who from the dull, muffled, or roaring sound of the bell
at services or in tolling, can foretell a death; the omen is
feared most if it occurs in a wedding-peal.[114] In "A Poor

---

[109] *The Changed Man.*
[110] *Human Shows.*
[111] G. E. Hadow, *Folk-Lore,* XXXV, 350; *Denham Tracts,* II, 51.
[112] Gurdon, 130.
[113] *Human Shows.*
[114] C. Latham, *Folk-Lore Record,* I, 51; E. Farrer, *Folk-Lore,* XII, 480;
E. J. Ladbury, *Folk-Lore,* XX, 344; Henderson, *Folk-Lore of the Northern
Counties,* 50.

Man and a Lady," the same omen hints at the coming estrangement.[115]

The night Fanny Robin disappeared from Weatherbury Farm, many gloomy conjectures were made as to her fate; some would have it, she was drowned, some that she had been murdered. Joseph Poorgrass held to the latter theory:

"What a night of horrors!" murmured Joseph Poorgrass, waving his hands spasmodically. "I've had the news-bell ringing in my left ear quite bad enough for a murder, and I've seen a magpie all alone!" [116]

The "dead bell" which Joseph heard is a very widespread omen, one of the omens connected with involuntary motions that played so important a rôle in Greek and Roman divination, and that remain almost unchanged to the present day.[117] The magpie is a form of *angang*—the meeting for good or ill luck which runs through Teutonic mythology.[118]

The Greeks believed in the "lucky right," just as we do, but the Roman augur prophesied happy auspices from the flight of birds to the left, or from visions seen over the left shoulder.[119] The ceremonial for cutting sacred plants like henbane also called for the left hand of the priest to be used.[120] By a trick of language the Latin word "sinister" has come to mean "left" in the sense of "inauspicious." In the British Isles the eminent folklorist Sir Laurence Gomme pointed out certain well-defined areas of survival of the Roman belief in the lucky left, finding it chiefly in the Roman Wall district of Northern England, and the Teutonic belief of the lucky right in the South.[121]

This interesting theory of the geographical distribution of a definite bit of folklore as a direct indication of Roman

---

[115] *Human Shows.*
[116] *Far from the Madding Crowd,* Chap. VIII.
[117] W. R. Halliday, *Greek and Roman Folk-Lore,* p. 140; Gregor, 27; James Napier, *Folk-Lore: or Superstitious Beliefs in the West of Scotland,* p. 57; J. G. Campbell, *Superstitions of the Scottish Highlands,* 258; J. C. Lawson, *Modern Greek Folklore and Ancient Greek Religion,* 329–30.
[118] Grimm-Stallybrass, III: 1117, 1119, 1123, 1125, 1126, 1129.
[119] Lawson, *op. cit.,* pp. 329–30; Browne, *Vulgar Errors,* IV, Ch. V.
[120] Grimm-Stallybrass, III, 1197–98.
[121] Gomme, Preface to *Denham Tracts,* Vol. II, p. 9.

and Teutonic influence will not weather all the conflicting evidence. In Dorset the Bishop's left hand in confirmation is held unlucky; in Northumberland, where we should expect to find our "lucky left," his left hand is thought to doom the recipient to single blessedness.[122] The left shoe, stocking, and foot are unlucky to the Scotch mind, yet in former times the bride's left stocking was thrown for luck, and a left stocking was wrapped round the neck of a sufferer from sore throat to effect a cure.[123] In northern counties the "even-ash" leaf must be placed in the left shoe for love-divination.[124] Spilled salt is tossed over the left shoulder to avert ill luck.[125] Holy water is sprinkled over the left shoulder, yet the witch was baptized thus with blood drawn by the devil from her left shoulder, and took her oath with uplifted left hand.[126] It is lucky, and it is unlucky to see the new moon over one's left shoulder; it depends on the place.[127] The left is a place of special luck and honor among the Hindoos and Northern Chinese.[128] We speak, however, of a morganatic or clandestine marriage as "left-handed": Dekker's *Honest Whore* has it, "I am the most wretched creature: sure some left-handed priest hath christened me, I am so unlucky." [129] It seems quite impossible to reconcile these conflicting beliefs on the score of Roman influence alone.

Hardy refers to the place of honor in the grave in the poem, "Her Late Husband," a story of a widow who willingly gives her place beside her husband to the woman he had loved, not, according to common custom, side by side, she on the right, and he on the left, in the place of honor.[130]

The single magpie which frightened Joseph Poorgrass

[122] Black, *Folk-Medicine*, 187; Henderson, *op. cit.*, 33; Gurdon, 133.
[123] Gregor, 30–31; N. Thomas, *Folk-Lore of Northumberland*, 47, 94–96, 98.
[124] Henderson, 110.
[125] H. Bateson, *Folk-Lore*, XXXIV, 242; C. Gurdon, 130.
[126] H. Bateson, *Folk-Lore*, XXXIV, pp. 241–42; Grimm-Stallybrass, IV, 1623.
[127] Gurdon, 162; C. Latham, *Folk-Lore Record*, I, p. 8.
[128] *Vulgar Errors*, Book IV, Chap. V, Dr. A. Clarke's note; Dennys, 25.
[129] Ellis's Brand, II, 79; *Folk-Lore*, XXXIV, 241–42; *Honest Whore*, Part II, III, ii, 136.
[130] *Poems of the Past and the Present.*

almost out of his wits—none too secure at any time!—
is pretty generally considered ominous. The most familiar
rhyme runs:

> One for sorrow, Two for mirth,
> Three for a wedding, and Four for a birth.

The variants are too numerous to mention.[131] At certain
times the magpie is harmless;[132] any time after forenoon,
or if seen to the right.[133] The nicknames given the magpie
betray its character; it is called "Tell-pie" or "Chatter-
pie";[134] and in the Highlands they say of a meddling chat-
terbox, "What a messenger of the Campbells (a magpie),
you have become!"[135] In more ruthless mood the devastat-
ing comment is, "Ye're like the pyot, ye're a' guts and
gyangals."[136] "It is little happiness to kill a magpie," runs
a widely known proverb.[137]

No doubt some of the magpie's ill fame is due to the fact
that, like the raven and crow, he has all through Aryan
folklore been a bird of dole and death. But his appearance,
habits, and extraordinary gifts also make him uncanny. The
Northumbrian story is that he alone refused to enter the
Ark; another says that Noah refused him admittance because he was a cross between a raven and a dove; the magpie
watched the Flood from an obliging rock, and has been
jabbering about it ever since.[138] A drop of human blood
in his tongue is said to give him human speech.[139] In Sussex
they say that the tree or house he perches on never falls.[140]

---

[131] Henderson, *Folk-Lore of the Northern Counties*, 127; J. Harland and
T. T. Wilkinson, *Lancashire Folk-Lore*, 144; C. J. Billson, *Folk-Lore of
Leicestershire and Rutland*, 35; Gurdon, *Folk-Lore of Suffolk*, 8.
[132] G. H. Kinahan, *Folk-Lore Record*, IV, 98; Gregor, 137; James Napier,
Superstitious Beliefs in the West of Scotland, 113.
[133] C. Latham, *Folk-Lore Record*, I, 9; G. H. Kinahan, *F. L. Record*, IV, 98;
Gregor, 137.
[134] *Denham Tracts*, II, 19–20; C. C. Robinson, *Eng. Dialect Soc.*, 1876, p. 142.
[135] J. G. Campbell, *Superstitions of the Scottish Highlands*, 227.
[136] *Ibid.*, p. 249.
[137] *Ibid.*, 249.
[138] Henderson, *Folk-Lore of the Northern Counties*, 126.
[139] Gregor, 138.
[140] C. Latham, *Folk-Lore Record*, Vol. I, p. 9; C. Liebrecht, *Folk-Lore
Record*, II, 228.

Yet he scents lurking disease in lambs; one he alights on is invariably doomed.[141] He is as good a judge of weather as of trees, and he still has an extensive cultus in Poitou.[142]

To avert the ill luck caused by meeting a magpie one may make the sign of the cross, bow and lift his hat politely, cross his thumbs, as in meeting a witch, and even spit over them for luck.[143] Or he may repeat this simple charm:

> Magpie, magpie, chatter and flee,
> Turn up thy tail, and good luck fall me.[144]

In the poem "Premonitions" Hardy mentions among birds of evil omen the owl which hoots from a nearby tree and the raven which flies over the house, bringing to the woman within the foreboding that some one dear to her is to die.[145]

Marie Louise, surprised by the secret visit from Napoleon, after his disastrous Russian campaign, took the dreadful news with simple, heartfelt grief. To his question, "What do they know about this in Paris?" she replied:

> "I cannot say. Black rumors fly and croak
> Like ravens through the streets, but come to me
> Thinned to the vague! . . ."[146]

Odin had two ravens who every day brought him word how the world fared.[147] The raven is universally considered a bird of death.[148] In Sweden night ravens are thought to be the ghosts of murdered men whose bodies have not yet been discovered; the hole in the nightjar's wing has been given as proof that he is the ghost of a man buried with the stake through his body; that is, a criminal.[149] The raven's longevity is uncanny; Medea's raven was nine hundred years

---

[141] C. Latham, *loc. cit.*
[142] Liebrecht, *Folk-Lore Record*, II, p. 228; Grimm-Stallybrass, I, 675.
[143] C. Latham, *loc. cit.;* Harland and Wilkinson, 144; Mrs. Whitehead, *Folk-Lore*, XXXVII, 77; *Denham Tracts*, II, 19–20; Billson, 35.
[144] *Denham Tracts*, II, 20.
[145] *Human Shows.*
[146] *The Dynasts*, Part Third, Act I, Scene XII.
[147] Latham, *Folk-Lore Record*, I, 55.
[148] Gurdon, 5; Henderson, 48; C. Swainson, *Folk-Lore and Provincial Names of British Birds*, pp. 89–92.
[149] *Henderson, 126.*

old.[150] Like the magpie, the raven scents lurking disease in lambs; when ravens appear in autumn in great numbers, shepherds fear large losses.[151] W. H. Hudson said that the presence of ravens near the house of illness and death is due to the instinct for carrion prey.[152] In Goethe's *Faust*, the witch asks Mephistopheles, "Where are your two ravens?"[153]

The screech owl, that is, the brown or tawny owl, is another dole-bird. Rome once underwent a lustration because one strayed into the Capitol.[154] To hear his ghostly hoot before one sees him is particularly unlucky.[155] When he frequents a town, a plague is not far off.[156] He is ghostly rather than malicious.[157]

"The Shiver" is a variation of the old theme, "If you shiver, some one is walking over your future grave." The woman, up early to watch her lover set out on a mysterious journey, shivers with sudden foreknowledge of their approaching estrangement.[158] A lovely poem, "In the Garden," tells the story of a simple, poignant incident; the sundial, the moment the sun comes out from the clouds, throws a sinister shadow on the woman who was first to die.[159]

Several omens seem to point to a sort of second sight in animals; after his abdication, Napoleon has refused to die on his sword, preferring to poison himself; his attendants, ignorant of his intention, are about to desert him:

> "Hark at them leaving me! So politic rats
> Desert the ship that's doomed. . . ."[160]

[150] C. Swainson, *Folk-Lore and Provincial Names of British Birds*, pp. 88–92.
[151] G. H. Kinahan, *Folk-Lore Record*, IV, 99.
[152] W. H. Hudson, *A Hind in Richmond Park*, Chap. VIII, pp. 107–8.
[153] Grimm-Stallybrass, IV, 1333, Supp. to Vol. I, p. 148; Goethe's *Faust*, Part I, Witch's Kitchen Scene.
[154] Ellis's Brand, III, 206.
[155] Richard Blakeborough, *Wit, Character, Folklore, and Customs of the North Ridings of Yorkshire*, pp. 130–31.
[156] C. Latham, *F. L. Record*, I, pp. 54–55.
[157] Grimm-Stallybrass, III, 1134–35.
[158] *Human Shows;* Gurdon, 134; Henderson, 113; Brand, III, 177, Note 1. A. Parker, *Folk-Lore*, XXIV, 91.
[159] *Moments of Vision.*
[160] *The Dynasts*, Part Third, Act IV, Scene IV; E. M. Wright, 216.

In "Signs and Tokens," we hear the sound of trotting
does in a deserted park, a ghostly reminder that the master
is to die.[161] In this poem the slothful flies are seen perched
on rotting fruit: they are wearing crape scarves! [161] It was
quite commonly believed that bees, at the death of a beloved
master, would die unless mourning "Snoos," or hoods, were
made for them to display upon each hive.[162]

The night Mr. Aldclyffe died, Cytherea Graye, a newcomer to Knapwater House, was frightened by the moaning
of the pet housedog, and the mournful howl of the great
watchdog in the court; in this chapter, in an otherwise crude
book,[163] Hardy's distinctive somber note is heard, a note
that is echoed again, for instance, in the episode in *Far
from the Madding Crowd* in which, by irony of circumstance, the dog that helped Fanny Robin to the Union, a
kindly creature that seemed the very personification of Night
in its solemn and compassionate aspect, was stoned away
from the door.[163] The dog is the sacred animal of death
and the guide to the underworld in Aryan mythology; the
dogs in the palace of Ithaca and their master Odysseus saw
Athena, though she was hidden from the eyes of all else;
and seeing her, the dogs did not bark, but whined lovingly.[164]
In West Sussex it is believed that the ghosts of dogs walk
abroad, seen only by their kind.[165] The Lowlanders say
that a dog will not approach one who is "fey," that is,
doomed to die.[166] Hardy's favorite dog, Wessex, once gave
an unmistakable death-warning: the dog rushed joyfully to
greet the visitor, Mr. William Watkins, but at sight of him,
began to whine piteously, and at intervals during the visit,
would paw his friend and then draw back in distress. The

---

[161] *Moments of Vision:* "Signs and Tokens."
[162] Henderson, 309.
[163] *Desperate Remedies,* Chap. VI; *Far from the Madding Crowd,*
Chap. XL.
[164] Halliday, *Greek and Roman Folklore,* 59; Black, *Folk-Medicine,* 150;
Aubrey's *Remaines,* 86, 163; Ellis's Brand, III, 184–186.
[165] C. Latham, *Folk-Lore Record,* I, 17.
[166] Gregor, 126.

next morning came the news of Mr. Watkins' death an hour after leaving Max Gate.[167]

Premonitions abound in Hardy's novels and poems. As Clym Yeobright struck into the path that led to the cottage of Susan Nunsuch, on his way to question little Johnny about his meeting with Mrs. Yeobright just before her death, he felt a creeping chilliness which, in after days, he held peculiarly ominous. It was at this interview that he learned of Eustacia's part in the tragedy.[168] Young Somerset was haunted by the fear that the de Stancys would rob him of Paula, and Paula herself at the last moment hastened her wedding to the architect from an inexplicable fear of estrangement.[169] Lady Constantine was alarmed when the curate came prepared for a funeral.[170] Later when she saw Swithin clad in her former husband's clothes, she felt a strong premonition that Sir Blount was not really dead.[171] She was warned of her approaching maternity by the waking dream of the golden-haired child in the tall fern.[172] In the same story, Granny Martin carefully prepared Swithin's room for him in his absence, knowing that she would be gone at his return; and it was Granny who used to go up into her "old country," where she found mother, father, and all she had known as a child as natural as when she had left them.[173] To my mind the most poignant moment in the book is St. Cleeve's mysterious reluctance to see Viviette after the long absence, foreseeing, as it were, all "Time's revenges." [174] Bathsheba was justified in her conviction that Troy was alive despite proof to the contrary.[175] Elfride, at the moment when Knight saved her from death on the falling tower, felt a premonition that something similar to

---

[167] F. E. Hardy, *The Later Years of Thomas Hardy,* 241.
[168] *The Return of the Native,* Book V, Chap. II.
[169] A *Laodicean,* Book IV, Chap. I; Book VI, Chap. III.
[170] *Two on a Tower,* Chap. XIX.
[171] *Ibid.,* Chap. XXII.
[172] *Ibid.,* Chap. XXXVI.
[173] *Ibid.,* Chaps. II, XXXIX.
[174] *Ibid.,* Chap. XLI.
[175] *Far from the Madding Crowd,* Chap. XLVIII.

this scene was again to happen to them, a premonition fulfilled when she saved his life on the Cliff-without-a-Name.[176] Tess was troubled by a thorn that pricked her breast after she had parted with Alec d'Urberville, and inexpressibly shocked by the damnatory text, "Thy, Damnation, Slumbereth, Not. 2 Pet. II, 3," [177] Lady Penelope's prophetic promise to marry her three lovers, each in his turn, was fulfilled to the letter, and is a matter of Dorset history.[178] A rather melodramatic omen occurs in *A Pair of Blue Eyes:* Elfride, in her pathetic eagerness to stem Knight's exclamation of bitterness when he learns of her affair with Stephen Smith, says softly, as she looks at the church tower, "Thou hast been my hope, and a strong tower for me against the enemy." A few moments later a flock of birds fly from the tower; suddenly the tower moves, and crumbles to earth.[179] Dramatic foreshadowing is used in "A Tragedy of Two Ambitions" : the two brothers, ambitious for their sister and themselves, have allowed their drunken father to drown, but are secretly remorseful. Some time later, as they are passing the sedge where their father had died, they see a straight little silver poplar rising from it:

"His walking-stick has grown!" said Cornelius. "It was a rough one—cut from the hedge, I remember." [180]

It reproached them and threatened all their peace. This simple incident haunts the memory after the tale is laid aside.

In "The Flirt's Tragedy," a little boy broods in the night over his mother's treachery; the guilty pair—the woman and her new spouse, hear him crying to himself because his false father had murdered his true.[181] "Near Lanivet," a favorite even with Hardy himself, is the tale of an odd premonition. The lovers, tired from a long walk, reach the

[176] *A Pair of Blue Eyes,* Chaps. XVIII, XXI.
[177] *Tess,* Chaps. VI, XII.
[178] *A Group of Noble Dames:* "The Lady Penelope"; R. Thurston Hopkins, *Thomas Hardy's Dorset,* 95.
[179] Chap. XXXI.
[180] *Life's Little Ironies.*
[181] *Time's Laughingstocks.*

crossways, and she rests her head upon the handpost, stretching out both her arms, as if crucified. Both of them are struck with an inexplicable fear, which they are unable to laugh away, try as they will.[182]

In "The Lady of Forebodings," a woman is visited by the premonition that she can no longer keep her lover as he is; some flaw has imperceptibly crept into their hitherto perfect confidence and happiness, some flaw which will destroy the whole.[183] In "Plena Timoris," the heroine, confronted with the body of the lovesick girl who has drowned herself, sees the outcome of her own affair.[184] In "The Announcement," the two brothers who have sat silent throughout a long visit, suddenly announce the death of a common friend.[185] One of Hardy's most beautiful lyrics records an incident in the life of his wife, Emma Lavinia Hardy. One day he heard her playing over her favorite old tunes; some time later, when he returned from town, she was about to finish her little concert. After her death he pondered the question of her foreknowledge of her death, and his brooding is heard in "The Last Performance."[186] The speaker in "The Interloper," while watching three friends out of sight, suddenly sees beside them, but apparently unseen by any of them, a ghostly figure, the embodiment, as it were, of that madness which is to befall one of the three. There is an accent and tone as macabre in "The Interloper" as in Poe's best work.[187] In "Before Marching and After," we have the story of a young soldier in the World War who, just as he is about to set out for the front, is strangely quiet at the foreknowledge that this is indeed the end.[188] The wind in "The Wind's Prophecy" keeps telling the lover that he is hastening to meet, not his sweetheart, but a love he had not yet known.[189]

[182] *Moments of Vision.*
[183] *Human Shows.*
[184] *Ibid.*
[185] *Moments of Vision.*
[186] *Ibid.;* F. E. Hardy, *The Later Years of Thomas Hardy,* p. 153.
[187] *Moments of Vision.*
[188] *Ibid.*
[189] *Ibid.*

Particularly poignant is the poem, "At a Fashionable Dinner": it is the poet's story of the strange premonition of her own death which came to the first Mrs. Hardy. At a dinner of thirteen guests, seated next to her husband, Lavine, the heroine of the episode, notices a shadow beyond the door—a shadow which looks, she says, like her own body lying there as servants glide in and out. When he says it is far more like satin sheen, she gloomily believes he is thinking of a new bride. The poem must be read to see how a trite theme may be touched to beauty with delicate and reticent art.[190]

The superstition is almost universal.[191] Lloyd George, Winston Churchill, and the great Parnell are said to have believed thirteen unlucky.[192] The number is taboo on many berths and staterooms today.[193] Thirteen was the number for a witches' coven; the cult may have chosen it for its existent uncanny associations.[194] Explanations of its unlucky character are comparatively modern; the most common explanation is that thirteen sat at the Paschal Supper.[195] The Scotch call it a "Deil's" or "Baker's dozen," alluding to the old legend hidden in Ophelia's saying, "The owl was a baker's daughter." [196] Bakers, according to the legend, are cursed because one of them, an old woman, once refused to do Christ a kindness.[197]

No reader of Hardy can forget the poem, "Who's in the Next Room?" It is Death who is in the next room; the speaker, in the gray dawn, hears his ghostly footsteps and sees his shadowy shape. This is more like a waking dream than an ordinary premonition.[198] "On a Heath" is a gloomy little poem in which two lovers are seeking each other on

---

190 *Human Shows.*
191 Napier, 138; Gregor, *F. L. Journal*, I, 364–66; Billson, 64; Fogel, 543; Gutch, 300.
192 A. R. Wright, *Folk-Lore*, XXXVIII, 307.
193 Wright, *Ibid.*, 306–8.
194 M. A. Murray, *The Witch Cult in Western Europe*, 191–94.
195 Brand, III, 264–65; Henderson, 49.
196 Gurdon, 131; *Hamlet*, IV, v, 40.
197 Rendel Harris, *The Ascent of Olympus*, pp. 2–3.
198 *Moments of Vision.*

the darkened heath, and the woman, feeling some chill presence, cries out and so brings her lover to her side; each feels an unspoken menace in the heath.[199]

Sometimes approaching death or misfortune is not sensed by those whom it concerns: neither the singer nor the listener sees the phantom shape between them in "At the Piano"; [200] neither the lady on the balcony nor the lover beneath feels Fate, like a masked face, creeping near in a poem called "On the Esplanade." [201] "The Three Tall Men" tells the grimly ironic tale of a very tall man who made, in turn, three coffins for himself: the first was used for his brother, the second for his son, and the third remained unused, as he was lost at sea.[202] A charming episode, which it is pleasant to know refers directly to Hardy's first wife, is told in "A Man Was Drawing Near to Me": the heroine of the poem is quite unaware that her future husband is on his way to visit her.[203] "In a London Flat" is perhaps too light a subject for Hardy's art: Browning would have made an admirable dramatic sketch of this sophisticated lady: the lady, lightly chaffing her visitor, says that he looks like a widower; in a year he is free, and she completely indifferent.[204]

Hardy gives us several instances of the old Greek fear of "insolence," the belief that "Whom the gods would destroy, they first make mad." It is this fear which prompts the bride, in "The Country Wedding," in her alarm at the wild merriment of the village bandsmen, to rebuke them: "Too gay! Clouds may gather, and sorrows come!" [205] A year to the day the bandsmen are burying the pair. The motif is more quietly sardonic in "He Fears His Good Fortune": In the face of extraordinary good fortune and radiant happiness, he feels

[199] *Ibid.*
[200] *Ibid.*
[201] *Human Shows.*
[202] *Winter Words.*
[203] *Late Lyrics;* F. E. Hardy, *The Early Life,* 92.
[204] *Late Lyrics.*
[205] *Ibid.*

"It is too full for me,
Too rare, too rapturous, rash. . . ."

He accepts his undeserved fortune philosophically:

"Well . . . let the end foreseen
Come duly!—I am serene."
—And it came.[206]

The same belief underlies Mr. Penny's answer to the
question,

"How's your daughter, Mrs. Brownjohn?"
"Well, I suppose I must say pretty fair. . . . But she'll be worse
before she's better, 'a b'lieve." [207]

This is the wisdom of the Maltster's reply to Gabriel Oak's
query as to his health, "Oh, neither sick nor sorry, shepherd; but no younger." [208] Many persons not otherwise
superstitious, are careful not to boast of the health of their
loved ones; we still see highly cultivated people touching
wood as they utter some trifling boast or polite fib.[209] The
motif is touched to grandeur in the Third Citizen's cry in
The Dynasts:

"Throw down the gage while God is fair to us;
He may be foul anon!" [210]

On the whole, Elizabeth-Jane's reluctance to believe her
great good fortune is the most striking use of this omen;
her mother's exemption from worry, her own happiness, and
Donald Farfrae's love all seem a miracle in which she
cannot believe for fear of tempting Providence. In modest
Elizabeth-Jane this is not superstition, but transcendent
common sense.[211] There is a general conviction, it seems,
that boasting about anything will cause the luck attaching

[206] *Moments of Vision.*
[207] *Under the Greenwood Tree,* Part I, Chap. II.
[208] *Far from the Madding Crowd,* Chap. XV.
[209] Prof. J. Rhys, *Folk-Lore,* III, 85–86; E. M. Wright, *Rustic Speech and
Folklore,* 237–38; E. S. Hartland, *Ritual and Belief,* 84; E. Clodd, *Magic
in Names,* 101.
[210] *The Dynasts,* Part Second, Act I, Scene III.
[211] *The Mayor of Casterbridge,* Chap. XIV.

to it to turn.[212] This reminds us of the Greek "insolence,"
and the lighter interpretation of the whole idea of Nemesis.
To the possession of costly things adheres, in life as in
folklore, the risk of loss and spiritual disaster.[213]

The most terrible of all premonitions of death come in
the form of wraiths. A wraith, or "waff," is usually the
shape of some living person whom the beholder knows to
be far away; it is sometimes the person's own double, alone
or accompanied by others; it may be the ghost of some
person who has met with sudden death.[214] The appearance
of wraiths is the result of second-sight, or, as we call it
today, thought-transference. The Scotch say that those
gifted with second-sight should not indulge in "strong and
undue wishes," and Campbell has many tales of Highland
tragedies brought about by the exercise of this dangerous
will power, tales in which a mere wish to see the absent makes
them visible, frightening the beholder to death.[215] W. H.
Hudson gives many striking stories from his own experience
of thought-transference.[216]

The heroine of "A Committee-Man of the Terror" was
about to elope with the man who had once condemned to
death her father, brother, cousin, and uncle when a procession of the dead passed before her eyes—all headless. She
renounced her lover.[217] At the moment of death Mrs. Aldclyffe appeared to Cytherea Graye.[218] Such poems as "The
Noble Lady's Tale," [219] "At the Dinner Table," [220] "What
Did It Mean?" [220] and "The Chosen" [220] treat the theme of
second-sight. "The Noble Lady's Tale" deals with the farewell appearance of an actor who had married above him.
His jealous wife's thoughts followed him to the theater

[212] C. J. Billson, 65; Gregor, 35; Clodd, *Magic in Names*, 101.
[213] Rhys, *Folk-Lore*, III, 85; Grimm-Stallybrass, IV, 1349, 1379, 1562.
[214] Gutch, 211; Henderson, 46–48; Denham II, 268; Aubrey's *Miscellanies*, 72–74, Grimm-Stallybrass, IV, 1571.
[215] J. G. Campbell, *Witchcraft and Second Sight in the Scottish Highlands*, 141.
[216] W. H. Hudson, *A Hind in Richmond Park*, Chap. IV, pp. 37–50.
[217] *A Changed Man.*
[218] *Desperate Remedies*, Chap. XXI, (4).
[219] *Time's Laughingstocks.*
[220] *Late Lyrics.*

and assumed her likeness. His performance was ruined, his heart broken. Even when he learned that she had not left home, he could not forgive her breach of faith.[221] This little poem would seem to say that sometimes "thoughts are things." In "What Did It Mean?" a lover asks his new betrothed to pluck a flower from his discarded sweetheart's garden. She yields innocently, suspecting no evil, intending no offense. The blossom itself shrinks from her; a pale face peers from a window nearby; as she gives him the flower, his face is shadowed by a sudden coldness and the suspicion that all along she had meant to separate him from the first woman, whom he realizes he loves. We are half convinced that the innocent girl in her secret heart had conspired against her rival merely by her deep admiration of the man.[222] "The Chosen" treats a theme similar to Pierston's pursuit of the "well-beloved," the artist's search for the ideal woman. When the chosen woman reads his thoughts, she flees from him; a benumbing spell, as if some one had ill-wished her, falls upon her; in vain does he try to atone.[223]

Two poems carry the belief in wraiths to the utmost limits of credence. A poem just twelve lines long tells a haunting tale: While at church the wife catches sight of her husband with a face of inexpressible sadness. She returns home to find that he had not left the house, but has been listening to the bell toll. Her involuntary exclamation is that the bell had not tolled at all! "She Saw Him, She Said" is a perfect short story in verse.[224] Still more ironic is "The Pair He Saw Pass," a tale of a man recently married, who sees the love he has jilted riding with him to their wedding in the parish church. It is with terror that he learns that no one has been seen at the church. The news comes that the jilted woman died at the moment he had seen her riding to her wedding. Did her thoughts project themselves into actual reality: did she ride to her wedding, as she had

---

221 *Time's Laughingstocks.*
222 *Late Lyrics.*
223 *Ibid.*
224 *Human Shows.*

hoped and planned? Was she reclaiming her lost lover? He soon sickened and died, at any rate.[225]

"At the Dinner Table" is a cruel incident in which the poet does not need to heighten the irony of circumstance. The young wife sees in a mirror an old woman strangely like herself; she recalls her husband's shocking and inexplicable malice, when fifty years later, now a widow, she recognizes herself and the image that had haunted her as one and the same.[226]

The sense of coming disaster is strong in *Jude;* it infects the reader as it fails to do in *Tess.* Widow Edlin's ghastly tale of the family curse prevents Jude's marriage to Sue; they are conscious of a tragic doom like that which overhung the house of Atreus or the house of Jeroboam.[227] Jude's prescience of death is a relief to the reader, for death is release to Jude.[228] The most solemn premonition in all Hardy is perhaps Eustacia Vye's hatred and fear of Egdon Heath. As of some implacable enemy, she says, " 'Tis my cross, my misery, and will be my death." [229]

Premonitions bulk large in *The Dynasts.* On the eve of Austerlitz, Napoleon felt, "as from an unseen monster haunting nigh" England's "hostile breath." [230] All through *The Dynasts* [231] Napoleon alone is conscious of the tremendous forces which urge him on. His premonition of the Moscow disaster [232] and the bloody apparition of Marshal Lannes, which appears to him before Waterloo,[233] are other proofs of the rapport between him and destiny.

The English, too, had their premonitions: Pitt died from inexpressible worry; [234] Nelson had warnings that the hours of his service for England were numbered, for he took

[225] *Ibid.*
[226] *Late Lyrics.*
[227] *Jude the Obscure,* Part V, Chap. IV.
[228] *Ibid.,* Part VI, Chap. IX.
[229] *The Return of the Native,* Book I, Chap. IX.
[230] Part First, Act VI, Scene II.
[231] Part Second, Act I, Scene VIII; Part Third, Act VII, Scene IX.
[232] *The Dynasts,* Part Third, Act I, Scene VIII.
[233] *Ibid.,* Part Third, Act VII, Scene VI.
[234] *Ibid.,* Part First, Act VI, Scene VIII; *The Trumpet-Major,* XXXIV.

aboard his flagship the coffin in which his body was brought
home after Trafalgar.[235] There is a masterly blend of
comedy and tragedy in the Boatman's story of how they
"broached the Adm'l!" [236] The Duke of Brunswick's pre-
occupation at the ball revealed the family gift of second-
sight.[237] General Prescott's wife suffered a premonition of
her widowhood.[238] At her wedding to Napoleon, Marie
Louise felt the dissuading touch of Marie Antoinette on her
arm; [239] and one hardly knows whether to smile or cry at
the scene where the little King of Rome refuses to leave the
palace where they have been so happy.[240] These glimpses
into the future enhance the mysterious splendor of *The
Dynasts.* The atmosphere of the drama is murky, like the
air before a thunderstorm; the sky is full of half-hidden
light that threatens any moment to blaze forth in terrible
glory.

Hardy's use of the prophetic and premonitory dream is
interesting. All the modern dream-books of Europe, and
such books as *Mother Shipton's Legacy* and *Napoleon's
Book of Fate,* used in Lancashire within the last half century,
are the lineal descendants of the *Oneirocriticon* of Artemi-
dorus.[241] Psychologists scorn the prophetic dream but grant
that the premonitory dream is another matter. Physicians
agree that the dreamer may become conscious in certain
types of dreams of morbid visceral conditions before these
reach the degree of intensity sufficient to attract the waking
consciousness.[242] Viviette's hallucination, the vision of the
golden-haired child, might well be taken as a physical premonitory dream.[243]

[235] *Ibid.,* Part First, Act II, Scene I.
[236] *Ibid.,* Part First, Act V, Scene VII.
[237] *Ibid.,* Part Second, Act I, Scene IV; Part Third, Act VI, Scenes II, VI,
VII.
[238] *Ibid.,* Part Third, Act I, Scene II.
[239] *Ibid.,* Part Second, Act. V, Scene VIII; Part Third, Act IV, Scene II.
[240] *Ibid.,* Part Third, Act IV, Scene III.
[241] Lawson, J. C., p. 553; Halliday, 138–39; Harland and Wilkinson,
145, Intro., p. 19.
[242] Havelock Ellis, *The World of Dreams,* pp. 157, 161–63.
[243] *Two on a Tower,* Chap. XXXVI.

Stephen Smith's dream of Elfride, in which she fails to appear for her wedding to Lord Luxellian, is vaguely prophetic of the fact that she has come to the end of her tangled romance, and is lost to all three of the men who have loved her.[244] Grace Melbury's dream of three crazed bells on the eve of her marriage to Fitzpiers was confirmed by the ill luck of the match.[245] Elfride scarcely knew whether to believe that her dream of the Widow Jethway's standing over her was a fact or a dream.[246] Napoleon's vision of the gory figure of his old marshal the night before Waterloo, is, like all dreams of those smeared with blood, to be interpreted as a sign of defeat and death. The spectre's reproachful cry has an almost Shakespearian ring: "What —blood again? Still blood!" [247]

Two poems, "At Waking" and "In The Night She Came," contain dreams which presage estrangement. The latter is the story of a lover who had sworn that he would love eternally; in the night his love appears to him, old and ugly, as Time must subdue her. The next day at meeting they seem divided by some shade.[248] "A Last Journey" treats of a dream in which the sick man, homesick for the woodlands, in dreams visits his father's orchard, and sees his father shaking the overripe apples from the boughs, a token, that he, like them, is to fall. He tells his little son of the dream, and dies happily.[249]

Eustacia Vye's dream, however, is easily the most striking in Hardy's writings. Every reader of *The Return of the Native* remembers how she danced to wondrous music with a knight in silver armor; how suddenly they "dived into one of the pools of the heath, and came out somewhere beneath an iridescent hollow, arched with rainbows," where, just as he was about to kiss her, "there was a cracking noise,

[244] *A Pair of Blue Eyes,* Chap. XXXIX.
[245] *The Woodlanders,* Chaps. XXIV, XXIX.
[246] *A Pair of Blue Eyes,* Chap. XXIX.
[247] *The Dynasts,* Part Third, Act VII, Sc. VI; Gregor, p. 29.
[248] *Time's Laughingstocks.*
[249] *Human Shows.*

and his figure fell into fragments like a pack of cards"; how she woke crying, " 'O that I had seen his face!' " [250] Taken bit by bit, this dream admits of several interpretations. To dream of dancing is to come into some great happiness; [251] to dream of music is to hear good news; [251] to dream of pleasant places is to be blessed with a devoted husband and children. [251] On the other hand, to dream of falling into a pit or pool is to lose one's sweetheart; [252] to dream of green fields is an omen of death, which is still another guess for the commentators for Falstaff's death: "a' babbled of green fields." [253] We who know Eustacia's story need not consult our dream-books to interpret her dream: The happiness she pictured fell, in truth, to pieces like a pack of cards; the heath she hated was at last to have its will of her.

Hardy occasionally indulges in a smile at the deeply superstitious rustic mind. Timothy Fairway's story of the coffin which was too short for George Yeobright, makes Christian Cantle, timid soul, wonder whether it is an evil omen to dream of one's shadow in the shape of a coffin. Any dream-book might have increased Christian's alarm; for, although it is lucky to dream of a corpse—that's a wedding—to dream of a coffin is unlucky at all times. [254] The student interested in Hardy's sources, so largely drawn from oral tradition, will find the basis of this incident in a story told the Hardys by their servant Ann, so interesting that he transcribed it carefully. [255]

Hardy reaches some of his most solemn effects in the use of personal and family fatality. Ovid tells us, *Omnium rerum est vicissitudo,* and again, *Fors sua cuique loco est.* [256] History records days unlucky to Becket, Cromwell, and Henry

---

[250] *The Return of the Native,* Book II, Chap. III.
[251] Ellis's Brand, III, 134.
[252] Ellis's Brand, III, 139.
[253] Lean, *Collectanea,* Vol. II, Pt. II, p. 552; *Henry V,* II, III, 16.
[254] *The Return of the Native,* Book II, Chap. VI; Harland and Wilkinson, p. 148.
[255] F. E. Hardy, *The Early Life of Thomas Hardy,* p. 206.
[256] Aubrey's *Miscellanies,* Bohn ed., p. 25; Ovid, Fast. Lib. 4.

VIII.[257] Nelson and the Duke of Brunswick came of families which received unmistakable death warnings.[258] Nelson's taking his coffin aboard the *Victory* is historical.[259] Second-sight is by no means, as commonly thought, restricted to certain Highland septs and Irish clans.[260] The d'Urberville ill luck is an inherited tendency, and perhaps the same is true of the Fawley curse in marriage. But a strong personal fatality attaches to Jude, Tess, and Eustacia Vye. Eustacia's every impulse and action is significant; she carries her fate with her. It is wholly true of Henchard, but not of Eustacia, that Character is Fate; the gods themselves conspire against the "Queen of Night."

. The fatality of places and weather plays a part in Hardy's novels. Elfride was uneasy as she and Knight were seated on young Jethway's tomb, and both her lovers noticed her pallor as she came from a glimpse of the Luxellian vault. The most somber meeting of the three, however, is the meeting at the railway station, as Elfride's coffin is carried away from the two rivals.[261] Even such a sensible girl as Elizabeth-Jane felt an uncanny fear of Lucetta in Casterbridge churchyard:

> Here, in a churchyard as old as civilization, in the worst of weathers, was a strange woman of curious fascinations never seen elsewhere; there might be some devilry about her presence.[262]

The sense of impending disaster is strong the night Eustacia and Wildeve are drowned in the weir:

> The gloom of the night was funereal; all nature seemed clothed in crape. The spiky points of the fir trees behind the house rose into the sky like the turrets and pinnacles of an abbey. Nothing below the horizon was visible save a light which was still burning in the cottage

---

[257] Aubrey's *Remaines,* Britten Ed., pp. 12–13; Mathew Paris, sub anno 1169; Ellis's Brand, II, pp. 47–48.
[258] *The Dynasts,* Part First, Act I, Scene I; Part Second, Act I, Scene IV; Part Third, Act VI, Scenes II, III, VII.
[259] *The Trumpet-Major,* Chap. XXXIV.
[260] Campbell, *Witchcraft and Second Sight,* 110, 121; Henderson, 344.
[261] *A Pair of Blue Eyes,* Chaps. VIII, XIX, XXVII, XL.
[262] *The Mayor of Casterbridge,* Chap. XXI.

of Susan Nunsuch. . . . The moon and stars were closed up by cloud and rain to the degree of extinction. It was a night which led the traveller's thoughts instinctively to dwell on all that is terrible and dark in history and legend—the last plague of Egypt, the destruction of Sennacherib's host, the agony in Gethsemane.[263]

This is the mien and voice of Egdon Heath in its blackest mood.

The fatalism of Hardy's people ranges from broad rustic comedy to high tragedy. It is one of the most characteristic qualities of Hardy's clowns. Humphrey is telling Fairway and Grandfer Cantle, for instance, why he no longer goes to church:

"I ha'nt been there these three years; for I'm so dead sleepy of a Sunday, and 'tis so terrible far to get there; and when you do get there 'tis such a mortal poor chance that you'll be chose for up above, that I bide at home and don't go at all." [264]

They agree, however, that George Yeobright's fate was happier; was he not "lucky enough to be God A'mighty's own man"? [265] The rustics at the malt-house in *Far from the Madding Crowd* speculate gloomily as to Charlotte Coggan's fate:

"Poor Charlotte! I wonder if she had the good fortune to get into Heaven when 'a died! But 'a was never much in luck's way, and perhaps 'a went downward after all, poor soul." [266]

As to the rustic view of Fate, let us use the exception to prove the rule; Geoffrey Day's second wife was a most extraordinary woman; what was true of her might safely work just the other way for common mortals, and Geoffrey's comment may thus pass:

"Doom? Doom is nothing beside a elderly woman—quite a chiel in her hands." [267]

[263] *The Return of the Native,* Book V, Chap. VII.
[264] *Ibid.,* Book I, Chap. III.
[265] *Ibid.,* Book I, Chap. V.
[266] *Far from the Madding Crowd,* Chap. VIII.
[267] *Under the Greenwood Tree,* Part II, Chap. VI.

Through the majority of Hardy's tales runs a darker view of fate. The Hardcomes are married each to the wrong woman: death rights the matter, and the two who are left accept their destiny quietly.[268] Sally Hall realizes that her wedding to Darton is put off, not for a week, nor a month, but forever.[269] Bathsheba's men do not tell her of Troy's reappearance, thinking she will learn all too soon.[270] When the Mellstock band are ousted by Fancy Day, they accept Parson Maybold's decision, and attend her début in a body. It is hard to forgive the parson for not allowing them to "fall glorious with a bit of a flourish at Christmas" instead of being "choked off" and "dwindling away" "at some nameless paltry Second-Sunday after." [271] The dairy maids at Tabothays bear no feminine malice when Tess carries off their adored Clare: "Such supplanting was to be." [272] There are times when we are out of patience with Tess's patience! This fatalism may be poignant and solemn: Farfrae and Henchard feel that they are ruled by mysterious powers.[273] Eustacia, ready to try to make up the misunderstanding with Clym's mother, yields to his dissuasion:

> "Let it be as you say then," she replied in the quiet way of one, who though willing to ward off evil consequences by a mild effort, would let events fall out as they might sooner than wrestle hard to direct them.[274]

Marie Louise, brooding over her lost happiness, muses,

> "Methinks that I was born
> Under an evil-coloured star, whose ray
> Darts death at joys!" [275]

And Napoleon, dimly conscious of the forces behind him, cries,

---

[268] *Life's Little Ironies:* "The History of the Hardcomes."
[269] *Wessex Tales:* "Interlopers at the Knap."
[270] *Far from the Madding Crowd,* Chap. LIII.
[271] *Under the Greenwood Tree,* Part II, Chap. IV; Part IV, Chap. V.
[272] *Tess,* Chaps. XI, XIV, XXII, XXIII.
[273] *The Mayor of Casterbridge,* Chaps. XIX, XX, XXXIV.
[274] *The Return of the Native,* Book IV, Chap. VII.
[275] *The Dynasts,* Part Third, Act. V, Scene II.

"Some force within me, baffling mine intent,
    Harries me onward, whether I will or no.
    My star, my star is what's to blame—not I." [276]

Hardy's use of omens, dreams, premonitions, and fatality
shows the somber tinge of his mind, the saturation of the
experiences of a long life in intimate contact with people
who still think in a primitive way. His understanding is deep
and sympathetic. At rare moments he allows his intelligence
and his humor to play over this superstitious way of looking
at life; but, on the whole, it is not the comedy, but the tragedy and the irony of life that move him most. Not because
he is himself superstitious—although most of us are in
some respect—but because, after all, there is a certain un-
deniable truth and beauty in this primitive way of thought
and feeling, does he dwell so constantly on omens and
superstitions. He saw, no doubt, that of all dogmatists the
man of science is the most terrible, because the most unconscious; and that the latter in all honesty must end in the
confession that the universe is an enigma. Hardy would
seem to say that to view the future with awe and a natural
touch of fear is not to lack quiet courage and strength. It
is possible, in many cases, to give a scientific explanation
for these accidental coincidences, these forebodings, but
Hardy does not trouble to give it. He gives us these omens
and premonitions for what they are worth in the lives of his
Wessex people; they are worth a great deal to them—and
to us. It is surprising to look back over this mass of superstition, as we call it, and to realize that in not a single instance have we been moved to scorn or contempt for the believer in omens. With the author we sometimes smile at
rustic credulity; oftener we are privileged to share a deep
understanding and sympathy. The fullness of a rich experience and a ripe spirit comes in time to the reader of Hardy.

[276] *The Dynasts,* Part Second, Act I, Scene VIII.

II

DIVINATION

Divination is the active counterpart to omens and premonitions. It is the *sortilegium* and *augurium* of the ancients, practised lawfully only by the priest or by the head of a family. Among the Germanic tribes, divination, like the priestly office, was hereditary. It was held unlawful when practised by any not recognized as priest of a cult. Such a practitioner was believed to use his knowledge chiefly for the selfish benefit or active hurt of individuals, rather than for the social weal. In the present chapter, we are concerned not with the professional conjuror or magician, but with the deep-seated beliefs and traditional methods used by the folk themselves to pierce the veil of the future, with love spells and charms of village maidens, the appeal to lots, and the ceremonial of divination at such seasons as Midsummer Eve, Hallowe'en, and Christmas. These divinations range from the simple plucking of a flower to the somber rite of watching in the church porch to see the ghosts of those who are to die within the year; they are futile and comic in some instances, and deeply tragic in others. There are two questions which men and women ask of the future: "Am I to marry?" and, "Am I to die soon?" These categorical questions seldom receive an unmistakable "Yes" or "No" in life, or in Hardy's fiction; the answer suggests a gleam of hope, it may be, or a shade of doubt which deepens despair.

There is a lovely scene in *Tess of the d'Urbervilles* in which Tess is gathering the buds of arum colloquially called "lords and ladies," and is stripping them absent-mindedly and half curiously as Angel Clare comes up to her. Tess holds up the last newly peeled bud to Clare, saying simply, "It is a lady again. . . . There are always more ladies than lords when you come to peel them." [1] Tess is the soul of simplicity; her speech lacks all the subtle implication a sophisticated girl would have given it. Although already in love with Clare, she is not capable of flirtation; but the poetry of her nature is a surer magnet than feminine coquetry. This gesture, these words of Tess's tug at Clare's heart and tempt him to stoop to the milkmaid. All that Tess did, she did as simply and fatalistically as she peeled the "lords and ladies"; hers is a nature that treasures whatever joy comes to it, but shows itself best in the patient acceptance of blight and sorrow. In this episode Hardy suggests Tess's whole quality and hints that she is to suffer bitterly for her quiet, adoring nature.

A different kind of divination is that practised by the matter-of-fact Mrs. Penny, wife of the village cobbler at Mellstock. Irresistibly comic is her assurance that Fate is about to send her a future partner, and her reward, the estimable Penny himself, sees the comedy he is made to furnish. As we listen to Mrs. Penny telling the guests at the Dewys' Christmas party how she came to marry her husband, we may indulge an imperceptible wink now and then or even an inaudible, "Mrs. Penny, how *could* you?"

"Ah, the first spirit ever I see on Midsummer-eve was a puzzle to me. . . . I sat up, quite determined to see if John Wildway was going to marry me or no. I put the bread-and-cheese and cider quite ready, as the witch's book ordered, and I opened the door, and I waited till the clock struck twelve, my nerves all alive, and so strained that I could feel every one of 'em twitching like bell-wires. Yes, sure! and when the clock had struck, lo and behold, I could see through the door a *little small* man in the lane wi' a shoemaker's apron on. . . . In he walks, and down he sits, and O my goodness me, didn't I flee upstairs, body and soul hardly hanging together! Well, to cut a long story short, by-long and by-late, John Wildway and I had a miff and parted; and lo and behold the coming man came! Penny asked me

[1] *Tess,* Chap. XIX; Dyer, *Folklore of Plants,* 173.

if I'd go snacks with him, and afore I knew what I was about a'most, the thing was done."

"I've fancied you never knew better in your life; but I may be mistaken," said Mr. Penny in a murmur.[2]

The "dumb cake" was a sort of dreaming-bread, made of certain traditional ingredients, baked, and cut into three pieces. Part of each was to be eaten, part placed under the pillow; when the clock struck twelve, the votary was to go to bed backwards, without uttering a single word to break the spell.[3] If she was to be married, her future husband would be seen hurrying after her; if she saw nothing, she was doomed to be an old maid. This mode of divination was practised up to comparatively recent times by Northumberland maidens. It is likely that the traditional bread-and-cheese and cider which figure in our story are not so primitive a survival as the "dumb cake." We would give much to know what "witch's book" the future Mrs. Penny used; was it *Mother Bunch's Closet Newly Broke Open,* a popular old chapbook, or merely traditional witching doggerel passed orally from generation to generation? Mother Bunch figures in old chapbooks as a keeper of old-world saws and choice matrimonial advice; like Mother Goose and Mother Shipton, her traditional name suggests both the "wise woman" and the witch.[4]

Proud Bathsheba Everdene undertook to read the future with her usual capricious indifference to the happiness of all save herself. On a Sunday afternoon, the thirteenth of February, Liddy was sitting with her mistress; "Liddy, like a little brook, though shallow, was always rippling. . . ." The sight of the old leather Bible on the table suggested to Liddy that Bathsheba find out whom she was to marry by Bible and key, but she was afraid to assist in the rite when she recalled that perhaps Sunday was an inauspicious time for divination. Bathsheba, however, was idly curious:

[2] *Under the Greenwood Tree,* Part I, Chap. VIII.
[3] Ellis's Brand, III, 331; N. Thomas, *Folklore of Northumberland,* 54–55.
[4] Lina B. Eckenstein, *Comparative Studies in Nursery Rhymes,* 5, 27.

The book was opened—the leaves, drab with age, being quite worn away at much-read verses by the forefingers of unpractised readers in former days, where they were moved along under the line as an aid to the vision. The special verse in the Book of Ruth was sought out by Bathsheba, and the sublime words met her eye. They slightly thrilled and abashed her. It was Wisdom in the abstract facing Folly in the concrete. Folly in the concrete persisted in her intention, and placed the key on the book. A rusty patch immediately upon the verse, caused by previous pressure of an iron substance thereon, told that this was not the first time the old volume had been used for the purpose.

"Now keep steady, and be silent," said Bathsheba.

The verse was repeated; the book turned round; Bathsheba blushed guiltily.

"Who did you try?" asked Liddy curiously.

"I shall not tell you." [5]

It was not long, however, before Liddy knew Bathsheba's secret; for, piqued by Boldwood's indifference to her beauty, Bathsheba was only seeking some pretext to send him the valentine she had bought for Teddy Coggan, and was, the reader suspects, rather pleased when the hymn-book, tossed into the air, came down shut, thus deciding the most momentous issue of Boldwood's life. The next morning, the proud and sensitive farmer received the valentine, sealed with a large red seal and bearing the inscription, "Marry Me." The fatal fascination had begun. [6]

Divination by Bible and key has continued up to recent times among the English, the Scotch and the Pennsylvania Dutch. [7] It is also used to detect the name of a thief; in fact, the sixteenth verse of the first chapter of *Ruth* is preferred for this detection of theft, and the *Song of Solomon,* the eighth chapter, the sixth and seventh verses, for love div-

---

[5] *Far from the Madding Crowd,* Chap. XIII.
[6] *Ibid.,* Chaps. XIII, XIV.
[7] Harland and Wilkinson, *Lancashire Folklore,* 7, 103–104. Napier, *Folk-Lore; or Superstitious Beliefs in the West of Scotland,* 106–107; Edwin C. Fogel, *Beliefs and Superstitions of the Pennsylvania Germans,* Proverb 201.

ination.[8] The Yorkshire belief is that the maiden trying the spell must fasten the key to the Bible with one of her garters;[9] another version has it that the charm works only when two sweethearts perform the rite.[10] In the nineteenth century, on the quay at Lynn, wives and sweethearts of seafaring men used to practise a peculiar sort of key-magic. They would turn a key with a winding motion, the stem towards them, to bring the expected vessel uptide; or would turn it in the opposite direction to bring good luck to those setting out on a voyage.[11] The records of Scottish witch trials show that Bible-and-key divination was charged against witches.[12]

"Tossing for it" is the basis of all games of chance like Chuck-farthing or Put.[13] It was characteristic of Bathsheba to "toss, as men do." She felt herself a match for any man; constantly arrogating to herself masculine privileges until the burden of their correspondent duties become unbearable, she finally fell back upon her feminine virtue of inconsistency, and called in Gabriel Oak. This story ends on a happier note than is usual in Hardy's novels; but it is none the less a note of irony. Bathsheba is chastened, it is true, but Boldwood is utterly destroyed, and the lack of poetic justice is the ironic close.

The most exquisite rite of divination is the maidens' sowing of hempseed on Midsummer Eve in *The Woodlanders*. Half the Hintocks were present to see the traditional ceremony. Marty South was not among the girls carrying each a handful of hempseed.

"I don't believe in it," she said laconically.

[8] *Folk-Lore Journal*, I, 333; Note; L. Salmon, *Folk-Lore*, XIII, 422–23; C. J. Billson, *Folklore of Leicestershire and Rutland*, 58; Lady Camilla Gurdon, *Folklore of Suffolk*, 96.
[9] Richard Blakeborough, *Wit, Character, Folklore, and Customs of the North Riding of Yorkshire*, 129.
[10] C. Latham, *Folk-Lore Record*, I, 31.
[11] W. B. Gerrish, *Folk-Lore*, IV, 391–92.
[12] J. G. Dalyell, *The Darker Superstitions of Scotland*, 522.
[13] Joseph Strutt, *Sports and Pastimes*, Bohn ed., 276–77; 386–87.

At midnight the girls appeared, some of them frightened.

"Directly we see anything, we'll run home as fast as we can," said one whose courage had begun to fail her.

"I wish we had not thought of trying this," said another, "but had contented ourselves with the hole-digging tomorrow at twelve, and hearing our husbands' trades. It is too much like having dealings with the Evil One to try to raise their forms." [14]

Off they went into the wood, but as the Great Hintock clock struck twelve, they came scurrying like frightened rabbits from the darkness; one declared they would never attempt it again, for instead of seeing their future partners, "We saw Satan pursuing us with his hourglass!" Grace Melbury had run straight into Fitzpiers' arms; perhaps the clever young doctor had hoped to use the girl's innocent superstition in his favor; we recall how seriously she took the dream of three crazed bells on her wedding eve as an evil omen. [15]

We do not know how the Hintock girls went about discovering their husbands' trades; half a dozen ways might have been chosen from. In the Isle of Man, vessels containing various things, such as clear water, meal, earth, and objects characteristic of certain callings were formerly placed around a room. The girls' eyes were bandaged; if one of them put her hands into the vessel of water, this was a sign her husband would be a handsome fellow; if she touched meal, he would be a miller; if earth, a farmer; if a net, a fisherman, and so on, through the most familiar trades. [16] A modified form of love-divination by nuts was practised in England: the maiden was to take a walnut, a hazel-nut, and nutmeg, grate and mix them with butter and sugar, and swallow the pellets lying down. If she was to marry a gentleman, her dreams would be happy; if a tradesman, she would hear "odd noises and tumults"; if a traveler, the sound of thunder and lightning would break up her sleep. [17] A much more common method was to take a small

---

[14] *The Woodlanders,* Chap. XX.
[15] *Ibid.,* Chaps. XXI, XXIV.
[16] *Folk-Lore,* II, 311.
[17] Ellis's Brand, I, 387.

lump of lead or pewter, put it in the left stocking before retiring, and place it under the pillow; on the next day, Midsummer Day, to place a pail of water so that the sun shone on it, and pour in the metal boiling hot, leaving it to form as it might. A ship meant a sailor-husband; tools, a common workman; a ring, a jeweler; a book, a parson.[18] German girls in medieval times were wont to wash their feet in a basin, throw out the water, and listen to it; the sound of scribbling or sewing meant respectively a clerk and a tailor or shoemaker.[19] All these methods involve sympathetic magic: washing in the basin falls under the principle whereby two persons are forbidden to wash in the same water, for fear of quarreling; the maiden who eats the nut-pellets literally eats her future, just as a "sin-eater" takes on himself the sins of the deceased by partaking of the funeral food. The Manx ceremony is fanciful, rather than primitive. Perhaps the Hintock maidens practised quite a different charm.

There is a crude matter-of-factness about this business of finding the husband's trade that repels the reader. The sowing of hempseed is in striking contrast to it. It goes back to the days when Teutonic women went out into the fields of flax at night, and leaped to make the flax grow high. From the ceremony of blessing the crop of flax came certain rites of divination. The rhyme which accompanies the sowing of hempseed is extremely old. One version runs:

> Hemp-seed I set, hemp-seed I sow,
> The young man whom I love, come after me and mow! [20]

The spell has been tried in many places in England within the last half century, sometimes on St. Mark's Eve, sometimes on Hallowe'en, but most commonly on Midsummer Eve.[21] The German bride in olden days put flax in her shoes

[18] Ellis's Brand, I, 336; E. M. Wright, *Rustic Speech and Folklore,* 260.
[19] Aubrey's *Remaines,* 24–25.
[20] Eckenstein, 65; Gurdon, 96.
[21] Billson, 32–33; Gurdon, 96; Gregor, 84; *Denham Tracts,* II, 278; Harland and Wilkinson, 140; C. Latham, *Folk-Lore Record,* I, 33.

for good luck.[22] The sowing and cutting of hemp were once associated all over Europe with peculiar dances, such as survive in the ancient game of Thread-the-Needle, and are plainly fertility rites.[23] Hemp is a narcotic, and was probably the herb that witches smoked in their clay pipes.[24] All the "wise women" of Teutonic antiquity had their spindles— Mother Goose, or Bertha of the Big Foot, Brunhilde, the Sleeping Beauty, and others pricked mysteriously by a sleeping-, or is it, a wishing-thorn, and swan-maidens—all play some important part in magic and divination. Even such a supreme folklorist as Jacob Grimm can do little more than point out here and there a striking likeness that needs further study.[25]

The simple rite in *The Woodlanders* has in it the pageant of the past. The older folk lent their unspoken sympathy by their presence; the mysterious beauty of the wood, the hushed suspense, the humor of Satan and his hourglass, the timid faith of the girls themselves—all make the scene memorable. The reader may well feel that he, too, is conspiring with unholy powers, and assisting for one night at the rites of the folk.

Hardy's use of folklore shows no straining for effect. He does not refer to certain modes of divination popular in Dorset: to the custom of peering down the Wooler Wishing-Well;[26] to Midsummer divination by the white of an egg in water, a method which the Hardy reader finds employed by Conjuror Trendle in "The Withered Arm," in his effort to discover Gertrude's persecutor;[27] to the simple act of placing the shoes in the shape of a lucky "T";[28] to fortune-telling by the wishbone or "merrythought" of a fowl, a di-

---

[22] Hilderic Friend, *Folk-Lore Journal,* II, 287.
[23] Eckenstein, 56; Mrs. Alice B. Gomme, *Traditional Games of England, Ireland and Scotland,* Memoir, Vol. II, pp. 502–503.
[24] Eckenstein, 56.
[25] Grimm-Stallybrass, I, pp. 278–81, 419–20, 429; III, 1240; IV, 1403.
[26] N. Thomas, *Folklore of Northumberland,* 6.
[27] H. J. Rose, *Folk-Lore,* XXXIV, 155; E. M. Wright, *Rustic Speech,* p. 260; J. C. Lawson, *Modern Greek Folklore and Ancient Greek Religion,* 331.
[28] Wm. Barnes, in Hone's *Year Book,* p. 1175; N. Thomas, 54; Denham, II, 279.

rect survival of divination by the shoulder-blade of a sheep in ancient times.[29] Hardy uses only such material as comes naturally into the action of the story he has to tell. His own interest in divination is perhaps revealed in the poem, "Yuletide in a Younger World," in the regretful thought that those who once liked divination now are "blinker-bound." [30]

One of the oldest modes of augury was from the flight of birds, a mode beautifully employed in "The Alarm." [31] A Wessex soldier, called south to the coast to fight Bonaparte, but sorely tempted to return to his childing wife, looses a little bird tangled in the sedge, and prays earnestly that he may be directed by its flight. He follows it southward, and finds that Napoleon has not landed and he is free to go home. In his simple piety we see an act of faith rather than of magic. The Greeks and Romans made a science of this mode of augury: to the Greeks flight to the right was lucky; to the Romans, flight to the left.[32]

Marie Louise was a believer in astrology, as we learn from her acceptance of the prophecy that Napoleon was to die at an inn called *The Red Crab*.[33] This is but one of the many passages in *The Dynasts* which reveal the intense popular hatred of "Boney," who kept soothsayers busy with prophecies of his downfall that always proved to be another "hope deferred."

There is a scene in *Far from the Madding Crowd* in which Joseph Poorgrass is telling the omen that had come to him just before the sheep on Weatherbury Farm had eaten of clover and blasted themselves:

"Yes, and I was sitting at home looking for Ephesians, and says I to myself, ' 'Tis nothing but Corinthians and Thessalonians in this danged Testament,' when who should come in but Henery here: 'Joseph,' he said, 'the sheep have blasted theirselves.' " [34]

[29] Grimm-Stallybrass, III, 1114; Lawson, 327.
[30] *Winter Words.*
[31] *Wessex Poems.*
[32] Lawson, 309–10; Grimm-Stallybrass, III, 1128–30.
[33] *The Dynasts,* Part First, Act III, Scene V.
[34] Chap. XXI.

This is not divination, but a comic use of sortes, the humor of the episode increased because the appeal to lots and sortes is one of the oldest and most dignified modes of divination. Aubrey tells us that lot-meads still existed in the the England of his day.[35] Lot-taking is referred to in *The Dynasts.*[36]

Divination of death is the theme of "The Superstitious Man's Story." The seedsman's father is recounting what a curious, silent sort of man William Privett, the hero of his tale, was—the sort of man to make one feel chilly the moment he entered a room. He goes on to tell how Mrs. Privett saw her husband go out, but not return; how she chalked a message for him on the door, "Mind and do the door"; how she found him sleeping, much mystified by the message on the door, and convinced that he had not gone out at all. Midsummer Day she met Nancy Weedle, who accounted for her sleepy look by confessing that she had been one of a party who watched in the church porch the night previous. Midsummer Eve was the time when the faint shapes of all who were going to be at death's door might be seen entering the church, and when those who are doomed to die would not come out of the church.

"What did you see?" asked William's wife.

"Well," says Nancy, backwardly— "We needn't tell what we saw, or who we saw."

"You saw my husband," said Betty Privett in a quiet way.

"Well, since you put it so," says Nancy, hanging fire, "we thought we did see him; but it was darkish and we was frightened, and of course, it might not have been he."

"Nancy, you needn't mind letting it out, though 'tis kept back in kindness. And he didn't come out of church again: I know it as well as you." [37]

Three days later Privett was found dead in the fields.

[35] Aubrey's *Remaines,* 92.
[36] Part Second, Act III, Scene I.
[37] *Life's Little Ironies:* "A Few Crusted Characters": "The Superstitious Man's Story."

Mrs. Privett's instant guess, and her complete belief in the superstition, reveal the attitude of a whole community. The belief was extremely common all over England up to the beginning of the present century.[38] Hardy does not allude to the gruesome rite of cauff-riddling.[39]

Midsummer Eve is the time when ghosts of dead lovers appear: Jude sat alone one night after Sue had gone, as watchers sit on Midsummer Eve, hoping to see the phantom of the Beloved.[40] A lovely poem, "On a Midsummer Eve," deals with this theme:

> I idly cut a parsley stalk,
> And blew therein towards the moon;
> I had not thought what ghosts would walk
> With shivering footsteps to my tune.[41]

There is, for the poet's purpose, a definite value in this unconquerable human desire to know what the future holds. It reveals unsuspected depths and shallows of human nature—hidden impulses, secret longings, and inexplicable strivings which rise and put reason aside. The comedy or tragedy of the issue lies, to some extent, in the mood and temperament of the questioner. Mrs. Penny's divination is told with Dickensian humor. Bathsheba Everdene's maddening caprice, the touchstone of her nature, is revealed in the cruel nonchalance of "tossing for it." Grace Melbury sowing the hempseed is a delicate slip of a girl, slow to know her own heart, timid to a fault, readily swayed against her own interests, yet always so exquisite that we love her even as we condemn her. Tess's slight gesture is full of the soft pathos that plays about her like a transfiguring mist. Hardy uses divination to paint the light and shade of character, and to secure a powerful and highly natural suspense.

---

[38] J. U. Powell, *Folk-Lore*, XII, 72–73; H. C. March, *Folk-Lore*, X, 481; M. Peacock, *Folk-Lore*, XIV, 94; Aubrey's *Remaines*, 26, 97, 133; Gurdon, 32; C. L. Wimberly, *Folklore in the English and Scottish Ballads*, 246.
[39] Wm. Henderson, *Folklore of the Northern Counties*, 51–52.
[40] *Jude the Obscure*, Part III, Chap. VIII.
[41] *Moments of Vision*.

III

GHOST AND FAIRY LORE

There is a large amount of ghost and fairy lore in the works of Thomas Hardy. There are the primitive conceptions of the soul as a moth, a bird, a tree, a light, or a name. There are suggested likenesses between ghosts, fairies, and witches. There are ghosts of every variety—happy, remorseful, malicious, plaintive, and ineffectual. The major part of our ceremonial of death and burial is a survival of a primitive cult based on the fear of the dead kinsmen; such, for instance, is the use of coins for the eyes of the dead, the burial of the unbaptized or unregenerate in the north side of the churchyard, the happily extinct practice of burying the suicide or criminal at the crossroads with a stake through his body, and the picturesque custom of "telling the bees." Certain animals, chiefly dogs and horses, have second-sight, and certain persons are born ghost-seers. There are times and seasons, notably Christmastide, Midsummer, and the autumn feast of All Souls, when ghosts are most likely to appear; there are lonely moors, woodlands, and family mansions which they tend to haunt. Hardy's ghosts are interesting in and of themselves: some of them go their placid way, following the pursuits they knew in life; others, their eyes opened, look back upon their earthly life as a curious affair; still others utter biting satire on a blind world.

In "The Souls of the Slain," Hardy pictures the spirits of those who have died in battle homing to England; they are night-moths, large and flamelike, moving like a Pentecostal wind, wailing in the storm:

52

Soon from out the Southward seemed nearing
A whirr, as of wings
Waved by mighty-vanned flies,
Or by night-moths of measureless size,
And in softness and smoothness well-nigh beyond hearing
Of corporal things.[1]

They are met by a "senior soul-flame," who tells them that they are remembered, not for their glorious death, but for the "little unremembered acts of love" that had endeared them to those at home. The scene is "The Race," a turbulent stretch of sea off Portland Bill; the whole conception is daring, Blakelike, but worked out with more care for detail than Blake would have bestowed on it. The quality of this poem is extremely rare in literature; it actually bodies forth spirit.

Another poem, "The Sheep Boy," [2] has something of the same eerie quality. The vast clouds that drive the sheep and all living things before them, impelling the bees to headlong flight, and mysteriously blotting out the whole landscape, seem to be full of "souls." The poet again suggests a moth-soul in "Friends Beyond," [3] where the speaker, musing on the past, is reminded of his dead friends of the Mellstock choir at "mothy curfew-tide." He suggests the same idea more directly in the poem, "Something Tapped": A bereaved lover, hearing a ghostly tap at the window, goes eagerly to find only a huge moth beating its wings against the pane.[4] But the most direct use of the motif is to be found in "The Superstitious Man's Story." [5] Some villagers watching in the church-porch on Midsummer Eve, had seen William Privett enter the church, not to reappear—a sure omen of death. Some weeks later, Privett and a fellow-laborer, tired out from a morning's haying, lay down in the fields to take a nap. John Chiles awoke suddenly just in time to see a white moth miller issue from Privett's mouth and fly away.

[1] *Poems of the Past and the Present.*
[2] *Human Shows.*
[3] *Wessex Poems.*
[4] *Moments of Vision.*
[5] *Life's Little Ironies:* "A Few Crusted Characters."

He was shocked to find his friend dead. The rest of the tale
is still more uncanny: at the very hour of his death, the form
of William Privett was seen at Longpuddle Spring, two
miles away, a spot he had carefully avoided for years, because of the painful memory of his little son who had been
drowned there.

The belief in an external soul capable of assuming a shape
and an existence independent of the body runs through all
folklore; there are savage tribes today who believe that the
soul is a bird, a bee, a moth, a tree, a light, a shadow, a stone,
and even a name.[6] The Greeks did not invent the myth of
Psyche; they merely gave her an exquisite story; her Teutonic counterpart, Freyja, had a butterfly avatar.[7] In Yorkshire and Gloucestershire, they still call night-flying moths
"souls"; [8] and when a moth flutters around a candle, Lith-
uanian peasant women say that some one's soul is going
hence.[9]

Modern savages think that the soul may escape through
the mouth, the eyes, the nose, the anterior fontanelle, or
even through the joints. Dreams are the adventures of the
soul out of the body; death is its refusal to be coaxed back
into the body.[10] Our lady-bird rhyme, which in some versions
substitutes "butterfly" for "ladybird," was probably originally a soul-catching charm, invoking the wandering soul to
return to its body by relating the misfortunes which require
its presence at home: philologists have no satisfactory deri-
vation for the words "ladybird," "lady-cow," or "butterfly." [11]

Closely connected with this conception of the soul is the

[6] Dr. James G. Frazer, *The Golden Bough,* one vol. ed., 1922, 674–75.
[7] J. Grimm, *Deutsche Mythologie,* J. S. Stallybrass, trans., II, 829–830;
IV, 1548; Donald Mackenzie, *Ancient Man in Britain,* 192.
[8] G. L. Gomme, *Ethnology in Folklore,* 158; E. M. Wright, *Rustic Speech
and Folklore,* 116.
[9] Grimm-Stallybrass, IV, 1548.
[10] Rev. Sabine Baring-Gould, *Strange Survivals,* 258; W. H. Rivers,
"The Concept of Soul-Substance in New Guinea and Melanesia," *Folk-Lore,*
XXXI, 49; Gudmund Schütte, "Danish Paganism," *Folk-Lore,* XXXV, 361–62.
[11] S. O. Addy, *Folk-Lore,* XIII, 432; N. W. Thomas, *Folk-Lore,* XIV, 182;
Harland and Wilkinson, *Lancashire Folklore,* 70–71; Grimm-Stallybrass, II,
694–95.

idea that moths or butterflies are the shapes assumed by
witches or their demon lovers: in Scotland moths were called
"witches," and were dreaded as uncanny; [12] in Northumberland red butterflies were killed as witches; [13] and this ghost-
like butterfly was known as an *alb* in German folklore.[14]
Witches were believed to take this form the more readily to
steal milk; witches, malicious dwarfs, and butterflies share
the name of *milchdieben;* they stole the milk from the udders
of kine, and could even force a mother to wean her child,
a belief that underlies the saying that German mothers have
when weaning a child, "The butterfly has taken the milk
away." [15] Nowhere is the connection between ghost, witch,
and fairy lore quite so close as in this particular belief; fairy
lore took over certain ideas of dead souls, and some of these
were still later transferred to witchcraft. At the bottom of
all of them lies the primitive idea that "soul-substance" resides in hair, teeth, blood, breath, spittle, and even in the
shadow or the name of a human being, an idea which also
explains most practices of sympathetic magic.[16]

All the weird tales of the nightjar with its one pierced
wing point to the belief in a bird-soul. Its wing is pierced, so
runs the story, because it is the spirit of a murderer, suicide,
or of one buried at the crossroads with a stake through his
body.[17] There are other tales of bird-souls, some exquisitely
poetic and remarkably like the fairy tales so familiar to
us.[18] There are also tales of tree-souls, illustrated in old
South's fear of the great elm; [19] tales of light-souls, like our
Jack-o'-Lent or will-o'-the-wisp; [20] tales of stone-souls,[21] and

---

[12] Rev. Walter Gregor, *Some Notes on the Folk-Lore of the North-East of
Scotland,* 147.
[13] *Denham Tracts,* II, 325.
[14] Grimm-Stallybrass, II, 462; III, 1072, 1074, 1082.
[15] Grimm-Stallybrass, III, 1072; N. Thomas, *Folk-Lore,* XIV, 182.
[16] W. H. R. Rivers, *Folk-Lore,* XXXI, 50–52.
[17] Gudmund Schütte, "Danish Paganism," *Folk-Lore,* XXXV, 364.
[18] M. J. MacCulloch, "The Folk-Lore of the Isle of Skye," *Folk-Lore,*
XXXIII, 311–12; G. L. Gomme, *Ethnology in Folklore,* 158, 159.
[19] *The Woodlanders,* Chaps. II, XIII, XIV; C. Lowry Wimberly, *Folklore
in the English and Scottish Ballads,* 38, 84.
[20] Wimberly, 82; Baring-Gould, *Strange Survivals,* 31; Grimm-Stallybrass,
II, 508, 512.
[21] Frazer, *The Golden Bough,* 680.

of name-souls.[22] We echo this primitive belief when we say,
"My heart was in my mouth." [23]

Hardy refers to the naughty fairy, the jack-o'-lantern, and
to pixies and their habits.[24] The jack-o'-lantern is the spirit
of a man who has removed landmarks, and is punished by
being forced to wander continually; [25] but he is also conceived as a sportive creature whose innate love of mischief
causes him to lead travelers astray, over moors and into
bogs, laughing heartily the while, and angered only by a
rival light, which he dashes to the ground.[26] Much like
pixies, he delights in playing tricks upon those who have
taken a drop too much at the inn and in knotting the manes
of horses.[27] Egdon Heath was full of pixies: Mrs. Yeobright
was warned not to lose her way home, for many had been
pixy-led on Egdon.[28] It was from the fear of pixies and such
terrifying visitors as the reddleman, the "red ghost," that
little Johnny Nunsuch eagerly accepted the crooked sixpence,
proof against witchcraft, which Eustacia Vye gave him for
tending her fire.[29] As Henchard was leaving Casterbridge for
the last time, he passed a green circle, which reminded him
that it was on that very pixy-ring that Susan must have stood
as she bade him farewell when she went off with the sailor
Newson.[30]

It is possible that tales of pixies represent an ancient memory of a small folk—perhaps non-Aryan, perhaps Stone Age
men—who once inhabited England.[31] The Vale of Black-
moor was full of "green-gowned" and "green-spangled"
fairies who whickered when their dense woods were invaded

[22] Wimberly, 84, 338; Edward Clodd, *Magic in Names,* 37, 44–45; E. S.
Hartland, *Ritual and Belief,* 131; Gregor, 30.
[23] Frazer, *The Golden Bough,* 181.
[24] *Wessex Tales:* "Interlopers at the Knap"; *Moments of Vision,* "To My
Father's Violin"; *The Dynasts,* Part Second, Act IV, Scene VIII, etc.
[25] Baring-Gould, *Strange Survivals,* 31; Grimm-Stallybrass, III, 918.
[26] Grimm-Stallybrass, II, 512–513; Lady Camilla Gurdon, *Folklore of
Suffolk,* 122.
[27] *Denham Tracts,* II, 84; E. M. Wright, *Rustic Speech,* 210–211.
[28] *The Return of the Native,* Book I, Chap. III.
[29] *Ibid.,* Book I, Chap. VIII.
[30] *The Mayor of Casterbridge,* Chap. XLIV.
[31] Grimm-Stallybrass, IV, 1409, 1414–17.

by prying human creatures.[32] Pixies, like all fairies, are green in color.[33]

Myrtle Petherwin, having torn her gown one night and found it neatly mended the next morning, was sure that her sister Ethelberta was a fairy, but Emmeline thought she was too tall for a fairy, and perhaps merely knew the fairy's godmother.[34] Again, when Picotee, another sister, had been indulged in her desire to see a real dinner party, the country maiden was frightened by the capers the servants were cutting belowstairs:

Her nerves were screwed up to the highest pitch of uneasiness by the grotesque habits of these men and maids who . . . resembled nothing so much as pixies, elves, or gnomes, peeping upon human beings from their haunts underground, sometimes for good, sometimes for ill—sometimes doing heavy work, sometimes none; teasing and worrying with impish laughter half-suppressed, and vanishing directly mortal eyes were bent upon them. . . .[35]

The relation between ghosts and witchcraft comes out plainly in the picturesque Dorset phantom, the Ooser. Betty Dornell, grieved at her lover's repugnance when he saw that she was sickening with smallpox, exclaimed indignantly that she would not so have treated him, had he been ugly as the Ooser in the church vestry itself![36] The Ooser seems to have been a sort of grotesque devil-mask with great horns attached which was formerly worn at the Melbury-Osmond Christmas Revel.[37] Witches were said to have worn such masks in order to induce a particularly hollow tone;[38] yet the classical witches, noted for their "stridor," or hollow

---

[32] *Poems of the Past and the Present:* "The Bullfinches"; *Tess*, Chap. L; Wm. Barnes, "The Veairies," *Poems of Rural Life in the Dorset Dialect*, 72.
[33] Wimberly, 176; J. B. Partridge, *Folk-Lore*, XXXVII, 307.
[34] *The Hand of Ethelberta*, Chap. XXV.
[35] *Ibid.*, Chap. XXIX.
[36] *A Group of Noble Dames:* Dame the First, "Betty, the First Countess of Wessex."
[37] D. H. M. Read, *Folk-Lore*, XXII, 302, Note 13; cf. Wm. Barnes, Glossary of the Dorset Dialect, *Transactions of the Philological Society*, 1864, p. 73.
[38] M. A. Murray, "Organizations of Witches in Great Britain," *Folk-Lore*, XXVIII, 236.

voices, cannot be proved to have donned masks.[39] Nevertheless, we know that the German witches wore some disguise,
and probably either blackened their faces or wore masks
in their ritual dances; in fact, the word *masca* in Romance
tongues means a mask, a blackened face, a helmet, and a
witch.[40] The play upon the satirical term "to wear horns,"
as applied to a cuckold, may serve to explain the use of the
word Ooser for the procession in which those unfaithful
in marriage are satirized by being carried in effigy, by rough
music, and by a serenade in which their misdeeds are publicly
recited. The Skimmington ride, as it is called in Dorset and
immortalized in *The Mayor,*[41] is, in other counties, dubbed
a Hooset- or Wooset-Hunting.[42]

The Ooser seems also to have some connection with headless ghosts: near Witney, in Oxfordshire, at Ousen Bottom,
there was long seen a ghost who carried his head under his
arm and alarmed the passengers of the mail-coach by sometimes climbing up to the carrier's seat! [43] We shall have more
to say on this subject when we consider physical ghosts.

Ghosts, fairies, and witches are intimately connected in
their lore. The sojourner in Fairyland, like the visitor to
Hades, must be careful to eat nothing.[44] Witches, like fairies,
have the power to make themselves invisible, to change their
shape at will, to steal the essence of milk, and other food-
stuffs, to ride cattle and horses at night, to steal away unsained children, to scatter "elf-shot," and to travel through
the air.[45] Witches hold their important assemblies at the
seasons when souls of the dead are drawn into the train
led by Odin, Freyja, and Bertha—that is, at May-Eve,
Midsummer-Eve, Hallowe'en, and the Twelve Days of
Christmas; they feast and dance by night, just as elves do,

[39] Wm. R. Halliday, *Folk-Lore,* XXXIII, 227–229.
[40] N. W. Thomas, *Folk-Lore,* XI, 264; Grimm-Stallybrass, IV, 1618.
[41] Chapter XXXIX.
[42] Ditchfield, *Old English Customs,* 178; D. H. M. Read, *Folk-Lore,* XXII, 302.
[43] Angelina Parker, "Oxfordshire Folklore," *Folk-Lore,* XXXIV, 323.
[44] E. S. Hartland, *The Science of Fairy Tales,* 43 ff.
[45] Canon J. A. MacCulloch, "The Mingling of Fairy and Witch Beliefs," *Folk-Lore,* XXXII, 228–230.

though they leave no "fairy rings" of green grass.[46] The music of which elves are so fond plays a large part in witches' revels; one pipes to them on a horse's head, and must play until some human creature happens upon the feast; he, in turn, is bound to play unless he invokes some sacred name to break the evil spell.[47] It is curious that Hardy gives us none of the familiar tales of the spirit-music which proceeds from the Wessex barrows.[48]

Ghosts are of many kinds: on the whole those tend most surely to return who are dissatisfied with the turn things have taken with the living, who are remorseful or reproachful; those whose love bridges the gap between flesh and spirit and draws them back to watch over those left behind; who, like family ghosts, return to give definite advice at a crisis in family affairs; and ghosts of those who have not long been dead, especially of those just buried or about to be buried. Hardy has a macabre little poem, "A January Night,"[49] in which the wild stormy weather is pictured as the work of the spirit of the dead man, not yet confined to its wooden cell. There are many stories of ghosts who return to reproach the living. "The Harvest Supper"[50] is such a tale: Nell, forgetting the lover she has lost only a month before, is singing and dancing with the gallant Scotch Greys in the barn when the phantom of her lover appears and reproaches her; the girl goes home ill, resolved never to wed. In "The Supplanter,"[51] the lover turns in anger against the woman who had supplanted his true love and broken her heart, and caused her ghost to return and plague him. "Something Tapped"[52] is a tale of a reproachful ghost who pleads with her lover to join her in her lonely bed.

The ballad, "A Trampwoman's Tragedy,"[53] paints a vivid picture of gypsy life; the trampwoman, in a fit of ca-

[46] MacCulloch, *Folk-Lore,* XXXII, 229–230.
[47] Grimm-Stallybrass, II, 516–517.
[48] Wilkinson Sherren, *The Wessex of Romance,* 25.
[49] *Moments of Vision.*
[50] *Human Shows.*
[51] *Poems of the Past and the Present.*
[52] *Moments of Vision.*
[53] *Time's Laughingstocks.*

price, had told her fancy-man that the child she was to bear
was not his; he had killed his rival and had hung for it, but
his ghost returned, unable to rest until he learned the truth,
when he "thinned away," content at last, leaving her alone
to haunt the Western Moor. The fable of the tale, the gypsy
life, the poet's insight into the feminine heart, have all conspired to make this ballad one of the most popular of Hardy's
poems. In "The Second Night," [54] we have a rather curious
tale: A false lover is keeping tryst with a new sweetheart;
the woman who loves him, overwhelmed by the discovery,
kills herself. Her ghost comes to reproach him for disloy-
alty in love; but, thinking it is merely a jealous woman, he
takes all her upbraiding coolly enough. As she turns to leave
him, a brilliant star streams through the sky, and for the
moment he fancies it is like the passing of a soul. Some hours
later he learns that the woman he had jilted is indeed dead;
and, as the realization comes that it was her ghost who had
come to reproach him, as if to confirm the truth, another
star shoots madly through the sky. "The Inscription" [55] has
an ironic fable: A widow had foolishly inscribed her name
upon her husband's tablet, omitting only the date: she was
afraid to marry, and her ghost comes night after night to
gaze on the fateful inscription. "A Sound in the Night" [56]
is the gruesome story of a man who, under the spell of a
"witch-woman," has murdered the woman he really loves,
and their child. Maddened by the thought of his crime, he
deserts the witch, leaving her, in turn, to be haunted by the
sound of a woman's crying and an infant's moan, which
come fitfully to her in the wind. Other poems on this theme
are "The Woman I Met" [57] and "The Church and the Wedding." [58] "At Shag's Heath" and "The Duke's Reappearance" tell the story of the ghost of the unfortunate Monmouth,[59] who returns to reproach his betrayer.

[54] *Late Lyrics, and Earlier.*
[55] *Ibid.*
[56] *Ibid.*
[57] *Ibid.*
[58] *Human Shows.*
[59] *A Changed Man, and Other Stories; Human Shows:* "At Shag's Heath."

"The Dead and the Living One" has an ironic twist: The woman who has lost her soldier-lover to a rival is gloating over her death; suddenly a gory phantom makes his presence felt at the grave; it is the soldier, who rebukes his former sweetheart, telling her that Death has willed that he and his true love should not be divided. The close of this poem is a thing of sheer perfection:

> There was a cry by the white-flowered mound,
> There was a laugh from underground,
> There was a deeper gloom around.[60]

Happy ghosts come also to haunt the places they have loved in life, and to be near their dear ones. In "The Phantom" [61] the spirit of the dead woman is gladly evoked by her bereft lover; in "The Old Neighbour and the New," [62] in the chair where the new vicar is seated, the speaker sees only the form of the dead vicar he had loved. "Her Immortality" [63] contains a characteristic Hardy theme: the ghost of the dead girl implores her lover to live for her, telling him that she lives only through him, and that with his surcease ends her lease of life. We have similar tales of living ghosts in "The To-Be-Forgotten" [64] and "His Immortality." [64] "The Dead Man Walking" [65] and "The Two Men" [66] are tales of "walking ghosts"; "Her Haunting Ground," [67] and "My Spirit Will Not Haunt the Mound" are memorable expressions of the idea that only those who wish to see the dead, will see them, and see them in the old, familiar places. One stanza sums up the thought best:

> My spirit will not haunt the mound
>   Above my breast,
> But travel, memory-possessed,

[60] *Moments of Vision:* "The Dead and the Living One."
[61] *Time's Laughingstocks.*
[62] *Late Lyrics.*
[63] *Wessex Poems.*
[64] *Poems of the Past and the Present.*
[65] *Time's Laughingstocks.*
[66] *Wessex Poems.*
[67] *Human Shows.*

To where my tremulous being found
Life largest, best.[68]

There are wistful ghosts, too, who come only when especially evoked: the ghost in "The Cheval-Glass" [69] wonders,
even in death, if separation has really changed the heart of
the beloved; there are the ghosts of "The Spell of the
Rose" [70] and "The Wistful Lady," [70] each of whom appears,
not to the beloved, but to the supplanter. Particularly delicate
is the ironic reminder of the "wistful lady" to her faithless
lover: time and time again she appears to the woman he has
wedded, scanning her face, not unkindly but curiously, pon-
dering her words, sometimes seeming to wish to speak to her,
sometimes beckoning to her, then disappearing as if fearful
of the encounter. At last the husband remembers his dead
love's playful threat to show herself, not to him, but to his
new love. We are also reminded of poor Fanny Robin, by
whose body even timid Liddy was not afraid to sit; Fanny
was too "nesh" to appear to any one.[71]

"The Grave at the Handpost" [72] introduces us to a new
kind of ghost, which it does not introduce in person, but in-
directly—the malicious, dangerous physical ghost of the suicide buried at the crossroads with a stake through his body.
The story is as gruesome as anything in Hardy. An aged
father, apparently deserted by his son, in a fit of despond-
ency kills himself, and is meted out the death then given a
suicide; he is buried at the crossroads with a new six-foot
hurdle-saul from a sheep-pen through his body. On his return
from the army, the son induces the kind-hearted Mellstock
folk to assist in moving his father's body to the churchyard,
where he intends to erect a stone. Then they discover the
mode of burial. The thought of his father pursues him; and
one Christmas Eve, hoping to share his shameful fate, he,
too, kills himself; by the irony of circumstance, he is buried

[68] *Satires of Circumstance.*
[69] *Ibid.*
[70] *Ibid.*
[71] *Far from the Madding Crowd,* Chap. XLIII.
[72] *A Changed Man, and Other Stories.*

quietly in the churchyard! The village waits who sing their plaintive carol over the suicide's body are the only relief in a story of almost unmitigated gloom.

This practice, now happily long extinct, is but one of several death and burial customs based on the fear of the dead. Our ceremonial of burial contains survivals of two distinct cults of the dead, one based on the love of dead kinsmen, the other, far more primitive, on the fear of them. The following customs are possibly to be explained as survivals based on a cult of fear of the dead: Opening doors and windows at the hour of death; feeding the bees funeral food and telling them of the death within the house; expelling all animals from the room of death, and killing any creature that strays into it; watching the corpse until burial; taking the corpse to the grave by regularly used "corpse-ways"; funeral feasts; shutting the eyes of the dead with coins; turning the mirrors in a room where a death has occurred; burial of the unregenerate and unbaptized in the north side of the churchyard; burial of suicides and criminals at the crossroads with a stake through the body; and the use of corpses, grave-clothes, grave-molds, coffin-nails, and the like for medical cures.[73] The passing-bell was originally intended to frighten off evil spirits lying in wait for the dying soul.[74] Mourning attire may have originated in the fear of the dead, and may have been a sort of disguise to deceive the dead,[75] but it is more likely that it was worn to indicate that those who had been polluted by touching the dead were taboo to the living until ceremonially purified.[76]

The mutilation of a corpse is a primitive device on the part of the living to rid themselves of the dead: Athenian suicides had their right hands cut off, and Clytemnastra, it will be remembered, lopped off her husband's hands and feet and tied them around his neck in order to cripple his

[73] *Ethnology in Folklore*, 114–126.
[74] Harland and Wilkinson, *Lancashire Folklore*, 41–42; Dalyell, *The Darker Superstitions of Scotland*, 136 ff.
[75] Baring-Gould, *Curiosities of Olden Times*, 12.
[76] E. S. Hartland, *Ritual and Belief*, 235 ff.

ghost.[77] This practice has existed from early times in Denmark: Saxo tells the story of Otho the impostor, who seized the throne in Odin's absence, but on the return of the latter, fled to Finland, where he was slain. The barrow in which he was buried smote all who approached it until his body was unearthed, beheaded, and impaled.[78] Our English and Scottish ballads abound in references to such mutilations.[79] At Royston Church, near Barnsley, a thigh-forked skeleton was found in 1886; elsewhere coffins have been found with a special place cut out for the decapitated head.[80] Mary Hill's Grave is one of several places in Oxfordshire said to be the burial-places of mutilated suicides.[81] During the World War, English war correspondents sent to the *London Times* accounts of how the Tommies buried German soldiers of great size and fierceness face downwards, to prevent the return of their ghosts![82] The Danes think that the *nat-rawn*, the nightjar with one pierced wing, is the ghost of a mutilated criminal.[83] Undoubtedly corpse mutilation has led to the numerous folk-tales of headless ghosts, and of ghosts carrying their heads under their arms. Most famous of all our headless ghosts is the debonair Green Knight of *Gawayne and the Grene Knyghte*. Hardy refers to the ghost who gave her name to the Quiet Woman Inn, a discreet lady who was pictured as carrying her head under her arm![84]

Crossroads play an important rôle in folklore: The Teutonic divinities of death, as well as fairies, elves, dwarfs, demons, witches, and ghosts of all sorts, were wont to gather at crossroads; at crossroads the soul of the dead was disputed for.[85] Crossroads were a place where charms and

---

[77] Wm. R. Halliday, *Greek and Roman Folklore*, 50.
[78] York-Powell's ed. *Saxo-Grammaticus*, Intro. LXI, LXVII.
[79] C. L. Wimberly, *Folklore in the English and Scottish Ballads*, 225–226.
[80] S. O. Addy, *Folk-Lore*, XII, 101–102; Dr. Karl Feilberg, "The Corpse-Door: A Danish Survival," *Folk-Lore*, XVIII, 364–365.
[81] Percy Manning, *Folk-Lore*, XIV, 73–74.
[82] *Folk-Lore*, XVII, 224–225, quoting *London Times*, July 29, 1915.
[83] Gudmund Schütte, "Danish Paganism," *Folk-Lore*, XXXV, 364–365; Grimm-Stallybrass, II, 828–829.
[84] *The Return of the Native*, Book I, Chap. V.
[85] Wimberly, 369; Grimm-Stallybrass, II, 838; III, 1074, 1115.

spells were tried to cure ailments; [86] a place where divinations were practised,[87] and altogether a most ghostly place.

Another survival based on the fear of the dead is the burial of the reprobate, the unbaptized, and the criminal on the north side of the churchyard in unconsecrated ground, the body lying north and south, not east and west and facing the east as does a normally buried body.[88] Old Aubrey notes that the way of coming into all great churches was formerly at the west door, so that the worshiper might face the altar at the East, which is the way for true Christians to pray.[89] The fox in the Roman de Renart prayed christianly, but the wolf, like the heathen he is, facing the north.[90] Cloten was buried face to the East, as Cymbeline had ordered; [91] only Ophelia's rank entitled her to any form of Christian burial, but the funeral train were bidden to throw on her grave:

> . . . For charitable prayers
> Shards, flints, and pebbles. . . .[92]

Fanny Robin, and Tess's baby, Sorrow the Undesired, were buried "behind church." [93]

Other practices probably originating in a cult based on the fear of the dead are the opening of the doors and windows, and the unlocking of all locks and bolts at the moment of death and after death. Nothing must impede the passing soul. There is also the custom of placing coins on the eyes of the dead, and the familiar omen that if the corpse will not keep its eyes closed, it is looking for the next one to follow. Mother Cuxsom was telling an interested circle at the Casterbridge town pump the details of Mrs. Henchard's death:

[86] W. Crooke, *Folk-Lore,* XX, 88–89.
[87] Grimm-Stallybrass, III, 1115, Notes 1, 2.
[88] Sir Thos. Browne, *Urn Burial,* Chap. III; *Denham Tracts,* II, 38, 65; Harland and Wilkinson, 275; Gurdon, 49; Ellis's Brand, II, 291; Gregor, 213; N. Thomas, *Folklore of Northumberland,* 100; Dennys, 65; Wm. Henderson, *Folklore of the Northern Counties,* 61.
[89] Aubrey's *Remaines,* 106; Grimm-Stallybrass, I, 34; IV, 1297.
[90] Grimm-Stallybrass, I, 34; Reinh. Fuchs, XLI.
[91] *Cymbeline,* V, 2.
[92] *Hamlet,* V. 1.
[93] *Far from the Madding Crowd,* Chap. XLVI; *Tess,* Chap. XIV.

"And she was white as marble-stone. . . . And likewise such a thoughtful woman, too—ah, poor soul—that 'a minded every little thing that wanted tending. . . . 'Yes' says she, 'when I'm gone, and my last breath's blowed, look in the top drawer o' the chest . . . and you'll find my coffin clothes. . . . And there's four ounce pennies, the heaviest I could find, a-tied up in bits of linen, for weights—two for my right eye and two for my left! And when you've used 'em, and my eyes don't open no more, bury the pennies, good souls, and don't ye go spending 'em, for I shouldn't like it. And open the windows as soon as I am carried out, and make it as cheerful as you can for Elizabeth-Jane!' "

"Ah, poor heart!"

"Well, and Martha did it, and buried the ounce pennies in the garden. But if ye'll believe words, that man, Christopher Coney, went and dug 'em up, and spent 'em at the Three Mariners. 'Faith,' he said, . . . 'Death's not of such good report that we should respect 'en to that extent,' says he."

" 'Twas a cannibal deed!" deprecated her listeners.

"Gad, then, I won't quite ha'e it," said Solomon Longways. "I say it today, and 'tis Sunday morning, and I wouldn't speak wrongfully for a zilver zixpence at such a time. I don't see noo harm in it. To respect the dead is sound doxology; and I wouldn't sell skellintons—leastwise respectable skellintons—to be varnished for 'natomies, except I were out of work. . . . But money is scarce, and throats get dry. . . . Why *should* death rob life o' fourpence? I say there was no treason in it."

"Well, poor soul, she's helpless to hinder that or anything now," answered Mother Cuxsom. "And all her shining keys will be took from her, and her cupboards opened; and the little things 'a didn't wish to be seen, anybody will see; and her wishes and ways will all be as nothing!" [94]

Thus Casterbridge comments on life and death and lesser matters. Opening doors and windows to permit the easy flight of the passing soul was formerly a widespread custom; [95] in North Country strict silence was also enjoined. [96]

[94] *The Mayor of Casterbridge,* Chap. XVIII.
[95] C. Latham, *Folk-Lore Record,* I, 60; J. G. Frazer, *Folk-Lore Journal,* III, 281; Gregor, 206; Billson, 104; Mrs. Gutch, *Folklore of Yorkshire,* 222.
[96] Mrs. Gutch, 222; Ellis's Brand, II, 231.

In Fuhkien, China, in the humbler homes, a hole was made in the roof as egress for the departing spirit.[97] The Pennsylvania Dutch even unlock all drawers, boxes, locks, and the like.[98] Homeopathic magic underlies all these precautions: In the past century Scotch and German peasants, like Sumatran savages today, were still accustomed to unlock doors and windows, and to uncork bottles to facilitate childbirth.[99]

The poetic interpretation of coins on the eyes or in the mouth of the dead is that they are the fare to the other world; this idea has been superimposed upon the original belief that the metal in these coins would keep evil spirits from seizing the dying soul. Charon's fee,[100] the Greek obolus, is essentially the same as our "Peter's Pence," as the North-Country folk call them, or "dead-pennies," in Dorset parlance.[101]

At Lulworth, a quarter of a century ago, the dead were still occasionally laid out with a penny in one hand, and a little wooden hammer in the other.[102] Keys have been found in English coffins still more recently,[103] a practice exactly paralleled by the natives of the Isle of Zacynthos, who lay a key on the breast of the dead, not content with the more customary precaution of placing a coin in the mouth of the corpse.[104] But the custom of placing coins on the eyes of the dead, as described by Hardy in *The Mayor*, is by far the most common one.[105]

"Telling the bees" is the most beautiful custom connected with death; Hardy describes it for us in the tale, "Interlopers at the Knap." [106] The night that Sally Hall's lover,

---

[97] N. B. Dennys, *Folklore* of China, 22.
[98] E. C. Fogel, *Beliefs and Superstitions of the Pennsylvania Germans*, Proverbs 606, 607.
[99] Wimberly, *Folklore in the English and Scottish Ballads*, 358–59.
[100] Halliday, *Greek and Roman Folklore*, 50–51; Grimm-Stallybrass, II, 831–32.
[101] Aubrey's *Remaines*, 159.
[102] W. Sherren, *The Wessex of Romance*, 19.
[103] E. Hull, *Folk-Lore*, XXXVIII, 207–208; M. M. Banks, *Folk-Lore*, XXXVIII, 399; M. Peacock, *Folklore of Lincolnshire*, 238.
[104] J. C. Lawson, *Modern Greek Folklore and Ancient Greek Religion*, 111–112.
[105] Chap. XVIII; Gregor, 207.
[106] *Wessex Tales*.

Darton, had come to make binding the tacit betrothal between them, Sally's brother, who had run away with a former sweetheart of Darton's, came home very ill. He died that night, and Sally, when about to break the news to Helene, his wife, and Darton, surprised them in a tender scene in which Darton, led by sympathy for her pitiable plight, was offering to help her take care of the children. Sally interpreted the scene as a declaration of love and broke off the engagement. As he was leaving the house, Darton caught sight of Mrs. Hall about to carry out a familiar rite; passing to the north wall, where the bees were hived, she tapped at each hive, waiting till she heard a buzzing within before she passed on to the next, thus passing down the whole row. Like many another countrywoman, she believed that if the bees were not "waked," or told of the death, they would pine away and die during the ensuing year.

"Telling the bees" is a custom common to all Germanic peoples. In some places the procedure was, as in this story, merely a tapping three or more times at the hive lest the bees die of a broken heart, refuse to make honey, or fly away.[107] But in Scotland and certain English shires, a special "snoo," or hood of crape was thrown over the hives.[108] A simpler way was merely to lift the hives as the body was borne to the churchyard,[109] and the most primitive custom, to feed the funeral cake to the bees.[110] In Cornwall the custom had an extremely primitive form: the bees must be "waked" by the son and heir, and the news was also broken to trees.[111] Oak worship and bee culture are intimately connected, and the woodpecker may be the connecting link.[112] At any rate, bees have uncanny, supernatural gifts; and at Christmas,

---

[107] C. Latham, *Folk-Lore Record*, I, 59; Fogel, Proverb 1096; *Folk-Lore Journal*, III, 379; *Folk-Lore Journal*, VI, 146.
[108] C. Latham, *Folk-Lore Record*, I, 59; G. E. Hadow, *Folk-Lore*, XXXV, 349.
[109] L. M. Eyre, *Folk-Lore*, XIII, 173; Fogel, Proverbs 594, 615.
[110] *Denham Tracts*, II, 213.
[111] G. L. Gomme, *Folklore as a Historical Science*, 162–63; Dyer, *Folklore of Plants*, 4.
[112] Rendel Harris, *Boanerges*, 357 ff.; *Picus Who is Also Zeus*, 52–56; *The Ascent of Olympus*, 8; Dyer, *Folklore of Plants*, 4.

when cattle are said to kneel in adoration, the bees hum a Christmas hymn! [113] It is a curious and perhaps a significant coincidence that bees, like the silent race of elves and dwarfs, obey a queen; certain it is that they have long been regarded as supernatural creatures with a touching affection for man.[114]

To return to the varieties of ghosts, there are some which are so convincing to the physical senses that they make themselves unmistakably known. "The Head Above the Fog" [115] has an odd specter, a mere ghostly head speeding along through the fog; "The Phantom Horsewoman" [116] describes a ghost who rides as madly as the lady rode in life. In "The Carrier," [117] the carrier's wife, much to the dismay of the passengers, was in the habit of climbing up to the seat beside her husband; this probably happened near haunted Vagg Hollow. William Privett's ghost was seen in broad daylight at Longpuddle Spring,[118] and the ghostly heroine of "The Glimpse" [119] showed herself to the visitor to an old house in the common light of day, afterwards flaunting her indifference by never appearing to him again. But the most indubitable physical ghost in Hardy is Sir William Blount; Swithin St. Cleeve, clad in Sir William's old clothes, was making his way home one night, when met by a group of rustics who were just then deep in a discussion of their old master's mysterious death. Next day Sammy Blore was telling the story:

". . . And the form was Sir Blount's. My nostrils told me, for— there, 'a smelled. Yes, I could smell'n being to leeward. . . . I don't say 'twere a low smell, mind ye. 'Twere a high smell, a sort of gamey flavour, calling to mind venison and hare, just as you'd expect of a great squire,—not like a poor man's 'natomy at all. . . ."

[113] Henderson, *Folklore of the Northern Counties,* 311.
[114] Grimm-Stallybrass, II, 696.
[115] *Moments of Vision.*
[116] *Satires of Circumstance.*
[117] *Human Shows;* cf. F. E. Hardy, *The Later Years of Thomas Hardy,* 96.
[118] *Life's Little Ironies:* "A Few Crusted Characters": "The Superstitious Man's Story."
[119] *Moments of Vision.*

"Well, well; I've not held out against the figure of starvation these twenty year, on nine shillings a week, to be afeard of a walking vapour, sweet or savoury," said Hezzy. . . .

". . . Well, when I found 'twas Sir Blount my spet dried up within my mouth; for neither hedge nor bush were there for refuge against any foul spring 'a might made at us." [120]

Rustic superstition would thus seem not only to expect, but also to hope for the worst from ghosts. Apparently ghosts are seen both by those who wish to see them and those who do not. But there are born ghost-seers, such as shepherds, single folk, persons gifted with second sight, and those prime ghost-seers, dogs and horses. Only witches and wizards were held to excel shepherds in this doubtful gift, and Hardy refers to their uncanny powers in several places, in such a poem as "The Spot," [121] in "The Sheep Boy," [122] where the great bank of fog that sweeps across the upland, driving the sheep and the bees before it, and enshrouding the lonely sheep boy, seems to be full of "souls," [122] and particularly in the tale, "What the Shepherd Saw." [123] Lambing Corner on Marlbury Downs was finally abandoned because shepherds said that during the nights of Christmas week they saw flitting shapes in the open space around the trilithon, the gleam of a weapon, and the shadow of a man dragging some mysterious burden into the hollow. It was a shepherd's boy, years before, who had witnessed a murder there, and had been forced by the squire to kiss the stone and swear to keep the secret. He kept it indeed, but the ghostly reënactment of the crime soon betrayed the affair to the shepherds who frequented Lambing Corner. Shepherds have always been regarded as possessing supernatural powers; they can cure cattle and human beings alike: [124] they share with witches the power to lead those astray who do not treat them with due courtesy; [125] they control the elements, bring-

---

[120] *Two on a Tower*, Chap. XXII.
[121] *Poems of the Past and the Present.*
[122] *Human Shows.*
[123] *A Changed Man.*
[124] Grimm-Stallybrass, IV, 1651.
[125] J. Britten, *Folk-Lore Record*, III, Pt. I, 135.

ing on rain and tempest. Because their occupation prevented their attending church, friends and relatives used to put a lock of wool into the coffin of a dead shepherd, to show his innocence of any willful neglect of the means of grace, when called to account at the Judgment Day.[126] In their lonely hours they must have thoughts which are not the thoughts of common men: ". . . We shepherds, cut off from the world, have our thoughts about many things while the silly sheep are grazing. . . ." [127]

Dogs are prime ghost-seers: the howl of the dog is a sure death-omen because he sees the wraith that is invisible to human eyes. The dogs at Knapwater House bewailed the death of their master hours before the household knew of it.[128] Hardy's favorite dog, Wessex, once greeted a family friend, Mr. Watkins, with mournful whines; an hour after his departure, their visitor was dead.[129]

When Christian Cantle was lamenting the fact that no woman would have him, because he was only the "rames" of a man, it suddenly occurred to his superstitious soul that he had full reason to be afraid of nights; Fairway had reminded him that it was not to married folk, but to single sleepers, that ghosts showed themselves.[130] This hardly seems to tally with the popular superstition that ghosts will not speak unless spoken to; [131] for timid Christian Cantle cannot be pictured as carrying on a conversation with even the most friendly of ghosts!

The common belief that ghosts appear in the twelve days of Christmas is a heathen idea harking back to the great progresses of Holda and Bertha, with their train of souls, and to Odin's "Furious Host." [132] The Christian idea superimposed upon it, that the sacredness of the season renders believers free from ghostly visitation at that time is best

[126] Miss Law, *Folk-Lore*, XI, 345.
[127] Grimm-Stallybrass, IV, 1618; Voss's *Idyls*, 9, 49.
[128] *Desperate Remedies*, Chap. VI; Ellis's Brand, III, 184–86; Halliday, 59.
[129] Florence E. Hardy, *The Later Years of Thomas Hardy*, 205.
[130] *The Return of the Native*, Book I, Chap. III.
[131] Ellis's Brand, III, 70.
[132] Grimm-Stallybrass, I, 268, Note 5; III, 921.

expressed by Marcellus.[133] But the Pennsylvania Dutch believe that one born on Christmas night or Midsummer Eve or Good Friday can see ghosts and hear cattle talk.[134]

There are several poems in which ghostly visitors appear at Christmas or at New Year's.[135] In "Yuletide in a Younger World," the poet looks back regretfully to his youthful days when they had eyes for phantoms, and ears for divination and prophecy. In "A New Year's Eve in War Time," [136] Death, like a ghost, comes astride a great horse, knocking at the homes he is to visit. "A Christmas Ghost-Story" [137] is Hardy in satiric vein: The ghost of an English soldier far from home wakes to ask the stars why the people on the earth still tack "Anno Domini" to the years: he sees no peace anywhere. "The House of Hospitalities" [138] paints an old house that has once rung with Christmas jollity, and now harbors wistful Christmas ghosts. "Her Late Husband" [139] refers to the belief that angels walk at Christmas. "The Dead Quire" and "The Paphian Ball" are tales of the Mellstock quire. The former is a story of great beauty: The Mellstock youth, now that the band and quire are gone, have forsaken their caroling, and have caroused all night at the inn. On their way home, they hear the quire singing "While Shepherds Watched"; they follow the familiar tones along the Froom to the bottom of Church Lane, to the very headstones of the graves, where the voices die away.[140] "The Paphian Ball" [141] relates a curious experience of the Mellstock quire: On their rounds they are met by a strange figure humming a weird tune, who offers to pay them well if they will play for a ball, to which, however, they must go blindfolded. They find themselves in a vast and sumptuous hall, playing for a drunken host; and as they play, their reward,

---

[133] *Hamlet*, I, 1, 158–164; cf. E. M. Wright, *Rustic Speech*, 192.
[134] Fogel, Proverb 1371.
[135] *Winter Words.*
[136] *Moments of Vision.*
[137] *Poems of the Past and the Present.*
[138] *Time's Laughingstocks.*
[139] *Poems of the Past and the Present.*
[140] *Time's Laughingstocks:* "The Dead Quire."
[141] *Human Shows.*

a pile of guineas, heaps ever higher before them. Becoming drowsy, however, they begin the Nativity hymn, "While Shepherds Watched"; the scene vanishes as if by magic, and they find themselves on dark Rainbarrow. At church next morning, they are congratulated for their wonderful playing the night before: a ghostly band had saved the day!

Ghosts also appear on Midsummer Eve and All Souls' Day and Eve. A lovely poem, "On a Midsummer Eve," treats this theme:

> I idly cut a parsley stalk,
> And blew therein towards the moon;
> I had not thought what ghosts would walk
> With shivering footsteps to my tune.[142]

Then it was, as the lover leaned at the brook about to drink, that a faint figure with a familiar aspect seemed to stand above him. The reader of *Jude* [143] will recall how Jude sat vainly hoping that Sue would return, waiting for her as lovers expect the phantom of the Beloved on Old Midsummer Eves. "I Rose up as my Custom Is" [144] tells the tale of a ghost who, as his custom is, rises up on the eve of All Souls' Day, only to find that he is unremembered and unregretted. "A Night of Questionings" [145] describes the complaints of a ghostly band who return to take account of the world, and find it little to their liking.

The reader of *Far from the Madding Crowd* will remember that when Bathsheba sent to the Union for Fanny Robin's body, she sent evergreens and flowers to cover the cheap coffin, and chose Old Pleasant to draw her, because Fanny had been fond of him. In spite of Joseph Poorgrass's "multiplying eye," Fanny was finally brought home in rustic state.[146] In all folklore we find certain recognized funeral plants: there are lettuce, parsley, and fennels; among ever-

---

[142] *Moments of Vision.*
[143] *Jude the Obscure,* Part III, Chap. VIII.
[144] *Satires of Circumstance.*
[145] *Human Shows.*
[146] Chap. XLI.

greens are the laurel, bay, box, rue, and rosemary; among
fruits, the apple, quince, and pomegranate. Lettuce, parsley,
and fennels were peculiarly sacred to death among the ancient Greeks.[147] Parsley is an unlucky plant: there is a widespread belief that if one transplants parsley, he will die or
bring misfortune upon the household; [148] and there is the
euphemism for an unborn child, who is said to be "hiding
. . . in the parsley bed." [149] Rosemary and bays were once
used for both funerals and weddings; and on the latter occasions, they were gilded.[150] In fact, rosemary and rue were
formerly used as disinfectants, and even as medicine and in
amulets against witchcraft.[151] In the poem, "The Childless
Father," [152] Wordsworth describes the common North-
Country custom at funerals, each mourner taking a sprig of
box and throwing it into the grave.[152] Modern Greek peasants bury a dead maiden in the robes of a bride, laying apples,
quinces, and pomegranates on the bier, and following it with
marriage songs to the grave,[153] a custom that is very similar
to the English funeral described by Hardy in such poems as
"The End of the Year," "Retty's Phases," and "Julie-
Jane."

Retty asked that on her burial day the six bells which
are rung as bridal honors, should be rung for her; [154] the
same peal is rung for the dead woman in the poem, "The
End of the Year." [155] The bearers at such funerals were
usually young unmarried women or young unmarried men.
Every Hardy reader remembers piquant Julie-Jane, who
chose her bearers from her fancy-men [156] before she died.
The custom of ringing the bell to denote the age and sex of

[147] Frazer, *The Golden Bough,* 341.
[148] Dyer, *The Folklore of Plants,* 26–27.
[149] *The Well-Beloved,* Part III, Chap. III.
[150] Ellis's Brand, II, 119–120; *Ram Alley* (1611); *A Faire Quarrell,* V, I.
[151] Ellis's Brand, II, 253.
[152] *Lyrical Ballads,* 1800 ed., II, 147; N. Thomas, *Folklore of Northumberland,* 7; C. S. Burne, *Folk-Lore,* XX, 219; G. E. N. Day, *Folk-Lore,* XX, 223.
[153] Lawson, 537–38; 556.
[154] *Human Shows:* "Retty's Phases."
[155] *Late Lyrics.*
[156] *Time's Laughingstocks:* "Julie-Jane." Cf. *Folk-Lore,* XXXIV, 325;
Human Shows: "Retty's Phases," Hardy's note.

the deceased was once very common in England—three short peals for a child, six for a woman, and nine for a man.[157] Hardy refers to the custom in *A Pair of Blue Eyes* [158] and in *Two on a Tower*,[159] where the head bell-ringer is delightfully self-important.

Bells were rung originally as a magic rite whose efficacy lay chiefly in the iron of which they were composed, which would effectually drive away witches, demons, and all evil spirits from the passing soul.[160] In the Middle Ages bells were also rung to keep off lightning,[161] to expedite childbirth,[162] and in any hour of crisis. Hallowing the bells was the churchmen's clever device to divert attention from the magic of the rite to its religious significance.[163]

Wessex places known to be haunted are Vagg Hollow,[164] Toller Down,[165] Yell'ham Firs,[166] all so-called Druid Altars,[167] Egdon Heath,[168] crossroads in general,[169] and old family mansions.[170] As a rule, ghosts tend to return to the places they knew in life; apparently some ghosts are not aware that the old house no longer contains those they lived with there. In the poem, "The Sailor's Mother," [171] and the story, "To Please His Wife," [172] the mother who has lost her favorite son at sea and been forced to give up her little shop, comes night after night to ask the new owner if her

---

[157] E. M. Wright, *Rustic Speech and Folklore*, 278; Thomas, 100, 102–103.
[158] Chap. XXIV.
[159] Chap. X.
[160] Gutch, 223; Harland and Wilkinson, 42–43; Grimm-Stallybrass, III, 1085.
[161] Grimm-Stallybrass, III, 1022, Note 1; IV, 1280; Aubrey's *Remaines*, 22; Harland and Wilkinson, 43.
[162] Black, *Folk-Medicine*, 178.
[163] Ellis's Brand, II, 206–207; Harland and Wilkinson, 43.
[164] *Late Lyrics:* "Vagg Hollow."
[165] *Time's Laughingstocks:* "The Homecoming."
[166] *Poems of the Past and the Present:* "The Mother Mourns"; *Satires of Circumstance:* "Wessex Heights."
[167] *Moments of Vision:* "The Shadow on the Stone"; *A Changed Man:* "What the Shepherd Saw."
[168] *The Return of the Native*, Book I, Chap. III.
[169] *Late Lyrics:* "Where Three Roads Joined."
[170] *The Woodlanders*, Chap. XIX; *Tess*, Chaps. XXXIV, XXXV; *A Laodicean*, Book III, Chap. II; Book VI, Chap V.
[171] *Late Lyrics.*
[172] *Life's Little Ironies.*

boy has returned. A more authentic case is to be found in "The Superstitious Man's Story"; [173] the ghost of William Privett was seen in broad daylight at Longpuddle Spring, where his boy had been drowned years before, and whither he would not go in life. Some ghosts apparently wander as they please; others seek only the places where they have been happy; still others are driven to seek spots positively painful to them.

Hardy is fond of the fancy that old houses which have sheltered many generations of a family are full of the presences of the departed, who take an active interest in the fortunes of their descendants.[174] In "Family Portraits," [175] the portraits take life, and act out the drama of their lives; when impatiently interrupted by the master of the house, they leave him with the disdainful prophecy that his own ways were to shape just as they had been about to show. In "Night in the Old Time," [176] the ghosts reproach their solitary and childless descendant by their reproachful gaze; in "She, I, and They," [177] a ghostly sigh reveals to the listening pair a world of ancestral disapproval! The most striking tale of ghostly pantomime is "The Re-Enactment": [178] A woman is waiting for her lover in an ancient house; a ghostly beau of a former day enters, intent on keeping tryst, and at first mistakes the living lady for his sweetheart. Soon discovering his mistake, and feeling ill at ease, he attempts a declaration of love to the ghostly fair one; it falls flat, and in embarrassment the phantoms seek a more auspicious spot. When the woman's lover comes, he feels at once the "intenser drama," falls strangely silent, and forgets the avowal he had come to make. Years pass; the lady still lives there alone, often aware of ghostly presences in the house, but

---

[173] *Life's Little Ironies:* "A Few Crusted Characters."
[174] *Late Lyrics:* "A House With a History"; "The Strange House"; "The Two Houses"; *Satires of Circumstance:* "Starlings on the Roof"; *Moments of Vision:* "The House of Silence."
[175] *Winter Words.*
[176] *Time's Laughingstocks.*
[177] *Moments of Vision.*
[178] *Satires of Circumstance.*

never vouchsafed another glimpse of the pair who had spoiled her romance; she often asked herself if they were living lovers, intruders in the house, or, as she knew in her heart, real phantoms. The poet's intense imaginative power carries the reader through the tale with a sweep of conviction.

Every Hardy reader knows the de Stancy ghosts who take a keen interest in pretty, plebeian Paula: they seem to move when she flippantly asks them to step down, and their aristocratic faces are distorted by righteous indignation as the old castle burns.[179] The d'Urberville ghosts are far more terrible; they seem to take delight in frightening Tess by their hideous and subtle likeness to her, and thus alienating Angel Clare.[180] Tess's fate runs here, as always, in a double pattern of dark and bright threads: in the wedding-coach with Clare, she could laugh away the ominous premonition of family doom, but with Alec, the sound of the ghostly carriage terrified her. Hardy touches this familiar theme to grotesque and awesome effects.

The very occupations of Hardy's ghosts bear a satiric implication: we see the Mellstock fiddlers fiddling away in the churchyard even as ghosts; we hear the voices of the dead quire singing their carols when the living have neglected the office of the waits; we see staid old ghosts dancing a minuet to "Eden New," or stepping merrily through the figures of a country-dance.[181] We see English sovereigns, awakened by the noise of a new coronation, commenting on statecraft wisely and wittily in "The Coronation,"[182] a poem which received some acid comment from the conservative British press when published. It hits off perfectly in a few lines the idiosyncrasies of each sovereign: Mary Stuart takes the noise for an execution, Elizabeth for an affair of state; Henry the Eighth is a little perturbed, hoping it is a wed-

---

[179] *A Laodicean,* Book III, Chap. II; Book VI, Chap. V.
[180] *Tess,* Chaps. XXXIII, XXXIV, XXXV, LI.
[181] *Moments of Vision:* "Jubilate," "The Choirmaster's Burial," "To My Father's Violin"; *Time's Laughingstocks,* "The Dead Quire"; *Human Shows,* "The Paphian Ball."
[182] *Satires of Circumstance.*

ding, if anything. The poem ends on a more solemn note, for all agree that kingship means little once it is done with. "A King's Soliloquy" [183] is another word on the same subject: The King, on the night of his funeral, muses on his thankless rôle, now completed, and thinks he would have been happier in the life of the average man.

"Channel Firing" is admirable ghostly comment on life. Hearing the gunnery practice at sea, and taking it for the trump of the Last Day, the ghosts awake, but soon learn to their disgust that the nations are busily preparing for still another war. Parson Thirdly sums up the general opinion:

> And many a skeleton shook his head.
> "Instead of preaching forty year,"
> My neighbour Parson Thirdly said,
> "I wish I had stuck to pipes and beer." [184]

There are ghosts who cannot rest because history holds them up to ignominy or misrepresentation they do not deserve.[185] As a pendant to "Spectres That Grieve," we might well take "Mute Opinion": [186] The poet is permitted in a vision to see the past, not as voiced by the historians, the orators, the prophets, but as the mutely great had thought, and he is awed indeed by the contrast in the two patterns. *The Dynasts* aims to present history in this way, through the medium of one unifying imagination, and that a poet's imagination.

Hardy sometimes permits himself a smile at the plight of unlucky ghosts: the folk in "The Levelled Churchyard," [187] a poem which must have come out of the poet's memories of his youthful adventures in church restoration, complain bitterly that their bones are mixed up in "human jam"; no one can find his own proper verse, in fact, no one knows who is who or what is what. The same theme is treated with eerie grotesquerie in another poem, "Voices from Things Grow-

[183] *Poems of the Past and the Present.*
[184] *Satires of Circumstance.*
[185] *Satires of Circumstance:* "Spectres that Grieve."
[186] *Poems of the Past and the Present.*
[187] *Ibid.*

ing in a Churchyard." Fanny Hurd, once a little girl, is now a plot of daisies; Bachelor Bowring, Gent., is a stately oak after a century below the sod; Thomas Voss flourishes in gay red berries; the high-bred Lady Gertrude, true to form, is a trifle stiff as a laurel-tree; Eve Greensleeves, light in death as in life, has climbed the wall to revel in wind and sun, and feel the kisses of the bees. Old Squire Audeley Grey may speak for himself:

> I'm old Squire Audeley Grey, who grew,
> > Sir or Madam,
> Aweary of life, and in scorn withdrew;
> Till anon I clambered up anew
> As ivy-green, when my ache was stayed,
> And in that attire I have longtime gayed,
> > All day cheerily,
> > All night eerily! [188]

The nonchalant lilt of the flowing stanza makes us hear the "murmurous accents" and the "radiant hum" of the happy ghosts. The lyric, "Regret Not Me," [189] plays with the same theme, and the ghosts in "Intra Sepulchrum" [190] have much the same tale to tell. "Who Is Digging on My Grave?" [191] is an ironic affair: the lady learns that it is not her lover, not her kindred, not even her rival, but her little dog: the honest soul confesses, with a woeful lack of tact, that he was only seeking a buried bone! [191]

"Friends Beyond" [192] recounts the conversation of happy ghosts of the Mellstock folk; forever deprived of their cherished possessions, they care little what the living now do with them.[192]

In "The Unborn," [193] it is the spirits of those not yet born who listen incredulously to the disillusioning story of a spirit newly come from earth. The poem, "In Childbed," [193] is

[188] *Late Lyrics.*
[189] *Satires of Circumstance.*
[190] *Late Lyrics.*
[191] *Satires of Circumstance.*
[192] *Wessex Poems.*
[193] *Time's Laughingstocks.*

another statement of the theme; a childing woman is visited
by the ghost of her mother, who pleads with her not to expect too much of the babe that is born into the world. "Fragment" [194] is a more bitter statement of the everlasting
problem, *Cui bono?* Little Father Time's utterances, which
are too often Hardy's, and not a little boy's, are never wiser
than on this particular theme:

"I think that whenever children be born that are not wanted, they
should be killed directly, before their souls come to 'em, and not be
allowed to grow big and walk about!" [195]

Certain poems seem to carry the inflections of Hardy's
voice. It is always dangerous to fix upon any poem and call
it a personal utterance, yet it is a temptation few critics can
resist. To interpret such a poem as "A Meeting with Despair" [196] as more than the record of a passing mood, to seek
to find in it the philosophy of a lifetime, would be manifestly
foolish. Nevertheless, "A Sign-Seeker," though it is another
voicing of despair, is one of those utterances whose utter
honesty and profound insight fully justify the gloom of the
poet's outlook. Hardy's despair is equaled only by his love
and pity for all that lives, and no one can read him without
feeling that the artist's joy in the pattern he weaves must
have mitigated to some degree the ugliness of the stuff of
which it is made. "A Sign-Seeker" is any honest doubter:

In graveyard green, where his pale dust lies pent
    To glimpse a phantom parent, friend,
    Wearing his smile, and "Not the end!"
Outbreathing softly: that were blest enlightenment . . .

.   .   .   .

. . . But none replies;
    No warnings loom, nor whisperings
    To open out my limitings,
And Nescience mutely muses: When a man falls he lies.[197]

[194] *Moments of Vision.*
[195] *Jude the Obscure,* Part VI, Chap. II.
[196] *Wessex Poems.*
[197] *Ibid.*

As to the old cynical query, *Cui bono?* Tess has an answer which is perhaps as good as any; life is illusion, is it therefore less precious?

"I don't know about ghosts," she was saying, "but I do know that our souls can be made to go outside our bodies when we are alive. . . . A very easy way to feel 'em go . . . is to lie on the grass at night and look straight up at some big bright star; and by fixing your mind upon it, you will soon find that you are hundreds o' miles from your body, which you don't seem to want at all." [198]

It is poetry, not philosophy, which must justify the ways of God to man.

[198] *Tess,* Chap. XVIII.

IV

MAGIC AND WITCHCRAFT

The belief in witchcraft has lingered in Wessex. In *The Early Life of Thomas Hardy,* Mrs. Hardy quotes passages from the poet's journal which show how deeply the theme of witchcraft and magic fascinated him. No incident was too trifling, no belief too obscure to record; many of these stories had been told Hardy by rustics at the village inn or by family servants who vouched for their truth.

Witchcraft is an underground religion which has been preserved through incredible vicissitudes all the way down from savage sorcery. It has the proverbial nine lives of the cat. Almost every organized religion in its day has warred with witchcraft of a sort, and come out a doubtful victor. When the early Christian church attacked heathenism, the people reluctantly gave up the worship of the old gods, without ceasing to believe in their supernatural powers. The opposition of church and state to witchcraft from the twelfth to the seventeenth century reached a state of frenzy which terrorized the witches, and wore out the civil and ecclesiastical courts; but, after the madness had subsided, the fires smouldered on. Sometimes, as in the hexe-murder in York, Pennsylvania, in 1929, the flames again break forth, revealing the volcano beneath the quiet surface of everyday life. Witchcraft has also survived a stronger force than persecution—the subtle undermining of popular education, with its smattering of applied science. In isolated places in England and America it still retains a hold on the imaginations of the people, who cling to it with instinctive trust in times of crisis. It is to them a deeper and more practical religion than the orthodox faith in which they have been reared.[1]

Hardy understood the Wessex peasant's feeling on the score of witchcraft, which might be worded something like this: the Church of England is all very well for Sunday worship, for tithes, for testimony to the fitness of the social order; but when the cows are bewitched and the butter won't come, when the horses of a morning are reeking with sweat, shall I then run to the vicar? It is pious and proper to pray for rain; it will help my crops more to have the weather-wizard try his spells. When I am "overlooked," it is no time to love my neighbor as myself, but a time to use magic against magic, white witchcraft against black. Failing this, there is only ill luck, sickness, and death.

This confession of faith on the part of the peasant reveals the fact that witchcraft is not only primitive, but a desperate faith, an appeal in time of stress to a power that is mightier, or at least more cunning and watchful, than the power employed by one's enemy.

Hardy was versed in popular ideas of magic, familiar with many actual and alleged cases of witchcraft, and acquainted from boyhood with persons who clung to these primitive beliefs. He attempted in his use of witchcraft as a theme to draw the distinction between white and black art. Black witchcraft aims to destroy property, to terrorize and even kill its victim; white witchcraft consists of charms and spells to counteract black art, to promote favorable weather, fertility of crops, flocks and herds, and general good luck. Black magic is anti-social, yet it is not easy to decide who is the white witch, and who the black. Hardy shows clearly what sort of persons fall naturally under neighborhood suspicion. The heroine of the tale, "The Withered Arm," for instance, got the reputation of a witch only by slow degrees.[2] Long before she was accused of "overlooking" Gertrude

---

[1] On the whole subject of the origins and evolution of witchcraft, see Grimm-Stallybrass, *Teutonic Mythology*, III, 1062–70.
[2] *Wessex Tales.*

Lodge, Rhoda had incurred the suspicions of her companions at the dairy. They feared her because of the apathetic patience with which she accepted Lodge's slights; an ordinary woman in Rhoda's situation would have been wildly jealous for her boy, if not for herself. In her indifference to their sympathy, there was something sinister. They sensed in Rhoda a strong and baleful personality, and readily took her for a black witch. Eustacia Vye was another matter. Eustacia was hated because she openly despised the social and moral standards of Egdon, and disdained what seemed to her a stupid and dull outlook on life. That she loved power we know from the boast she uttered when she brought Wildeve across the heath to her fire; she told him she had done it merely to triumph over him as the Witch of Endor called up Samuel. Eustacia had a religion of her own, but it was not the religion of Egdon. It was rather a passionate epicureanism, in which her extraordinary beauty and her powerful will exercised over the rustic mind a fascination that seemed utterly malevolent.[3] Mrs. Winter, also suspected of black witchcraft, was not a true witch at all, but an unfortunate old woman, to whose tragic loss of her son the villagers ascribed the misfortunes which fell upon her persecutors. Was it not proud Harriet Palmley who laughed at Jack Winter's crabbed love letters until, beside himself, he broke into her house to steal them and was caught and hanged, when a word from her would have cleared him? So reasoned the villagers. The tall, gaunt old woman who, on her rare appearances, frightened the children half out of their wits, was a fit subject for dark fancies: her history and appearance were both against her.[4]

Hardy's description of Elizabeth Endorfield, the white witch of *Under the Greenwood Tree,* reveals his delight in this creation. Particularly satanic were certain characteristics of hers: she did not attend church; she wore her bonnet indoors, and always wore a red cloak; she had a pointed

[3] *The Return of the Native,* Book I, Chap. VI.
[4] *Life's Little Ironies:* "A Few Crusted Characters."

chin; she was extremely shrewd and gifted in insight. But her friends protested that she was not a witch, merely a "Deep Body"; and they urged in proof that she was not gaunt and ugly, nor unusually odd in her manner.[5] Of such slight things as these were witches made! We can well believe that the witches of the sixteenth as well as the thirteenth century were little more than the product of popular fancy, born of their knowledge of drugs and midwifery, their unusual ugliness, their idleness and abject poverty.[6] The reader will recall the whimsical rhyme in which Elizabeth disclaims all magical powers, and pretends to use nothing more than common sense:

> "This fear of Lizz—whatever 'tis—
> By great and small;
> She makes pretence to common sense,
> And that's all." [7]

So saying, she advises Fancy Day to feign sickness, and thus win over her obdurate father to the match with Dick Dewy. Many a Deep Body like Elizabeth Endorfield has lacked the wit to plead her own cause effectively, and so lost her head! This is Hardy's most delightful comment on witchcraft.

Mere white witchcraft, of course, are the love charms which the village maidens and anxious widows procure from the "wise woman." In "The Catching Ballet of the Wedding Clothes," [8] a village girl consults a white witch as to whether she shall marry the honest sailor to whom she is betrothed, or the rich admirer who has sent her fine wedding clothes and a ring. The witch's advice is a bit of worldly wisdom—nothing more: Take the better match of the two as the world sees it. The girl marries Jack, the sailor, in the clothes and with the ring sent by his rival. That night the rich lover appears to her in a dream and claims her for his

---

[5] *Under the Greenwood Tree,* Part IV, Chap. III.
[6] Grimm-Stallybrass, *Teutonic Mythology,* III, 1039, 1075; M. A. Murray, *The Witch Cult in Western Europe,* 170.
[7] *Under the Greenwood Tree,* Part IV, Chap. III.
[8] *Winter Words.*

bride; for is he not the owner of the ring? The girl believes herself married to him, and steals away from Jack, to spend a lifetime of regret in penance for her superstition.

The village "wise man" ranges in his abilities and functions all the way from a gifted amateur to a strict professional. Hardy's conjurors, Fall, Trendle, and Mynterne of Owlscombe, are professional mediators between supernatural powers and men, practitioners of the arts of divination, folkmedicine, and magic in a way approved, though not openly countenanced, by the community in which they live. Most of their apparatus and many of their methods go back to the polemic of the Greek Hippolytus; the same paraphernalia and technic appear in Reginald Scot's *Discoverie of Witchcraft*.[9] Trendle was able to show Gertrude Lodge the form of her enemy in the white of an egg dissolved in a glass of water, and to recommend to her the famous "corpse-cure" which caused her death;[10] Fall, popularly known as "Wide-O" and universally considered the greatest of Wessex magicians, prophesied the weather for Henchard;[11] Dairyman Crick was about to consult Trendle's son when the witchcraft in his dairy ceased as mysteriously as it had begun.[12] These incidents are typical illustrations of folkmagic, yet the most primitive bit of magic in Hardy, the waxen image, is used, not by a witch or professional conjuror, but by a fear-crazed and deeply superstitious woman. Hardy's most haunting tale of witchcraft is found in the episode where Susan Nunsuch literally charms her enemy Eustacia to death.[13] Equally macabre, however, is the story of "The Withered Arm." Rhoda Brook's boy, sent to watch the homecoming of the new bride, had made report of the lady's beauty, and the picture was eating at Rhoda's heart, as she brooded over the embers of her fire before going to bed:

[9] Wm. R. Halliday, *Greek and Roman Folklore,* 125; Sir Laurence Gomme, *Ethnology in Folklore,* 112–13.
[10] *Wessex Tales:* "The Withered Arm."
[11] *The Mayor of Casterbridge,* Chap. XXVI.
[12] *Tess of the d'Urbervilles,* Chap. XVII.
[13] *The Return of the Native,* Book V, Chap. VIII.

. . . For the first time Gertrude Lodge visited the supplanted woman in her dreams. Rhoda Brook dreamed—since her assertion that she really saw, before falling asleep, was not to be believed—that the young wife, in the pale silk dress and white bonnet, but with features shockingly distorted as by age, was sitting on her chest as she lay. The pressure of Mrs. Lodge's person grew heavier; the blue eyes peered cruelly into her face; and then the figure thrust forward its left hand mockingly, so as to make the wedding-ring it wore glitter in Rhoda's eyes. Maddened mentally, and nearly suffocated by pressure, the sleeper struggled; the incubus, still regarding her, withdrew to the foot of the bed, only, however, to come forward by degrees, resume her seat, and flash her left hand as before.

Gasping for breath, Rhoda, in a last desperate effort, swung out her right hand, seized the confronting spectre by its obtrusive left arm, and whirled it backward to the floor, starting up herself as she did so with a low cry.

"O, merciful heaven!" she cried, sitting on the edge of the bed in a cold sweat; "that was not a dream—she was here!" [14]

Next morning her hand still retained the feel of the specter's arm; she milked and came home to breakfast wearily; her son had heard the sound of a fall in her room the night before.

Then came Gertrude's gracious visit, and her confession of the strange pain in her arm. The details of her story fitted perfectly into Rhoda's nightmare, and the young wife's left arm showed the faint impress of Rhoda's hand. The supplanted woman shrunk in horror from the thought that she might be, after all, a witch with a malignant power to harm. She had wished her rival less beautiful; she had not wished to harm her. In spite of her sincere repentance, however, only torturing conscience induced her to take Gertrude to see Trendle; perhaps the fear of self-discovery detained her.

The exact status of the conjuror is indicated in this visit of the two women to Trendle. The conjuror affected not to believe greatly in his own powers. When credited with a cure, he would reply that he merely drank a glass of grog

[14] *Wessex Tales.*

upon them, and that perhaps the whole thing was chance.[15]
When Trendle saw the withered arm, however, he confessed
the case beyond his skill. He resorted to an ancient mode of
divination, showing Gertrude Lodge the form of her enemy
assumed by the white of an egg dissolved in a glass of water.
This mode of "Scrying the future" was once used by lovesick maidens in the Scotch Lowlands.[16]

As time went on, the rumors of Rhoda's evil eye grew unbearable; Rhoda and her son left Holmstoke. Years passed;
Gertrude's health and beauty failed. Trendle advised her to
try the corpse-cure, that is, touch the body of a man who had
been hanged while the body was still warm, and by a "turn
in the blood" effect a cure. The hangman took pity upon the
unfortunate lady; but at the very moment when she thought
her cure achieved, came the horrible discovery that the
hanged man was the son of Lodge and Rhoda Brook. Gertrude's death completes the circle of tragic irony.[17]

The belief that a witch could blast a limb is very old; this
was the charge brought by Richard the Third against Jane
Shore.[18] The evil eye is a world superstition; amulets are
worn against it in modern Greece and Italy, and babies wear
the magic coral just as in Vergil's day.[19] Savages fear it as
much as do the highly civilized Chinese.[20] Extravagant
praise is unlucky; it not only incurs the envy of the gods but
conceals secret malice;[21] hence the wise mother in such a
case, justly suspicious, had best disparage the baby, or, crossing her thumbs, spit across them for luck![22] Curious instances of popular belief in the evil eye until quite recently
kept coming up in the Dorset courts; one of the most amusing was that of an old laborer applying for admission to the

[15] *Ibid.*, "The Withered Arm."
[16] Prof. Samuel C. Chew, *Thomas Hardy, Poet and Novelist*, 119; Rev.
Walter Gregor, *Notes on the Folk-Lore of the North-East of Scotland*, 165.
[17] *Wessex Tales:* "The Withered Arm."
[18] Prof. Samuel C. Chew, *op. cit.*, 118.
[19] R. F. Gunther, "The Cimaruta": *Folk-Lore*, XVI, 132–61; Wm. R. Halliday, *Greek and Roman Folklore*, 36; Dalyell, *The Darker Superstitions of
Scotland*, 45.
[20] N. B. Dennys, *The Folklore of China*, 49.
[21] Grimm-Stallybrass, III, 1100–1103; Gregor, 35.
[22] Grimm-Stallybrass, III, 1102; Halliday, *op. cit.*, 36.

poorhouse, who claimed to be so badly bewitched by his sister-in-law that he was unable to work, and that even the famous "Toad-Doctor" who sold his toad-bags every year at Stalbridge Fair, and was known to Hardy and Barnes, was unable to cure him.[23]

The oppression which Rhoda Brook felt in her nightmare, and which she took for an incubus, or witch, sitting on her chest, riding her, is a virulent work of black witchcraft; the hag-ridden woman could not believe that her rival had not actually visited her.[24] The rustic belief runs that horses found reeking with sweat of a morning have been hag-ridden by witches all night.[25]

The closest approach to popular ideas and practices of witchcraft is the series of incidents in *The Return of the Native* in which Susan Nunsuch struggles to combat Eustacia Vye's evil spells. Susan's use of the deadly image is the climax of a universal resentment against Eustacia; it is a piece of pure folk magic. The reader will recall how Eustacia, determined to bring Wildeve across the heath, had kept timid Johnny Nunsuch tending the fire against his will, telling him to listen for the splash of a frog in the pool, and bustling him off with his crooked sixpence for luck the moment the familiar signal was heard. Johnny's meeting with the reddleman increased his fright, and shortly afterwards, he fell ill. The boy's mother guessed that the splash was a signal for a rendezvous, and half believed that it was a tryst with the powers of darkness. Some time later, Eustacia Vye, drawn by curiosity, attended church. In the midst of service, she screamed aloud; Susan had pricked her with a long stocking needle, to bring blood and so end her spells over Johnny. At last the year in which the story unfolds itself is almost completed. The tragic estrangement of Clym and Eustacia begins to loom in the distance, as Clym broods over

[23] J. G. Black, *Folk-Medicine,* 22; H. Colley March, *Folk-Lore,* XI, 107–12; *Folk-Lore Record,* Vol. III, Pt. II, pp. 288, 289, quoting *The Standard,* 22 Sept. 1880.
[24] *Wessex Tales:* "The Withered Arm."
[25] *The Woodlanders,* Chap. XXVIII.

his mother's dying words with their hint of cruel ingratitude. Unaware of Eustacia's guilty part in his mother's death, Clym visits Susan Nunsuch, to question Johnny, who had talked to Mrs. Yeobright before her death. The boy is sick again; when Clym inquires for him, Susan "regarded him in a peculiar and criticizing manner" as if to say, "You want another of the knocks which have already laid you so low." [26]

All the concentrated fear of an intensely superstitious woman was in the look Susan Nunsuch gave Clym Yeobright; and as the truth of his mother's death dawned upon him, her suspicions of Eustacia must have seemed justified. Clym's alienation from his mother, his blindness, poverty, and tragic loss, seemed the veritable result of black witchcraft. Thus Hardy prepares us for the dreadful image. On the night that Eustacia had appointed for her flight with Wildeve, Johnny Nunsuch was dangerously ill. Susan had made a wax image of Eustacia, which she stuck full of pins and slowly melted before the fire, praying that as it melted away, even so might her enemy waste and perish. The subtle story is full of unspoken implications. The most casual reader cannot escape the feeling that the image is partly responsible for Eustacia's death. Eustacia despised Wildeve; why did she go out into the storm to meet him? Why was her absence not discovered sooner? Why did she not receive Clym's letter pleading for the reconciliation for which she had longed but had ceased to hope? What kept her steps in the direction of the weir? The story rises into the rhythms of poetry as it approaches its climax; it rises and falls like the slow incantations of the weird sisters. Susan Nunsuch, roasting the waxen image before the fire, seems to have taken to herself deadly allies, the storm and the dark heathen impulses of the heath. Egdon Heath seems to say, "She has scorned me, too. Come, let us destroy her." Eustacia has none the less a woman's last word; it is the smile on her face, calm and beautiful.[27]

[26] *The Return of the Native,* Book V, Chap. II.
[27] *Ibid.,* Book V, Chap. VIII.

The total effect of this story is so magnificent that one shrinks from tearing it apart to examine the fragments of witch lore it contains. Susan's "pricking the witch" is a device that has long been held most efficacious among the simpler countercharms against witchcraft. In the sixteenth century in English and Scottish witch trials certain official prickers drew blood from the accused victims. A malignant witch was said to bleed but little.[28] "Pricking the witch" was a common occurrence up to a quarter of a century ago in many English rural districts.[29] A gentler mode of counteracting witchcraft was, on meeting the witch, to "cruch-yor-thumb," that is, double it inside the palm;[30] to answer no questions, respond to no compliments, and avoid the use of such expressions as "please" or "thank you."[31] A crooked sixpence is proof against witchcraft; Johnny Nunsuch prized the one given him by Eustacia Vye for tending her fire, and was doubly frightened at the sight of the reddleman, because, in his flurry, he dropped his lucky sixpence.[32]

Hardy also uses the image with fine effect in *The Mayor of Casterbridge*: when misfortunes were heaping high upon Henchard, he was seized by superstitious fears:

"I wonder," he asked himself with eerie misgiving, "I wonder if it can be that somebody has been roasting a waxen image of me, or stirring an unholy brew to confound me. I don't believe in such power; and yet what if they should ha' been doing it!"[33]

Henchard at heart was much like Farmer Lodge, who was angry, we remember, at his wife Gertrude because she had had recourse to Conjuror Trendle, yet himself firmly be-

---

[28] J. G. Dalyell, *The Darker Superstitions of Scotland,* 637–44; John Denham, *Denham Tracts,* II, 324–25; N. Thomas, *Folk-Lore of Northumberland,* 27–28, 39, 53; Wm. Henderson, *Folk-Lore of the Northern Counties,* 181–82.
[29] *Folk-Lore Journal,* II, 349–50; C. Latham, *Folk-Lore Record,* I, 23–24.
[30] N. Thomas, *op. cit.,* 53–54; *Denham Tracts,* II, 325.
[31] Grimm-Stallybrass, III, 1102–3; Lady Camilla Gurdon, *Folk-Lore of Suffolk,* 12–13.
[32] *The Return of the Native,* Book I, Chap. VIII; N. Thomas, 54.
[33] *The Mayor of Casterbridge,* Chap. XXVII.

lieved in the wise man's powers.[34] Henchard was seized
with horrible fears when he caught sight of a mysterious
image of himself, absolutely faithful to him in form, feature,
and dress, floating in Ten Hatches; his first thought was
that some sinister agency beyond his ken had sent it to him
as an omen of some mysterious punishment in store for him.
It was Elizabeth-Jane who discovered that this was no
"miracle"; the sight was saddening, but in no sense "appalling," as he had felt. When Henchard realized that it was his
effigy, the gruesome relic of the skimmity ride, that was
floating in Ten Hatches, and that Elizabeth-Jane forgave
him, he cried, "Who is such a reprobate as I! And yet it
seems that even I be in Somebody's hand!" [35] And this mood
of Henchard's, coming, as it does, on the eve of his final
downfall, is infinitely touching. The touch of superstition in
Michael Henchard is a telling bit of characterization: when
luck is with him, the mayor is self-willed and confident to a
fault; when misfortunes come upon him, he is ready to believe himself the victim of black magic, and, on the other
hand, eager to employ the same evil powers to his own ad-
vantage. Hence the subtle contrast between his braggadocio
and his fears.

The history of the wax and clay image as an amatory or
deadly device is too complex to be outlined here. Simathea,
the Theocritean witch, made a wax image of her lover,
pricked it with needles, and melted it, throwing into the fire
also a shred of his cloak.[36] The same procedure was followed by the Duchess of Gloucester, who employed Roger
Bolingbroke and the notorious witch Marjery Jourdain, to
help her through this device recall the wandering affections
of her husband; the unfortunate Duchess was thus impli-
cated in a plot against the life of Henry the Sixth, and was
exiled to Calais.[37]

[34] *Wessex Tales:* "The Withered Arm."
[35] *The Mayor of Casterbridge*, Chap. XLI.
[36] Wm. R. Halliday, *op. cit.*, 66; Frazer, *Golden Bough*, one vol. ed. 1922, 44.
[37] J. Harland and T. T. Wilkinson, *Lancashire Folklore*, 174–75; *2 Henry VI*, I, 4.

The amatory image is not nearly so common as the use of the device to impair the health or take the life of the victim. The *Grettis Saga* refers to this deadly use of the image.[38] The ballad of "Willie's Lady" tells a story of Billy Blind's deception of his witch mother-in-law by a child of wax, over which she recites her spells, and thus saves the life of his child.[39] Records of the trials of the famous witches of Pendle Forest—Old Demdike, Young Demdike, and the rest—read like a romance of horror. All were charged with destroying their enemies by means of such images.[40] James the First, a rabid witch-hunter, persecuted the astrologer Dee, who once had rendered innocuous a waxen image of Elizabeth found buried in Lincoln's Inn Fields.[41] James's *Demonologie* and the numerous statutes against witchcraft passed in his reign, reveal the common use of the image. Had witchcraft been the organized cult he held, it would have been completely uprooted; the very fact that it lived on in out-of-the-way communities, practised by isolated individuals, is proof that it was never a true religious cult.

The amazing feature about the image is that it has persisted up to our own day. As late as 1910, it was in use in the Isle of Skye;[42] and among the English people of Prince Edward's Island only a decade ago, there were still persons who shaped a potato like an old woman, filled it with pins, and roasted it against witchcraft.[43] Sometimes the image was thrown into a stream of water, a practice that may, in fact, go back to the Stone Age in Scotland.[44] It was said that Satan himself taught the medieval witches to make these images, and stuck the first thorn or pin in them; the accusation has its roots in savage sorcery.[45] Our Teutonic ancestors placed such images at the door, at crossroads, and

---

[38] York Powell's ed. *Saxo-Grammaticus,* Intro., LXXX.
[39] C. Lowry Wimberly, *Folklore in the English and Scottish Ballads,* 356.
[40] Harland and Wilkinson, *op. cit.,* 164–191.
[41] Harland and Wilkinson, *op. cit.,* 178–79.
[42] Canon M. J. MacCulloch, *Folk-Lore,* XXXIV, 92.
[43] H. J. Rose, *Folk-Lore,* XXXII, 126.
[44] R. C. Maclagen, M.D., *Folk-Lore,* VI, 144–48; *Gomme, Folk-Lore,* II, 23; Dalyell, 173; Bryan J. Jones, *Folk-Lore,* VI, 302.
[45] M. A. Murray, *The Witch Cult in Western Europe,* 116–17; 196.

on the graves of parents; although they came to be a deadly
device, they were originally employed as a preventive measure in folk-medicine.[46] The Pennsylvania Dutch today still
bury a stillborn calf at the stable door to prevent further
deaths; and Hardy himself was familiar with the English
practice of hanging the heart of a sheep or calf, stuck full
of black thorns, over the chimney, the one spot in the house
sacred to Donar, god of medicine, as well as the hearth and
family.[47]

The deadly image is not a new theme in literature. *The
Lancashire Witches,* a Jacobean play, and Ainsworth's romance of the same name, present the theme.[48] William
Barnes's poem, "A Witch," is a humorous treatment. But
with the exception of Rossetti's magnificent ballad of "Sister
Helen," no one has handled the image with such fine effect
as Hardy in *The Return of the Native.*

Dairy witchcraft is treated in *Tess* with broad humor.
Soon after Tess's arrival at Talbothays, the cows did not
give down their milk as usual, and the presence of a newcomer was blamed for the phenomenon, one milker assert-
ing that the milk went straight into the cows' horns at such
a time. Crick thought that even witchcraft might be limited
by anatomical possibilities. The maids and men then resorted to songs, a favorite device in dairies.[49] Some time
later, when the butter would not come, Crick contemplated
recourse to white witchcraft:

" 'Tis years since I went to Conjuror Trendle's in Egdon . . .
and he was nothing to what his father had been . . . I don't believe
in him . . . but I shall have to go to 'n . . . if this sort of thing
continnys!"

"Conjuror Fall, 'tother side of Casterbridge . . . was a very good

[46] Grimm-Stallybrass, *op. cit.,* III, 1073, 1091–93; IV, 1628–29.
[47] Edwin M. Fogel, *Beliefs and Superstitions of the Pennsylvania Germans,*
Intro. p. 13; F. E. Hardy, *The Early Life of Thomas Hardy,* 147; *Folk-Lore,*
XXVIII, 100, quoting *The London Times,* 5th March, 1917; Ellis's Brand, III,
167.
[48] Prof. Samuel C. Chew, *op. cit.,* 116.
[49] *Tess of the d'Urbervilles,* Chap. XVII.

man when I was a boy," said Jonathan Kail, "but he's rotten as touchwood by now."

"My grandfather used to go to Conjuror Mynterne, out at Owlscombe, and a clever man 'a were. . . . But there's no such genuine folk about nowadays!"

. . . .

"Perhaps somebody in the house is in love . . . I've heard tell . . . that that will cause it. . . ." [50]

The dairy is the witch's happy hunting-ground. If skilled she can keep the butter from coming and even avoid the usually fatal countercharm of the hot poker plunged into the churn. To circumvent dairy witchcraft in many English rural districts, they repeat this charm:

> Come, butter, come,
> Come, butter, come,
> Peter stands at the gate,
> Waiting for a butter'd cake,
> Come, butter, come. [51]

In Scotland and Northumbria, they make the churn staff of rowan, or mountain ash, which is sure proof against witchcraft; or they place a cross of rowan, a crooked sixpence, or a horseshoe at the bottom of the churn. [52] Certain "badhanded" persons who should never set hens and are fatal to churnings, if by chance present in the dairy, must lay their hands upon the churn, speak a good word to it, and leave as quickly as possible. [53] A less innocent mode of counteracting dairy witchcraft is to plunge a hot poker into the churn, maiming or killing the witch; and many gruesome tales are told of this deadly spell. [54] There is a widespread belief that witches, in the shape of hares, can creep into the byres at

[50] *Ibid.*, Chap. XXI.
[51] John Brand, *Popular Antiquities,* Sir Henry Ellis's ed. III, 312–13; Mrs. Gutch, *Folklore of Yorkshire,* 214.
[52] Wm. Henderson, *op. cit.,* 183; N. Thomas, *op. cit.,* 53; G. F. Black, *Folk-Medicine,* 112; Rev. W. Gregor, *op. cit.,* 194.
[53] Gregor, *op. cit.,* 194; *Denham Tracts,* II, 274, 326.
[54] Wimberly, *op. cit.,* 387; Harland and Wilkinson, *op. cit.,* 154, 166; *Folk-Lore Record,* III, Pt. I, p. 134; *Folk-Lore Journal,* I, 123.

night and suck the cows dry.[55] The close relation of witches
and fairies comes out clearly in dairy lore: milk, particularly
human milk, was grateful to fairies; hence their abduction
of unsained young mothers.[56] The common-sense explanation of dairy witchcraft lies in the obvious fact that the
witch did not attack the byres of the wealthy, where due
regard was paid to cleanliness, but those of the struggling
tenant farmer.

Witches were almost as fond of the stable as of the dairy.
Readers of *The Woodlanders* will recall the consternation
in Melbury's stables the morning that Grace's favorite mare
Darling was found reeking with sweat from a night's riding.
Fitzpiers had ridden her hard to reach home before daybreak, but the man who tended Darling insisted that she had
been "hag-rid," thus starting a series of reminiscences about
riding witches.[57] When Marian saw Tess's white face after
one of her encounters with Alec d'Urberville, she vowed
she looked "hag-rode." [58] In a figurative sense Hardy uses
the phrases "hag-ridden" and "nightmare" in "The Ruined
Maid," [59] and "A Nightmare and the Next Thing." [60] But
the meaning is literal in the macabre little poem, "I Rose
Up as My Custom Is":

> Her words benumbed my fond faint ghost:
> The nightmares neighed from their stalls,
> The vampires screeched, the harpies flew,
> And under the dim dawn I withdrew
> To Death's inviolate halls.[61]

To prevent horses from witches' riding, holed stones,
called lucky stones, or horseshoes were hung up in stables.[62]

[55] J. G. Campbell, *Witchcraft and Second Sight in the Scottish Highlands,*
pp. 7–8.
[56] Gregor, *op. cit.,* 62.
[57] Chap. XXVIII.
[58] *Tess,* Chap. XLVII.
[59] *Poems of the Past and the Present.*
[60] *Winter Words.*
[61] *Satires of Circumstance.*
[62] Gurdon, 35; *Denham Tracts,* II, pp. 43, 325–26; Thomas Pettigrew, M.D.,
Superstitions connected with . . . Medicine and Surgery, 88; J. F. Payne,
M.D., *Medicine in Anglo-Saxon Times,* 46.

Horseshoes were efficacious because witches abhorred the iron of which they are made, because of their shape (a broken circle), and the ghost-seeing horse from whom they are taken. Our Southern darkies say that the witch has to travel all over the road the horseshoe has ever been over before she can get in the house, and by the time she gets back, it is day! [63] The nailing of horseshoes to the stalls reminds us of the Roman antidote against the plague, in which nails were driven into the walls of the cottage, and also recalls the Dorset practice of nailing the heart of a dead sheep or calf over the chimney to prevent future losses in flocks and herds.[64] Holed stones were thought to prevent nightmare. Nightmare, that is, the oppression felt at such times, was believed to be a sort of incubus; our Teutonic ancestors called the night-riding spirit an "alb," which also means a witch; and still more picturesquely, the "On-leaper." [65] Rhoda Brook was hag-ridden, a victim of a dreadful nightmare.[66] Tales of incubi multiplied throughout the Middle Ages; the literal-minded clergy transformed the old Teutonic gods and goddesses to evil spirits, and their attendant train of dead spirits into wizards, witches, and demons of all sorts.

The attitude of Hardy's folk toward the professional conjuror is illustrated in Henchard's visit to "Wide-O." Half ashamed of his superstition, Henchard first assured himself that Fall knew all the standard cures, for warts, for instance, and for the evil eye; yet he was unwilling to eat with the wizard as man with man. Hardy comments on this attitude as follows:

People supported him with their backs turned. . . . Those who consulted him uttered the formula, "There's nothing in 'im." . . . They consulted him . . . "for a fancy!" When they paid him, they

---

[63] N. N. Puckett, *Folk-Beliefs of the Southern Negro,* 158.
[64] F. E. Hardy, *Early Life,* 147; Ellis's Brand, III, 17–18; *Folk-Lore Journal,* I, 91–92; Harland and Wilkinson, *op. cit.,* 208–9; *Folk-Lore,* X, 482–87, XXVIII, 100.
[65] Grimm-Stallybrass, II, 443; III, 1155; IV, 1419.
[66] *Wessex Tales:* "The Withered Arm."

said, "Just a trifle for Christmas," or "Candlemas," as the case might be.[67]

Trendle was in the habit of modestly waiving all claim to supernatural skill: when credited with cures, he would say he merely drank a glass of grog upon them; yet this was the conjuror who showed Gertrude Lodge the form of her enemy in the glass by the simple device of a white of an egg dissolved in water, who advised her to try the corpse-cure, and who was famed for his skill in combating dairy witch-craft.[68] Both Fall and Trendle made modest claims to control and predict weather, to effect many medical cures, and to counteract ordinary black witchcraft with white. Trendle's son inherited his father's practice and fame much as up to recent times certain Manx families were held in repute as magicians and folk-physicians, claiming their descent from ancient Druids.[69]

Witches have always been credited with power to raise winds and foul weather; in one sense, the Eumenides were glorified witches; bringing hailstorms and blasting crops with their poisonous slaver.[70] Malicious meddling with weather was a standard charge against medieval witches: the charms used by the witches, their grotesque dances, and their rites of burning the god's sacrificial animal and scattering abroad his ashes, point to a fertility cult.[71] We have tales of a repentant witch who begged that her ashes be strewn on water, not on the air, where they would breed storm or drought; it is easy to trace this degenerate myth to its pure source, the progresses of stately gods and goddesses through the air at certain seasons, bringing abundance of crops and herds to men, or if needed, the rebuke of pestilence and death.[72] The belief persisted up to modern times that certain Manx families were weather wizards: they

[67] *The Mayor of Casterbridge,* Chap. XXVI.
[68] *Wessex Tales:* "The Withered Arm"; *Tess,* Chaps. XVII, XXI.
[69] Prof. J. Rhys, *Folk-Lore,* II, 297.
[70] Grimm-Stallybrass, III, 1086–87.
[71] M. A. Murray, *The Witch Cult in Western Europe,* 117, 169, 172–173; Dalyell, *op. cit.,* 267; York Powell, ed. *Saxo-Grammaticus,* Intro. lxxviii.
[72] Grimm-Stallybrass, III, 1087.

were once said to sell mariners winds on a thread tied with knots.[73] An appeal to the local weather wizard was as familiar in Hardy's day as several generations earlier. Denham records the familiar saying, heard during an unusual windstorm, "There's been somebody at t' wise man this morning, and he's raised t' wind." [74] Hardy records in his journal a curious case of a farmer at Puddlehinton who abused a fellow farmer because the latter had induced the parson to pray for rain; he complained that it was a trick to catch God, as it were, off his guard, in generous mood! [75] Shepherds, in particular, are still feared as wizards in many English country districts, wizards with power to control the weather, exercise the gift of the evil eye, and effect notable cures.[76]

The payment of the witch or conjuror is a vexed question: Scotch witches appear to have insisted upon prompt payment for their services,[77] whereas Sussex "wise men" followed the more usual practice of refusing pay.[78] On the whole, the tradition is one of service rendered without set reward; but Hardy's conjurors are never averse to a "trifle" or a "gift."

There are several references in Hardy to books of witchcraft: Tess's mother set great store by her copy of the *Compleat Fortune-Teller*, by which she read Tess's fortune, and which, in superstitious fear, she insisted on having carried out of the house at night.[79] A certain *Universal Fortune-Teller* was still very popular in England within the past century.[80] We do not know what "witch's book" was used by Mrs. Penny to catch a glimpse of her future husband,[81] nor what the maidens in the Hintocks consulted to divine their future husbands' trades.[82] It is useless to ask if the

---

[73] Ellis's Brand, III, 5.
[74] *Denham Tracts*, II, 29.
[75] F. E. Hardy, *The Early Life of Thomas Hardy*, 206.
[76] *Folk-Lore Record*, Vol. III, Pt. I, p. 135; Grimm-Stallybrass, IV, 1618.
[77] J. G. Campbell, *Witchcraft and Second Sight in the Scottish Highlands*, page 4.
[78] Lady C. Gurdon, *Folklore of Suffolk*, 13; Grimm-Stallybrass, III, 1165.
[79] *Tess*, Chaps. I, III, IV.
[80] W. Henderson, *Folklore of the Northern Counties*, 102, 107–9.
[81] *Under the Greenwood Tree*, Part I, Chap. VIII.
[82] *The Woodlanders*, Chap. XX.

great "Wide-O" had a book from which he had his lore,
but probably Trendle's son inherited from his father some
book of magic, just as many an English witch has passed her
book on to her daughter.[83] The most famous English book
of magic was the *Red Book of Appin,* said to have been
wrested from the Devil himself, and last heard of in the
possession of the Stewarts of Invernnahyle, now unhappily
extinct.[84] Most so-called "witch's books," however, were
largely collections of simple love charms and ordinary herbals. From such may have come such innocent spells as the
cure for voluptuous widows that was told Arabella, by
which she was advised to wear a mourning brooch containing her husband's hair;[85] or the cure tried by the Widow
Peach, in which she stood barefoot upon her husband's grave
to let the sense of it enter her soul, and also wove love-knots
made from the grasses of his grave.[86]

Love-knots in amatory spells are closely allied to the general use of knots in magic and the superstitions regarding
them. In fact, the love- or marriage-knot tied in garter or
girdle, the caduceus of Hermes, and the *nodus Herculeanus*
are similar examples of the old magical principle by which,
when one desires a certain effect, he does something which
in some way resembles or imitates it, and which thus acts as
an actual cause.[87] Hence, the belief that sitting cross-legged
at cards brings ill luck to one's opponent;[88] that crossing the
thumb under the hand stops witchcraft;[89] that the muttered
spells of a witch at a wedding will cause the marriage to be
childless;[90] that unlocking doors, windows, and bolts will

[83] M. Eyre, *Folk-Lore,* XVI, 170.
[84] M. A. Murray, *op. cit.,* 170, 194; C. L. Wimberly, *op. cit.,* 222; J. G.
Campbell, *Superstitions of the Scottish Highlands,* 293–94.
[85] *Jude the Obscure,* Part V, Chap. VIII.
[86] *A Changed Man, and Other Stories:* "The Romantic Adventures of a
Milkmaid."
[87] Sir Thomas Browne, *Vulgar Errors,* Book V, Chap. XXIII; *Denham
Tracts,* II, 279–80; Dalyell, *Darker Superstitions,* 302–9.
[88] N. Thomas, *Folk-Lore of Northumberland,* 54; *Vulgar Errors,* Book V,
Chap. XXIII, Sect. 9.
[89] N. Thomas, *op. cit.,* 53.
[90] Grimm-Stallybrass, III, 1175.

permit the dying soul to take flight more easily; [91] and hence the picturesque use of rush rings in the handfestings of the fifteenth, sixteenth and seventeenth centuries.[92]

Rustic witchcraft is not always deadly and terrible. One of a group of rustics discussing Lady Constantine's fond meetings with St. Cleeve on the astronomical tower, summed up the affair admirably:

"If they get up in this tower ruling plannards together much longer, their plannards will soon rule them, in my way of thinking." [93]

The phrase, "Ruling the planets," was heard not so long ago in English country districts, referring to a man of the elder generation, with superior knowledge and powers, hence, a bit of a wizard.[94] Hardy gives us no rustic astrologer of so clear-cut a type as Jerry Gamm in Kipling's "Marlake Witches." [95]

Hardy treats the theme of devil pacts with broad humor in *The Woodlanders:* Dr. Fitzpiers' books of philosophy, known to the Hintock rustics as "black art," had been sent from London to the parson; this mistake threw the parson's wife into hysterics, and drew from the parson a clerical rebuke in the form of a message written on the package delivered to the doctor. Timothy Tangs, however, was disposed to side with the doctor:

"Well, 'tis a strange thing about doctors that the worse they be, the better they be. I mean that if you hear anything of the sort about 'em, ten to one they can cure ye as nobody else can." [96]

The rustic has no objections to "black art" if it enables his physician to know as much as the village "wise man." Dorset countrymen had a name for magic, which like the medieval

---

[91] Gregor, 206; W. Sherren, *Wessex of Romance,* 19; Mrs. Gutch, 222; C. J. Billson, *Folk-Lore of Leicestershire and Rutland,* 104.
[92] Ellis's Brand, II, 107.
[93] *Two on a Tower,* Chap. XIII.
[94] York U. Powell, *Folk-Lore,* XII, 75; Richard Blakeborough, *Wit, Character, Folk-Lore, and Customs of the North Riding of Yorkshire,* 200.
[95] *Rewards and Fairies.*
[96] *The Woodlanders,* Chap. IV.

term "gramarye," reminds us of days when those with book-knowledge were regarded with awe and fear: they called it "jommetry." [97] Grammer Oliver was not one to be fooled by a mere youngster, saying that if such young whipper-snappers as Fitzpiers should live to her age, they'd see how clever they were at five-and-twenty.[98] But the consolations of philosophy availed Grammer little some time later, when, having sold her skeleton to the doctor and spent part of the money, she was seized by the fear that she had made a veritable devil's pact which would cost her her immortal soul. With a lovable tyranny that reminds us somewhat of Juliet's nurse, Grammer coaxed Grace Melbury:

> "It do wherrit me terribly; and I shall die o' the thought of that paper I signed with my holy cross. . . . If you only knew how he do chevy me round the chimmer in my dreams, you'd pity me!" . . .
>
> .   .   .   .
>
> "Ah, if I were a young lady, and could save a poor old woman's skellington from a heathen doctor instead of a Christian grave, I would do it. . . . But nobody will do anything for a poor old familiar friend but push her out of the way." [99]

This is the plea that beats down Grace's reluctance. She visits him, charming him with her delicate beauty; and the sad story begins to move slowly, as if with reluctance, to its destined close.

Another legend of a pact with the Devil is found in one of the stories connected with Batcombe Cross in *Tess,* not to be confused with the more beautiful legend of the same place in "The Lost Pyx." [100] After Tess had sworn on the stone pillar called the "Cross-in-Hand," she met a solitary shepherd, and in reply to her question as to whether it was really a Holy Cross, received the reply:

> "Cross—no; 'Twer not a cross! 'Tis a thing of ill-omen, Miss. It was put up in wuld times by the relations of a malefactor who was

[97] E. M. Wright, *Rustic Speech and Folklore,* 30–34; Wimberly, *op. cit.,* 222; *Folk-Lore,* XXXIII, 66.
[98] *The Woodlanders,* Chap. VI.
[99] *Ibid.,* Chap. XVII.
[100] *Poems of the Past and the Present.*

tortured there by nailing his hand to a post, and afterwards hung. The bones lie underneath. They say he sold his soul to the devil, and that he walks at times." [101]

Another interesting legend, this time of Batcombe Church, relates how Conjuror Mynterne, mounted on his steed in the air, knocked from the church one of the pinnacles, which to this day will not remain in place.[102] Hardy does not tell this story. The idea of a male devil is essentially foreign to Teutonic mythology, and the idea of a repulsive covenant between devil and witch is no part of primitive magic, but the debased product of the too literal imagination of the medieval clergy.[103] What the church did to stamp out witchcraft was to associate the witches with certain heretical sects such as the Templars and the Waldenses, to make witchcraft heresy, and heresy sorcery.[104] In the end heretics were punished for sorcery, but the fate of the witches was more terrible than that of any heretical sect. Nothing came of this engrafted clerical demonism but tales of amorous alliances between witches and devils, such as the Widow Edlin refers to:

"I've heard strange tales o' husbands in my time. They say that when the saints were upon earth, devils used to take husbands' forms o' night, and get women into all sorts of trouble." [105]

Stories of devil-pacts are still occasionally heard: in Weardale they tell how one may cheat the Devil at the moment of reckoning by giving him a black cock, cat, or dog instead of one's soul.[106] Hardy records in his journal a story of a drunken parson who fell off his horse one night, was seen being hoisted to his saddle by a dark figure with a cloven

---

101 *Tess,* Chap. XLV.
102 *Folk-Lore,* X, 481; Hopkins, *Thomas Hardy's Dorset,* 233–36.
103 Grimm-Stallybrass, III, 1015–17, 1030–31, 1044–45, 1055–56, 1062–68, 1076, 1104; Thomas Wright, *Essays on Subjects Connected with the Literature, Popular Superstitions and History of England in the Middle Ages,* Vol. II, pp. 250 ff.; Dalyell, 577 ff.
104 Grimm-Stallybrass, III, 1065. The entire chapter on Witchcraft throws light on the origin of medieval ideas of witches.
105 *Jude,* Part VI, Chap. IX.
106 *Denham Tracts,* II, 67–68.

foot, and who finally disappeared mysteriously another night in a thunderstorm.[107]

The Devil's cloven foot is one of several popular ideas about him which reveal his heathen, mythological origin: he is like the Teutonic giants in his rare moments of stupidity, and like the *skratti,* or woodsprites, in his cunning and passion for mischief; his cloven hoof may be the hoof the he-goat or the horse, sacred to Odin.[108] Hardy's rustics speak of the Devil with respect mixed at times with affectionate familiarity. The hostler in *The Hand of Ethelberta* rebuked a cursing groom thus:

"Never mind the cursing and swearing, or somebody who's never out of hearing may clap yer name down in his black book." [109]

Coggan, in reminiscent mood, lamented the decay of the times, so different from the days in which a "wet in Father Everdene's kitchen . . . brought you no nearer the horned man than you were afore you begun"; [110] and he echoes this sentiment again. English country folk use several euphemisms for the Devil, chief among them "Auld Horny," "Auld Scrat," "The very old 'Un." [111] These euphemisms are a reminder of the magical power of names, a superstition which persists in the custom of plain folk calling at a house, who will refuse to give their name to a servant, and insist on seeing the person they have called to see, a custom which reminds us of the account Gabriel Oak gave of himself the first time he called upon Bathsheba:

"Would you tell Miss Everdene that somebody would be glad to speak to her?" [112]

Hardy's rustics are fond of the expression "son of a witch" and "son of a sinner," not in a sinister sense, but merely

[107] F. E. Hardy, *Early Life of Thomas Hardy,* 203.
[108] Ellis's Brand, II, 517–22; Grimm-Stallybrass, II, 480–81; III, 994–95; 1004–1005, 1014, 1029, 1064; IV, 1310.
[109] Chap. I.
[110] *Far from the Madding Crowd,* Chap. VIII.
[111] A. Parker, *Folk-Lore,* XXIV, 84; E. M. Wright, *Rustic Speech.* 198–203; Mrs. Gutch, *Folk-Lore of Yorkshire,* 128.
[112] *Far from the Madding Crowd,* Chap. IV; C. L. Wimberley, 338; Edward Clodd, *Magic in Names,* p. 101; Gregor, 35.

to denote a weak, foolish person.[113] In a superstitious regard for names, Joseph Poorgrass stands supreme. When he could not open the gate at Lambing-Down, he knelt and said the Lord's Prayer, the Belief, the Ten Commandments, and the Dearly Beloved Brethren; this sufficed to break the evil spell.[114] It was Joseph, too, who in his reproof of Cainy Ball, urged him always to say "Please God" before saying or doing anything.[115] Joseph is the true *homo superstitiosus;* untroubled by the vexed questions of the world beyond Weatherbury, he goes his placid way, his religion pure magic, his devotions charms and spells. There is no guile in him; he is rusticity reduced to its simplest terms.

The Romantic Adventures of a Milkmaid, in many respects quite un-Hardyesque, treats the theme of fascination with an undercurrent of humor. The Baron who is the villain of the piece exercises an inexplicable power over Marjery: at the Yeomanry Ball, she goes through intricate steps new to her with perfect ease; her infatuation reaches such a height that she rejects her betrothed. All through the story runs the suggestion that the Baron is not quite what he seems to be; how else explain the coal-black horses which draw his coach, the whole equipage vanishing mysteriously from sight as if by a stroke of black art?[116] Even when Marjery is freed from the Baron's spell, a happy wife and mother, she confesses that only the thought of her baby would suffice to save her, should her evil genius return. Upon his disappearance, the Baron became the center of a group of dark legends, hinting that he was a limb of the Devil, if not the Evil One himself.

"The Fiddler of the Reels" treats a similar theme with greater skill. Mop, the fiddler, with his cruel delight in his uncanny power over Car'line Aspect, is a haunting figure.

---

[113] *Return of the Native,* Book I, Chap. III; *Far from the Madding Crowd,* Chaps. XV, XXVI; cf. J. G. Campbell, *Witchcraft and Second Sight,* 4–5, and J. Abercromby, *Folk-Lore,* XIV, 98, who questions Campbell's Gaelic derivations.
[114] *Far from the Madding Crowd,* Chap. VIII.
[115] *Ibid.,* Chap. XXXIII.
[116] *A Changed Man.*

One would think he had his fill of pranks when she has lost
her true lover, and borne Mop a child. After several years,
when she has won back her one-time betrothed by his affection for her little girl, Car'line has the ill luck to fall in with
Mop. The fiddler takes a picturesque revenge: Car'line,
after heavy drinking, is drawn into the dance; and even
when the figures are completed and the dancers withdrawn,
she dances on under Mop's spell until she falls exhausted.
Mop makes off with the child; the husband is broken-
hearted at torturing rumors that the little girl is forced to
perform with Mop in an American circus. But Car'line feels
that she is the most persecuted of women. The humor of
this little tale is exceedingly grim.[117] Here is a sort of witchcraft which is never old-fashioned. Modern medicine attempts to deal with it as hypnotism, but is it not, at bottom,
witchcraft? The Scotch have an expressive word for this
sort of fascination; they call it "glamour." [118]

Several poems treat this theme of "glamour." "The
Wanderer" [119] is the complaint of one drawn on and on
quite without reason. "A Sound in the Night" [120] is the story
of a husband who has fallen under an evil woman's spell,
murdered his true love and their child, and to escape further
disaster, flees from the witch. Closely akin to such fascination is the theme of fiendish and inexplicable impulses. In
"The Face at the Casement" the accepted lover has accompanied his betrothed in a visit to a dying man who has long
loved her; as they drive away, he puts his arm about her to
wound the sick man who is watching from the window. This
hellish deed tortures him in later days.[121]

There is a solemn passage in *Desperate Remedies* [122]
which Hardy used again in *The Mayor,* suggesting that he
could not easily say the thing and let it go. Henchard had

---

[117] *Life's Little Ironies.*
[118] James Napier, *Folk-Lore: or Superstitious Beliefs in the West of Scotland* . . . 132.
[119] *Late Lyrics, and Earlier.*
[120] *Late Lyrics.*
[121] *Satires of Circumstance.*
[122] Chap. XVI.

told Newson that Elizabeth-Jane was dead; and when he had let the sailor go, he was shocked at the evil impulse he had blindly followed. He was soon assailed by another temptation, the desire to break the match between Farfrae and Elizabeth-Jane by merely telling the Scotchman the truth as to her parentage: Hardy comments thus on Henchard's inexplicable impulse:

There is an outer chamber of the brain in which thoughts unowned, unsolicited, and of noxious kind, are sometimes allowed to wander for a moment prior to be sent off whence they came. One of these thoughts sailed into Henchard's ken now.[123]

Here is the blackest sort of witchcraft, but no sign of a witch; here is horror of soul beyond the power of magician to inflict, a something which fills us with a sense of the pathetic helplessness of the human will when the buried lower nature comes to the surface. Each of us at times exercises this sort of witchcraft over himself, against his better nature, his will, and his reason.

It was not Hardy's way to approve or condemn; he recorded and re-created what he saw with heightened effectiveness. In no other field of folklore, however, does the comedy of the human spectacle merge more grotesquely with the tragedy. On the whole, Hardy concerned himself principally with the darker impulses of our nature; but witchcraft of every sort was interesting to him because it involves a common strain in widely different types of persons. He realized that magic is a primitive religion whose roots go incalculably deep; and, as always, he indicts nothing in the human heart, but meets every new discovery with unfailing understanding and sympathy. It is we who weep over Eustacia Vye; it is we who shudder at Susan Nunsuch. Hardy's Olympian calm was born of a great pity, a pity that "doth lie too deep for tears."

[123] *The Mayor,* Chap. XLII.

V

FOLK-MEDICINE

Folk-Medicine, as it exists today, is by no means altogether "folk." Many of the familiar remedies and practices that linger in Wessex are to be traced to regular medicine, which has fallen more or less away from the best opinion, has put on country dress, and is masquerading as pure folk-medicine. The fine empiric school of Greek medicine was corrupted by Oriental influences, and throughout the Middle Ages slowly accumulated a large amount of superstitious practice. If we could go far enough into antiquity, we should no doubt discover the origins of many a current folk-remedy in classical medicine or in Egyptian or Babylonian medicine. The application of fried adder's fat to an adder bite which we find in *The Return of the Native,* for instance, harks back to the days of Nero: Andromachus, physician to Nero, used the flesh of vipers as a basic constituent in theriaca, a specific against snake bite, and the amazing part of the matter is that this selfsame specific occurs in our modern pharmacopœia.[1] One could not ask for an apter illustration of the way in which true medical lore, either discredited or allowed to fall into comparative disuse, keeps its place in the book of drugs, or in folk-memory and folk-practice. It is perhaps safe to surmise that Greek and Roman physicians took the idea for this remedy from the folk themselves, for this particular instance is but one of many cases of application of the old magical principle, "Take a hair of the dog that bit you." [2] The love-potions sold by the Wessex quack

[1] *The Return of the Native,* Book IV, Chap. VII; Wm. R. Halliday, *Greek and Roman Folklore,* 131–133.
[2] E. Selons, *Folk-Lore,* XXIII, 229–230.

Vilbert are part of a long and tough tradition. Such potions were prohibited by Greek and Roman legislation; but long before such laws were thought of, our Teutonic ancestors were drinking the *minne* of the dead and of the gods with whom the dead passed the first three nights, hoping through the draught to partake of the virtues of the dead, and enjoy a magical communion.[3] The enchanted beaker drained by Tristram and Iseult had magic virtues which doomed the pair to a tragic love. The mass of legends about the mandrake, closely related to the beliefs in corpse and gallows-cures, and the paralyzing effect of "The Hand of Glory" have as a basis in actual fact the medieval use of mandrake as an anæsthetic in surgery.[4] The stock in trade of the village quack contains remedies once held highly scientific, but now discredited in the best medical practice: Vilbert's bright-colored lard, concocted to cure miscellaneous ills, like the red hangings in the room of the smallpox patient in olden days, or a hundred other similar practices, was based on the old principle that like cures like.[5]

A study of the Anglo-Saxon leechbooks, the Leechbook of Bald, for instance, shows a curious mixture of fine herbal lore and superstitious spells, in which, in many instances, the names of the heathen gods in various incantations have merely been replaced by the names of Christ, the Virgin, and favorite saints. These charms lessen, no doubt, the noble scientific achievement of the leechbooks, but we could ill spare them, for they afford us a glimpse of the world of heathen poetry. Much of this herbal lore has descended almost unchanged to the "wise men" and "wise women" of Dorset and other shires. When the medieval clergy were ousted from the practice of medicine, they retaliated cruelly upon the humbler practitioners, the village "wise women" and conjurors, who thus fell under the dreadful charge of sorcery. Medicine on its popular side arose slowly out of

---

[3] *Jude the Obscure,* Part V, Chap. V; Grimm-Stallybrass, I, 59–62.
[4] James J. Walsh, *Mediæval Medicine,* p. 120 and note.
[5] *Jude the Obscure,* Part I, Chap. V; T. J. Pettigrew, *On Superstitions connected with . . . Medicine and Surgery,* 18–19.

primitive magic, and after a long evolution into pure science,
drifted to its original source, mixing itself with witchcraft
and magical formulas and rites. It is to be regretted that we
have no adequate study of the sixteenth and seventeenth
century witchcraft cults on their medical side. The "wise
man" of today is the possessor of much true herbal lore,
much common sense, preventive medicine, and well-tested
veterinary lore; but he casts aspersion on his claims of supernatural power by methods which too often smack of the
charlatan.[6]

Hardy's references to folk-medicine, although not numerous, are extremely interesting. The most striking bit of medical folklore in Hardy's writing is the tale of "The Withered Arm."[7] The reader will recall how Rhoda Brook,
Farmer Lodge's discarded sweetheart, tortured by a terrible dream in which her rival seemed to be sitting on her
chest, crushing the life from her body, roused herself, and
striking out wildly, left the print of her hand on the phan
tom's arm. Gertrude Lodge's left arm withered mysteriously.
Sincerely sorry, and half afraid of her own dark nature,
Rhoda accompanied the young wife on a secret visit to Conjuror Trendle, who let Gertrude see her persecutor in the
white of an egg as it dissolved in water. As the years passed,
the sick woman grew weaker; she grieved over the loss of
her health, her beauty, and her husband's affection. In des-
peration, she again had recourse to Trendle, who told her
that she must try the corpse-cure; that is, must touch with
the withered limb the neck of a man who had just been
hanged. Thus only, by a "turn in the blood" could she hope
for a change in her constitution, and eventual recovery. By
an ironic twist of circumstance, the body Gertrude Lodge
touched to effect her ghastly cure was the body of the son

---

[6] On the whole subject of the relation of charms and spells in the Anglo-
Saxon leechbooks to classic medicine, on one side, and true folk-medicine,
on the other, see J. F. Payne, M.D., *English Medicine in Anglo-Saxon
Times*, pp. 57–59, 62, 108–109, 119–120, 135–136.
[7] *Wessex Tales*.

of Lodge and Rhoda Brook, and the shock finished the work of witchcraft, curing all Gertrude's ills at one swift stroke.

The widespread use of the dead hand for various cures well up to 1900 must have suggested the theme of this tale to Hardy; hangmen made a business, for fees, of admitting several persons at a time to the scaffold at the time of executions.[8] Wens and goiters were commonly believed to be curable by the "dead touch." [9] The hand of Father Arrowsmith, a Catholic martyr of the time of William the Third, was until recently still kept at Ashton-in-Makerfield, and was said to perform remarkable cures.[10] Even the halter or pieces of the gibbet used in the execution of a criminal were held highly efficacious; [11] and the modern Sicilians have an elaborate cult of executed criminals recalling the Greek *pharmakos*.[12] Whether the *pharmakos*, or scapegoat, was actually killed, or merely driven out of Athens by whips as a rite of formal purification, he is representative of a whole community, whose sins and diseases he takes upon himself. This rite, essentially magical, has reached sublime heights of interpretation in every great world-religion.[13] Odin hung for nine days and nights between heaven and earth to learn the runes of magic might, and since then all who die on the gallows are his chosen ones.[14] In the sacred grove at Upsala horses and men were hanged in dedication to Odin; the sacrificial victim, in sharing the fate of the god, was believed to take on his divine nature and powers; hence the whole series of superstitions in the cult of executed criminals, and hence the belief that storms follow in the wake of a suicide

[8] W. G. Black, *Folk-Medicine*, 101; Pettigrew, *op. cit.*, 74.
[9] Lady Camilla Gurdon, *The Folklore of Suffolk*, pp. 18–20; W. W. Groome, M.D., *Folk-Lore*, VI, 124–25.
[10] Wm. Harland and T. T. Wilkinson, *Lancashire Folklore*, 158–163.
[11] Halliday, *Greek and Roman Folklore*, 49; C. Latham, *Folk-Lore Record*, I, 48; Rev. Sabine Baring-Gould, *Strange Survivals*, 243; Black, *op. cit.*, 100.
[12] Mabel Peacock, *Folk-Lore*, VII, 268–83; E. Sidney Hartland, *Folk-Lore*, XXI, 168–179; J. C. Lawson, *Modern Greek Folklore and Ancient Greek Religion*, 355–360.
[13] Lawson, *op. cit.*, 355–360; E. M. Roberts, *Folk-Lore*, XXVII, 220–221; Jane Harrison, *Folk-Lore*, XXVII, 298–99; S. Baring-Gould, *Strange Survivals*, 240, 251.
[14] Baring-Gould, *Strange Survivals*, 239–40.

or an execution, for in the storm Odin is riding to claim a
newcomer to the ranks of the Furious Host.[15]

Corpse-cures take many revolting forms. On the basis of
the magical efficacy of anything connected with the executed
man, we find bits of hangman's rope, pieces of the gibbet,
gravestone chips, graveyard mold, pieces of the shroud,
and even mock burials resorted to for cures for ailments
ranging all the way from corns, warts, and headache to
gout, epilepsy, goiter, and paralysis.[16] Cramp-rings made
from coffin-handles and nails were popular in the last century, and were firmly believed to cure the sufferer.[17] Modern
Russian gamblers believe that a piece of a halter brings
good luck at play; the superstition reminds us of the fact
that Odin, Lord of the Gallows, was also the god of dicing
and gambling.[18] Sufferers from epilepsy believed that they
might be cured simply by wearing the unwashed clothes of
the dead, or by carrying about them a remnant of his
shroud.[19] Superstitious Scots formerly used to lay earth
taken from a churchyard upon a malignant ulcer.[20] The Chinese, revering the dead too much to desecrate the grave, are
believers in the magical healing properties of water from a
grave.[21] In England up to comparatively recent times mock
burials were occasionally tried by sufferers from rheumatism.[22] In the Middle Ages, long after physicians had discredited them, *usnea,* the moss from a dead man's skull,
and *mummy,* an unguent made from the flesh of a corpse,
continued to be employed by those who mixed sorcery and

[15] *Ibid.,* 242–43.
[16] Harland and Wilkinson, 75, 158–63; Pettigrew, 64, 68, 162; Dalyell,
Darker Superstitions of Scotland, 126–128; Aubrey's *Miscellanies,* Bohn ed.,
124–126; Aubrey's *Remaines,* Britten ed., 197–198; Gregor, *Notes on the
Folk-Lore of the North-East of Scotland,* 48; E. Fogel, *Beliefs and Superstitions of the Pennsylvania Germans,* Proverbs Nos. 93, 1429, 1479, 1534,
1539, 1548, 1565, 1567, 1580, 2070; J. J. Walsh, M.D., *Mediæval Medicine,* 22;
Sir Henry Ellis's ed. John Brand's *Popular Antiquities of Great Britain,* III,
276–78; etc.
[17] Pettigrew, 61, 87; N. Thomas, *The Folk-Lore of Northumberland,* 45.
[18] Grimm-Stallybrass, I, 159–160; III, 1007; IV, 1334; *Folk-Lore Record,*
Vol. III, Pt. I, 137; *Daily Telegraph,* March 27, 1880.
[19] Fogel, Proverbs 1534, 1539; Gregor, 45.
[20] Dalyell, 126.
[21] Dennys, *Folklore of China,* 25, 48.
[22] Alice B. Keary, *Folk-Lore,* XII, 351–52.

medicine; in fact, this revolting practice lasted well into the eighteenth century.[23]

The whole subject of corpse-cures shades almost imperceptibly into the legends of the mandrake, and that version of the faith in the magical powers of the criminal's hand which is called "The Hand of Glory." The classical and medieval belief was that the mandrake was to be found beneath the gallows, and was nourished by the juices and humors of the corpse which hung there; that it was instinct with life and feeling, shrieked when torn from the ground, bringing death and madness to the dogs who were used to uproot it; that it was to be found in male and female forms, and had the power to propagate itself.[24] It is highly probable that the powerful narcotic odor of the mandrake root lies at the bottom of both the superstitious and the purely scientific view of this strangest of plants. On the side of superstition we may put the belief that the hand of a dead criminal may be used by housebreakers to stupefy the inmates of a house.[25] The German name for mandragora is *Alraun,* which is also the name of the Teutonic wise woman, or witch, and before the dawn of witchcraft, the name of a great goddess. Viewed another way, the alraun witch was one who operated by the use of alraun; originally she was the root itself, a medicine which brought blessed relief from pain and the boon of sleep. The goddess degenerated into the witch at the coming of Christianity.[26] The name *main de gloire* is derived linguistically from *mandragore;* hence our "Hand of Glory." Perhaps the connection with the cult of the executed criminal is a late invention based upon the fanciful similarity of names. But mandrake was the basic constituent of the anæsthetics used by medieval surgeons; it was com-

[23] J. J. Walsh, M.D., *Mediæval Medicine,* 22; Dalyell, 375-83.
[24] Rendel Harris, The Origin of the Cult of Aphrodite: *The Ascent of Olympus,* 109-110.
[25] J. S. Payne, *English Medicine in Anglo-Saxon Times,* 75; Ellis's Brand, III, 278-79; Aubrey's *Remaines,* Britten ed., 103; Grimm-Stallybrass, III, 1073, Note 3; Richard Blakeborough, *Wit, Character, Folklore, and Customs of the North Ridings of Yorkshire,* 201.
[26] Grimm-Stallybrass, I, 404; III, 1202; Rendel Harris, *The Ascent of Olympus,* 123-124.

bined with opium, or ivy or hemlock juice, but was invariably present.[27] Justice has never been done the art of these medieval surgeons, who performed successfully major operations by the use of such anæsthetics. Strange to say, although the use of anæsthetics died out in regular practice, the memory and tradition of it lingered on in the works of Elizabethan dramatists.[28] The mandrake, in its female form, has been ingeniously identified with the Black Aphrodite whose worship was brought from Cyprus to Greece by Phœnician sailors. According to this hypothesis, Aphrodite's magic cestus is nothing more or less than a belt of mandrake roots, powerfully aphrodisiac in effect.[29] English herbals reveal the fact that mandrake was imported—seeds, roots, and fruits —from Cyprus. We are familiar with the story of Leah and Rachel: Rachel, Jacob's favorite wife, begged Leah to give her the mandrakes Leah's son Reuben had gathered; Leah had been using them in love charms to win back Jacob's favor; Rachel wanted them, it is likely, for purposes of abortion.[30] The use of the mandrake in amatory charms and for Rachel's purpose was common enough in England and Scotland up to the early nineteenth century; it is still used for certain medical purposes even today.[31] It is said that in certain London districts, Jewish parents rub the man-shaped root upon the gums of girl-babies to promote teething, and vice versa; and that in London as late as 1913 a familiar figure could still be seen at certain times selling mandrake at a penny a slice, retailing marvelous tales of its remarkable cures.[32] Other aspects of the mandrake tradition, particularly its malignity, lingered until modern times: In 1908, for instance, a laborer digging in a neglected garden cut

[27] Walsh, *Mediæval Medicine,* 104–105; 120.

[28] Walsh, 120, Note; Thomas Middleton, *Women Beware Women,* IV, 1; *Romeo and Juliet,* II, 3; IV, 2; IV, 3.

[29] Rendel Harris, *The Ascent of Olympus,* 120–30.

[30] Genesis, Chap. XXX; Thomas Browne, *Vulgar Errors,* Book V, Chap. VII; Pettigrew, 84; Dalyell, 216–217.

[31] Dalyell, *Darker Superstitions of Scotland,* 216–217; James Napier, *Folk-Lore: or Superstitions in the West of Scotland,* 90; E. Lovett, "Folk Medicine in London," *Folk-Lore,* XXIV, 121.

[32] E. Lovett, *Folk-Lore,* XXIV, 121.

through a white bryony root which he took for mandrake; sick with worry, he went home, brooded upon his "awful bad luck," and a week after the accident, fell down a stairway and was instantly killed.[33]

It would be interesting to know whether mandrake is the "herb" referred to in the poem, "A Sunday Morning Tragedy." This poem tells a story of a mother who seeks a shepherd's aid in behalf of her daughter, who is apparently deserted by her lover and is soon to bear a child. The shepherd, a subtle man, gives her an herb he uses in his flocks to balk "ill-motherings." The tale ends on a grimly ironic note: the lover, who all along had meant to surprise his sweetheart, comes with a host of friends from the village church where the banns have just been called, only to find that the girl he hopes to wed is dead.[34] In the poem, "The Mother Mourns," the poet suggests the old belief that Mother Nature herself shudders at the birth of the mysterious mandrake.[35]

Legends of the mandrake and of the "Hand of Glory" are closely connected with love-potions. The quack Vilbert traveled the Wessex roads year after year, selling his golden salves to ailing dames, and his love-potions to eager maidens. Meeting Arabella at the Great Wessex Agricultural Show, Vilbert induced her to buy a potion distilled from pigeons' hearts.[36] These ingredients were familiar enough in the *pocula amatoria* of the Greeks and Romans, and are immortalized in the stern edicts which they evoked.[37] *The Lay of Gudrun* reveals a use of love-philters among the Scandinavians which may possibly be due to Celtic influence.[38] The Pennsylvania Dutch say that kissing a girl with the heart of a turtledove in one's mouth will surely procure her love; and we are quite willing to believe them![39] In

[33] Ella M. Leather, *Folk-Lore*, XXIV, 240.
[34] *Time's Laughingstocks.*
[35] *Poems of the Past and the Present.*
[36] *Jude the Obscure*, Part V, Chap. V.
[37] Dalyell, *Darker Superstitions of Scotland*, 213–214.
[38] York-Powell, ed. *Saxo-Grammaticus*, Intro. lxxvii.
[39] Fogel, *The Beliefs and Superstitions of the Pennsylvania Germans*, Proverb 192.

The Anatomy of Melancholy moody Burton describes phil-
ters made of the "dust of doves' hearts," and gruesome potions of mandrake roots and mandrake apples, dead men's
shrouds, and corpse-candles, said to be very efficacious, but
"not fit to be made common." [40] There is some extremely
close connection between love-philters of this sort and
corpse-cures, if we could but unravel the tangle. Medea gave
to Jason a magic unguent made from flowers nourished on
the ichor which dripped from the martyred Prometheus.
She was equally skilled with a love-potion as a poison, this
classic witch in her herb garden; did she invoke one and the
same principle of magic in all her potions? And is this the
the principle invoked by both Gertrude Lodge and Arabella? [41] At any rate, the reader of *Jude* is keenly alive to
the exquisite irony of Vilbert's fate; there is a certain justice, poetic or otherwise, in Vilbert's assuming the rôle of
Arabella's husband. Arabella was crafty, after the way of
her kind; with this single touch of finesse Hardy redeems
an otherwise infinitely coarse animal.

Vilbert must have depended for a regular income on something more in demand by steady customers than love-potions.
Jude saw him one day, we remember, selling a pot of golden
ointment, really yellow lard, to an old woman as a specific
cure for a bad leg. The old woman paid a guinea in install-
ments of a shilling a fortnight for the precious salve which
Vilbert assured her could only be obtained from a certain
animal which grazed on Mount Sinai and could only be
captured at the risk of one's life.[42] One wonders instantly if
this animal which grazed on Mount Sinai could possibly be
that choice medieval absurdity, the Vegetable Lamb? This
strangest of creatures, pictured on Parkinson's *Theatrum
Botanicum,* and described for us in the fabulous *Travels of
Sir John Mandeville,* was thought to be both an animal and
a plant native to Scythia. The usual theory was that the

---

[40] Part III, Sect. II, Mem. III, Subs. 1.
[41] Rendel Harris, *The Ascent of Olympus,* 110; *Wessex Tales:* "The
Withered Arm"; *Jude the Obscure,* Part V, Chap. V; Part VI, Chap. X.
[42] *Jude the Obscure,* Part I, Chap. IV.

lamb was a seedpod of a tree, which, when ripe, burst open, disclosing a little lamb. The creature lived suspended from the tree by a flexible stalk; when the nearby herbage was exhausted, it withered and died. Probably the myth preserves an interpretation of the cotton plant; at any rate, the belief lingered well into the eighteenth century.[43] We know that drugs and precious herbs came to England from the East at an early day; for Asser, in his *Life of Alfred,* states that Alfred sent envoys to the Patriarch of Jerusalem, and received from him drugs and directions for their use.[44] *The Leechbook of Bald,* moreover, specifies a number of Syrian and Armenian drugs, among them the famous Balm of Gilead, a product of Asia Minor.[45] It is quite possible, however, that the mysterious animal referred to by Vilbert might well have been merely the figment of a ready imagination, built on existent tradition of the great efficacy of Eastern drugs.

The "golden ointment" the quack sold runs true to form: in folk medicine, the drug should harmonize with the malady. Certain colors, however, were believed to be particularly efficacious for medicines: red and yellow were favorites, but black ran a close second.[46]

A fascinating problem is presented by the itinerant leeches of the Middle Ages, who went about the country selling their drugs, usually attended by some monster or performing animal, and were an invariable feature of country fairs.[47] Their lineal descendants are such men as the Toad Doctor who for years was seen at "Toad Fair" at Stalbridge, selling his patients a bag containing a live toad, whose twitchings were thought to give the wearer a turn of the blood and a complete change of constitution.[48] This fellow was known

[43] E. S. Rohde, "The Folk-Lore of Herbals," *Folk-Lore,* XXXIII, 261–63.
[44] J. F. Payne, M.D., *English Medicine in Anglo-Saxon Times,* 60.
[45] Payne, 60; Dalyell, 612; Black, 195.
[46] J. Black, *Folk-Medicine,* 112; Grimm-Stallybrass, I, 177; Rev. Oswald Cockayne, *Leechdoms, Wortcunnings, and Starcraft of Early England,* I, XXXI–XXXII, 307; E. Dyer, *Folklore of Plants,* 201; Pettigrew, 18–19.
[47] Grimm-Stallybrass, III, 1151.
[48] W. Sherren, *The Wessex of Romance,* 22–23.

to both William Barnes and Hardy,[49] and it may have been he who suggested to Hardy the cure prescribed by "Wide-O," the conjuror in *The Mayor*. When Henchard questions him as to his skill, he assures him that he is master of all the standard cures: He can charm away warts, and can cure the evil, if his patient will only wear the toad-bag.[50] The most extreme cure for warts is the familiar corpse-cure, but also efficacious are such simple cures as rubbing the warts on some animal or object, all the while repeating a charm.[51]

Nowhere is the principle of sympathetic magic which lies at the bottom of folk-medicine more clearly seen than in the remedy offered the dying Mrs. Yeobright. When the rustics have discovered that she has been bitten by an adder, their old-time remedy comes at once to their minds: the fat of adders, caught alive if possible, must be laid upon it. They catch one alive, and two which have been killed that day, but which, according to the superstition that an adder cannot really die until sundown, are still half alive: [52]

The live adder regarded the assembled group with a sinister look in its small black eyes, and the beautiful brown and jet pattern on its back seemed to intensify with indignation. Mrs. Yeobright saw the creature, and the creature saw her; she quivered throughout, and averted her eyes.[53]

This barbarous remedy, in use up to comparatively recent times in Wessex, is an application of the same principle on which an ancient Roman, bitten by a viper, took a draught of viper wine.[54] English gypsies apply literally the proverb, Take

[49] Ernest Brennecke's ed. *Life and Art*, a collection of miscellaneous essays by Thomas Hardy: "The Rev. William Barnes, D.D."; F. E. Hardy, *The Early Life of Thomas Hardy*, 148.

[50] *The Mayor of Casterbridge*, Chap. XXVI.

[51] James Hardy, "Wart and Wen Cures": *Folk-Lore Record*, I, 227 ff.; Pettigrew, 80.

[52] *The Return of the Native*, Book IV, Chap. VII; C. Latham, *Folk-Lore Record*, I, 15.

[53] *Ibid.*, Book IV, Chap. VII.

[54] Sherren, *The Wessex of Romance*, 22; D. H. M. Read, *Folk-Lore*, XXII, 305; Wm. Halliday, *Folk-Lore*, XXXII, 263–64, Note 2; Pliny, *Nat. Hist.* XXXIX (22) 71.

a hair of the dog that bit you; they fry the hairs, and apply them to the wound.[55] Snake's tongue and arvel were formerly prized for headache cures, for ease in extracting a thorn, and for immunity from disease.[56] Similarly, a stone which in any way resembles a snake, was thought to have magic properties: by its shape, perhaps, as does the ammonite, or fossil shark's tooth; or by its markings, as does the serpentine and ophite.[57] The serpent is worshiped by most primitive peoples; the Hindoos, Egyptians, Greeks, Romans, and Celts credited the serpent with healing powers as well as wisdom; Christianity is the first great religion to desert at one and the same time the worship of the serpent and the principle that the gods can cure the evils they send, and even Christianity does not entirely renounce this rule of magic. Hebrew mythology degrades the beautiful and gifted serpent, which among primitive races still calls forth fear and awe, and lives in the caduceus of Æsculapius.[58]

Verbal charms play an important rôle in folk-medicine: Christian Cantle, timid soul, hearing a suspicious sound on the heath one night, straightway invoked supernatural aid in an ancient charm:

"Matthew, Mark, Luke and John, bless the bed that I lie on; four angels guard. . . ."

but at this point he was silenced by Fairway.[59] This sleep-charm is familiar to most of us, and is still occasionally heard. Children and aged women alike murmured it to charm their bed. It may well have come from a moon-charm; for Irish midwives used to charm the four corners of the house and bed of a childing woman, ending the spell with the words,

---

[55] Edmond Selons, *Folk-Lore,* XXIII, 229–30; Gregor, 127.
[56] Gurdon, 23–24; Aubrey's *Remaines,* Britten ed., 38; *Folk-Lore Journal,* IV, 185; C. J. Billson, *Folk-Lore of Leicestershire* . . . , 40.
[57] Halliday, *Folk-Lore,* XXXII, 264; M. J. MacCulloch, *Folk-Lore,* XXXIV, 91; Dalyell, 140–141.
[58] Grimm-Stallybrass, II, 684–85; IV, 1492; W. H. Hudson, *The Book of a Naturalist,* 153–171, 172–185; Gurdon, 10.
[59] *The Return of the Native,* Book I, Chap. III.

"New moon, new moon, God bless me,
God bless this house and family." [60]

Of course, an old moon-charm may have become mixed with
a sleep-spell, but the antiquity of both parts of the rhyme
seems clear enough; the names of the four Evangelists need
not mislead us, for they are a late "improvement." A favorite medieval charm against flying venom invoked the four
cardinal points, each protected by one of the four Evangelists; it may have originated in the Apocrypha, but, if so, how
shall we explain the same charm, without the Evangelists'
names, as it occurs in the *Atharva Veda?* [61] This charm,
which is far older than Christianity, is familiar all over
Great Britain and the United States.[62] Many of the charms
in the Anglo-Saxon leechbooks which we usually ascribe to
Teutonic or Celtic folklore, may be traced to Oriental or
Greek sources; some *carmina* were undoubtedly medico-
magical formulas in origin.[63] Christian Cantle's prayer, like
many Christian prayers, was an appeal to magic: he invoked, not a Supreme Intelligence nor a Divine Will, but a
law of cause and effect which he thought to set working
through a specific formula.

Hardy employs the waxen image as a device of magic in
The Return of the Native, but gives no parallel medical use
of it.[64] Our Teutonic ancestors believed in the medical efficacy of the image; for they were wont to hang up an image
of that part of the body which was restored to health in
their groves, or at crossroads; the church, at first antagonistic
to this practice, later established the worship of sacred relics
capable of cures.[65]

The reader of *Far from the Madding Crowd* will recall

[60] Black, 128.
[61] E. S. Rohde, "The Folk-Lore of Herbals," *Folk-Lore,* XXXIII, 252–53;
Payne, 119, 135–36.
[62] Mrs. Gutch, *Folklore of Yorkshire,* 128, 214; Harland and Wilkinson,
68; *Denham Tracts,* II, 11; Ellis's Brand, III, 312.
[63] J. F. Payne, M.D., *English Medicine in Anglo-Saxon Times,* 108–9,
119–22, 135–36, 99–101, Cockayne, Vol. I, Preface, x.
[64] *The Return of the Native,* Book V, Chaps. VII, VIII.
[65] Grimm-Stallybrass, III, 1179–80; Pettigrew, 44, 59.

the amazing swiftness and accuracy with which Gabriel Oak pierced the flanks of the blasted sheep, giving them instant release from agony, and Laban Tall's undisguised admiration of this skill in ovine surgery, a skill which was all the rarer among shepherds because the fraction of an inch to the right or left of the exact spot meant the death of the ewe.[66] A large part of the medical superstitions connected with sheep and shepherds find no place in Hardy's writings: We do not hear, for instance, that sufferers from consumption will benefit from sleeping in a sheepfold, or even walking around one; [67] nor that a baby with whooping-cough should be laid in one of the sheep's forms; [68] nor again, that the patella of a sheep is the surest cure for cramp,[69] nor a dozen other remedies. But shepherds from the earliest times have passed for wizards with power to control weather, effect cures of man and beast, the power to see ghosts, and general supernatural gifts of a high order.[70]

Hardy recognized the similarity of certain folk-beliefs to the tenets of modern medicine. The theme of the story, "An Imaginative Woman," is based on a medical hypothesis that is still being debated by physicians, the question of prenatal influence. It deals with the love of a romantic woman for a poet whose verses she admires to excess. She broods over his picture, corresponds with him, and, in an access of desperate courage, runs away from her husband, only to be brought home, fatally ill. She makes a clean breast of the affair; the poet, whom she has never seen, is dead. The child born at her death has the hair and eyes of the poet, and is despised as a bastard. Hardy's preface note reveals the fact that he believes more firmly in prenatal influence than the best medical opinion of today will seem to

[66] Chap. XXI.
[67] Mrs. E. Wright, *Folk-Lore*, XX, 218.
[68] W. W. Fowler, *Folk-Lore*, XIX, 345.
[69] C. J. Billson, *Folklore of Leicestershire and Rutland*, 40; Gurdon, 21.
[70] Grimm-Stallybrass, III, 1151; M. Gaster, *Folk-Lore*, XXXIII, 415–20; T. W. E. Higgins, *Folk-Lore*, VII, 298–99; *Folk-Lore Record*, III, Pt. I, 135.

warrant.[71] He uses the same theme far more effectively in "San Sebastian," where the medium of poetry instantly converts an unconvincing tale to beauty:

> Maybe we shape our offspring's guise
> From fancy, or we know not what,
> And that no deep impression dies—
> For the mother of my child is not
> The mother of her eyes.[72]

The story of the poem is even more incredible than "An Imaginative Woman": the sergeant who had wronged a woman at San Sebastian, had never been able to forget her "beseeching eyes"; his daughter by his English wife has the eyes and bearing of the unknown Spanish girl. We are left with the suggestion that his tortured conscience is to blame for the fancied resemblance.

Hippocrates, the great Greek physician, held to the belief in prenatal influence, and Jacob, master-trickster, practised it in his device to increase his flocks by affecting the ewes with mental impressions, and so causing them to imitate the color seen in their offspring! [73] But the best medical opinion of our day is flatly against the whole theory that the unborn child is directly affected by prenatal maternal impressions.[74]

Hallucinations are closely allied to the subject of prenatal maternal impressions. Hardy relates an ironic tale of a notable hallucination in "A Group of Noble Dames": Timothy Petrick has come to excuse the shortcomings of his grandson, Rupert, on the score of his noble paternity; for Annetta had made a dying confession that he was the natural son of the Earl of Christminster. Years later, the physician who had attended Annetta when Rupert was born told Petrick of the delusion under which both Annetta and her

---

[71] *Wessex Tales:* "An Imaginative Woman."
[72] *Wessex Poems.*
[73] Havelock Ellis, *Studies in the Psychology of Sex,* 1923 ed. I, 221–23.
[74] Joseph De Lee, M.D., W. B. Saunders Company, Section V, *The Hygiene and Conduct of Pregnancy and Labor,* Chap. XVII, "The Hygiene of Pregnancy," pp. 238–243.

mother had suffered as victims of a form of hallucination in which they took vivid dreams for actual happenings. The Squire was at once disgusted and relieved at this explanation of Rupert's ingrained plebeian traits.[75]

Hardy is particularly fond of the study of hereditary family traits. In the story, "For Conscience' Sake," he reveals the uncanny resemblance between Frances Millbourne and her supposed stepfather, who is, of course, her father. The resemblance is brought out by nausea on a sea-voyage. Hardy says:

Nausea, in such circumstances, like midnight watching, fatigue, trouble, fright, has this marked effect upon the countenance—that it brings out strongly the divergences of the individual from the norm of his race. . . . Unexpected physiognomies will uncover themselves at these times in well-known faces; the aspect becomes invested with the spectral presence of entombed and forgotten ancestors. . . .[76]

He restates the belief in *The Mayor of Casterbridge:*

In sleep there come to the surface buried genealogical facts, ancestral curves, dead men's traits. . . .[77]

In "Heredity" and in "The Pedigree" the poet celebrates the "family face": [78] a similar idea is expressed in the maternal resemblance Bob Loveday suddenly develops after his long years at sea, a likeness which overshadows all other impressions of travel and adventure.[79] The same idea is still more beautifully expressed in the poem, "The Rover Comes Home." [80] But let us confess it, Hardy's studies of heredity in Jude and Sue, in the d'Urbervilles and Jocelyn Pierston, are pathological in large part, and do not come into the field of folk-medicine.[81]

There is much fascinating medicine still in use in Hardy's

---

[75] *A Group of Noble Dames:* "Squire Petrick's Lady."
[76] *Life's Little Ironies:* "For Conscience' Sake."
[77] *The Mayor of Casterbridge,* Chap. XIX.
[78] *Moments of Vision.*
[79] *The Trumpet-Major,* Chap. XV.
[80] *Human Shows.*
[81] See particularly *Tess,* Chaps. XI, XXXVII, XLVII, LVII: *Jude,* Part I, Chap. XI; Part V, Chap. VI.

Wessex that he does not give us: the wishing-well at Cerne Abbas with its marvelous cures, for instance; [82] the annual Toad Fair at Stalbridge, whither came the famous Toad Doctor that Barnes and Hardy knew; [83] the mouse-medicine, at least as old as the Greeks, which some Wessex folk give their children; [84] the ancient custom of passing a child with the whooping-cough or rickets through a shrew-ash or a perforated stone; [85] the belief that the seventh son of a seventh son possesses marvelous medical powers: [86] the fear of the "venomous" forefinger of the right hand as applied to a wound or sore; [87] and a dozen other curiosities of folkmedicine. None of these fragments fitted into the mosaic Hardy created. As always, he used folklore here, not for its own sake, but to produce a definite artistic effect. But the episodes of folk-medicine he gives us by the way, as it were, are none the less interesting in themselves. They reveal to us a people who think and act in a primitive way, a people who mix medicine with magic, as in the earliest days.

[82] *Folk-Lore Journal*, VI, 118; *Folk-Lore*, X, 479–80.
[83] F. E. Hardy, *The Early Life of Thomas Hardy*, 148.
[84] Rendel Harris, *The Ascent of Olympus*, 83–84.
[85] Black, 53; Grimm-Stallybrass, III, 1166–68.
[86] *Denham Tracts*, II, 39.
[87] *Ibid.*, II, 24.

VI

WEATHER LORE AND THE LAN- GUAGE OF COUNTRY THINGS

~~~~~~

The Reverend Mr. Swancourt once asserted that the farmers of Endelstow could tell time to the fraction of an hour "by means of shadows, winds, clouds, the movements of sheep and oxen, the singing of birds, the crowing of cocks. . . ." [1] The amiable vicar had another "tall story" of a countryman who could prophesy with barometric exactness a change of weather simply by the braying of an ass and the temper of his wife! We must allow every teller of tales his legitimate margin of artistic heightening; and the vicar is no exception.[2] Many weather proverbs testify to the English rustic's skill in reading the weather. Gabriel Oak could tell time by his observation of the stars, just as today the shepherds still gauge time by the shadows on the sundials cut in the turf.[3] The Hintock dwellers knew every tree in the woodlands, knew the smell and savor of every variety of apple: to their minds, Mrs. Charmond must be a wretched landlord, because she couldn't tell a beech from an oak.[4] The farmer's intimate knowledge of the ways of his livestock extends even to the belief that if a pig is carted home, he will stay, but if allowed to see where he is going, will find his way back like a cat. There are many habits of sheep, cattle, poultry, birds, and insects which indicate the advent of a storm or "rainy spell." Diggory Venn knew instantly that

[1] *A Pair of Blue Eyes,* Chap. XIV.
[2] *Ibid.,* Chap. XIV.
[3] *Far from the Madding Crowd,* Chaps. II, VI; E. Lovett, "Superstitions and Survivals Among Shepherds": *Folk-Lore,* XX, 67–70.
[4] *The Woodlanders,* Chap. VI.

the sound Johnny Nunsuch took for a frog was only a stone
flung into the pool: November was too late for Johnny's
statement.[5] Not only the look of the sky and the ominous
stillness of the air, but the toad that crossed Oak's path, the
brown slug that crept indoors, and the black spider which
dropped from the cottage ceiling, were infallible indications
of the approaching storm and the desolating rain which was
to follow it.[6]

The reader will recall Oak's massive and highly inacces-
sible watch whose hour hand had a habit of slipping ahead
several hours, so that the shepherd had constantly to correct
its recordings by observations of the sun and stars. At lambing time, one St. Thomas's Eve, Oak was busy on Norcombe
Down. The feeling that he and the great hill were riding
eastward through space made him give himself up for a
moment to the sheer poetry of motion. The sheep-bell called
him away; and when he returned, it was with a new-born
lamb, which he warmed by the fire. He fell asleep from
weariness, but was soon awakened by the bleating of the
lamb. Finding the hour hand had shifted, he looked at the
stars.

The Dog-star and Aldebaran, pointing to the restless Pleiades,
were half-way up the Southern sky, and between them hung Orion,
which gorgeous constellation never burnt more vividly than now, as
it soared above the rim of the landscape. Castor and Pollux with
their quiet shine were almost on the meridian; the barren and gloomy
Square of Pegasus was creeping round to the northwest; far away
through the plantation Vega sparkled like a lamp suspended amid the
leafless trees, and Cassiopœia's chair stood daintily poised on the
uppermost boughs.

"One o'clock," said Gabriel.[7]

Some months later, having lost all his sheep at one swoop,
Oak had tried in vain at the Casterbridge Fair to hire himself out as a shepherd or bailiff, and had taken refuge in

[5] *The Return of the Native,* Book I, Chap. VI.
[6] *Far from the Madding Crowd,* Chap. XXXVI.
[7] *Ibid.,* Chap. II.

a van beside the road. After a nap, he awoke to find the van in motion, and, as usual, took his bearings by the stars, concluding that it was nine o'clock, and that he had slept two hours—a simple astronomical calculation that was the birthright of the skilled shepherd.[8]

English shepherds today make excellent estimates of time without watch, sundial, or even visible sun. Some of them still cut in the turf simple dials, made in a circle of eighteen inches in diameter, with sticks about twelve inches long placed at regular distances from each other, causing the sun to cast a shadow in now one, and now another quadrant, thus showing them when it is time to start for home.[9] Shepherds have always had the reputation of being weather-wizards,[10] and when one consider feats like these, he is not surprised.

The rustic's close observation of the sun originated the familiar saying, "At New Year's tide, the days lengthen a cock's stride." [11] The phrase is used in connection with the superstition that ghosts travel towards their old haunts at the rate of a "cock's stride" on New Year's, Old Style—a belief that we find on the lips of one of the Hintock rustics, in his version of the story of the two ghost-brothers, who are returning to Hintock House slowly but surely in spite of the exorcism of the priest.[12] As a weather proverb, the phrase means simply that the countryman, observing the place where the shadow of the upper lintel of the door falls at twelve o'clock, makes a mark there; the sun in its meridian being higher on New Year's Day, its shadow comes nearer the door by five or six inches, that is, by a "cock's stride." [13]

Christopher Julian had a taste of the countryman's impatience with city folk who do not know Mother Nature's

---

[8] *Ibid.,* Chap. VI.
[9] E. Lovett, "Superstitions and Survivals Among Shepherds," *Folk-Lore,* XX, 67–70.
[10] *Denham Tracts,* II, 337.
[11] Ellis's Brand, I, 20; C. Gurdon, *Folk-Lore of Suffolk,* 165.
[12] *The Woodlanders,* Chap. XIX.
[13] *Denham Tracts,* II, 99.

most elementary lessons. Directed to sight his destination by means of some elms in the distance, Julian exclaimed in dismay that he could not tell oaks from elms at such a distance, and received a curt reply.

"But a man can hardly tell oaks from elms at that distance. . . ."

"That 'a can very well—leastwise, if he's got the sense. . . . When you get there, you bear away smart to nor'west. . . ."

"How the deuce am I to know which is northwest in a strange place, with no sun to tell me?"

"What, not know nor'west? Well, I should think a boy could never live and grow up to be a man without knowing the four quarters. I knowed 'em when I was a mossel of a chiel." [14]

The people of the Hintocks knew their trees as intimately as they knew each other. As Giles Winterborne was driving Grace Melbury home, on her arrival from school, he pointed out the various orchards and commented on their crop:

"They had a good crop of bitter-sweets; they couldn't grind them all" (nodding towards an orchard where some heaps of apples had been left since the ingathering).

She said "Yes," but looking at another orchard. "Why, you are looking at John-apple trees! You know bitter-sweets—you used to well enough!"

"I am afraid I have forgotten, and it is getting too dark to distinguish." [15]

In this exquisite scene, Hardy sounds the prelude to Winterborne's ill-fated love story. In a very different scene he shows us Giles and Marty South planting trees: Marty has sacrificed her beautiful hair for money for her father, has caught cold, and is feeling the bleakness of the day and of life in general. The wind faintly stirs the saplings as Giles put them into the ground, and the sound is like a sigh: Marty says, "It seems to me as if they sigh because they are very sorry to begin life in earnest—just as we be." [16] But Giles goes right on planting the young trees, spreading the roots with gentle caressing touch, and setting

[14] *The Hand of Ethelberta,* Chap. XII.
[15] *The Woodlanders,* Chap. VI.
[16] *Ibid.,* Chap. VIII.

the roots towards the southwest, because they will need a strong holdfast in that direction from future gales. The same theme is treated with greater poignancy in the poem, "The Pine Planters: Marty South's Reverie."[17] Sensitive Jude Fawley could not bear to see trees cut down, or even lopped, from a fancy that it hurt them.[18] It would be possible to multiply instances of still greater and more inexplicable sympathy between man and nature; the case of Old South, Marty's father, whose life ended when his "enemy," the great elm, was felled, comes at once to mind.[19]

A keen knowledge of the ways of livestock is one result of farm life: Arabella, for instance, flew into a rage when one of the newly bought pigs ran away and found its way home, laying the blame on Jude because he had driven them home, allowing them to see the road over which they traveled rather than carting them over.[20]

Hardy refers several times to the common superstition that the cuckoo is the greatest liar among the birds, delighting to deceive credulous listeners by his mocking cries.[21] He speaks, for instance, of false reports as cuckoo-cries, heard but not heeded.[22] Legend says that the cuckoo, the bird of Thor, is an enemy to matrimonial bliss, and his reputation on this score is certainly unsavory.[23] It was once commonly believed that if one were to ask the cuckoo the first time one hears him in the spring how many years one has to live, he would for once tell the truth.[24] Hardy refers to the belief dear to children that there is but one cuckoo: in "Boys Then and Now," the little fellow feels all the joy go out of the spring day when he learns that there is more than one cuckoo;[25] and Johnny Nunsuch believed this, much to Diggory Venn's disgust:

[17] *Time's Laughingstocks.*
[18] *Jude the Obscure,* Part I, Chap. II.
[19] *The Woodlanders,* Chap. XIV.
[20] *Jude the Obscure,* Part I, Chap. VIII.
[21] Grimm-Stallybrass, IV, 1488.
[22] *A Pair of Blue Eyes,* Chap. XXXII; *The Hand of Ethelberta,* Chap. XXV.
[23] Lina B. Eckenstein, *Comparative Studies in Nursery Rhymes,* 205.
[24] Grimm-Stallybrass, II, 676–77; III, 1129.
[25] *Winter Words.*

"You are rather afraid of me. Do you know what I be?" . . .
"The reddleman!" . . .
"Yes, that's what I be. Though there's more than one. You little
.children think there's only one cuckoo, one fox, one giant, one devil,
and one reddleman, when there's lots of us all." [26]

Country folk hold by St. Swithin, and believe that rain
upon his day, moreover, means a plentiful apple crop; in
such an event they say that the saint is christening the apples.[27] Bob Loveday's intended bride, wishing to impress
her country relations with her knowledge of rustic life, remarked upon this belief; [28] and this was the time of year
when Margery, the milkmaid, was to marry Jim Hayward;
the Baron, although a man of the world, was little the
wiser at hearing that the wedding was to be "not long after
the time when God A'mighty christens the little apples." [28]
In the poem "We Sat at the Window," the lovers are de-
pressed by the incessant rain that St. Swithin's day.[29] The
French have a rain-maker of their own, St. Medard: and
the Chinese believe that if it rains on February third, the
first day of Spring, it will rain "more or less" for forty
days.[30] There is shrewd wisdom in this "more or less"! This
looks like a world superstition.[31]

There is the wisdom born of experience, too, in Hostler
John's prognostications of rain by the rustiness of his joints,
which he declares are a veritable weathercock after a man
has reached threescore.[32] The countryman is fool-proof on
the score of the weather and the habits of livestock and of
all living creatures. When Johnny Nunsuch, having heard

[26] *The Return of the Native,* Book I, Chap. VIII.
[27] N. Thomas, *Folk-Lore of Northumberland,* 178; *Folk-Lore,* XXIV, 237;
Ellis's Brand, I, 312.
[28] *The Trumpet-Major,* Chap. XVII; *A Changed Man,* "The Romantic
Adventures of a Milkmaid."
[29] *Moments of Vision.*
[30] M. T. Mansfield, *Folk-Lore Journal,* V, 129; Dennys, *Folk-Lore of
China,* 32.
[31] *Folk-Lore Journal,* I, 267–68; *Folk-Lore,* XXIV, 237; C. Gurdon, *Folk-
Lore of Suffolk,* 164.
[32] *The Hand of Ethelberta,* Chap. XLIV.

the splash of Wildeve's pebble flung into the pool, had duly reported to Eustacia Vye that a frog had hopped into the water, and had been sent off across the heath with his precious crooked sixpence for luck, he met the reddleman. The little fellow was terribly frightened, particularly because at first sight of the reddleman he had dropped the sixpence. Diggory Venn's impatient queries were not reassuring; but as the boy proceeded with his story, the reddleman pricked up his ears:

"Hopfrogs don't jump into ponds this time of year."

"They do, for I heard one."

"Certain-sure?"

"Yes. She told me afore that I should hear'n; and so I did. They say she's clever and deep, and perhaps she charmed 'en to come." [33]

The intimate association of frogs and toads with water earned for them a reputation among primitive peoples as custodians of rain. Every rustic knows that the croaking of frogs is a sure sign of rain.[34] In "Night-Time in Mid-Fall," the poet pictures a night so stormy that the eels, in their eagerness to reach shelter, are bold enough to cross the turnpike itself! [35] When Gabriel Oak found a toad crossing his path, his fears of a storm were confirmed.[36] To those versed in country things, the unusual stillness and clearness of the atmosphere before a storm or rain speak in no uncertain terms: the young countryman told the keeper of Rainbarrow Beacon that a change of weather was coming, because he could hear the cows moo all the way from the Froom Valley, and could see the lantern of Max Turnpike shining brightly.[37]

Familiar weather-sayings still occasionally heard are as follows: If you hear sheep at night, rain is coming; [38] when

[33] *The Return of the Native,* Book I, Chap. VIII.
[34] Ellis's Brand, III, 204; J. G. Frazer, *Golden Bough,* 73.
[35] *Late Lyrics.*
[36] *Far from the Madding Crowd,* Chap. XXXVI; E. J. Ladbury, *Folk-Lore,* XX, 344.
[37] *The Dynasts,* Part First, Act. II, Sc. V.
[38] F. L. Ramsey, *Folk-Lore,* XXXVII, 368.

cows lie down all facing the same way, rain is coming;[39] and the saying that pigs can smell the wind.[40]

It is Gabriel Oak who sums up all the countryman's extraordinary weather lore. Oak's was an elemental sympathy with nature; he spoke and understood her familiar language. The sky, the air, the behavior of every living creature he met, spoke of the approaching thunderstorm, and the cold rain which was to follow. This memorable prelude fills the reader himself with an almost electric nervousness. The sheep knew all about the thunderstorm, but nothing of the cold rain; the creeping things were well aware of the discomfort of the rain, and were doing their best to hide away from it.

The night had a sinister aspect. A heated breeze from the south . . . slowly fanned the summits of lofty objects, and in the sky dashes of buoyant cloud were sailing in a course at right angles to that of another stratum, neither of them in the direction of the breeze below. The moon, as seen through these films, had a lurid, metallic look. The fields were sallow with the impure light, and all were tinged in monochrome, as if beheld through a stained glass. The same evening the sheep had trailed homeward head to tail, the behavior of the rooks had been confused, and the horses had moved with timidity and caution.

Thunder was imminent, and . . . it was likely to be followed by one of the lengthened rains which mark the close of dry weather for the season. . . .[41]

After Oak had warned Troy that rain was coming, and had been laughed at for his pains, and after the hands had started drinking the grog Troy had forced upon them, Oak left the hall with a sick heart.

Gabriel proceeded towards his home. In approaching the door, his toe kicked something which felt and sounded soft, leathery and distended, like a boxing-glove. It was a large toad humbly travelling across the path. Oak took it up, thinking it might be better to kill the creature to save it from pain; but finding it uninjured, he placed it

---

[39] *Ibid.*, 368.
[40] L. M. Eyre, *Folk-Lore*, XIII, 172.
[41] *Far from the Madding Crowd*, Chap. XXXVI.

again among the grass. He knew what this direct message from the Great Mother meant. And soon came another.

When he struck a light indoors there appeared upon the table a thin, glistening streak, as if a brush of varnish had been lightly dragged across it. Oak's eyes followed the serpentine sheen to the other side, where it led up to a huge brown garden-slug, which had come indoors to-night for reasons of its own. It was Nature's second way of hinting to him that he was to prepare for foul weather.

Oak sat down meditating for nearly an hour. During this time two black spiders, of the kind common in thatched houses, promenaded the ceiling, ultimately dropping to the floor. This reminded him if there was one class of manifestation on this matter that he thoroughly understood, it was the instincts of sheep. He left the room, ran across two or three fields towards the flock, got upon a hedge, and looked over among them.

They were crowded close together on the other side around some furze bushes, and the first peculiarity observable was that, on the sudden appearance of Oak's head over the fence, they did not stir or run away. They had now a terror greater than their terror of man. But all this was not the most noteworthy feature; they were all grouped in such a way that their tails, without a single exception, were towards that half of the horizon from which the storm threatened. There was an inner circle closely huddled, and outside these they radiated farther apart, the pattern formed by the flock as a whole not being unlike a vandyked lace collar, to which the clump of furze-bushes stood in the position of a wearer's neck.

This was enough to re-establish him in his original opinion. He knew now he was right, and that Troy was wrong. Every voice in nature was unanimous in bespeaking change. But two distinct translations attached to these dumb expressions. Apparently there was to be a thunder-storm, and afterwards a cold continuous rain. The creeping things seemed to know all about the later rain, but little of the interpolated thunder-storm; whilst the sheep knew all about the thunder-storm, and nothing of the later rain.[42]

The magnificence of the storm in *Far from the Madding Crowd* is not to be described in any words but Hardy's. In a scene like this, or with Oak scanning the silent heavens on

[42] *Ibid.,* Chap. XXXVI.

Norcombe Down, the grandeur of the forces of nature must strike the heart of the dullest reader. Thus the Psalmist must have felt in the stillness of the night and the terror of the storm, when he cried, "The heavens declare the glory of God; and the firmament showeth his handiwork. Day unto day uttereth speech; and night unto night showeth knowledge." And again, "Bow thy heavens, O Lord, and come down; touch the mountains, and they shall smoke. . . ." [43]

If one would know Hardy's feeling for country things, he need only turn to the poem, "Afterwards," [44] or to an utterance that has the poet's characteristic humility in the face of the unknowable, the poem, "An August Midnight." The speaker watches the longlegs, the moth, the dumbledore, and the pariah fly as they meet around his lamp, and muses:

> "God's humblest they!" I muse. Yet why?
> They know Earth-secrets that know not I. [45]

The familiar sights and sounds of Nature, the habits of plants and animals, all speak an unmistakable language to those versed in country things. Robert Frost has caught the whole meaning of a country landscape in which a deserted farmhouse tells its own story; he calls it "The Need of Being Versed in Country Things." [46] Hardy's folk are happily so versed.

[43] *Psalms* XIX, CXLIV.
[44] *Moments of Vision.*
[45] *Poems of the Past and the Present.*
[46] Robert Frost, *New Hampshire.*

VII
SEASONAL FESTIVALS AND CUSTOMS

Despite school-board efforts to revive folk-songs and country-dances, merry England is almost entirely a thing of the past. Much of the charm of Hardy's art lies in his pictures of Maypole dances, Guy Fawkes bonfires, sheepshearings, rustic randies, and mummers' plays at Yuletide. Scenes like these were familiar to Hardy as a boy; he describes them with gusto, preferring the simpler pleasures of the folk to the pomp and circumstance of festivals in court and hall. He never ceased to love the ancient carols, the stately Tate-and-Brady hymns. Through his eyes we glimpse the changing figures of the country-dance, a maze of line and color, a medley of happy voices. The dance is now decorous and stately, now wildly exuberant, and over it all presides the Genius of the dance, impishly matchmaking for weal or woe.

The May festival, now practically extinct in England to-day,[1] lives for us in *The Return of the Native*. Diggory Venn's unfailing solicitude had made sure that the festivity to be held opposite Thomasin's home would not arouse painful memories. Clym Yeobright, however, coming suddenly upon the folk busily wreathing the Maypole with flowers, was swept into sudden and bitter regret.

It was a lovely May sunset, and the birch trees . . . had put on their new leaves, delicate as butterflies' wings, and diaphanous as amber. . . . The pole lay with one end supported on a trestle, and

[1] H. C. March, *Folk-Lore*, X, 481, Hardy's note; E. M. Wright, *Rustic Speech and Folklore*, 296.

women were engaged in wreathing it from the top downwards with
wild-flowers. The instincts of merry England lingered on here with
exceptional vitality. . . . Indeed, the impulses of all such outlandish
hamlets are pagan still: in these spots homage to nature, self-
adoration, frantic gaieties, fragments of Teutonic rites to divinities
whose names are forgotten, seem . . . to have survived mediæval
doctrine.

   . . . The next morning, when Thomasin withdrew the curtains
of her bedroom window, there stood the Maypole, in the middle of
the green, its top cutting into the sky. It had sprung up in the night
. . . like Jack's bean-stalk. . . . The sweet perfume of the flowers
had already spread into the surrounding air, which, being free of
every taint, conducted to her lips a full measure of the fragrance received from the spire of blossom in its midst. At the top of the pole
were crossed hoops decked with small flowers; beneath these came a
milk-white zone of Maybloom; then a zone of bluebells, then of cow-
slips, then of lilacs, then of ragged-robins, daffodils, and so on, till
the lowest stage was reached. Thomasin . . . was delighted that the
May-revel was to be so near.[2]

Natural high spirits which even her sense of propriety
could not subdue led Thomasin to dress for the revel so
gayly that Clym suspected a mood of coquetry with himself
for object. According to her calendric system of braiding her
hair—in fours on ordinary Sundays, in fives for Maypolings
and gypsyings, and in sevens the day she was married—
Thomasin with her golden braids must have been a charming sight. Charming, too, is the story of the lost glove for
which Diggory Venn searched, and which proved to be
Thomasin's. The ending of *The Return of the Native* was
a concession on Hardy's part to popular taste; yet the note
of quiet comedy on which it closes is admirable as un-
obtrusive philosophic comment. Perhaps the author would
have us echo the words of Mrs. Yeobright, "Cry about
one thing in life, cry about all; one thread runs through the
piece. . . ."[3]

   [2] *Return of the Native,* Book VI, Chap. I.
   [3] *Ibid.,* Book III, Chap. VII.

The wild revelry which once characterized May rites is pictured most vividly, not in the Maypole festivity near Thomasin's home, but in the moonlight gypsying to which Eustacia Vye was irresistibly drawn. In reckless contempt of Clym's opinion, in loneliness and anger, Eustacia sought the village picnic at East Egdon. She was determined to "be bitterly merry, and ironically gay and . . . laugh in derision!" In this mood Eustacia reached the scene that August afternoon:

She now beheld the musicians themselves, sitting in a blue waggon with red wheels scrubbed as bright as new, and arched with sticks, to which boughs and flowers were tied. In front of this was the grand central dance of fifteen couples. . . .

The young men wore blue and white rosettes, and with a flush on their faces footed it to the girls, who, with the excitement and the exercise, blushed deeper than the pink of their numerous ribbons. Fair ones with long curls, fair ones with short curls, fair ones with love-locks, fair ones with braids, flew round and round. . . . In the background was one happy man dancing by himself, totally oblivious of all the rest. . . .[4]

Eustacia, not seeing the lady who was to receive her, went away. When she returned the scene had changed; a great yellow moon had risen and was beginning to exert a subtle power:

A whole village-full of sensuous emotion, scattered abroad all the year long, surged here in a focus for an hour. The forty hearts of those waving couples were beating as they had not done since . . . they had come together in similar jollity. For the time being Paganism was revived in their hearts, the pride of life was all in all, and they adored none other than themselves.[5]

The fascination of the scene led Eustacia to accept Wildeve's invitation to enter the dance. Beginning at the bottom of the figure, they work their way up to the top, and here their beauty and grace attract universal admiration.

[4] *Ibid.*, Book IV, Chap. III.
[5] *Ibid.*

Through the length of five and twenty couples they threaded their giddy way. . . . The pale ray of evening lent a fascination to the experience. There is a certain degree and tone of light which tends to disturb the equilibrium of the senses, and to promote dangerously the tenderer moods; added to the movement, it drives the emotions to rankness, the reason becoming sleepy . . . and the light fell now upon these two from the disc of the moon. All the dancing girls felt the symptoms, but Eustacia most of all. The grass under their feet became trodden away, and the hard, beaten surface of the sod . . . shone like a polished table. The air became quite still; the flag above the waggon which held the musicians clung to the pole, and the players appeared only in outline against the sky. . . . The pretty dresses of the maids lost their subtler day colours and showed more or less of a misty white. Eustacia floated round and round on Wildeve's arm, her face rapt and statuesque; her soul had passed away and forgotten her features, which were empty and quiescent, as they always are when feeling goes beyond their register.

How near she was to Wildeve! it was terrible to think of. She could feel his breathing, and he, of course, could feel hers. How badly she had treated him! Yet here they were, treading one measure. The enchantment of the dance surprised her. . . . She had entered the dance from the troubled hours of her late life as one might enter a brilliant chamber after a night walk in a wood. Wildeve by himself would have been merely an agitation; Wildeve added to the dance, and the moonlight, and the secrecy, began to be a delight. . . .[6]

Such a passage could have come only from a dancing man. Beneath all the refinements of the country-dance, lies a certain abandon, a primitive desire to dance in the open, under the moon, if possible, with other young people who yield themselves to the mazy spell of the changing figures and the drawing power of the moon. Midsummer Eve is still celebrated in some parts of the state of Pennsylvania with scenes of unrestrained revelry, culminating in orgies in which no woman would be safe. The gypsying on Egdon is the nearest approach to the primitive orgiastic May rites.

Survivals of May customs are found, however, no longer associated with May Day, but scattered about in frag-

[6] *Ibid.*

mentary state in the observance of other festivals. The club-walking described in *Tess* is really a survival of May rites; and so are the folk-play, the sword dance, the pageants and civic processions which linger even today. Christian teaching has shifted the communal May-walking or riding to Whitsuntide, but cannot conceal the original nature of the feast as a sort of local Cerealia. The men's clubs were the first to disappear; the Marlott club, of which Tess was a member, was one of the last of the women's clubs to go, after a life of many centuries.[7] This club-walking is extremely picturesque: The women, young and old, were dressed in white; each carried in her right hand a carefully peeled willow wand, and in her left a bunch of white flowers. The elderly women looked a bit grotesque; but the young girls, who far outnumbered them, seemed to shine with a new beauty in the realization that they were thus publicly and with social approval displaying their charms. They were awkward and somewhat self-conscious, but they were also naïve and unspoiled. Each maiden seemed to be basking in her own little sun—some dream or affection, some remote and cherished hope. It is a passage that reveals Hardy's amazing insight into the feminine heart, and seems to suggest in the universal rustic desire to display one's beauty in a way sanctioned by tradition, the old Teutonic custom of choosing brides at Maytide. The pretty scene with all its innocent pleasure was quite spoiled for Tess by the spectacle of her father riding home in drunken state from the Pure Drop Inn. He had just learned of his illustrious ancestors, and was returning home to break the news in truly grotesque splendor. In the dance that followed the May-walking, there were at first no male partners; but after a time, the Clare brothers passed by the green and paused to watch. Angel Clare danced with one of the bolder girls, not espying Tess until called away by his companions, but startled by the girl's reproachful eyes. As he turned to take his last look at the scene, it seemed to him that all the girls were dancing gayly—

[7] *Tess of the d'Urbervilles*, Chap. II.

All of them except, perhaps, one. This white shape stood apart by
the hedge alone. From her position he knew it to be the pretty maiden
with whom he had not danced. Trifling as the matter was, he yet
felt instinctively that she was hurt by his oversight. He wished that
he had asked her; he wished that he had inquired her name. She was
so modest, so expressive, she had looked so soft in her thin white gown
that he felt he had acted stupidly.[8]

Thus ended Tess's club-walking and her romance—ended
before it was well begun.

May rites are extremely old. The Greeks had their
Daphnephoria at Thebes and the Eiresione customs at
Athens; there were rather obscene dances in connection with
the bringing in of the Dorian May-wreath.[9] The Romans
kept the Floralia from April 28 to May 1 with songs,
games and dances.[10] Among the heathen Teutonic tribes the
first of May was sacred to Donar, and the eve preceding was
a time of wild revelry.[11] In lower Saxony and in parts of
England, the rite was at one time a simple "May-Riding," a
fetching in of the May-wagon, a community walking which
gradually became a civic procession. On the Rhine, there
was no such procession; here the May was celebrated by a
mock combat, in which two actors impersonated the giants
Winter and Summer, fighting until Winter was killed, a
combat which survives in the sword dances of northern England, in the Pace-Egg play, and the Christmas mummers'
play.[12]

In primitive Teutonic society, the approach of summer
was not only a holy tide to be welcomed in with feasting,
sacrifice, and communal dances or processions, but a time of
civil importance: May Day was the time when brides were
chosen, when servants hired out, tenants took land, and

---

[8] *Tess of the d'Urbervilles,* Chap. II.
[9] Wm. R. Halliday, *Greek and Roman Folklore,* p. 70; James Frazer, *The
Golden Bough,* one vol. ed. 1922, p. 360.
[10] John Brand, *Popular Antiquities of Great Britain* . . . Sir Henry Ellis,
ed., Vol. I, p. 258; Jacob Grimm, *Deutsche Mythologie,* J. S. Stallybrass, Tr.,
Vol. II, p. 781.
[11] Edwin M. Fogel, *Beliefs and Superstitions of the Pennsylvania Germans,*
Intro. p. 10.
[12] Grimm-Stallybrass, *Teutonic Mythology,* II, 776–79; II, 784–88.

folkmoots were formally held.[13] The same was true of the tribes of Britain which, for lack of an accurate scientific name, we call Celtic. Up to comparatively recent times in the East Riding of Yorkshire,[14] and in certain English shires, servants hired out and tenants took over new land or houses in May and November, that is, by the Celtic year, which differs from the Teutonic solstitial year, in being truly pastoral.[15] Sheep sacrifice is a thing of the past among the Manx farmers, but the great need-fires are still made on the gorse-covered slopes, and mayflowers adorn the houses, while rowan is tied to the tails of cattle to preserve them from witchcraft.[16] There are Lady-Day hirings, Old Style, in *Tess of the d'Urbervilles,*[17] and from both William Barnes and Hardy we learn that May-November "flittings" were the accepted thing in their day for both servants and tenant farmers.[18]

Saint Valentine's Day plays a rather minor rôle in English folklore. In *Far from the Madding Crowd,*[19] Bathsheba Everdene, piqued by Boldwood's indifference to her beauty, "tossed for it" to see whether the newly bought valentine should go to him or to naughty Teddy Coggan. When chance would seem to have it Boldwood, she affixed a seal which read, "Marry Me!" and much amused at the motto which had idly come to hand, sent it off to the post. It was the caprice of a moment, for which four persons were to pay long and bitterly.

Valentine's Eve is the setting of a somber scene in the romance of Elfride Swancourt. Stephen Smith and Henry Knight are on their way to Endelstow, each regretful of the long misunderstanding, each hopeful of a reconciliation. At Chippenham the rivals see attached to their train a grand,

[13] Grimm-Stallybrass, *op. cit.,* II, 788.
[14] C. S. Burne, *Folk-Lore,* XXIII, 423.
[15] *Folk-Lore,* XXIII, 425: J. Rhys, *Folk-Lore,* II, 302, 313; Frazer, *Golden Bough,* one vol. ed., 633.
[16] J. Rhys, *Folk-Lore,* II, 302, 313.
[17] Chap. LI.
[18] Ernest Brennecke, Jr.'s, ed. *Life and Art,* collected essays of Hardy: "The Dorsetshire Labourer."
[19] Chap. XIII.

dark carriage, which, unknown to them, contains Elfride's body. By the irony which draws all who love Elfride into a charmed circle of frustrated hopes, this was the eve of St. Valentine's, that "bishop of blessed memory to youthful lovers." [20]

The truth is that the saint has nothing to do with the sending of love messages, but that his festival day merely happened to be also the day before the feast of the goddess Februata Juno, February fifteenth, on which Roman boys were wont to draw lots for the names of girls whom they might admire and attend for a year. It is thought that the early Church attempted to root out this custom by renaming the day in honor of a saint particularly famed for his purity of life.[21] Ophelia's broken song [22] is probably a snatch of an old folk-song preserving some traditional custom which at one time permitted maidens to visit and bespeak bachelors in marriage on St. Valentine's Day; and we know that in Scotland and on the Continent during the Middle Ages, marriages based on such proposals were upheld as strictly legal.[23] Perhaps we have in this custom a survival of the privileges accorded the women of the great Valentinian gens, who were in all probability unmarried, and whose power to heal by their very presence made it possible for them to visit their patients, men or women, unaccompanied; on the other hand, it is difficult to explain the process by which the Gnostic St. Valentine, whose disciples affected bridal dress to symbolize a mystical union with the Deity, came to be the patron saint of lovers.[24] Whatever the origin of the day, it was a favorite time in England and Scotland for love divinations of many sorts and for love messages.[25]

Far from the Madding Crowd contains some of Hardy's most memorable rustic scenes. It was Cainy Ball

[20] *A Pair of Blue Eyes,* Chap. XXXIX.
[21] Brand's *Popular Antiquities,* Ellis ed., I, 59.
[22] *Hamlet,* I, IV, 48–55.
[23] H. A. Rose, *Folk-Lore,* XXX, 63.
[24] H. A. Rose, *loc. cit.,* 64–65.
[25] H. A. Rose, *loc. cit.,* 65; Brand, I, 58.

who brought the sheep-shearers news of preparations for the feast, lumps of fat as big as a man's thumb and biffins for apple pies; and it was Joseph Poorgrass who vowed to do justice to it all:

"Yes; victuals and drink is a cheerful thing, and gives nerves to the nerveless, if the form of words may be used. 'Tis the gospel of the body, without which we perish, so to speak it." [26]

The shearing-supper, however, was more than a matter of dumplings. Bathsheba sat within the deep window at one end of the long table spread upon the grass plot. Supper over, Coggan contributed a lyric which was received with the appreciative silence of rustic approval. Poorgrass, almost overpowered by his young mistress's gaze, contrived to sing, but was quite thrown out by young Coggan's gasps of mirth. The candles were brought in; a hush of anticipation fell over the workfolk. Then Bathsheba graciously consented to sing "The Banks of Allan Water"; one of the verses was long remembered:

"For his bride a soldier sought her,
    And a winning tongue had he;
On the banks of Allan Water
    None was so gay as she!"

"In addition to the dulcet piping of Gabriel's flute Boldwood supplied a bass in his customary profound voice, uttering his notes so softly, however, as to abstain entirely from making anything like an ordinary duet of the song; they rather formed a rich, unexplored shadow, which threw her tones into relief. The shearers reclined against each other as in the early ages of the world, and so silent and absorbed were they that her breathing could be heard between the bars; and at the end of the ballad, when the last tone loitered on to an inexpressible close, there arose that buzz of pleasure which is the attar of applause.[27]

In striking contrast to this idyllic scene is the harvest supper which Sergeant Troy turns into a drinking orgy. At

[26] *Far from the Madding Crowd,* Chap. XXII.
[27] *Ibid.,* Chap. XXIII.

first the supper proceeded gayly enough; and as Oak neared the barn, he heard the sound of violins, a tambourine, and jigging feet. One end of the barn was piled to the ceiling with oats, but a large central space was cleared for dancing; tufts of green foliage covered the timbers above. On a platform sat three fiddlers bowing away vigorously, and beside them stood a tambourine player frantically wielding his instrument. The dance was "The Soldier's Joy," in compliment to Troy and Bathsheba, who led the figures as top couple. At its close, Oak contrived to tell Troy about the menace of the approaching storm; Troy pooh-poohed the idea of rain, and in spite of Bathsheba's protests, had every man supplied with brandy-and-water. Bathsheba, the women, and the musicians left the barn indignantly. The treble-strong brandy-and-water, an innovation unwelcome to most of the hands themselves, wrought its work completely in an hour. When Oak returned again, he found the men lying about in a drunken stupor, utterly incapable of helping him to shelter the ricks before the storm would be upon them. Hardy implies quite clearly that orgies like this at Weatherbury were not the accepted harvest festival.[28]

"The Harvest Supper" [29] describes a rustic dance in the barn, the red-coated Scotch Greys footing it to the village girls with their customary gallantry, and winning a song or a kiss in return. The "Ploughman's Feasting Days," were Sheep-Shearing, Plough Monday, Shrovetide, Harvest Home, the local Wake-Day, Seed-Cake Day, and the Twice-a-Week-Roast.[30] Frumenty and cheese were an essential part of the feast.[31] In Vermont today sheep-shearings are occasions of the utmost gayety. That a sheep-shearing might be taken very seriously even by a great lord is shown in an episode in *The Dynasts,* in which the Duke of Bedford narrowly missed the Regent's Fête at Carlton House because

---

[28] *Ibid.,* Chap. XXVI.
[29] *Human Shows.*
[30] Ellis's Brand, II, 34–37; Lady C. Gurdon, *The Folk-Lore of Suffolk,* 113–5.
[31] Ellis's Brand, II, 37; Aubrey's *Remaines of Gentilisme and Judaisme,* James Britten, ed. p. 34.

he would not put off his sheep-shearing dinner.[32] Who does not remember the four-and-twenty sheep-shearers in *The Winter's Tale,* "all good catch-singers, with but one Puritan among them, and he sings psalms to hornpipes." [33]

The Wessex harvest, as described by Hardy, is not so picturesque nor so interesting a survival of agricultural folklore as the corresponding customs in Devon, Cornwall, and the Border counties. There is no trace in Hardy's pages of the fascinating rite of bringing in the last ear of wheat, "Bringing in the old wife," "Crying the neck," "Shouting the Mell," and "Bringing in Summer." [34] It was once the custom to carry home the last sheaf fantastically dressed as an old woman, and keep it until the following harvest, or burn it amid much boisterous mirth. The traditional mode of communal harvesting, on this occasion by moonlight, is well illustrated in *The Mayor,* in a scene where townsmen work feverishly side by side with farmers to save the threatened crops.[35]

Country weddings in Wessex are described in the poem, "The Country Wedding," in Fancy Day's marriage to Dick Dewy, and in "The Bride-Night Fire," earlier called "The Fire at Tranter Sweatley's." [36] Other novels and poems contain references to such wedding customs as the bride-peal, the serenade, and the randy. In "The Country Wedding," [37] the fiddlers, contrary to accepted village custom, preceded the wedding party instead of bringing up the rear, and the bride was uneasy at this breach of tradition. A wedding peal of six bells, termed a "ring o' grandsire triples" or a "Triple bob-major" by the ringers, was

---

[32] *The Dynasts,* Part Second, Act VI, Sc. VII.
[33] Act IV, Sc. 3.
[34] Aubrey's *Remaines,* 34; J. Frazer, *The Golden Bough,* one vol. ed. 1922, pp. 405, 466–67; C. Gurdon, *op. cit.,* p. 72; Wm. Henderson, *Folklore of the Northern Counties of England,* . . . pp. 87–90; N. Thomas, *Folk-Lore of Northumberland,* pp. 124–28; W. Gregor, *Notes on the Folk-Lore of the North-East of Scotland,* pp. 178–97; *Folk-Lore:* V, 167–69; VI, 148–54; XII, 215, 350; XIII, 177–180; XV, 194–96; 221; etc.; *Denham Tracts,* II, 3.
[35] Chap. XXVII.
[36] *Wessex Poems.*
[37] *Late Lyrics.*

rung in honor of Cytherea Graye's second marriage.[38]
Fancy Day's wedding discloses the custom, already old-
fashioned in Fancy's day, of bridesmen's walking "arm in
crook" with bridesmaids.[39] The serenade for the newly
married couple is treated with broad humor in *The Return
of the Native:* great is the dismay of the serenaders when
they learn that Wildeve and Thomasin are not married,
after all.[40] At the close of *Far from the Madding Crowd,*
the farm hands, who were genuinely devoted to Oak
and Bathsheba, gave them the equivalent of a serenade,
saluting them with cannon, a fanfare of trumpets, and
selections from the Weatherbury band; the usual randy was
reduced to the colorless formality of Oak's sending some
drink for the farm folk down to Warren's.[41] Tess had no
wedding randy, either, when she was married to Angel
Clare, but jovial Dairyman Crick insisted upon some refreshments and entertainment.[42] The serenade is glimpsed
again in the poem, "In the Nuptial Chamber:" the bride,
hearing the air to which she had waltzed with her former
lover, rises distraught from bed; her dull husband insists
that it is only a compliment paid to them.[43] Wedding-
randies were almost as choice occasions for the jolly village
bandsmen as Christmas itself; they were privileged, if
church musicians, to attend all christenings, weddings, and
funeral parties.[44] "The Three Strangers" gives us a notable
picture of a christening party, in which the sheep thief
happily escapes the hangman's clutches.[45]

Hardy tells us nothing of traditional wedding sports,
such as racing for the bride's garter,[46] "lifting the bride,"
or of the fine old sport of running at the quintain.[47]

[38] *Desperate Remedies,* Epilogue; cf. *A Group of Noble Dames:* "Dame
the Ninth."
[39] *Under the Greenwood Tree,* Part V, Chap. I.
[40] Book First, Chap. V.
[41] Chap. LXVII.
[42] *Tess of the d'Urbervilles,* Chap. XXIII.
[43] *Satires of Circumstance:* "Fifteen Glimpses" (X).
[44] *Life's Little Ironies:* "The History of the Hardcomes."
[45] *Wessex Tales.*
[46] Wm. Henderson, *Folklore of the Northern Counties,* 37.
[47] Ellis's Brand, II, 163.

Hardy opens the massive story of the *Return of the Native* with a scene of pagan revelry—the whole heath alive with suns of fire, some pale and distant, some red, like dreadful wounds, some "Mænades, with winy faces, and blown hair." [48]

It was as if the bonfire-makers were standing in some radiant upper storey of 'the world. . . . The heath down there was now a vast abyss, and no longer a continuation of what they stood on. . . . Occasionally, it is true, a more vigorous flare than usual sent darting lights like aides-de-camp down the inclines to some distant bush, pool, or patch of white sand, kindling these to replies of the same colour, till all was lost in darkness again. . . .

It was as if these men and boys had suddenly dived into past ages, and fetched therefrom an hour and deed which had before been familiar with the spot. The ashes of the original British pyre which blazed from that summit lay fresh and undisturbed in the barrow beneath their tread. . . . Festival fires to Thor and Woden had followed on the same ground and duly had their day. . . .

Moreover to light a fire is the instinctive and resistant act of man when, at the winter ingress, the curfew is sounded throughout Nature. It indicates a spontaneous Promethean rebelliousness against the fiat that this recurrent season shall bring foul times, cold darkness, misery and death. Black chaos comes, and the fettered gods of the earth say, Let there be light.[49]

One knows not which to admire more, the magnificence of the description, or the essential justice of the interpretation of the fires. All the findings of recent anthropological research tend to prove that prehistoric man in Britain included as a distinct race a round-headed people, who may or may not be the same folk who brought in the Bronze Age, but who are, at least, the people that, in contrast to the mode of burial practised by the long-headed folk, burned their dead, and very probably offered animals and human beings as human sacrifices.[50] These round-headed

[48] Book First, Chap. III.
[49] *Ibid.*
[50] Donald Mackenzie, *Ancient Man in Britain,* p. 109; E. Pittard, *Race and History,* pp. 84, 187–88, 192–94; T. D. Kendrick, *The Axe Age: A Study in Keltic Prehistory,* pp. 52, 79, 120.

folk survive in certain racial English types today. The great fires on Egdon go back to a people who were in England at least by 2000 B. C., and probably much earlier.[51]

Apparently the Guy Fawkes celebration took over pre-existing customs and transferred them to a fixed date. The day is observed in varying ways in England; for instance, it was formerly a day for rioting at Guildford;[52] at Folkstone there was a procession like that of a medieval Corpus Christi guild;[53] at Lewes, however, there was a regular Saturnalia, with dangerous fires, and effigies of the Guy, the Pope, or any criminal of local notoriety.[54] The only essential feature of the festivity is the bonfire, which is far older than the processions and orgies; the effigy itself is no older than 1605, although, of course, the carrying of images harks back to pagan pageantry.[55] Guy Fawkes is burnt in effigy only in those parishes where the Reformation was popular, not in the Roman Catholic portions of Lancashire or Yorkshire, nor in Ireland, where the autumnal bonfires which are the basis of Guy Fawkes celebrations are held on Hallowe'en and Hallowmas.[56] In the latter, we have a survival of the May-November pastoral year; for these fires are the relic of original need-fires and the Bel-tein fires of a people we carelessly call Celtic.[57] The Roman Church was quick to seize upon an important feature of the autumnal festival, and to adapt it to its needs, making it, as in Roman times, a true Feast of the Dead; it may be that Britain derived from Roman sources their ceremonies of eating certain "soul-cakes," funeral foods, in commemoration of the dead at the feast of Pomona the first two days of November. In the Roman festival, as in modern Scotch Hallow-

[51] Kendrick, *op. cit.*, p. 120.
[52] C. S. Burne, Folk-Lore, XXIII, pp. 415–16.
[53] C. S. Burne, *op. cit.*, V, pp. 38–40; *Folk-Lore*, XXIII, pp. 412–13.
[54] C. S. Burne, *op. cit.*, XXIII, 414.
[55] C. S. Burne, *op. cit.*, XXIII, 419.
[56] C. S. Burne, *loc. cit.*; Mabel Peacock, *Folk-Lore*, XIV, 90.
[57] C. S. Burne, *op. cit.*, XXIII, 423.

e'en, divination by apples and nuts was practised; [58] and in Lancashire and Herefordshire devout Catholic folk used to prepare special oatcakes on All Souls', repeating the couplet, "God have your soul, Beans and all." Beans were a funeral food among the ancients.

The feast of the coming of winter includes the following elements of varied source and nature; the purifying fire, through which cattle were driven in primitive times, and from which fire was taken for use throughout the coming year, and into which horses, cattle, and perhaps human sacrifices were once thrown; ceremonies in commemoration of the dead; and finally, processions carrying effigies of the dying year, which easily degenerated into mere satirical demonstrations in honor of some historical villain. In Protestant shires, the season is one of wild revelry, the political aspect of the festival affording an excuse to indulge in merrymaking and to yield to the age-old impulse to build great fires; among Roman Catholic peasants the sadness of the Feast of the Dead still lingers.

The autumnal fire was one of the seasonal fires known to our heathen ancestors. The primitive Teutonic tribes had a solstitial year with great fires at Midsummer and Midwinter, the latter of which survive in our Yule "blazes." [59] The people who held to a pastoral year beginning in late April and reaching its middle point at the beginning of November, are sometimes called Celtic. Whoever they are —a question for anthropologists to answer—their twice-a-year fires came in the spring and fall. The tradition of Bel-worship (not to be confused with a distinct deity, the Semitic Baal) still lingers in parts of Ireland, Scotland, and northern England, and may have some connection not yet cleared up with the mysterious Druid religion. The Palilia, the Roman Feast of Shepherds, held from April 21 to the Kalends of May, was characterized by huge need-fires,

[58] On the general relation of the modern to the Greek and Roman Feast of the Dead, see Ellis's Brand, I, 378, 391–94.
[59] Grimm-Stallybrass, I, 42, II, 758; Ellis's Brand, I, 298.

over which shepherds leaped and around which they drove
their flocks to secure immunity from sickness and death in
the coming year.[60]

The fires on Edgon Heath were not need-fires, not an act
of orgiastic worship, but a timid act of rebellion. Beneath the
rude revelry of the Egdon folk lay a half-acknowledged
fear; but once a year they took this liberty with their ancient
enemy. Egdon accepted their sole gesture of defiance with
easy indifference, but upon Eustacia Vye it poured the vials
of its wrath. Here was an enemy who had built herself a
solitary fire, and from it viewed in cold disdain all the ter-
rors of the heath. Egdon's revenge is quiet and terrible; in
a year and a day it has its will of Eustacia. At the close of
this tremendous story, and not until then, does the design
appear, like some vast temple half hidden by a mist. It is
then that the reader asks himself, Is Egdon indeed the
Spirit Sinister, one of the most terrible of all Nature's mani-
festations to man's heart and senses? Is she, in truth, a Gor-
gon to those who have beheld her, those whose hearts she
has turned to stone?

Around Christmas gather many folk-beliefs and customs,
one of the most exquisite of which is the picturesque idea
that the whole creation worships at the season of Christ's
birth. In "The Oxen" [61] the poet looks back regretfully to
his boyhood days when he believed in miracles, and it
charmed him to know that at twelve of the clock on Christmas Eve, the oxen were kneeling in their stalls. The same
theme is handled, this time with broad humor, in Dairyman
Crick's story of William Dewy and the pious bull. When
the conversation turned to the subject of the power of music
over dumb creatures, Crick told the story of how William
Dewy fooled the bull. While on his way home from a wedding, the famous fiddler had cut across Forty-acres, and was
chased by a bull. It was three o'clock in the morning; it was

---

[60] Wm. R. Halliday, *Greek and Roman Folklore,* 68; Ellis's Brand, I, 306;
Grimm-Stallybrass, I, 42, II, 625–26.
[61] *Moments of Vision.*

no use to hope for chance aid. William struck up a jig, and a sort of a smile stole over the bull's face. But the moment William tried to climb the hedge, the bull lowered his horns:

"When he had scraped till about four o'clock he felt that he verily would have to give over soon, and he said to himself, 'There's only this last tune between me and eternal welfare! Heaven save me, or I'm a done man.' Well, then he called to mind how he'd seen the cattle kneel o' Christmas Eves in the dead o' night. It was not Christmas Eve then, but it came into his head to play a trick upon the bull. So he broke into the 'Tivity Hymn, just as at Christmas carol-singing; when lo, and behold, down went the bull on his bended knees, in his ignorance, just as if 'twere the true 'Tivity night and hour. As soon as his horned friend were down, William turned, clinked off like a lone-dog, and jumped safe over the hedge, before the praying bull got on his feet again. . . . William used to say that he'd seen a man look a fool . . . but never such a fool as that bull looked when he found his pious feelings had been played upon, and 'twas not Christmas Eve. . . ."

"It's a curious story; it carries us back to mediæval times, when faith was a living thing!" [62]

As no one else received the tale with the slightest skepticism, it is small wonder that Angel Clare turned to catch sight of the girl who murmured this comment: it was Tess, the milk-maid.

The belief that the animal creation worships at the season of Christ's birth is familiar and widespread; [63] only those who can see ghosts at Christmas have the power of hearing the cattle, sheep, and horses talk, as they do talk at this holy season. [64] Another part of the same folk-belief is the lovely legend of the blossoming Glastonbury thorn. [65]

---

[62] *Tess of the d'Urbervilles,* Chap. XVII.
[63] Thomas Wright, *Essays on the Popular Superstitions . . . of the Middle Ages,* Vol. I, Chap. IV; Grimm-Stallybrass, IV, 1481; Ellis's Brand, I, 473–74; J. U. Powell, *Folk-Lore,* XII, 76; L. M. Eyre, *Folk-Lore,* XIII, 174; H. A. Rose, *Folk-Lore,* XXXII, 126.
[64] Edwin M. Fogel, *Beliefs and Superstitions of the Pennsylvania Germans,* Proverbs, 1284, 1371; T. Wright, *op. cit.,* I, 128.
[65] Fogel, *op. cit.,* Proverb 1363; Grimm-Stallybrass, IV, 1479; Ellis's Brand, III, 376; L. M. Eyre, *Folk-Lore,* XIII, 174.

The story also runs that on Christmas Eve exactly at midnight, the water in wells for three minutes is turned into
wine.[66] Bees—admirable creatures that they are—are
thought to hum the Nativity hymn![67] Old Aubrey records
the curious interest he felt in one of the memoranda so
characteristic of him: "Mdm. at Twelve-tyde at night they
use in the Countrey to wassaile their Oxen. . . . Gett the
song which is sung in the ox-house when they wassel the
oxen."[68]

Hardy describes three Christmas parties, the one Boldwood gave in Bathsheba's honor in *Far from the Madding
Crowd,* the festivity at the Yeobrights', in *The Return of
the Native,* and the gay dance at Tranter Dewy's in *Under
the Greenwood Tree.* Boldwood's party was prepared with
elaborate fidelity to tradition. Huge boughs of mistletoe
had been hung from the rafters in the hall; holly and ivy
lent color to the scene. All day a great fire had roared in
the kitchen; the three-legged pots had simmered with tempting puddings. The long hall had been cleared for dancing;
at one end was the back-brand for the fire, the uncleft trunk
of a large tree. But nothing could enliven the company:
Bathsheba's men had seen Troy and were fearful of the outcome; Bathsheba herself was trying to leave gracefully before the dancing should begin, but Boldwood detained her
and forced her promise to marry him. At this moment Troy,
cloaked to the eyes, walked in, and Boldwood, with feverish
joviality, welcomed him. The party ended in tragedy; from
the start a sinister gloom had hung over it.[69]

The party at Mrs. Yeobright's, to which Eustacia Vye
went as Turkish Knight in the mummers' play, is interesting
for the glimpse it affords us of folk-drama presented in a
strictly traditional manner. A six-handed reel delayed the
entrance of the mummers for a time. After the play, they
were offered refreshments, but Eustacia, fearful of detec-

[66] Fogel, *op. cit.,* Prov. 1343; Grimm-Stallybrass, II, 585.
[67] John Harland and T. T. Wilkinson, *Lancashire Folklore,* p. 253.
[68] John Aubrey's *Remaines . . .,* J. Britten ed., pp. 9, 40.
[69] *Far from the Madding Crowd,* Chaps. LII, LIII.

tion, could only sip some elder wine through her beribboned casque, and slip a glance now and then at Clym Yeobright.[70]

Hardy celebrates old-fashioned observance of Christmas in such poems as "The House of Hospitalities" [71] and the wistful "We Were Burning the Holly." [72] But the jolliest of all rustic Christmas festivities is the dance at the Dewys'. At midnight the fiddlers tuned up, and for several hours joy was unbounded. Dick was lucky enough to secure Fancy Day for "Triumph, or Follow My Lover"; the dancing grew wilder and wilder until the stout men stripped off coats and vests, leaving love-smitten Dick to swelter rather than forfeit a particle of Fancy's esteem. Hardy must have seen many a randy like the one at the Dewys'; as a boy he accompanied his father as fancy-fiddler for many country parties and all his life he loved the dances with their quickly changing figures. The party in *Under the Greenwood Tree* [73] ended with a feast, where every one, we may feel sure, did noble trencher duty.

Among traditional Christmas victuals are the Yule doughs. At the tables of the gentry these are served up with the boar's head, decked with greens, and steaming with burning liquor. At rustic tables, the boar's head is absent, but the Yule doughs are there, though in sadly altered form. They are no longer finely molded images; they are mere plum puddings and mince pies. It is a far cry from the "little images" of the manger and of the Virgin and Child, which were made from the time of the Early Fathers all through the Middle Ages, to the plum pudding and Jack Horner's pie! [74] A favorite dish at Christmas parties in Wessex was frumenty, a mixture of boiled wheat, eggs, sugar, and spices, into which rum or gin was sometimes poured.[75] Henchard

[70] *Return of the Native,* Book II, Chap. VI.
[71] *Time's Laughingstocks.*
[72] *Winter Words.*
[73] Chaps. VII, VIII; F. E. Hardy, *The Early Life of Thomas Hardy,* 29–31.
[74] Ellis's Brand, I, pp. 27, 526–27; Grimm-Stallybrass, I, 63; I, 63, Note 2; I, 215, 501, 501 Note.
[75] *Folk-Lore,* XXXV, 347; M. Peacock, *Folk-Lore,* XIII, 92; Brand, II, 10–11.

preferred his frumenty "laced" when he took it at Weydon Priors Fair.[76] Its use as a traditional Christmas drink is indicated in the familiar proverb on a silly woman, "She simpers like a furmety kettle at Christmas." [77]

Yule logs are survivals of the Midwinter festival fires of our Teutonic ancestors. Their similarity to the Midsummer rite of bringing in the last sheaf, "the old wife," is seen in the belief that each year's log should be kindled with a fragment of the last year's log.[78] It was held unlucky to bring in the log until the proper time, or the Christmas greens until very soon before Christmas.[79] The belief that a fragment of the Yule log would preserve a house from lightning points directly to the worship of the sacred oak and of Woden.[80] In the northern counties, as long as the Yule brand was burning, servants were treated to ale.[81]

Evergreen-decking at Christmas also hails from heathen times. Ivy, holly, bays, laurel, and other greens are traditional; but the Christmas bough, which Frazer would tell us is also the Golden Bough of Dante, is the sacred mistletoe. Medieval carols on the contest between the Holly and the Ivy show that the greens became symbols for the sexes, putting forth their respective claims to mastery. A gibing carol of the time of Henry the Sixth gives the victory to Holly, the youth.[82] At Lincoln College, Oxford, it was long the custom to drink an Ivy-beer, but this was on Ascension Day.[83] Holly is sacred, if for no other reason than for its red berries, which like the rowan-berries, were sacred to Donar, the god of the hearth and of medicine, and therefore had distinct medicinal and magical value.[84]

---

[76] *The Mayor of Casterbridge,* Chap. I.
[77] V. S. Lean, *Collectanea,* Vol. II, Pt. II, p. 794; Denham Tracts, II, 92.
[78] Ellis's Brand, I, 471; *Denham Tracts,* II 25–26; Aubrey's *Remaines,* p. 172.
[79] *Denham Tracts,* II, 25.
[80] Frazer, *The Golden Bough,* one vol. ed., 638.
[81] Ellis's Brand, I, 468.
[82] W. J. Phillips, *Carols,* 12, 56–58; Brand, I, 68.
[83] Rendel Harris, *The Ascent of Olympus,* p. 26.
[84] Fogel, *op. cit.,* Intro. pp. 9–10.

The worship of the mistletoe as the plant sacred to the god of the oak, as an all-heal and bringer of luck, goes back to prehistory; we don't know how old it is. It is not particularly Celtic; we find it preserving its ancient reputation of an all-heal among the Aino of Japan today.[85] We have associated it with the Druids, but we do not know who the Druids were. Rendel Harris ingeniously interprets Ixion on his wheel as a solar symbol![86] The name for mistletoe, "Guy l'an-neuf," once a favorite cry with small children begging small Christmas gifts from door to door, is unhappily a thing of the past.[87] The origin of the custom of mumming at Christmas is considered in the present study in relation to folk-drama as a whole.

The Christmas carol, so essential a part of the traditional Christmas, was faithfully served by the famous Mellstock "quire." The wassail singers go back to the early Middle Ages; the carol, originally a dance with song, rose to the height of its popularity in the fifteenth century.[88] The wassail songs are among our oldest and most beautiful carols. Much as Hardy loved the old carols, he puts no really old carol on the lips of his Wessex folk, but represents them as faithful to standard hymns of the English Church, which, with very few exceptions, are not derived from true folk-songs. But of the "waits" themselves he has much to say. Such poems as "The Rash Bride," "Seen by the Waits," "The Dead Quire" and "The Paphian Ball" show the Mellstock band on its yearly rounds. Particularly Hardyesque are the last two. "The Rash Bride" is the story of a young widow, a bit of a flirt, whose romance is blighted by an innocent disclosure of one of the singers.[89] On another Christmas Eve, the singers glimpse the lady of the manor

---

[85] Sir Thomas Browne, *Vulgar Errors,* Book II, Chap. VI; T. F. T. Dyer, *The Folklore of Plants,* p. 47; Grimm-Stallybrass, III, 1205–6; Rendel Harris, *The Ascent of Olympus,* pp. 45 ff.

[86] *The Ascent of Olympus,* p. 35.

[87] Grimm-Stallybrass, IV, 1525; Aubrey's *Remaines,* 89; Brand I, 458.

[88] W. J. Phillips, *Carols,* pp. 12, 95, 128.

[89] *Time's Laughingstocks.*

dancing for joy before her glass; she has just received word of her husband's death.[90] We have a medieval legend in modern setting in "The Paphian Ball"; [91] we see the "quire" faithful to their duties even after death; when those who have taken their places carouse at the inn, the ghostly singers perform the office of waits. This is the fable of "The Dead Quire." [92] Most memorable of all carolings are the yearly rounds made by the famous Mellstock band and quire. Hardy's grandfather, father, and uncle, were gifted string players, and formed the nucleus of the Stinsford church band, and their Christmas rounds must have been much like those of our performers in *Under the Greenwood Tree*. Hardy drew them from hearsay, as they ended their office when he was only a year old; and, although they are purely fictitious, they approach certain personages and incidents from actual life closely enough to have caused the poet real regret that he had, as he thought, unduly burlesqued them, robbing them of the poetry and romance which colored their time-honored service.[93] This rehearsal at Tranter Dewy's in which the Mellstock band conquer the toughness of that "teaser" but nonetheless "Splendid carrel," Number Seventy-eight, might well be drawn from accounts heard in boyhood of the notable rehearsals at Stinsford House, presided over by the eager, music-loving vicar Murray; and this argument as to the relative merits of strings and brass and wind may well sum up the Stinsford band's reasons for their supremacy of long standing:

". . . Your brass-man is brass—well and good; your reed-man is reed—well and good; your percussion-man is percussion—good again. But I don't care who hears me say it, nothing will speak to your heart wi' the sweetness of the man of strings!" [94]

[90] *Satires of Circumstance.*
[91] *Human Shows.*
[92] *Time's Laughingstocks.*
[93] F. E. Hardy, *The Early Life of Thomas Hardy*, 12–16.
[94] *Under the Greenwood Tree*, Part I, Chap. IV; cf. F. E. Hardy, *The Early Life of Thomas Hardy*, p. 12.

Their gracious reception at Fancy Day's, and their re-
buff at Farmer Shinar's, are no doubt echoes of experiences
of Hardy's own folk. There is, however, a marked note of
caricature in the latter episode, although it serves to throw
into deeper relief the tragedy which is to befall the quire.
They had given Shinar Number Thirty-two, "Behold the
morning star," but, far from appreciating it, he had roared
at them—

"Shut up! Don't make your blaring row here. A feller wi' a head-
ache enough to split likes a quiet night."
Slam went the window.
"Hullo, that's an ugly blow for we artists!" said the tranter. . . .
"Finish the carrel, all who be friends of harmony!" said old
William, commandingly, and they continued to the end.
"Forty breaths, and number nineteen!" said William firmly. "Give
it him well; the choir can't be insulted in this manner!"
A light now flashed into existence, the window opened, and the
farmer stood revealed as one in a terrific passion.
"Drown en'—Drown en' " the tranter cried, fiddling frantically.
"Play fortissimy, and drown his spaking!"
"Fortissimy," said Michael Mail, and the music and singing waxed
so loud that it was impossible to know what Mr. Shinar had said, was
saying, or was about to say; but wildly flinging his arms and body
about in the form of capital X's and Y's, he appeared to utter enough
invectives to consign the whole parish to perdition.
"Very unseemly— Very!" said old William, as they retired.
"Never such a dreadful scene in the whole round of my carrel practice—never!" [95]

As if this shocking episode were not quite enough, they
were pained next morning to find arising from the school-
girls' section of the church such a flood of melody as put
their exhausted efforts to shame. Spinks' bitter comment,
"Really, I think we useless ones had better march out of
church, fiddles and all," contains the prophecy of the passing
of the gallery.[96]
At the passing of the gallery one hardly knows whether

[95] Part I, Chap. V.
[96] *Ibid.,* Chap. VI.

to laugh or cry, but at bottom, the story is sad. The whole affair is typical of the passing of good old customs full of savor into the limbo of forgotten things. The Hardy reader will, of course, side with the quire; he will look back upon these old gatherings where spirits were high, and simple joys enough to warm the heart, and he will regret their passing. The most old-fashioned among us are moved to dub our stereotyped and highly dull pleasures of today as indeed "miserable dumbledores." But even the word is lost to us; there is more in Fancy's organ that meets the eye— and ear. *Under the Greenwood Tree* is an idyl in prose. All Hardy's use of folklore and folk-custom is poetic. Here he does not probe the human heart to its depths; he does not give us a profound reading of life. He paints for us ever fresh and charming genre pictures; he shows us the great zest his Wessex folk have for life.

VIII

SPORTS AND PASTIMES

One who loves fine old games will find in Hardy an embarrassment of riches. There are children's games which
preserve memories of tribal warfare and ancient wooing
customs; decorous, graceful diversions like bowls or chess;
rustic merrymakings where the fun is fast and furious.
Scene after scene unrolls before us in these Hardy tales like
the painted cloths of the oldtime peep-shows. Now it is the
swish of maidens' skirts in the race for smockfrocks; now
some brave buckler-play well laid on; now the kaleidoscopic
sights of the country fair; and now the baiting of the gallant bull in the crowded square. It is a rich and passing
pageant after which the reader casts a regretful glance,
wishing he might detain it a moment longer, but forced to
hear its music ever fainter in the distance.

Dick Dewy had denied himself the exquisite pleasure of
seeing Fancy Day again until, fortified by the necessity of
returning her handkerchief, his head awhirl with eager anticipation, he found himself at her cottage gate. It was
locked to keep the children, who were playing Prisoners'
Base in the front, from running into the schoolmistress's
grounds. Fancy was at the farther end of the garden with
spade and gloves, trying to root out a bramble; she did not
see nor hear him until, after a third attempt, his courage
oozed away, and he retreated to some little distance, trying
to look as if he had merely chanced to pass that way. But
the third call, shouted with desperate vehemence, had
drawn the pretty schoolmistress to the door. In a moment
she had taken the handkerchief with dainty thanks and had
shut the door, leaving Dick to meditate bitterly on the folly

of the conventions.[1] The delightful comedy is over all too soon. The ancient game of Prisoners' Base is a setting for a quite different scene in *Far from the Madding Crowd:* [2] Bathsheba, after a night's wandering in the fern hollow, in terror of Troy and herself, had gone quietly home with Liddy and taken up her residence in the attic. Here she sat trying to read, listlessly taking in the sounds without. A blood-red sun was casting a lustrous glare upon the west front of the church tower; it was six o'clock, the time when the young men of the village were wont to gather for their game of Prisoners' Base:

> The spot had been consecrated to this ancient diversion from time immemorial, the old stocks conveniently forming a base facing the boundary of the churchyard, in front of which the ground was trodden hard and bare as a pavement by the players. She could see the brown and black heads of the young lads darting about right and left, their white shirt-sleeves gleaming in the sun; whilst occasionally a peal of hearty laughter varied the stillness of the evening air. They continued playing for a quarter of an hour or so, when the game concluded abruptly, and the players leapt over the wall and vanished round to the other side behind a yew-tree. . . .[3]

Bathsheba, startled out of her listlessness, was curious to know why the base-players had broken off so suddenly. Liddy's reply was that they had gone to see the two men from Casterbridge put up a grand carved tombstone. It was the stone to Fanny Robin's memory—Troy's one sincere gesture. Like the sunset in which it occurs, this scene is a spot of fading light before the gloom which is to fall on the village and on the heart of proud Bathsheba Troy.

Prisoners' Base, elsewhere called Biddy-Base or Billy-Base,[4] is mentioned by both Spenser [5] and Shakespeare.[6] In

---

[1] *Under the Greenwood Tree,* Part I, Chap. IX.
[2] Chap. XLIV.
[3] *Far from the Madding Crowd,* Chap. XLIV.
[4] Alice B. Gomme, *Traditional Games of England, Scotland and Ireland,* I, 28–29, 34; II, 80 ff.
[5] *The Shepherd's Calendar,* "October," line 5.
[6] *Cymbeline,* V. 3.

modern London [7] the game varies a good deal from the ancient game described by Strutt,[8] on the one hand, and from the Dorsetshire version, on the other. But at one point in the modern game, the struggle proceeds in the fashion described by Strutt, by the players on both sides taking hold of hands, always remembering that one of them must touch the base. Any player is free to leave the line and give an opponent chase; he who is touched first becomes the other's prisoner, and so on until the fixed number agreed on at the start of the game, usually twenty, are safely "in prison." The formation of the players in opposite lines, careful always that one of their number is touching base, harks back to primitive tribal war-formation, the object of which was not, of course, to take prisoners, but to knock down and kill as many of the enemy as possible,[9] a rough-and-ready attack which must have been highly effective.

When Picotee came to peep at the fashionable dinner at which her sister was guest of honor and her father head butler, she was frightened in the servants' quarters by the roughness and abandon with which the maids and men played Cat-after-Mouse; they seemed to her grotesque and terrifying.[10] This favorite game of British and American schoolchildren [11] was played in Dorsetshire by children forming a ring, their arms extended and their hands clasped; the one playing the Mouse left the circle and pulled at the dress of another player who straightway became the Cat, in duty bound to follow the Mouse in and out of the ring until caught, when she took the place formerly occupied in the ring by the Cat, who in turn became the Mouse, and so the game went merrily on.[12] From this game our Drop-the-Handkerchief and Kiss-in-the-Ring originated, al-

---

[7] A. B. Gomme, *Traditional Games,* II, 481–82, Memoir.
[8] Joseph Strutt, *Sports and Pastimes of the English People,* 78–80.
[9] A. B. Gomme, *Traditional Games,* II, 481–82; Strutt, 80.
[10] *The Hand of Ethelberta,* Chap. XXIX.
[11] A. B. Gomme, *Traditional Games,* I, 64.
[12] J. S. Udal, *Folk-Lore Journal,* VII, 212–214; *Traditional Games,* I, 64.

though it must be said that kissing is a modern innovation absent from the old game.[13]

Festus Derriman, having privately learned that the French had not landed, decided to withhold this information from his men; with sudden belligerence, he flourished his sword, winning an unwilling admiration. Festus could not refrain from tormenting his comrades still further; he reminded them, "No grinning matches at Mai-dun Castle this summer; no thread-the-needle at Greenhill Fair, and going into shows and driving the showman crazy with cock-a-doodle-doo." [14] Small wonder that the troopers gave him chase when they learned the truth, and that Uncle Benjy preferred a whole regiment of French to the sight of his rapscallion nephew.

The game of Thread-the-Needle, called in Dorset "Dred-the-wold-woman's needle," [15] and formerly "Threading the Tailor's Needle," [16] was played on Shrove Monday or Tuesday, and concluded with a custom which suggests a ritual origin. When pair after pair of children had passed under the arched hands of the players until the original first couple was reached, they would then run to the churchyard, and, joining hands, "clip the church" by dancing around it three times. This clearly recalls the primitive practice of going through an arch at certain seasons, the creeping through holed stones or trees to propitiate the god or secure some boon, after which the suppliants would dance around the sacred spot.[17] In "outstep" places a sick child is still occasionally passed through a hollow ash tree, or some large holed stone.[18] The wedding ring itself is a relic of the ancient ordeal of the bride wherein she proved her virginity by her ability to pass through a small orifice.[19] Some folk-

[13] Strutt, 381; J. S. Udal, *Folk-Lore Journal,* VII, 212; Gomme, I, 64.
[14] *The Trumpet-Major,* Chap. XXVI.
[15] Wm. Barnes, Dorset Glossary, *Trans. Philological Soc.,* Vol. 73; Gomme, *Traditional Games,* II, 232.
[16] Strutt, 381.
[17] A. B. Gomme, *Traditional Games,* II, Memoir, 502–503.
[18] Grimm-Stallybrass, *Teutonic Mythology,* II, 645; *Denham Tracts,* II, 325; Black, *Folk-Medicine,* 66–68.
[19] Baring-Gould, *Strange Survivals,* 266–268.

lorists interpret the game of Thread-the-Needle as a survival of the parley held at the narrow gate to the town, called the "needle," before strangers were admitted by the gatekeeper.[20] Whatever our choice of explanation, the fact remains that children's games are palimpsests that, for sheer antiquity, put the ordinary folk-tale to the blush.

When the Widow Edlin learned that Jude and Sue had not carried out their resolve to be married, she scolded them severely and lamented the good old days when folk thought no more of getting married than a game of dibs,[21] but kept up the junketing for a week, then borrowed half a crown to begin housekeeping with! Dibs, under many different names, has been played the world over from prehistoric times down to our own day. It is the old game of Hucklebones or Cockall, and is identical with Fivestones, Checkstones or Chucks, Jackstones or Jacks, Dabs, Snobs, or Gobs, in the lingo of the London cockney.[22] It was apparently once used in marriage divinations both by the Druidess and the Roman sorceress. A picture found in Herculaneum is described by Vallancey, and gives us the following scene. The Roman sorceress has cast up the five stones in the first and principal cast of the Irish Purin; all five lie on the back of her hand, and the onlookers are intently examining the cast; the whole seems to indicate one of the divinations so commonly practised before the Roman marriage ceremony.[23] The Irish name for the game, Seic Seona, sounded to English ears like Jackstones. We have some evidence that the game was prehistoric in Ireland: when old women are called away from the game today, they usually place the stones in or near the hearth; stones similar to these in use at present have been found in the crannogs, or lake-dwellings, usually in some hole near the primitive hearth.[24] The Japanese Tedama is

---

[20] Gomme, *Traditional Games*, II, 503.
[21] *Jude the Obscure*, Part V, Chap. IV; Part VI, Chap. V.
[22] A. B. Gomme, *Traditional Games*, I, 96–97, 127, 152; Brand, II, 412–413.
[23] W. H. Hazlitt, *Faiths and Folklore*, II, 344.
[24] G. F. Kinahan, *Folk-Lore Journal*, II, 266.

a similar and very ancient game.[25] The game was originally played with the small knucklebones of sheep, and still is in certain English country districts.[26]

In a charming scene in *Two on a Tower,* the Bishop of Melchester and Lady Constantine's brother begin a game of bowls on the green. Having bowled one in a curve toward the jack, the Bishop turned to his hostess:

"Do you follow us?" he asked gaily.

"I am not skillful," she said. "I always bowl narrow."

The Bishop meditatively paused.

"This moment reminds one of the scene in *Richard the Second,"* he said. "I mean the Duke of York's garden, where the queen and her two ladies play, and the queen says—

'What sport shall we devise here in this garden,
To drive away the heavy thought of care?'

"To which her lady answers,

'Madam, we'll play at bowls.' "

"That's an unfortunate quotation for you," said Lady Constantine; "for if I don't forget, the queen declines, saying,

" ' 'Twill make me think the world is full of rubs, and that my fortune runs against the bias.' "

"Then I cite *mal à propos.* But it is an interesting old game, and might have been played at that very date on this very green." [27]

Another great Wessex dame, Lady Penelope, was fond of promenading between the pleasaunce and the bowling green.[28] The Spirit of the Pities, looking down upon the English Channel, viewed it as a playground for Napoleon's "bowling hands." [29] Even the job of errand-man at the Women's Skittle Alley was not enough to cure Joseph Poorgrass of his bashfulness.[30]

---

[25] Hazlitt, *Faiths and Folklore,* II, 344.
[26] Gomme, *Traditional Games,* I, 96–97.
[27] *Two on a Tower,* Chap. XXVII: Richard II, III, iv.
[28] *A Group of Noble Dames:* "Dame the Ninth, Lady Penelope."
[29] *The Dynasts,* Part Second, Act I, Scene II.
[30] *Far from the Madding Crowd,* Chap. VIII.

Ninepins was a favorite game with the Teutonic gods and heroes; bowls, as well as our modern games of marbles and billiards, are probably derived from the same source.[31] There are few bowling greens left in England; from the sixteenth century on these were rapidly displaced by indoor alleys, which soon became the haunts of idle, dissolute youth.[32] Hamlet's cry, "There's the rub!" refers to the slope, or bias in the bowling green.[33] Hamlet alludes also to the game of Kayles, or Ninepins, played with the knucklebones of sheep, and commonly called Loggats: he reproves the gravediggers:

"Did these bones cost no more the breeding but to play at loggats with 'em?" [34]

The kayle-pins were called kettle or kittle-pins, which was easily corrupted into Skittle-pins.[35] In Skittles the pins could be beaten down both by bowling and by tipping them over; a player had to have thirty-six fair pins, or chalks, to win; less gave the game to the antagonist, and more necessitated his beginning over.[36] Hone records the feat of a farmer of Croydon who wagered to bowl a skittle-pin five hundred times from Croydon to London Bridge, a distance of eleven miles. He lost his wager, but performed the feat four hundred and forty-five times! [37]

Elfride Swancourt naïvely betrayed a secret of her father's when she asked Stephen Smith:

"Did you ever play a game of forfeits called 'When is it? Where is it? What is it?'"

"No, never!"

"Ah, that's a pity, because writing a sermon is very much like playing that game. You take the text. You think, why is it? and so on.

---

[31] Grimm-Stallybrass, III, 947; Gomme, *Traditional Games,* II, 115–17; Brand, II, 432; Strutt, 270, 272, 384.
[32] Strutt, 268–269.
[33] *Hamlet,* III, 1, 65.
[34] *Ibid.,* V, 1, 95.
[35] Strutt, 272.
[36] *Ibid.,* 272–273.
[37] Hone's *Every-Day Book and Table Book,* II, 1070.

You put that down under 'Generally.' Then you proceed to the First, Secondly, and Thirdly. Papa won't have Fourthlys—says they're all my eye. Then you have a final Collectively, several pages of this being put in great black brackets, writing opposite, *'Leave this out if the farmers are falling asleep.'* Then comes your In Conclusion, then A Few Words and I Have Done. . . . !" [38]

This is one of many varieties of Forfeits.[39] The forfeits of the children's game—to stand in the corner on one leg, to call up the chimney, to kiss every one in the room—are faint reminiscences of terrible forfeits of primitive society, of days when the man who lost a contest of wit paid with his life, a woman with her honor.[40] Odin won a contest of wit, which has been taken as a symbol of the Scandinavian conquest of the Jutes; [41] Alvis the Dwarf, a beehive hut dweller, lost his bride because he could not read the riddles set him, and the tale sums up perhaps the fate of the small, broad-headed, metal-working folk of the Bronze Age.[42] Alvis, the prototype of the Elfin Knight, is an unsuccessful contestant; a whole group of English, Scottish, and Cornish ballads revolve about riddling,[43] and most brilliant of all are the Irish contests of wit in such a tale as that of *The Feast of Briucriu,* in the Red Branch Cycle.[44] Shakespeare's allusion to the forfeits in a barber shop, recreates the days when the barber-surgeon, busied with bleeding a patient, could ill afford to be distracted by some jocular fool's toying with his tools.[45] Forfeits are said to have existed up to recent times in certain Anglian barber shops and in inn yards, where those who dabble in water cisterns or carry candles into stables must pay the forfeit of a drink around.[46]

It was at Tony Kytes' wedding randy that the Hard-

[38] *A Pair of Blue Eyes,* Chap. IV.
[39] Brand, I, 517; Gomme, *Traditional Games,* 1, 137–39.
[40] Sabine Baring-Gould, *Strange Survivals,* 233–234.
[41] *Vafthrudnismal, Elder Edda,* Bellows' Trans., 68–83.
[42] *Strange Survivals,* 321–32.
[43] *Ibid.,* 225.
[44] M. Jubainville, *L'Épopée Celtique en Irlande,* 174.
[45] *Measure for Measure,* V, I, 323.
[46] Lady C. Gurdon, *Folklore of Suffolk,* 104–105.

comes danced with the girls they liked best; all the young folk danced, while the old people played Put or All-fours in the parlor.[47] After Anne's discovery of Bob Loveday's love scrapes, she sent him angrily away, then spent some unhappy hours over her cruelty. Before long Bob came in, owning that he had been playing Put with Festus Derriman at the Duke of York.[48] Put is a rather difficult rooking-game, referred to by various Restoration writers as popular at Christmastide; at first a polite game, by Queen Anne's day it seems to have become the property of the humbler classes.[49] The first player, if blessed with a good hand, may "put it" to his opponent to let him see his hand; if the latter demurs, he takes the trick; if the contrary, they play it out; he must take two tricks to win the game, and is in high luck if he holds the best possible hand with three treys in it.[50] All-fours takes its name from its four chances, each of which scores a point: high, the best trump out; low, the lowest trump dealt; jack, the knave of trumps; and pips, in which certain other cards of fixed value are counted in the scores of the players holding them. On the whole, the cards rank as at whist.[51] Like Put and Cribbage it was popular among the lower orders in Queen Anne's day.[52]

Pitch-and-toss, played with any coin bearing a head on one side, goes back to the Roman game of *Capita aut Navia;* [53] it is not to be confused with Chuck-halfpenny or Chuck-farthing, or Pitch-and-Hustle.[54] The countryman who described Bathsheba, the new owner of Weatherbury Farm, to Oak, felt that he was saying the last word when he

[47] *Life's Little Ironies,* A Few Crusted Characters: "The History of the Hardcomes."
[48] *The Trumpet-Major,* Chap. XL.
[49] W. C. Hazlitt, *Faiths and Folklore,* II, 502: *Rump Songs,* 1662; Speed's *Batt Upon Batt,* 1694; Nabbs' *Springs Glory,* A Masque, 1639; Chatto, *Facts and Speculations,* 1848, page 166; Brand, I, 516.
[50] *Bohn's Handbook of Games,* 322–323, quoting Hoyle; Ellis's Brand, I, 516.
[51] *Bohn's Handbook of Games,* 323–324.
[52] Hazlitt, *Faiths and Folklore,* I, 265; Chatto, *Facts and Speculations,* 1848, p. 166.
[53] Brand, II, 421: Macrobius, Saturn. lib. I. c. 7; *Faiths and Folklore,* I, 309.
[54] Strutt, 276–77, 337, 386–387; Gomme, *Traditional Games,* II, 43–45.

remarked that she would think no more of playing pitch-
and-toss sovereign than such humble folk as they would
think of playing pitch-halfpenny! [55]

The fascination of gaming and gamesters plays a large
rôle in *A Laodicean:* [56] moreover, the conception of life as
a game in which men are forced to accept the cast of
"Doomsters" beyond their ken is a favorite with Hardy
even in so early a poem as "Hap." [57] The most memorable
gambling scene is the grotesque dice-play on Egdon Heath
in which Diggory Venn recovers the money Christian Cantle
has gambled away. Poor Christian, to whom the mysterious
little cubes seemed indeed "the devil's playthings," has gone
off scolding Wildeve as a "regular sharper"; and Diggory
Venn, who has been watching the play, challenges Wildeve
to continue. The grotesquerie of the scene is extreme—the
dark heath, the heathcroppers edging nearer to see what
these queer human creatures are up to, the thirteen glow-
worms for light—all are part of a scene which Hardy has
perhaps touched up too highly.[58] Perhaps Hardy's intention
was to suggest the ancient association of the Evil One with
gaming.

Odin was the inventor of dice as well as of runes: the
space between the thumb and the forefinger, held particularly sacred by the Greeks, was called the *Woedenspanne* in
the Netherlands, and men lucky at play were said to have
the game "running on their thumb." [59] In witch trials the
Devil was called the Dicer, *Schenzerlein*, and Player Jack's
soul, like that of every gamester, was held the peculiar
property of the Devil.[60] The attributes of Odin carry over
to our Christian Devil, but always with a marked loss of
dignity and power: the Devil's partiality for cards is proverbial to such a degree that we still find cropping up

[55] *Far from the Madding Crowd,* Chap. VI; cf. *The Hand of Ethelberta,*
Chap. XLV.
[56] See especially Book IV, Chap. IV.
[57] *Wessex Poems.*
[58] *The Return of the Native,* Book Third, Chap. VIII.
[59] Grimm-Stallybrass, I, 159–160; III, 1007.
[60] *Ibid.,* III, 1007; IV, 1583.

modern stories of his Satanic Majesty's participation in card-games, particularly those played on the Sabbath.[61] Certain cards are peculiar to the Devil, the "deuce," an unlucky cast, being a euphemism for his name.[62] In Dorset the unlucky four of clubs is sometimes called the "old 'un" or "the old 'un's bedstead"! [63] Every card player knows that sitting cross-legged or crossing the thumbs will bring him good luck and his opponent bad.[64] On the whole, Hardy's rustics prefer the simplest sort of card games, like Put or All-Fours, and simple tossing of coins to more elaborate play.

There is a memorable game of chess in *A Pair of Blue Eyes,* in which Elfride, a skillful player, quick to detect Stephen Smith's unfamiliarity with the pieces, tenderly allows him to win two games; then, forgetting herself in a fascinating move, checkmates him. How different her game with Henry Knight a few months later—the game for which Elfride had sat up half the night studying the Praxis! Elfride's little tragedy is clearly foreshadowed in this, her first serious defeat; Knight took possession of her heart as easily as he demolished her false moves.[65]

Chess is an extremely ancient game, some tell us Oriental in origin; certainly Arabs are adepts in the game.[66] That it was a favorite game with the Greeks and Romans we know,[67] also that it occurs in the tales of the Gaelic Red Branch Cycle,[68] and in many English and Scottish ballads.[69] Many an English king since Canute has been a devotee of chess.[70]

Tippling amounts to an English institution, involves

[61] Harland and Wilkinson, *Lancashire Folklore,* 81–82; *Folk-Lore,* XXXVIII, 162; XXXIII, 395; XXXVII, 162.
[62] Aubrey's *Remaines,* Britten ed., 60.
[63] Hopkins, *Thomas Hardy's Dorset,* 22.
[64] Sir Thomas Browne, *Vulgar Errors,* Book V, Chap. XXIII.
[65] *A Pair of Blue Eyes,* Chaps. VII, XVII, XVIII.
[66] Strutt, 304–306.
[67] Aubrey's *Remaines,* 209; Pliny, *Natural History,* Lib. XXXVII. cap. 2.
[68] Hazlitt, *Faiths and Folklore,* I, 110: Dr. Douglas Hyde, *A Literary History of Ireland,* 314.
[69] C. L. Wimberly, *Folklore in the English and Scottish Ballads,* 194.
[70] Strutt, 309.

quaint old customs, and brings us to many fascinating old inns. Among the latter mentioned by Hardy are the Buck's Head, near Weatherbury, scene of many "lovely drunks"; the Quiet Woman at Egdon with its curious sign of a woman carrying her head under her arm; the King's Arms, the Tailor's Arms, the Three Choughs, the Three Mariners, and Peter's Finger in Casterbridge—the latter a corruption of St. Peter ad Vincula, the calendar name for Lammas Day, August 1, on which certain service originally had to be done for the lord of this manor in return for the land-tenure; [71] lone inns like those the trampwoman and her fancy-man loved—King's Stag, Windwhistle, Lornton Inn, and Wynyard's Gap; the Hit-or-Miss at Durnover, the Sow-and-Acorn near King's Hintock; the Old Greyhound, the Pure Drop, where Tess's father took his ease; the Traveller's Rest, the Ring of Bells, and—most delightful name—the Load of Hay! The grandest "wet" in all Hardy is that enjoyed by Joseph Poorgrass and his cronies at the Buck's Head, while Fanny Robin's body waited outside in lonely state. It was here that Joseph's "multiplying eye" got the best of him. Here Oak found him and rated him soundly, and received reply:

"Yes; I see two of every sort, as if I were some holy man living in the times of King Noah, and entering the ark. . . . I feel too good for England; I ought to have lived in Genesis by rights, like the other men of sacrifice, and then I shouldn't have b-b-been called a d-d-drunkard in such a way!" [72]

Nor can the reader of *Far from the Madding Crowd* forget the jolly "wets" at the Maltster's, particularly Oak's first visit, on which he was offered the huge mug, cracked and scarred from being set in the fire, and incrusted with cider and ashes baked hard, which bore the picturesque name of the "God-forgive-me," probably, Hardy suggests, because "its size makes any given toper feel ashamed of

[71] Hopkins, *Thomas Hardy's Dorset,* 165–166.
[72] *Far from the Madding Crowd,* Chap. XLII.

himself when he sees its bottom. . . ." [73] In "The Three Strangers" the visitors are treated to a drink from a huge brown ware vessel bearing the inscription:

> There is No Fun
> Untill i Cum.[74]

Hardy is out of sympathy with the English fox-hunting tradition; it is said that he would not allow the hunt to cross his property, and his heart is plainly with the fleeing fox.[75] But he is too much the artist to miss the fox-hunter's picturesque quality and point of view: the irate farmer, who had missed the scent, scolded Grace Melbury for not crying Halloa when she had seen the tired fox slip quietly into the dead fern. All the contempt of the sportsman for the hind who does not play the royal game is in this little scene.[76] Hardy makes admirable use of the fox-hunt in the uproarious tale of "Andrey Satchel and the Parson and the Clerk," in which the parson, who boasts that he has been in at the death of three thousand foxes, and the clerk, who is as great a devotee as the parson himself, after the hunt of their lives, run the fox to earth in a truly spectacular finish:

"At last, late in the day, the hunting came to an end by the fox running into a' old woman's cottage, under her table, and up her clock-case. The pa'son and clerk were among the first in at the death, their faces a-staring in at the old woman's winder, and the clock striking as he'd never been heard to strik' before." [77]

Hardy's sympathy for the trapped creature is revealed in passage after passage; on one side he sees the horror of the deadly man-traps set for the poacher, who after all is only exercising a privilege tacitly admitted by the English landed proprietors for many centuries; on the other, the tragedy of preying on defenseless creatures for pure sport.

---

[73] Chap. VIII.
[74] *Wessex Tales.*
[75] *Human Shows,* "Lady Vi"; "Winter Night in Woodland"; *Wessex Poems,* "She to Him."
[76] *The Woodlanders,* Chap. XII.
[77] *Life's Little Ironies:* "A Few Crusted Characters."

There is an allusion to the noble sport of hawking in *The Dynasts*:

Spirit of the Pities

Yet is it but Napoléon who has failed.
The pale pathetic peoples still plod on
Through hoodwinkings to light! [78]

The phrase calls up a picture of the hawk on a high-born lady's wrist, with hooded head and small, musical bells that sound a semitone apart when it takes flight! [79] Hardy also describes a "ratting" scene in *Tess,* the harvesters inexorably driving the hidden hares, rabbits, snakes, and fieldmice into the last clump of uncut grain, there to be slaughtered by their knives, sticks, and stones.[80] Crab-catching, a favorite rustic sport, is described in the poem "Aquatic Sports." [81]

When Lucetta looked from her window at High Place Hall, she looked down the large arched street which led into Bull-stake Square, in the middle of which rose the stone post to which oxen were tied in former days and baited by dogs, as the saying went, to make them tender.[82] In a corner of this square stood the old stocks; and in another quarter of the town the long disused cockpit.[83] The lords of Wessex who figure in *A Group of Noble Dames,* and who, therefore, go back to an earlier day than the Mayor, were devotees of cocking and ratting and bull-baiting. Lord Icenway and the Duke of Hamptonshire enjoyed these savage sports much as did Elizabeth and her nobles in the lusty age when they flourished in their heyday.[84] The Vagrancy Act of Elizabeth's reign struck at the jugglers, tumblers, and bear-wards who neither worked at a trade nor wore the

[78] Part Third, Act IV, Scene IV.
[79] Strutt, 42–43.
[80] *Tess,* Chap. XIV.
[81] *Human Shows.*
[82] The *Mayor of Casterbridge,* Chap. XXVII.
[83] *Ibid.,* Chap. XXI.
[84] "Dame the Fifth, Lady Icenway"; "Dame the Eighth, The Duchess of Hamptonshire."

livery of a noble patron, but did not put a stop to the huge bear gardens which long rivaled the Bankside theaters for popular favor.[85] Up to a century ago bull-baitings were held at Morpeth, and still more recently there were bull-runnings at Stamford.[86] Cock-fighting is a still more ancient sport: the Greeks and Romans were fond of it, and the chances are that it was already a familiar game in Britain at the coming of the Romans.[87] Henry the Eighth built a great cockpit at Whitehall; Cromwell prohibited cock-fights, but the Restoration brought a speedy return to the fleshpots of Egypt.[88] The English sport was peculiar to Shrovetide; and when cock-fighting was abolished, its place was taken by "cocking," "cock-throwing," "cock-squailing," or "cock-kibbet," as it was variously called.[89] In this sport a cock was put into an earthern vessel, with only his head and his tail exposed to view, and hung high in the air as a target; four throws were granted for twopence, and he who freed the cock won him.[90] In the Kentucky and Tennessee mountains the descendants of our American "Long Hunters" today shoot thus at wild turkeys at forty yards range, and it was this sort of markmanship which made possible Alvin York's spectacular capture of an entire German machine-gun battalion in the Argonne Forest in the World War.[91] Cocks of lead were set up in booths in English fairs; thus the phrase, a Jack-a-Lent, or target, became a nickname for a scarecrow or butt of ridicule.[92] Cock-throwing is one form of *Hahnenschlag;* another form survives in our game of Blindman's Buff.[93]

[85] J. Q. Adams, *Shakesperean Playhouses,* 118–133; Thomas Frost, *The Old Showmen and the London Fairs,* 25.

[86] Brand, II, 63–64; N. Thomas, *Folklore of Northumberland,* 122; W. Crooke, *Folk-Lore,* XXVIII, 141–163; M. Peacock, *Folk-Lore,* XV, 199–202; Strutt, 278.

[87] Brand, II, 57.

[88] *Ibid.,* II, 62, and Note 2.

[89] M. E. Wright, *Rustic Speech and Folklore,* 293; *Folk-Lore,* XXXI, 240–242; *Folk-Lore,* XXVII, 202; etc.

[90] Strutt, 283–284.

[91] Tom Skeyhill, *Sergeant York: His Own Life Story and War Diary,* Doubleday, Doran, and Co., 1930.

[92] Brand, I, 101–102; Jonson's *Tale of a Tub.*

[93] N. W. Thomas, *Folk-Lore,* XI, 251; 264–265; 272.

The most hilarious rustic sports were entered into heart and soul at various fairs which happily combined barter and recreation. Hardy has described the once famous sheep fairs at Greenhill and Pummery Tout, the horse-and-sheep fair at Weydon Priors, the cattle fair at Casterbridge, the spring trade-fair at Kennet-bridge, and the Casterbridge Candlemas hiring-fair. He shows us scene after scene, gay with the yellow and green vans of the earthware venders; the nicknack, nut, apple, and gingerbread stands, where one may eat if he hits the target; the peep shows, wax-works showmen, and jugglers of every description; the "thimbleriggers," fortune-tellers, and exhibitors of "inspired" monsters, giants, dwarfs, and animal mimics; the medical quacks with their wonderful "patter"; the frumenty woman and her "laced" and savory stuff; the Jerry-go-nimble, and the large tent in which, perhaps, the heroic tale of Dick Turpin is to be enacted. A strange and colorful medley this! There are sports aplenty, too—smock races for young women, the prize a shift of fine Holland linen—races to which country girls, victors in the Ascensiontide and Whitsuntide revels at home, eagerly give themselves.[94] For men there are footraces; wheelbarrow races run blindfold;[95] jumping over hurdles—a feature of Henchard's entertainment, as well as of village meets for centuries;[96] donkey races;[97] hopping races, in which youths in sacks tumble about blindly, to the merriment of the onlookers;[98] and wrestling and boxing matches.[99] There is the old-time chase for the greased pig, or climbing a greased pole, or clambering over a pole over a

---

[94] Brand, I, 210; II, 2; *Folk-Lore*, XIII, 175; *Folk-Lore*, XXIV, 237–238; N. Thomas, *Folk-Lore of Northumberland*, 75; *The Return of the Native*, Book I, Chap. V.

[95] Article signed "T," Hone's *Every-Day Book*, II, 674–675.

[96] *The Mayor of Casterbridge*, Chap. XVI; Hone's *Every-Day Book*, II, 674; *Folk-Lore*, XXIV, 238.

[97] *The Mayor of Casterbridge*, Chap. XVI; Brand, II, 9.

[98] *The Mayor of Casterbridge*, Chap. XVI; *A Changed Man*, "The Romantic Adventures of a Milkmaid"; Article signed "K" in Hone's *Every-Day Book*, II, 674–675; Wm. Barnes, Hone's *Year Book*, 1176, 1525–1526.

[99] *The Mayor of Casterbridge*, Chap. XVI; Strutt, 80–84; Hone's *Every-Day Book*, II, 674.

small stream (as in Henchard's entertainment again) [100]—
a curious sport which survives from ancient May revels,
in which the pole was originally the Maypole itself! Here
are games of single-stick, or quarter-staff, laid on with all
the gusto of a Little John or a Scarlet.[101] If we watch long
enough, we may see one of these fellows tear off his "pot,"
or wicker helmet, drop his "ladle," or staff, and take to
honest boxing; many a singlestick bout has ended thus, with
one combatant in glorious disgrace, and the other, ignomini-
ously beaten, left to hobble off on his staff.[102] Here too are
grinning matches, each contestant seeing if he can make
the most grotesque face through his horse-collar; jingling
matches, smoking and hot-hasty-pudding matches, and even
yawning matches! [103] Not all of these are described by
Hardy, but some of them play a part in the Wessex celebration of Napoleon's downfall.[104]

There is something at the fair for every taste, something to mar melancholy, something mad and merry for
every Jack and Joan. If we are going to the fair, it will be
foolish to try to find our way about in any methodical
fashion; we had best take the sights and sounds, the smells
and savors as they come. Firmly resolved then, not to be
taken in by any nimble wit, not to spend a penny on mere
frippery, let us set out. It is the last statute day of the fair,
Pack-and-Penny Day. The sober tradesmen and farmers
have sold their horses, sheep, or cattle, have bought their
earthenware, hardware, and drygoods, and gone home. The
gentry are nowhere to be seen. But there are plenty of
journeymen and apprentices, soldiers and sailors on fur-
lough, and shopkeepers out to get a pretty bargain or two.

---

[100] *The Mayor of Casterbridge,* Chap. XVI; *A Changed Man,* "The
Romantic Adventures of a Milkmaid"; Frazer, *The Golden Bough,* one vol.
ed., 1922, p. 124; *Folk-Lore,* XXIV, 237–238.
[101] *The Dynasts,* Part First, Act IV, Scene I; Part First, Act II, Scene IV;
Wm. Barnes, Hone's *Year Book,* 1525–26; Brand, II, 400; Strutt, 264.
[102] Wm. Barnes, Hone's *Year Book,* 1525–1526.
[103] Brand, II, 9; Strutt, 370–373; Hone's *Year Book,* 1525–26; Hone's
Every-Day Book and Table Book (1838), II, 669–676; II, 1307–1309.
[104] *The Dynasts,* Part First, Act II, Scene IV; Act IV, Scene I; *The
Trumpet-Major,* Chap. XXVI.

On the whole, it is a holiday crowd out for all the "jolly
fun of the fair." Country boys and girls are here in little
groups, all eyes and ears for the "humors of the fair."
And humors aplenty there are! We soon catch sight of the
nicknack vender crying his toys and gimcracks.[105] Here
Cheap Jack is about to sell a blooming country girl a brilliant shawl; her eyes shine with happiness, and her lover
pays the price asked; as they turn away, the hawker again
begins his harangue, *prestissimo e fortissimo*.[106] Not far
off stands a rival in eloquence, a quack offering the crowd
a wonderful yellow salve that will cure your rheumatism; if
you can get his ear, he'll sell you a love-philter, one of his
own concocted of the "dust of doves' hearts," after old
Burton's recipe! [107] There are many gypsies about—some
lounging idly in front of their tents, their dark eyes lighted
with swift and languorous contempt for the credulous
crowd.[108] Ballad singers, who have paid well for their
license to hawk ballads, will sing the latest broadside
through once for us, but they expect us to buy their gayly
painted sheets; we are seized with regret that they should
proffer us this when they might sing their lovely folk-
songs! [109] We have passed the gingerbread stalls with their
quaint and curious figures—gloves, dogs and cats, houses
and towers, and luscious dolls, and our minds go back to
Tiddy-Dol, greatest of Gingerbread men, in Hogarth's
print of the Idle Apprentice at Tyburn.[110] Nearby there is
going on a game of Thimble-rig.[111] The sleight-of-hand man
has his confidence men in the audience who risk a wager and
lose gallantly; the rustics take the bait and begin to bid.

[105] *The Mayor of Casterbridge,* Chap. I.
[106] *The Dynasts,* Part First, Act IV, Scene VI.
[107] *Jude the Obscure,* Part V, Chap. V.
[108] *The Mayor of Casterbridge,* Chaps. I and II.
[109] *Time's Laughingstocks:* "At Casterbridge Fair," I, VII; *The Mayor
of Casterbridge,* Chap. 1; *The Dynasts,* Part First, Act V, Scene VII;
Thomas Frost, *The Old Showmen,* 50.
[110] *Jude,* Part V, Chap. VII; *Human Shows,* "A Last Journey"; Hone's
Every-Day Book, II, 1309; *Folk-Lore,* XXIV, 237–38; Frost, *The Old
Showmen and the London Fairs,* 99–100.
[111] *Desperate Remedies,* Chap. XVII; *The Dynasts,* Part First, Act IV,
Scene VII; Hone's *Every-Day Book,* I, 767–770.

One countryman who had guffawed loudly when the rigger let the pea roll out from under the nutshell, or "thimble," after the last bad guess, wagers that the pea is not under that shell, at least; the rigger lifts the shell, revealing the pea which he has cleverly inserted! As we pass on, the shouts of laughter behind us die away; a tired and very pretty girl is setting up nuts and apples for targets; the lads who are shooting are well on the way to beggaring her.[112] The larger booths, with huge flaps that serve as doors, are full of varied exhibitions, we know. Were we to enter, we might find a horse who taps the answers to his master's questions, descendant, may we guess, of Shakespeare's "dancing horse";[113] or, it may be a learned pig named Toby—for be sure if he is not Toby, he is a simpleton![114] We draw the line at the bearded woman, the Cornish giant-ess, the Waterloo giant, the Corsican dwarf, and all the other "inspired monsters"; it is still true, we perceive, that folk will give more to see a dead Indian than to relieve a lame beggar![115] We cannot resist the wax-works—Othello the Moor, Bluebeard in a dreadful rage, Mother Shipton, and sweet Jane Shore; peep shows with their gayly painted cloths will show you who'll-have-you lying in state, and even Wellington at Waterloo![116] The Punch-and-Judy show we have always with us, and the pranks of the serio-comic little devil, with whom we have always sympathized, are as "tragi-cal mirth" as they were in Pepys' day.[117] But it is useless to look for those admirable puppet-shows of which Edmund Kean was once an exhibitor and Fielding himself a proud proprietor.[118]

Familiar enough is the primitive Jerry-go-nimble with its

[112] *Human Shows,* "A Last Look Around St. Martin's Fair"; *"A Last Journey."*
[113] *The Mayor of Casterbridge,* Chap. I; Frost, 22–23; *Love's Labour's Lost,* I, 2.
[114] Hone's *Every-Day Book,* II, 1307–1310; Frost, 239, 243, 314–315.
[115] *Moments of Vision,* "At a Country Fair"; Frost, 60, 155, 188, 299, etc.: Hone's *Every-Day Book,* II, 1307–1310; *The Tempest,* II, 2.
[116] Frost, 31, 138–143, 292–293, 310.
[117] Frost, 289, 305, 307.
[118] *A Pair of Blue Eyes,* Chap. I; Frost, 103–110, 216.

wooden horses and gay coaches, the organ, and the inviting cry "A coach or a horse for a halfpenny!" It was one
of these roundabouts that poor Joseph was taken to see—
the womenfolk standing on horses "with hardly anything
on but their smocks," but after all, he wasn't cured of his
bashfulness.[119] And it was on one of these that Raye, the
young lawyer, fell deeply in love with a pretty girl who rose
rhythmically and happily with the horses and seemed to
wish the ride might never come to an end.[120] But the high
light of the fair is still before us. It is the "Royal Hippo-
drome Performance of Turpin's Ride to York, and the
Death of Black Bess." Here our make-believe must come to
an end; it is impossible to see this play except through the
eyes of Joseph Poorgrass and Jan Coggan.

Turpin was, we know, one of the fascinating "gentlemen
of the road" of the eighteenth century, perhaps greater
than all the others—Captain Jemmy Hind, the French Du
Val, Old Mob, Tom Cox, Will Holloway, Neddy Wicks,
and Jack Sheppard. He was a large dark Essex man, his
face marked by smallpox, but gallant, kind, loyal to his
cronies, and contemptuous of folk in stagecoaches. For years
he was the terror of the North Road; and a great oak,
Turpin's Oak, at Finchley, on the road to Barnet, was
full of the bullets shot at him.[121] His ride to York in
twelve hours—a four days' journey by stage—is the climax
of one of his and Tom King's adventures. The two cronies
had been bowling at Kilburn; King, a brilliant rogue, was
suddenly saddened as he looked back at his days at Harrow;
he was filled with regret and presentiment of death. Surprised suddenly by the constable, both mounted in haste,
but King fell and was dragged down by the constable. Turpin
fired, fatally wounding his friend, then took to flight, the
officers at his heels. Cruikshank has immortalized the tale—

---

[119] *Far from the Madding Crowd,* Chap. VIII; Hone's *Every-Day Book,*
II, 1307–1310.
[120] *Life's Little Ironies,* "On The Western Circuit."
[121] For the historicity of Turpin see John Timbs, *The Romance of
London,* 247–248; cf. Wm. Ainsworth's Romance, *"Rookwood,"* preface pp.
34–37; Book I, Chap. IX; Book IV, Chap. VII.

the leap over the spiked toll gate at Hornsey, the mad ride through Edmonton, the swim across the Cawood ferry. As York's minsters come into view, Black Bess, Turpin's gallant horse, falls and dies—her heart has burst! Later, dressed as a countryman in a smock, Turpin misdirects the officers and makes his escape.[122] Turpin's historical end is almost as good as his legendary: he was hanged at York in 1739, as the account goes:

His firmness deserted him not at the last. When he mounted the fatal tree his left leg trembled; he stamped it impatiently down, and, after a brief chat with the hangman, threw himself suddenly and resolutely from the ladder. His sufferings would appear to have been slight, as he himself sang,

"He died, not as other men, *by degrees,*
But at once, without wincing, and quite at his ease!"[123]

This is the hero of the great show which delighted Joseph Poorgrass, Jan Coggan, and hundreds of other rustics; they did not miss the speeches, which Troy, for fear of betraying his identity, was forced to omit:

. . . accordingly the play began, and at the appointed time Black Bess leapt into the grassy circle amid the plaudits of the spectators. At the turnpike scene, where Bess and Turpin are hotly pursued by the officers, and the half-awake gatekeeper denies that any horseman has passed, Coggan uttered a broad-chested, "Well done!" which could be heard all over the fair above the bleating, and Poorgrass smiled delightedly with a nice sense of dramatic contrast between our hero, who coolly leaps the gate, and halting justice in the form of his enemies, who must needs pull up cumbersomely, and wait to be let through. At the death of Tom King, he could not refrain from seizing Coggan by the hand, and whispering, with tears in his eyes, "Of course he's not really shot, Jan—only seemingly!" And when the last sad scene came on, and the body of the gallant Bess had to be carried out on a shutter by twelve volunteers from among the spectators, nothing could restrain Poorgrass from lending a hand, exclaiming as he asked Jan to join him, " 'Twill be something to tell of at Warren's

[122] *Rookwood,* Chap. IV and XII.
[123] *Rookwood,* L'Envoi; cf. L. O. Pike, *The History of Crime in England,* II, 277 ff.

in future years, Jan, and hand down to our children." For many a
year in Weatherbury, Joseph told, with the air of a man who had
had experiences in his time, that he touched with his own hand the
hoof of Bess. . . .[124]

But it is time to leave the fair. We shall have no time
to see the "hoppings" at the village inns nearby. We have
not kept our resolve not to buy any frippery, but we have
not been taken in by any nimble wit. What is this? Our
pockets are picked, indeed. What's an empty pocket to the
jolly fun of the fair? They are playing that very air as we
turn away, and we resolve to whistle it on our way home.

[124] *Far from the Madding Crowd,* Chap. L.

IX
FOLK-SONGS, COUNTRY-DANCES,
AND FOLK-DRAMA

Folk-songs and "ballads," quaint Christmas carols rendered by the waits, and country-dances of all sorts were familiar to Hardy·from his earliest youth. The Stinsford Hardys— Thomas Hardy the First and his two sons, one of whom was our poet's father, for forty years were the heart of the famous Stinsford string band.[1] The rehearsal of the Mellstock band at Tranter Dewy's is a gentle caricature of the rehearsals that took place at the home of Thomas Hardy the Second;[2] and Hardy's grandfather's virtuosity on the bass viol is admirably pictured in the account of the playing of Thomasin's father in *The Return of the Native*.[3] His mother's reminiscence of her first glimpse of Thomas the Second bowing away in the gallery is charmingly recorded in "A Church Romance: Mellstock, ca. 1836."[4] The poet as late as 1923 confessed to Mr. Brennecke that the spell of the old carols and hymns was as strong and inexplicable as ever.[5] Hardy once expressed the regret that he had not followed the career of cathedral organist; he was typically English in this passion for the organ.[6] As a boy he had a most unusual ear, tuning fiddles and the family piano, and finding the "wolf" in the octave

---

[1] Florence E. Hardy, *The Early Life of Thomas Hardy*, 12–14.
[2] *Ibid.*, 15–17.
[3] Book I, Chap. V.
[4] *Time's Laughingstocks*; cf. *Early Life*, 16–17.
[5] Ernest Brennecke, Jr., *The Life of Thomas Hardy*, 5, 79.
[6] Florence E. Hardy, *The Later Years of Thomas Hardy*, 211.

a very real annoyance.[7] He grew to know the folk- and country-dances thoroughly, for he both played and danced them, playing second fiddle to his father's first at many a village randy near Bockhampton.[8] Only a dancing man could have caught the intoxication of the dance with its odd mixture of dignity and abandon. The mummers' play in *The Return of the Native*,[9] of course, is based on memories supplied him by the older generation; but "O Jan! O Jan! O Jan!" an old folk-play presented by the Dorchester Players in 1923, was based on an ancient song-and-dance act which Hardy witnessed as a boy of four.[10] Hardy, like Shakespeare, had an "experiencing nature," and seems never to have forgotten anything that happened to him.

The tradition of the Christmas waits is immortalized in many poems, and particularly in *Under the Greenwood Tree*. The Mellstock band and choir, in their Christmas rounds, gave such familiar carols as "Remember Adam's Fall," "Behold the Morning Star," O, What Unbounded Goodness," "Rejoice, Ye Tenants of the Earth," and the favorite Nativity Hymn, "When Shepherds Watch'd Their Flocks." [11] It was the latter carol with which William Dewy fooled the pious bull! [12] It was the solemn air, "He Comes the Prisoners to Release," which the kindly Chalk-Newton choir sang as a sort of substitute funeral service over the grave of the poor suicide buried at the crossroads with a stake through his heart.[13] Poems like "The Dead Quire" [14] and "The Paphian Ball" [15] recount traditions of the strange experiences which befell the Mellstock choir and kept their memory green even among those who failed to live up to their inherited office of the waits. The uproarious tale, "Absentmindedness in a Parish Choir," gives us the other

---

[7] Florence E. Hardy, *Early Life . . .* , 28.
[8] *Ibid.*, 29–31.
[9] Book II, Chap. V.
[10] E. Brennecke, Jr., *The Life of Thomas Hardy*, 19–20, 79.
[11] *Under the Greenwood Tree*, Part I, Chap. II.
[12] *Tess*, Chap. XVII.
[13] *A Changed Man:* "The Grave by the Handpost."
[14] *Time's Laughingstocks.*
[15] *Human Shows.*

side of the picture; the wearied Longpuddle fiddlers, having played at an all-night randy, took a bit of hot brandy-and-beer to keep warm in the gallery one Christmas morning, fell fast asleep, and when rudely awakened, forgetting time, place, and decorum, swung into a rousing dance-tune:

. . . " 'Begin! Begin!'
" 'Hey? What?' says Nicholas, starting up; and the church being so dark, and his head so muddled he thought he was at the party . . . and away they went, bow and fiddle, at 'The Devil Among the Tailors.'. . . The rest of the band . . . followed their leader with all their strength, according to custom. They poured out that there tune till the lower bass notes of 'The Devil Among the Tailors' made the cobwebs in the roof shiver like ghosts; then Nicholas, seeing nobody moved, shouted out as he scraped. . . . 'Top Couples cross hands! And when I make the fiddle squeak at the end, every man kiss his pardner under the mistletoe!' " [16]

Small wonder that this was the last of the Longpuddle church-band; a barrel-organ was sent for—one that would play two-and-twenty psalm-tunes, and not a sinful tune among them! The musician will look in vain among these Wessex carols for any really old and choice fourteenth- or fifteenth-century carols; most of those mentioned by Hardy are the work of seventeenth- or eighteenth-century composers,[17] and in all of them, of course, the term carol, like roundel, jig, or ballad, has long since lost its original meaning of a singing dance.[18]

Hardy loved the old Tate-and-Brady psalm-tunes, some of them closely allied to or actually descended from Gregorian plainsong, and written in the noble and plaintive Greek modes. Particularly beloved airs were "Saint Stephen's," "New Sabbath," "Lydia," "Eden New," and "Barthélémon" and "Tallis" played to Ken's Morning and Evening

---

[16] *Life's Little Ironies:* "A Few Crusted Characters"; cf. Ellis's Brand, II, 140, for antiquity of custom of kissing at close of dance.
[17] Cecil J. Sharp, *English Folk-Song: Some Conclusions,* 100–101.
[18] W. J. Phillips, *Carols* 24, C. R. Baskerville, *The Elizabethan Jig,* 10–11; Lina B. Eckenstein, *Comparative Studies in Nursery Rhymes,* 58; Ellis's Brand, I, 480–492.

Hymns respectively every Sunday in the year.[19] Hardy celebrates favorite hymn-tunes in "Apostrophe to an Old Psalm-Tune," [20] "Afternoon Service at Mellstock," [20] "Genetrix Laesa," [21] "On the Tune Called the Old-Hundred-and-Fourth." [22] In "Places" he recalls the chimes at Castle Boterel which used to stammer out the quaint Old-Hundred-and-Thirteenth; [23] in *The Return of the Native,* he celebrates the virtuosity of Thomasin's father who sawed a bass viol quite in two while playing the One-Hundred-and-Thirty-third to "Lydia"! [24] The reader shares Henchard's contempt for the Fourth Psalm set to Wakely's; every one knew that the Fourth has always been sung to "Oxford." Just as Farfrae and Lucetta passed the Three Mariners, the band played the terrible One-Hundred-Ninth to "Wiltshire," the denunciatory words full of ironic import not fully clear until the close of Henchard's career:

> "And the next age his hated name
> Shall utterly deface." [25]

Old as are some of the carols, rich in tradition as are certain hymns, they are scarcely to be termed true folk-music. Nor can we call many of the songs which the country folk call "ballads" either traditional ballads or true folk-airs; most of them are degenerate versions of old ballads, in which the words, printed in the form of broadside sheets and hawked about in streets and fairs by professional ballad-singers from the fifteenth century on, rapidly became extremely corrupt.[26] The airs which once accompanied the traditional ballads, thus divorced from their words, suffered less change for the worse, but are considerably altered from

[19] *Early Life of Thomas Hardy,* 14; cf. *Late Lyrics,* "The Chapel Organist."
[20] *Moments of Vision.*
[21] *Human Shows.*
[22] *Late Lyrics.*
[23] *Satires of Circumstance.*
[24] Book I, Chap. V.
[25] *The Mayor of Casterbridge,* Chap. XXXII.
[26] Sabine Baring-Gould, *Strange Survivals,* Chap. IX, 191–212; Baskervill, *The Elizabethan Jig,* 101–102.

their original form,[27] each singer having subjected them to his own idiosyncrasies of ear and intonation. Hardy refers to the professional ballad-singer and his ballets, or ballet-sheets, time and time again; [28] he was a familiar figure at all country fairs. In time many of these "ballads" came to be mere snatches of light operas, cheap "composed songs" of the London music halls which arrived a trifle late in the country or true folk-melodies sadly tortured out of their original modes.[29] To this class of spurious folk-song belongs, of course, "The Mistletoe Bough" which Paula played for Somerset,[30] and practically all English patriotic songs.[31] We may be sure that Joan Durbeyfield, with her excellent ear, added to her large repertoire of true folk-songs many of these music-hall "ballads," but we never hear them on Tess's lips.

Some true traditional ballads survive, however, among Hardy's Wessex folk. Grandfer Cantle's interminable favorite, "The Jovial Crew," [32] is the old ballad of "Earl Marshall," often called "Queen Eleanor's Confession," a ribald song which has defied time, and is still current in Dorset today.[33] The old ballad sung by Shinar, "King Arthur Had Three Sons," is a serio-comic tale of the farmer and his three scapegrace sons, the miller who was drowned in his millpond, the weaver who was hung in his yarn, and the little tailor, with whom the devil ran away.[34] "Dame Durden," [35] rendered by Gabriel Oak on the flute with appropriate grimaces, is an anonymous old song of broad humor; when all Dame Durden's servants on Saint Valentine's Day

[27] Cecil J. Sharp, *English Folk-Song: Some Conclusions,* 23–29.
[28] *The Dynasts,* Part First, Act V, Scene VII; *The Mayor of Casterbridge,* Chaps. I, XLIV; *Time's Laughingstocks,* "At Casterbridge Fair."
[29] C. J. Sharp, *English Folk-Song: Some Conclusions,* 110–115.
[30] *A Laodicean,* Chap. X.
[31] C. J. Sharp, *English Folk-Song: Some Conclusions,* 112.
[32] *The Return of the Native,* Book I, Chap. III.
[33] Child, *The English and Scottish Popular Ballads,* ed. 1888, III, 259 ff; IV, 498–499; V, 241–242, 297; *Cambridge History of English Literature,* II, 414.
[34] *Under the Greenwood Tree,* Part IV, Chap. II; Sharp, *One Hundred English Folk-Songs,* No. 80 and p. xxxviii; *The Oxford Song-Book,* I, No. 67, pp. 110–111; *English County Songs,* 20.
[35] *Madding Crowd,* Chap. VIII; *Book of English Songs,* 93–95.

"began to mate," the honest dame was not filled with unmixed joy. "The Harvest Supper" records Hardy's memories of a harvest-dance to which he stole away as a boy of about five: he remembered vividly the dancers ranged on both sides of the big barn between the dancing, one after the other singing some traditional ballad, this one of "the parrot and the cage of glittering gold" among them.[36] This ballad, called in Dorset by various names—"The Outlandish Knight," "May Colvine," "The Western Tragedy," and other titles—is known to us best as "Lady Isabel and the Elf Knight," and was recently found on the lips of an old Nova Scotian peasant woman, "Easter Ann," who sang the tale of the maiden who drowned the false lord of Amberton and bribed her parrot by hanging him on a willow tree in a cage of glittering gold, or "ivorie," the tale slightly altered, but the lineal descendant of "Lady Isabel. . . ."[37]

There are true folk-songs, however, which do not have the fine antiquity of the traditional English and Scottish ballads. A century ago these were still on the lips of the country people; they were heard in the fields, on the harvest-wagons, at sheep-shearings, at "sing-songs" in village taverns, at weddings, christenings, and randies of all kinds. Today the patient collector has only a few aged folk-singers left from whom to note down words and airs. Tess's favorites were folk-songs; "The Break o' Day" was used in Dorset dairies to induce the cows to let down their milk. Angel Clare loved this song and "Down in Cupid's Gardens" so well that Tess, in her pathetic hope of a reconciliation, practised them for him.[38] She also delighted to sing "The Spotted Cow," "I Have Parks, I Have Hounds," "Such a Beauty I Did Grow," and a song which was as much disliked by Angel Clare as adored by Tony Kytes—"The Tailor's

---

[36] *Human Shows:* "The Harvest Supper"; F. E. Hardy, *The Early Life of Thomas Hardy,* 26.
[37] W. Roy Mackenzie, *The Quest of the Ballad,* Princeton University Press, 1919, pp. 8–9, 93–95; F. E. Hardy, *The Early Life,* 26.
[38] *Tess,* Chap. XLIX.

Breeches." [39] "Down in Cupid's Gardens" was probably sung both by Grandfer Cantle and Tess with the usual 2-4 measure thrown into common time.[40] The folk-singer is often impatient of full-measure rests or pauses, a tendency which accounts for most of the irregular measures in folk-song. As a rule, too, the singer is more concerned with the words than the air of the song, and is eager to be on with his story. The tune comes to him apparently by a sort of instinct or second nature along with the words, just as the dance tunes come to the fiddler the moment he recalls the figures of the dance.[41]

The refrain sung by Dick Dewy in *Under the Greenwood Tree* [42] is the close of a sheep-shearing song which, in many variations, is found in every English county. A lovely Dorian melody for these words was sung by William King, a Somerset folk-singer, so successfully that he won first prize at the Mid-Somerset Musical Festival at Frome in 1904.[43] We cannot help wondering whether this was the tune to which Dick sang happily:

> "With the rose and the lily
> And the daffadowndilly,
> The lads and lasses a-sheep-shearing go." [44]

Sheep-shearing songs were always much in demand; Joseph Poorgrass regaled the company at Bathsheba's shearing-supper with a "ballet" of his own "composure," a tune consisting of two notes, the keynote and another; and next with the famous folk-song, "The Seeds of Love," into which he plunged after several false starts:

[39] *Tess*, Chaps. III, XLIX; *Life's Little Ironies:* "A Few Crusted Characters."
[40] *Tess*, Chap. XLIX; *The Return of the Native*, Book VI, Chap. IV; C. J. Sharp, *English Folk-Song: Some Conclusions*, 79.
[41] Sharp, *English Folk-Song: Some Conclusions*, 20-21.
[42] Part I, Chap. I.
[43] C. J. Sharp, *One Hundred English Folk-Songs*, No. 93; C. J. Sharp, *Folk-Songs from Somerset*, XVIII, p. 36.
[44] *Under the Greenwood Tree*, Part I, Chap. I.

"I sow-ed the-e . . .
I sow-ed . . .
I sow-ed the-e seeds of love,
 I-it was all i-in the-e spring,
 I-in A-pril, Ma-ay, a-and sun-ny June,
 When sma-all bi-urds they do sing!"

"Well put out of hand," said Coggan, at the end of the verse.
" 'They do sing' was a very taking paragraph."

"Ay; and there was a pretty place at 'seeds of love,' and 'twas well
heaved out. Though 'love' is a nasty high corner when a man's voice
is getting crazed. Next verse, Master Poorgrass." [45]

But at this point young Coggan exploded in his mirth, and
was sent away in disgrace, after which Poorgrass could not
be set going again. The whole passage is highly descriptive
of the folk-singer's traditional mode of rendering a song.
He usually pitches his song quite high, throws back his head,
fixes his features in rigid composure, closes his eyes, and sings
away.[46] Jan Coggan's and Jacob Smallbury's songs were received without applause—the correct traditional attitude of
audience and singer, just as cut-and-dried as the presentation
and acceptance of the mummers' play in *The Return of the
Native.*[47] Bathsheba's song was received with a buzz of applause, but Bathsheba, in the eyes of her farm-people, was
not a folk-singer. "The Seeds of Love," which Joseph Poorgrass was unable to finish, is a very popular modern version
of the old song "The Sprig of Thyme," the lament of a wife
for the extravagance and vices of her husband.[48] The song
has been erroneously attributed to a Mrs. Habergam, *circa*
1689, who seems to have suffered as does the heroine of the
song; [49] this legend gives evidence of the song's antiquity.
   It was at the sheep-shearing supper at Weatherbury farm-

---

[45] *Far from the Madding Crowd,* Chap. XXIII.
[46] Cf. *The Woodlanders,* Chap. XLVIII; C. J. Sharp, *English-Folk-Song:
Some Conclusions,* 106–108.
[47] Book II, Chap. VI.
[48] Grimshaw, *Old English Songs,* No. 93; *Folk-Lore,* VIII, 321; C. J.
Sharp, *One Hundred English Folk-Songs,* No. 33, 34, Notes, pp. xxix ff.; C.
J. Sharp, *Folk-Songs from Somerset,* 2–4.
[49] Sharp, *Folk-Songs from Somerset,* 2–4.

house that Bathsheba, to the piping of Oak's flute and the
rich, unexplored background of Boldwood's bass, sang "The
Banks of Allan Water." In the light of her subsequent marriage to Troy, the following verse lingered long in the memory of all present:

> "For his bride a soldier sought her,
>   And a winning tongue had he:
> On the banks of Allan Water,
>   None was so gay as she!" [50]

"Allan Water" is one of the beautiful songs claimed by the
Scotch as their peculiar property, but, like most of these,
probably of English origin.[51]

Farfrae charmed the company at the Three Mariners
with "My Ain Countree," "O, Nannie," "Auld Lang Syne,"
and "As I Came Down Through Cannobie." [52] When he
brought the monstrous seed-mill to Casterbridge, Lucetta
knew who was driving it from the strains of "The Lass o'
Gowrie" which proceeded from its interior.[53] Donald and
Elizabeth-Jane danced to the skipping tune of "Miss
McLeod of Ayr," a tune which may have been as great a
favorite with Robert Burns as with Hardy as a boy.[54]
Among Irish folk-airs Hardy mentions "The Irishwoman's
Capers," a jig tune,[55] "Nancy Dawson," [56] and the Derry
tune, "The Light of the Moon," [56] familiar to us as one of
John McCormack's songs.

The most famous of all cumulative folk-songs, formerly
much in demand at harvest festivals, and a favorite of
Grandfer Cantle's is "The Barley Mow." [57] A good singer,
to show his memory, would often lengthen the song by divid-
ing the measures of drink into half-quart, half-pint, and so

[50] *Far from the Madding Crowd,* Chap. XXIII.
[51] *Oxford Song Book,* Vol. I, Dr. Percy Buck, ed., No. 10, page 13.
[52] *The Mayor of Casterbridge,* Chaps. VIII, XIV.
[53] *Ibid.,* Chap. XXIV.
[54] *The Mayor of Casterbridge,* Chap. XVI; F. E. Hardy, *The Early Life
of Thomas Hardy,* 18.
[55] *Human Shows:* "Donaghadee."
[56] *The Dynasts,* Part Second, Act. III, Scene I; *Irish County Songs,* II,
64–69.
[57] *The Return of the Native,* Book VI, Chap. IV.

on, singing alternately with the rousing chorus, "So here's a good health to the barley mow!" [58]

Some of Hardy's most charming lyrics are written on rhyme and stanza patterns derived from elusive old half-remembered folk-airs. It is easy enough to find songs with a similar refrain in any given case, but one can never be sure that this is the song which ran in Hardy's mind. Contagious folk-rhythms run through such poems as "Meditations on a Holiday," "The Colour," "O, I Won't Lead a Homely Life," [59] "The Song of Hope," [60] and "The Vagrant's Song," with its refrain, echoing an old Dorset song:

> O, a hollow tree
> Is as good for me
> As a house where the back-brand glows!
> *Che-hane, mother; che-hane, mother,*
> As a house where the back-brand glows! [61]

Folk-rhythms probably underlie many of the songs in *The Dynasts*—"The Mad Soldier's Song," [62] the marching song, "We Be the King's Men, Hale and Hearty," [63] and "Budmouth Dears"; the last-mentioned Sergeant Young had from the bandmaster at Gloucester Lodge, and he, in turn, no doubt, from some folk-air.[64] Some rollicking refrain from folk-tunes no doubt gave rise to the ballad of "Boney," with its refrain which Festus Derriman gave with great gusto at the miller's party, "Rollicum-rorum, tol-lol-lorum": members of the Loveday family and other old folk had sung this for Hardy when he was a small boy.[65] In the Granville Barker production of *The Dynasts*, the song "My Love's Gone a-Fighting" was sung to a folk-air in the Dorian mode,

[58] C. J. Sharp, *English Folk-Song: Some Conclusions,* 99–100; C. J. Sharp, *One Hundred English Folk-Songs,* No. 99, pp. 232–233; Lady Camilla Gurdon, *The Folklore of Suffolk,* 72.
[59] *Late Lyrics.*
[60] *Poems of the Past and the Present.*
[61] *Human Shows.*
[62] *The Dynasts,* Part Third, Act I, Scene XI.
[63] *Ibid.,* Part First, Act I, Scene I.
[64] *Ibid.,* Part Third, Act II, Scene I.
[65] *The Trumpet-Major,* Chap. V; Preface, Hardy's note.

"Sweet Kitty." [66] Hardy's tenacious memory and excellent ear detected in the patriotic, military, and dance-tunes of the Regency and the Napoleonic era fine old jigs, reels, and "favourite quicksteps" ingeniously doctored and disguised.[67] He knew that airs like "The Bridge of Lodi," [68] "The Plains of Vitoria," [69] introduced at the Vauxhall fête and "Marlborough s'en va-t-en guerre!" [70] were not folk-airs, but he loved them as he loved brilliant uniforms, for their dash and glamour. For the same reason he cared for "Life's a Bumper," [71] "Take Me Paddy, Will You Now?" [72] "The Dashing White Sergeant," a composition of Henry Bishop's,[73] and the Worcestershire favorite, "Drink Little England Dry." [74] "Brighton Camp: or The Girl I Left Behind Me," however, is an ancient morris-dance tune to which modern words have been set.[75] The airs of the Napoleonic era, which, to Hardy's ear, contained so many echoes of folk-tunes, are perhaps among the airs played in "Music in a Snowy Street" [76]—melodies whose passing the poet laments.

"Timing Her" is written to an old folk-tune:

> Lalage's coming:
> Where is she now, O?
> Turning to bow, O,
> And smile, is she,
> Just at parting,
> Parting, parting,

[66] C. J. Sharp, *One Hundred English Folk-Songs,* No. 31, Notes p. xxix; *The Dynasts,* Part Third, Act V, Scene VI.
[67] Prof. Samuel Chew, *Thomas Hardy, Poet and Novelist,* 112.
[68] *Poems of the Past and the Present:* "The Bridge of Lodi"; *Wessex Poems:* "The Dance at the Phoenix."
[69] *The Dynasts,* Part Third, Act. II, Scene IV.
[70] *Ibid.,* Part Third, Act III, Scene V.
[71] *Late Lyrics:* "The Chimes Play, 'Life's a Bumper.' "
[72] *Moments of Vision:* "Sitting on the Bridge."
[73] *Human Shows:* "At a Pause in a Country Dance"; *Life's Little Ironies,* "Absentmindedness in a Parish Choir"; Granville Bantock, *One Hundred Songs of England,* No. 99.
[74] *Folk-Songs from Various Counties,* p. 9.
[75] C. J. Sharp, *Morris-Dance Tunes,* Set. No. VI, No. 2.
[76] *Human Shows.*

As she is starting
To come to me? [77]

The short lines give a light, airy sweep to the verse, and portray the eager anticipation of the waiting lover. The same lilting swing runs through the country-dance tunes, most of which Hardy knew by heart. The dance is indeed a "great thing" to the people of Hardy's novels and poems:

> The dance it is a great thing,
>   A great thing to me,
> With candles lit and partners fit
>   For night-long revelry;
> And going home when day-dawning
>   Peeps pale upon the lea:
> O dancing is a great thing,
>   A great thing to me! [78]

"The Night of the Dance" [79] describes typical preparations for a dance. Of all fancy fiddlers most famous were the Mellstock and Longpuddle bands; of the latter it was said:

". . . one half-hour they could be playing a Christmas carol in the squire's hall to the ladies and gentlemen, and drinking tay and coffee with 'em as modest as saints; and the next, at the *Turk's Arms,* blazing away like wild horses with 'The Dashing White Sergeant,' to nine couples of dancers and more, and swallowing rum-and-cider hot as flame!" [80]

There were dances to go with the Whitsuntide walkings, mayings, summer "gypsyings," christenings and weddings, harvest and shearing-suppers and "hoppings" in connection with the great trade- and hiring-fairs. The passion for the dance enters into such lyrics as "At the Entering of the New Year (Old Style)," [81] "Song to an Old Burden," [82] and the

[77] *Moments of Vision.*
[78] *Moments of Vision:* "Great Things."
[79] *Time's Laughingstocks.*
[80] *Life's Little Ironies:* "A Few Crusted Characters," "Absentmindedness in a Parish Choir."
[81] *Late Lyrics.*
[82] *Human Shows.*

group, "At the Casterbridge Fair." [83] Of all the dances in Hardy's writings, none has the hearty social glow of the Christmas party at the Dewys'; [84] but for sheer fascination the moonlight dance in which Eustacia and Wildeve moved as top couple, dominating the figures, is supreme.[85] Hardy portrays the fiddler's exultation in his power to sway a whole assembly:

> The fiddler knows what's brewing
>> To the lilt of his lyric wiles:
> The fiddler knows what rueing
>> Will come of this night's smiles! [86]

"After the Club-Dance" describes one sort of "rueing":

> Black'on frowns east on Maidon,
>> And westward to the sea,
> But on neither is his frown laden
>> With scorn as his frown on me!
>
> . . . . .
>
> The roadside elms pass by me,—
>> Why do I sink with shame
> When the birds a-perch there eye me?
>> They, too, have done the same! [87]

"The History of the Hardcomes" is a tragic story of mismating under the spell of the dance.[88] But as Jenny danced with the King's-Own at the Phœnix, she recked little of remorse:

> Hour chased each hour, and night advanced;
>> She sped as shod with wings;
> Each time and every time she danced—
>> Reels, jigs, poussettes, and flings:
> They cheered her as she soared and swooped,
> (She had learnt ere art in dancing drooped
>> From hops to slothful swings).[89]

[83] *Time's Laughingstocks.*
[84] *Under the Greenwood Tree,* Part I, Chaps. VII, VIII.
[85] *The Return of the Native,* Book IV, Chap. III.
[86] *Time's Laughingstocks:* "The Fiddler."
[87] *Time's Laughingstocks.*
[88] *Life's Little Ironies.*
[89] *Wessex Poems.*

Julie-Jane knew nothing of regrets:

> Dance; how 'a would dance!
> If a fiddlestring did but sound
> She would hold out her coats, give a slanting glance,
> And go round and round.[90]

Mop Ollamoor, the fiddler, exercised a cruel power over poor Car'line Aspect; he lured her into dancing "My Fancy Lad," a five-handed reel; and when this dwindled to a three-handed reel, he began "The Fairy Dance," another prime favorite. Car'line, forgetting her little girl, her journey, and her husband, danced wildly until she fell, mercifully exhausted.[91] Hardy knew a country-dance might well be an orgy; the older folk agreed, no doubt, with Timothy Fairway's contention:

> "You be bound to dance at Christmas because 'tis the time o' year; you must dance at weddings because 'tis the time o' life. At christenings folk will even smuggle in a reel or two, if 'tis no further on than the first or second chiel. . . . For my part I like a good hearty funeral as well as anything. You've splendid victuals and drink as at other times, and even better. And it don't wear your legs to stumps in talking over a poor fellow's ways as it do to stand up in hornpipes." [92]

The six-handed reel is the most common of country-dances, usually danced longways by six couples, that is, with the women on one side and the men on the other at the beginning formation. All true country-dances have no fixed succession of figures. The fiddler called the figures according to his own skill and fancy, making sure that the dance ended with the end of the tune. These old dance-tunes, like rounds, and many Gregorian melodies, end on the dominant, looking forward to a continuation of the tune.[93] Popular six-handed reels were "Hands-Across," so called because of its most frequently recurring figure, and danced at the tranter's party

---

90 *Time's Laughingstocks:* "Julie-Jane."
91 *Life's Little Ironies:* "The Fiddler of the Reels."
92 *The Return of the Native,* Book I, Chap. III.
93 C. J. Sharp, *English Folk-Song: Some Conclusions,* 62–63.

by Dick and Fancy as top couple; [94] "Speed the Plough," a dance still popular in New England; [95] "Triumph, or Follow-My-Lover," a pretty dance with set figures; [96] "The White Cockade," which has several charming crossing-figures for the first and third couples,[97] and which was used to open the Duke of Richmond's ball; [98] "Haste to the Wedding," known to New Englanders today as "The Green Mountain Volunteers"; [99] "The College Hornpipe"; [100] "Brighton Camp, or The Girl I Left Behind Me," [101] and "Jockey to the Fair" [102]—both great favorites with morris-dancers. Perhaps the most famous six-handed-reel air is "The Devil's Dream," or "The Devil Among the Tailors" —the tune which kept the mummers out in the cold at the Yeobrights' Christmas party,[103] and sealed the doom of the Longpuddle string-band! [103]

"My Fancy Lad; or Johnny's Gone to Sea" is a charming tune used for five-handed reels. This was the tune that Car'line Aspect could not resist [104] and was a favorite with Hardy from boyhood. "Major Malley's Reel" is four-handed: the reader will recall the four old men, bowed and grim, who footed it outside the door of Host Trencher's tent at Greenhill Fair! [105] "The Soldier's Joy," a dance for any number of couples, was played in compliment to Troy and Bathsheba upon their recent marriage.[106] Fine old tunes are

[94] *Under the Greenwood Tree,* Part I, Chap. VIII.
[95] *A Changed Man:* "The Waiting Supper"; Elizabeth Burchenal, *American Country-Dances,* Vol. I, 37–38.
[96] *Under the Greenwood Tree,* Part I, Chap. VII; *Time's Laughingstocks:* "One We Knew"; Thomas Wilson, *The Complete System of Country-Dancing,* 89–90.
[97] Burchenal, *American Country-Dances,* I, 18–19.
[98] *The Dynasts,* Part Third, Act VI, Scene II.
[99] *Under the Greenwood Tree,* Part V, Chap. II; Burchenal, I, 42–44.
[100] *A Changed Man:* "The Romantic Adventures of a Milkmaid"; Burchenal, I, 45.
[101] C.. J. Sharp, *Morris-Dance Tunes,* Set VI, No. 2; *The Dynasts,* Part Third, Act VI, Scene IV.
[102] *Far from the Madding Crowd,* Chap. VIII; Sharp, *Morris-Dance Tunes,* Set IV, No. 2.
[103] *The Return of the Native,* Book II, Chap. V; *Life's Little Ironies,* "Absentmindedness in a Parish Choir"; Burchenal, I, 14–15.
[104] *Life's Little Ironies:* "The Fiddler of the Reels."
[105] *Far from the Madding Crowd,* Chap. L.
[106] *Ibid.,* Chap. XVII.

"Nancy's Fancy," [107] "The Honeymoon," [108] "The New-Rigged Ship," [109] "The Prime of Life," [110] the "Maiden Coy," "The Duke of York's Reel," "The Sylph," "The Fall of Paris," which is probably identical with the air whose final phrase Hardy has written out for us in *The Dynasts,* and many others.[111] Quite electrifying in effect must have been Jenny's dancing at the Phœnix to the "Row-dow-dow," a tune with a rhythmic drum-roll at the beginning of each phrase! [112] Many old airs were rechristened during the Napoleonic era and the Regency: this explains such titles, perhaps, as "Lord Wellington's Hornpipe," [113] "The Regency Hornpipe," [114] "The Hanoverian," [115] and the like. Hardy no more failed to detect the folk-tunes beneath the superimposed names than did his hero, Pierston, who identified a barrel-organ air with "The Jilt's Hornpipe." [116] He was moreover fond, not only of true folk-dances, but also of the more formal social dances derived from them. He speaks affectionately of "Weippert's First Set" [117] and "Jullien's grand quadrilles." [118] Weippert's First Set was one of several general sets with a longways formation for any number of couples; originally country-dances might be danced in round, square, or longways formation; Playford's *Dancing-Master* shows the country-dance in its heyday, before it was adopted and sophisticated by the English court, giving clear evidence of figures derived directly from the morris- and sword dances.[119] The artificial restriction of formations to

[107] *The Return of the Native,* Book II, Chap. VII.
[108] *A Changed Man:* "The Waiting Supper."
[109] *Time's Laughingstocks:* "One We Knew"; *A Changed Man:* "The Romantic Adventures of a Milkmaid."
[110] *The Dynasts,* Part Third, Act VI, Scene II.
[111] *Wessex Poems:* "The Dance at the Phœnix"; *The Dynasts,* Part Third, Act II, Scene IV.
[112] *The Oxford Song-Book,* Vol. II, Thomas Wood, ed., No. 6.
[113] *The Dynasts,* Part Third, Act V, Scene VI.
[114] *Ibid.,* Part Second, Act VI, Scene VII.
[115] *Ibid.,* Part Third, Act VI, Scene IV.
[116] *The Well-Beloved,* Part II, Chap. II.
[117] *Late Lyrics:* "A Gentleman's Epitaph."
[118] *Time's Laughingstocks:* "Reminiscences of a Dancing-Man."
[119] Baskervill, *The Elizabethan Jig,* 349–350; C. J. Sharp, *Country Dance Book,* Part II, 16–18.

longways became more general as time went on, and reached
its height in such a longways dance as the "Sir Roger de
Coverley," [120] a dance of set figures often given at the close
of the evening, and the basis of our Virginia Reel.[121] The old
motions and gestures—clapping, shaking hands, kissing
partners at the close of the dance, stamping, snapping fingers, jumping, and so on, have paled into such conventional
postures and movements as are familiar to all of us; [121] they
lost their variety, spontaneity, and strong dramatic quality,
to gain decorum and stately grace. The quadrille is a beautiful dance derived from the cotillon, and goes further back
to the old Cushion Dance itself.[122]

In the early nineteenth century the polka swept through
Europe and England, and was danced chiefly at Hunt and
Yeomanry Balls.[123] About the middle of the century the
waltz supplanted it. The country-dances were still danced in
Hardy's day, with their heys, their allemands, their pous-
settes, and joyous flings. No dancer who had ever done a
hey, it seems, would rest content with formal steps: the hey
was a cipher of S's, a number of serpentine lines interlacing
in intricate delicacy and beauty.[124] One has only to think of
Dick Dewy and Fancy Day, of Eustacia Vye and Wildeve
as top couples, to regret that the days of the merry, graceful
social country-dances are behind us.

The mummers' play in *The Return of the Native*,[125] is a
locus classicus for folk-drama. Hardy based it mainly upon
the memories of his elders. He has meticulously preserved
details of costuming, gesture, and mode of declamation. A
short preliminary explanation of the origins and evolution
of the mummers' play will be necessary.

---

[120] *Late Lyrics:* "An Ancient to Ancients."
[121] Baskervill, *The Elizabethan Jig*, 350.
[122] Lina B. Eckenstein, *Comparative Studies in Nursery Rhymes*, 64–65;
Thomas Wilson, *Complete System of Country-Dancing*, 323.
[123] *A Changed Man:* "The Romantic Adventures of a Milkmaid"; cf.
Barrett, *English Folk-Songs*, 38–39, "Polka-Mad."
[124] Thomas Wilson, *Complete System of Country-Dancing*, 75.
[125] Book II, Chaps. IV, V, VI.

The word mummer is probably from the Danish "Momme," and signifies "one wearing a mask." [126] It harks back to a ritual origin, to dances in which men in animal masks performed the ceremonial of the death of the old year, and resurrection of the new, dances which resulted in the Greek feasts which preceded the Roman Saturnalia, and helped to give the latter what religious significance they possessed. These ritual dances were magical in a twofold sense: the killing of the old year, and bringing him to life again in the form of a dramatic presentation is on the old principle of sympathetic magic, that by imitating processes of nature, one can actually influence and direct them; and this part of the ceremonial survives in the sword dances of Northern England today. The second ceremonial rite—the securing of fertility by eating the representative of this spirit of life, and the acquiring of his vitality by actual contact with or assimilation of him survives in the Feast of the Kidlington Lamb, in Oxfordshire.[127] The one central fact in folk-drama is the death and revivification of one of the characters—a rite once magical in nature, accompanied by the dancing of men with faces blackened or hidden with animal masks. In these ritual dances, common to the primitive religion of all Europe and the British Isles, the victim was originally a sacred sacrificial animal, or, even earlier, a human representative of the tribe chosen for this high martyrdom.[128] The English sword dance contains a figure in which the dancers pretend to decapitate one of their number within the circle, who later rises and joins in the dance.[129] The sword dance recalls the procession at Dent, where Frigg and Wodan, giants symbolic of the opposing seasons, were carried through the town, and a sword dance hovered about a victim, who was finally allowed to go unharmed.[130] The

[126] Joseph Strutt, *Sports and Pastimes,* (Hone ed.) 251; Ellis's Brand, I, 461–62; Grimm-Stallybrass, II, 505–506.

[127] On the subject of the origins of drama in ritual dances see Reginald J. Tiddy, *The Mummers' Play,* 70–72; Ellis's Brand, I, 283.

[128] Grimm-Stallybrass, II, 764–784.

[129] R. J. Tiddy, *The Mummers' Play,* 71–72.

[130] T. F. Ordish, *Folk-Lore,* "Folk-Drama," II, 332; Grimm-Stallybrass, I, 304; II, 761–762.

English Plough Monday Play preserves this bit of ritual in the swordplay about the fool's neck and in his pleas for mercy, now farcically funny, but once a solemn ceremony.[131] In origin the mummers' play was dance and dumb-show, without dialogue or dramatic action suited to words.

The pagan New Year festivities, although vigorously denounced by the early Church, persisted in quite primitive form for over a thousand years; on the Continent, the Feast of Fools and in England, the mummers' play, in its simplest form, were celebrated by masking and wild merrymaking: animal masks indicated the ritual origin of the feast.[132] The pagan and new Christian elements in folk-drama were not harmonized until the time of the Crusades; this folk-drama, which we should more properly term dumb-show with ceremonial dance, continued side by side with the rapidly developing religious drama.[133] It may have debased the miracle play to some extent: there is some evidence that the Croxton "Play of the Sacrament" was influenced by it, a fact that needs further authentication, but if accepted, has surprising implications.[134] A saner view is that, on the whole, it could not compete with the immensely popular miracle play, and, therefore, in time, was relegated entirely to the lower classes.[135] We do not know when dialogue entered the mummers' play, but what dialogue we have today indicates the enormous part played by the experiences of the Crusades. The really significant fact is that the dialogue originally had nothing whatever to do with the dumb-show, which, having lost its ritual import, gave the participants an opportunity to explain the killing and revivification of the principal character.[136] According to the laws of dramatic suspense, however, they had to invent an action in which the villain, the victim of the sacrificial rite, was killed by the

[131] T. F. Ordish, *Folk-Lore*, II, 332; Ordish, *Folk-Lore Journal*, VII, 331–335, "Revesby Plough Monday Play."
[132] J. B. Jevons, *Folk-Lore*, XXVII, 182–190.
[133] T. F. Ordish, *Folk-Lore*, IV, 160, "English Folk-Drama."
[134] R. J. E. Tiddy, *The Mummers' Play*, 104–105.
[135] Tiddy, 104–105.
[136] J. B. Jevons, *Folk-Lore*, XXVIII, 182–184.

hero. But the illogical revivification of the dead and wounded persisted; poetic justice is not done, and a magical rite is thinly veiled by a crude dramatic action. In about one-half of the mummers' plays, the villain is killed, then revived, and his revivification apologized for; in the remainder the hero is killed.[137] About the time of the Renaissance the actors in this popular drama became provided with—one dare not assert that they actually wrote—secular plays founded on themes from Greek and Roman legend and from the cycles of the romances, and in them they found an admirable hero for their purpose—Saint George, a happy combination of a death-and-revival hero, a Christian champion against Mohammedan heathendom, and a fit person to make over into an English national hero.[138]

According to Oriental legend, Saint George was torn into ten pieces, which were collected by the Archangel Michael, and restored to life. Saint George took the place of Summer in the ancient ritual, and the Saracen or Turkish Knight, the place of Winter. We are not surprised to see Saint George transform himself into Prince George and King George under the Hanoverians; nor the Saracen into Napoleon, the standard English bogeyman from 1790 to 1815. We should like to know more of the pageant given before Emperor Sigismund and Henry V at Windsor in 1416—a pageant, probably a pantomime of Saint George; we should welcome evidence of dialogue, but we have no such evidence.[139] The Guilds of Saint George all over England, which every year gave elaborate processions in honor of their patron, must eagerly have seized upon dialogue, whatever its source and authorship. From 1400 to 1550 civic records mention the interest of the gentry in the Saint George and Robin Hood plays; from this time on these plays seem to have become the traditional amusement of the humbler classes.[140]

[137] J. B. Jevons, Folk-Lore, XXVII, 186–187.
[138] T. F. Ordish, Folk-Lore, II, 321–322; Tiddy, The Mummers' Play, 75.
[139] Ordish, Folk-Lore, II, 327.
[140] Tiddy, 91.

We shall probably never know the ultimate authorship of the texts of the mummers' plays. Their striking similarity in certain details, however, even in evident corruptions, which in many cases are corruptions of passages which, because unintelligible to the unlettered folk who repeated them, easily became garbled in various ways in various localities, is proof that there must have been one or more versions which met with pretty general approval. This is nowhere more plainly seen than in the Doctor's traditional chatter about "The itch, the stitch, the palsy and the gout," to which the fancy of the folk in its love of topsy-turveydom has added a mass of nonsense cures.[141] The folk-play seems to have borrowed the vice, or fool, from the miracle-play; a mass of miscellaneous matter from romance, pseudo-history, and local legends; and even, in some Dorset versions, ballads and bits of regularly composed plays and operas.[142] The mummers' play is a carryall—a mixture which accurately represents folk-taste; whereas the variations in a given folk-song show a true artistic impulse on the part of the singer, his choice of a particularly fine phrase or plaintive cadence, the mummers' plays show no conscious artistic improvement.[143] They are everywhere corrupted, but nowhere in exactly the same way. In *The Return of the Native*, for instance, we do not find characters which are present in many folk-plays: the fool, or jester, usually called Jack Finney, or Vinney; Old Bet, the shrewish wife of Father Christmas, Fair Sabra, the King of Egypt's daughter, and the Dragon. But in the Saint George play which the Hardy Players presented at Dorchester in 1923, all these were present except Old Bet.[144] Neither of these plays exhibits the corruptions of some other Dorset plays: one of the latter contains the ballad of the "Serving-Man and the Husbandman"; another, an extended quotation from Ad-

---

[141] Tiddy, 88–89.
[142] *Ibid.*, 82–83, 85.
[143] *Ibid.*, 85.
[144] J. S. Brennecke, Jr. *Life of Thomas Hardy*, 20; Tiddy, 163–168; J. S. Udal, *Folk-Lore Record*, III, Pt. I, 97–102.

dison's *Rosamunde*.[145] Nor is either of these versions composite, in the sense that a Dorset play collected by Mr. Udal is composite. In this version, after Saint George has slain one after the other Captain Bluster, Gracious King, General Valentine, and Colonel Spring, Saint Patrick—who belongs to an entirely different story, the story of the Seven Champions of Christendom—intervenes and gets the doctor, who as always proceeds to bring the victims to life. Then enters Old Bet, who as Father Christmas's wife, is only a duplication of the old fellow himself, both of them representing the Old Year; and a scene of broad farce follows.[146] Saint George is the victor in the play in *The Return of the Native;* in other folk-plays the victor may be King George or Prince George, both Hanoverian "improvements"; George the Third, as in a Somerset play; the "Royal Prussian King," Bold Robin Hood, Slasher, Sergeant Slaughter, and so on![147] The unsuccessful champion, who was originally the ritual victim, is variously called the Turkish Knight, the Turkey Champion, the King of Egypt, the Indian King, Alexander, Bold Slasher (although in some plays he is the victor), the Valiant Soldier, Jack Finney or Vinney, and Beelzebub or Belsey Bob![148] In one Oxfordshire play, Bonaparte enters, stick in hand, announcing that he has just come from Thumberloo—a portmanteau word that indicates the mixture of Cumberland and Waterloo, and shows how a text may be filled with mere amusing nonsense.[149] In the plays of the southern counties, where Napoleon was most feared, Boney plays an important part.[150] Strange to say, the Corsican ogre does not find his way into Hardy's mummers' plays.

On the whole, the mummers' play in *The Return of the Native* is considerably closer to the primitive source of folk-drama, we may safely believe, than the majority of extant

[145] Tiddy, 83–85.
[146] J. S. Udal, *Folk-Lore Record,* Vol. III, Pt. I, 93–97.
[147] A. R. Wright, *Folk-Lore,* XXXV, 97.
[148] *Ibid.,* XXXV, 97.
[149] Tiddy, 219–221.
[150] *Ibid.,* 81.

folk-plays. It has more dignity, less boisterous humor, and almost no scenes of sheer nonsense and topsy-turveydom. It begins with the entrance of Father Christmas, whose apology for his sudden entrance, "welcome or welcome not," may well date back to Puritan days.[151] His plea, ". . . give us space to rhyme," may once have run, "give us space to ride," and so may derive from an original connection of dialogue with the old Saint George Ridings.[152] But the boasting speeches of the combatants are an unvarying feature of all folk-plays. In Hardy's play we do not have the excuse given in so many other Dorset plays that the victors call in the doctor and allow the victims to be resuscitated because they "feel for the wives and families of those men you have slain." [153] This excuse, be it remembered, is the surest indication of the ritual origin of the folk-play.

It has been said that the mummers' play is not all Saint George and the Dragon; it is not all anything, but an amalgam of primitive ritual with many different elements. In one respect, however, it is antiquity itself; we refer to the manner of acting, the use of strictly traditional gestures, costumes, and mode of declamation. Father Christmas is always a humpbacked old man. A solemn gait, gesture, or tone of voice may accompany a funny speech, giving an air of unmistakable grotesquerie to the performance. It matters not; the acting is as old as the sword dance itself, and has been kept as strictly traditional as the most ardent devotee of ritual could desire.[154] Hardy shows us the preparations for the mummers' play, the unenthusiastic but careful adherence to tradition, and the exclusion of women, a difficulty which Eustacia avoided by bribing Charley to let her play the Turkish Knight. The usual white linen costumes were worn, but they were gayly decorated with rosettes and bows of bright ribbons, each girl trying to make her sweetheart's costume more effective than the others', much to the dismay

---

151 Tiddy, 81; *The Return of the Native,* Book II, Chap. V.
152 *The Return of the Native,* Book II, Chap. V; Tiddy, 86.
153 J. S. Udal, *F. L. Record,* III, Pt. I, 96–97.
154 Ordish, *Folk-Lore,* II, 334.

of the unfortunate mummers. Only the Doctor in his long, dark gown, carrying his inevitable bottle of physic, and old Father Christmas were exempt from this shameful feminine tyranny. The older generation of mummers undertook to coach the new players; Fairway prompted from memory, now stopping frequently to relate stories of the glorious presentations of an earlier day, now correcting a false gait or gesture.[155] Let us look on at the moment the Egdon mummers, Eustacia among them, are admitted to the Yeobrights' front sitting-room, at the conclusion of the dance of "The Devil's Dream":

Hump-backed Father Christmas then made a complete entry, swinging his huge club, and in a general way clearing the stage for the actors proper, while he informed the company in smart verse that he was come, welcome or welcome not; concluding his speech with:

"Make room, make room, my gallant boys,
    And give us space to rhyme;
    We've come to show Saint George's play,
    Upon this Christmas time."

The guests were now arranging themselves at one end of the room . . . and the play began. First of those outside the Valiant Soldier entered, in the interest of Saint George—

"Here come I, the valiant soldier;
    Slasher is my name:"

and so on. This speech concluded with a challenge to the infidel, at the end of which it was Eustacia's duty to enter as the Turkish Knight. . . . With no apparent effort or backwardness she came in, beginning—

"Here come I, a Turkish Knight,
    Who learnt in Turkish land to fight;
    I'll fight this man with courage bold:
    If his blood's hot, I'll make it cold!"

. . . Meanwhile Jim Starks as the Valiant Soldier had come forward, and, with a glare upon the Turk, replied—

"If, then, thou art that Turkish Knight,
    Draw out thy sword, and let us fight!"

[155] *The Return of the Native,* Book II, Chap. IV.

And fight they did; the issue of the combat being that the Valiant Soldier was slain by a preternaturally inadequate thrust from Eustacia, Jim, in his ardour for genuine histrionic art, coming down like a log upon the stone floor with force enough to dislocate his shoulder. Then, after more words from the Turkish Knight, rather too faintly delivered, and statements that he'd fight Saint George and all his crew, Saint George himself magnificently entered with the well-known flourish—

> "Here come I, Saint George, the valiant man,
>> With naked sword and spear in hand,
> Who fought the dragon and brought him to the slaughter,
> And by this won fair Sabra, the King of Egypt's daughter;
>> What mortal man would dare to stand
>> Before me with my sword in hand?"

This was the lad who had first recognized Eustacia; and when she now, as the Turk, replied with suitable defiance, and at once began the combat, the young fellow took especial care to use his sword as gently as possible. Being wounded, the Knight fell upon one knee, according to the direction. The Doctor now entered, restored the Knight by giving him a draught from the bottle which he carried, and the fight was again resumed, the Turk sinking by degrees until quite overcome—dying as hard in this venerable drama as he is said to do at the present day.

This gradual sinking to earth was, in fact, one reason why Eustacia had thought that the part of the Turkish Knight, though not the shortest, would suit her best. A direct fall from upright to horizontal, which was the end of the other fighting characters, was not an elegant nor decorous part for a girl. But it was easy to die like a Turk, by a dogged decline.[156]

The play proceeded between the Saracen, the Doctor, Saint George, and Father Christmas; Eustacia had no further part nor interest in it. Her eyes fixed upon Clym Yeobright's face, whose sadness and brooding mystery troubled her. The traditional close to the play, and the polite, but phlegmatic reception accorded it are admirably recorded by Hardy:

---

[156] *Ibid.*, Book II, Chap. V.

The remainder of the play ended: the Saracen's head was cut off, and Saint George stood as victor. Nobody commented, any more than they would have commented on the fact of mushrooms coming in autumn or snowdrops in spring. They took the piece as phlegmatically as did the actors themselves. It was a phase of cheerfulness which was, as a matter of course, to be passed through every Christmas; and there was no more to be said.

They sang the plaintive chant which follows the play, during which all the dead men rise to their feet in a silent and awful manner, like the ghosts of Napoleon's soldiers in the Midnight Review. . . . [157]

In this impressive close, the victims are, as in so many folk-plays, revivified. Their resurrection is not, in this case, a particularly jolly matter; nor is this a typical present-day folk-play. It is more dignified and solemn, less farcical, quite lacking in the nonsense that abounds in most extant mummers' plays. Hardy was present in 1923 at the Dorchester presentation of a more elaborate play than this version in *The Return of the Native.* Here were the players in the conventional white linen costumes gayly bedecked with rosettes of ribbons, their visors covered with streamers. Here was old Father Christmas, club in hand, the Prologue, the Dragon, his tail carefully carried in his hand, the luscious Sabra herself, the four valiant British saints—George, Andrew, Patrick, and David—Captain Slasher, the Doctor who brought all the fallen to life with his wonderful pills, and the Black Prince of Paradine. Even the critics, hardened to theatrical thrills, enjoyed the whole-hearted fun of the performance.[158]

In a conversation with William Archer, Hardy described the manner in which the mummers whom his elders remembered used to enter, long staff in one hand and a wooden sword in the other; they would, he said, intone their words, punctuating them at times by nicking the sword vigorously

---

[157] *Ibid.,* Book II, Chap. VI.

[158] Ivor Brown, *Saturday Review* (London), Dec. 8, 1923, p. 614; Ernest Brennecke, Jr., *The Life of Thomas Hardy,* 20; Authorized programme of the presentation of The Play of Saint George by the Hardy Players, Dorchester, Nov. 29, 1923: Version arranged by Mr. T. H. Tilley, Hon. Stage Mgr.

against the staff.[159] At the same interview he described the
old-time popularity of the mummers, so great that well-to-do
farmers did not disdain to take part. Fair Sabra was always
played by a boy, women were excluded as a matter of course,
and if the mummers of one village attempted to play in another, there was sure to be a fight! [160]

At this memorable Dorchester performance by the Hardy
Players in 1923, another folk-play was presented. "O Jan!
O Jan! O Jan!" has come down directly from the wooing
dialogue of the Middle Ages, as found in the dramatic song,
"The Keys of Canterbury," sometimes called "The Keys
of Heaven." [161] It recounts the familiar situation of the distracted lover, who, having offered the fair lady all that he
possesses—houses, lands, gowns, and jewels—is advised by
the old rustic Jan to offer her the keys to his heart, and need-
less to say, is duly accepted. The old folk-song, "The Keys of
Heaven," used to be danced with appropriate dramatic action by a man and wife.[162] It is still found as a children's
singing-game: one tune is a lovely Æolian air built on five
ascending notes of the scale.[163] Mr. W. R. Bawler, gorgeous
in velveteens, mimed Jan admirably, his broad Wessex vow-
els making the wooing all the jollier.[164] The piece was a
recension of a performance Hardy witnessed as a boy of
four at his father's house.[165]

Although written expressly for the 1923 presentation of
the Dorchester Hardy Players, *The Famous Tragedy of the
Queen of Cornwall at Tintagel in Lyonesse* can hardly be
termed a folk-play. The complaint of the critics who witnessed the performance that the theme and mode of presentation were, to some degree, incongruous, has probably

[159] William Archer, *Real Conversations* . . . 34–36.
[160] *Ibid.*
[161] C. R. Baskervill, *The Elizabethan Jig*, 249–252; Sharp, *English Folk-Song: Some Conclusions*, 106; E. T. Bell, *Music for One Hundred Figure and Character Dances*, 50.
[162] Sharp, *English Folk-Song: Some Conclusions*, 106.
[163] C. J. Sharp, *One Hundred English Folk-Songs*, No. 66, Notes, pp. xxxiv–xxxv.
[164] Programme, Part II, Corn Exchange, Dorchester, Nov. 29, 1923; Ivor Brown, *Saturday Review* (London), Dec. 8, 1923.
[165] Ernest Brennecke, Jr., *The Life of Thomas Hardy*, 19–20, 79.

some foundation, but betrays also a failure to grasp the poet's conception of his subject. Hardy chose to treat the theme not as a drama of passion and heartbreak sweeping us into its turbulent torrent of sorrow, but as a ghostly puppet-show conjured up for us by Merlin the Enchanter and interpreted to us by the shades of dead Cornishmen and Cornish women. Hardy was drawn to the theme in several ways. Tintagel Castle held tender memories for him; once while going through the castle, he and Miss Gifford were inadvertently locked in, and only escaped spending the night there by waving their handkerchiefs to the cottagers in the valley.[166] Tintagel had also a purely antiquarian interest for the poet.

The folklorist Jacob Grimm describes for us a thirteenth-century *wihtelspiel* in which ghostly puppets were set in action before the eyes of spectators, and explains its origin as perhaps due to the small lares, kobolds, or household sprites, exquisitely carved of boxwood, which were kept in the innermost part of the ancient Teutonic dwelling.[167] The word "wight" originally signifying "creature," came on one hand to mean "little creature," or "thing," in an affectionate sense, and was applied to children; on the other, to mean a "demon," "ghost." It is a fascinating hypothesis that these household gods, on the coming of Christianity, were hidden away out of a lingering sense of their power and sacredness, then were brought forth and used in a mere ghostly puppet-play! [168]

The Queen of Cornwall contains many folklore motifs already familiar to Hardy readers. Here is the love-potion,[169] the master-enchanter, omens and premonitions of death,[170] and Nature's travail in sympathy with the persons of the tragedy. Here are ancient minstrels, Tristram dis-

---

[166] F. E. Hardy, *The Early Life of Thomas Hardy*, 103.
[167] Grimm-Stallybrass, III, 441, Note.
[168] *Ibid.*, II, 441–442, Note; II, 501; III, 1034.
[169] Scene VI.
[170] Scenes XIX, XX.

guised as a harper, and some of the rude "historical music" we heard in the skimmity-ride in *The Mayor of Caster-bridge*—rams'-horns, crouds, humstrums [171]—here is that court rudeness which lasted well into medieval times—rudeness so great that at the time of the marriage of Mary, daughter of Henry IV of France, the Queen herself could hardly pass by the King's room or the men's halls without receiving some affront.[172] The life at the court of Mark is extremely primitive, and the drama exhibits old folklore motifs stripped bare of their trappings of romance, and freed from all subtle psychological analysis of human emotions and motives. This version of the story is less beautiful and polished than many others, but it is also stronger, for it aims at a totally different effect. Its action is extremely simple, in spite of the poet's somewhat unsuccessful attempt to telescope two conflicting versions of the tale. The unities are carefully preserved; the time of presentation conforms very closely to the time-scheme of the action itself. The style and diction are extremely archaic, sometimes to harshness and awkwardness. There is constant play of alliteration, and the occasional echo of a refrain already familiar to us, as in Tristram's echoing of Deor's lament, "That was o'ercome; so may this be!" [173] There is an effect of starkness and grandeur rather than of passion, in this short and broken action. The shades of dead old Cornishmen and dead Cornish women chant the events up to the beginning of the action; they are a chorus supplying needed information and interpreting the whole. At the close of the play it is Merlin, a ghostly figure with a white wand, who still seems to dominate the scene. The drama seems a strange dream conjured up by the enchanter. Is he not inviting us to pause and muse a moment on the irony of life and the exquisite irony of love?

[171] *The Queen of Cornwall*, Scene II; *The Mayor of Casterbridge*, Chap. XXXIX.
[172] *The Queen of Cornwall*, Scene XII; Wm. Hone's *Table-Book*, I, 389–390, quoting Ex. Ms. Coll. Ashmol. Mus. Oxford, John Aubrey, 1678.
[173] Scene XVIII.

Is he not performing before our very eyes a piece of magic?
His words are noble, reminding us of that other enchanter
Prospero:

> "I saw these times I represent,
> Watched, gauged them as they came and went,
> Being ageless, deathless. . . ." [174]

The Queen of Cornwall was a remarkable achievement for
a poet eighty-three years of age. It is folk only in the sense
that it was written for the mummers and performed by
them.

Hardy's interest in folk-music and folk-plays was keen
and profound. He made no attempt to gloss over the cru-
dities of either; he took both as he found them and gave
them the rôles in novel, poem, and play that they filled in
life. Joseph Poorgrass at the sheep-shearing supper trilling
out his song with crazed voice, Dick Dewy and Fancy Day
leading the dance to "Follow My Lover," the mummers sol-
emnly going through their play for the quiet delectation of
the Egdon folk—all are genre pictures of simplicity and
charm. No one who has experienced the charm of the old
ballads and songs but will feel grateful to Hardy for the antiquarian spirit which prized old airs, old dances, and old
plays. This antiquarianism is a sort of humanism—it is a confession that whatever has pleased the folk century after
century must needs be worth cherishing.

[174] Prologue: *The Queen of Cornwall.*

X

FOLK WIT AND WISDOM

~~~~~~

Much of peasant speech is distinguished by the quality of good conversation the world over—by keen observation, spontaneous feeling, and a fresh use of words. Dialect speakers often give us phrases instinct with passion and imagination, a sort of unshaped poetry powerfully sincere and unforced. Let us grant that this free use of imagery draws upon an extremely limited world; let us admit, however, that, although it does not roam to distant places and heretofore unimagined things, it is intensely immediate and has the seal of a living experience upon it. The humor of the folk, for instance, is sometimes too heavy, too unequal to the keen observation of character which underlies it; but occasionally a phrase is dropped which shows all the countryman's genius for sensing fine shades of temperament and personality. This passionate faith in the force and sincerity of peasant speech was a religion with Wordsworth and a delight to Synge. Both poets knew better than to sentimentalize over "humble life"; both exulted in the courage with which a leech-gatherer or a hunted, wildly romancing boy could meet life. It will not do for us to view the raciest country wit with overmuch surprise. While we smile patronizingly, some dialect speaker may be hitting us off to perfection, putting his finger instinctively upon the very idiosyncrasy which we prided ourselves was a mark of high sophistication. This folk wit is the salt of most of our proverbs; what more are they than essentially sound observation touched to finer form? Many of our best proverbs come to us with the smell of the field and the barn upon them. We have the saying, for instance, "God never sends mouths but he sends meat,"[1] which Hardy uses in the early novel, *Desperate Remedies:* The scullery-maid has remarked that, "God A'mighty always sends bread as well as children," and is met with the rejoinder, "But 'tis bread to one house, and the children to another!"[2] Mother Cuxsom says it best of all when she remarks, "Ay, where the pigs be many, the wash runs thin."[3]

It is remarkable how much new life rustic wording can give a proverb which has grown stale with use. There is grim satisfaction in the aged maltster's reflection that "Crooked folk will last a long while."[4] There is sound common sense in Granny Martin's comment on her grandson St. Cleeve's aristocratic aloofness from all village pursuits:

"But I told his mother how 'twould be—marrying a man so many notches above her. The child would be sure to chaw high, like his father!"[5]

The familiar saying that "It is better to bow than to break"[6] is closely related to a curious West African proverb, " 'I have forgotten thy name' is better than 'I know thee not.' "[7] It is in this spirit that Coggan advised Oak to be friends with Troy, when in the bitterness of the realization that Troy had married Bathsheba, the shepherd had angrily refused the half-crown tossed him to drink the married couple's health. Pocketing the coin, Coggan remarked that Troy was going to be their master, and therefore, . . . " 'Tis well to say 'Friend' outwardly, though you say 'Troublehouse' within!"[8] When Phillotson had allowed Sue

---

[1] F. Ray, *Collection of Proverbs,* 1678 ed., page 178.
[2] Chap. XIII.
[3] *The Mayor of Casterbridge,* Chap. XIII.
[4] *Far from the Madding Crowd,* Chap. VIII.
[5] *Two on a Tower,* Chap. II; Wright, *English Dial. Dict.,* I, 570, Note.
[6] Ray, 104, 363.
[7] Dwight E. Marvin, *Curiosities in Proverbs,* 357.
[8] *Far from the Madding Crowd,* Chap. XXXV.

to go away to Jude, Arabella reproached him coarsely;[9] the proverb "It's a foul bird that fyleth his own nest" is as old as Saxo Grammaticus [10] and *The Owl and the Nightingale*,[11] and is merely veneered, not changed by Gallic wit in a favorite saying of Napoleon, "Il faut laver son linge en famille." [12] Geoffrey Day betters the common proverb that "Beauty draws more than oxen" [13] when, having perceived Dick Dewy's surreptitious attempts to hold Fancy's hand under the tablecloth, he decides to nip this infatuation in the bud, and remarks with the melancholy air of one who has just made a philosophical discovery, "A young woman's face will turn the north wind, Master Richard; my heart if 'twon't!" [14] We may know that "Penniless is impotent" [15] and that "A man without money is a bow without an arrow," [16] but neither comes home so keenly to us as does Enoch's musing excuse for suffocating the bees: "But 'tis the money . . . without money man is a shadder!" [17] Both flighty Joan Durbeyfield and sensible Elizabeth-Jane felt that it was well to "be kin to a coach," [18] or as the Scotch have it, to "be sib to siller!" [19]

Squire Everard's indignation with his daughter for refusing a prudent match was full of homely wisdom: he warns her, "Better a little fire to warm 'ee than a great fire to burn 'ee!" [20] The countryman has his own way of saying things: Tranter Dewy warned Dick not to fall in love with a girl whom he could not hope to marry, and met his fretful reproach with true folk wit:

"Pooh, father! You just repeat what all the common world says; that's all you do."

[9] *Jude*, Part V, Chap. VIII.
[10] Saxo, V, 30; York-Powell's ed., Intro. lxxxv.
[11] Vv. 99–100.
[12] W. K. Kelly, *Proverbs of All Nations*, 109.
[13] Ray, 2; J. Long, *Folk-Lore Record*, Pt.. I, Vol. III, page 76.
[14] *Under the Greenwood Tree*, Part II, Chap. VI.
[15] Capt. R. C. Temple, *Folk-Lore Journal*, III, 25.
[16] Bohn's *Handbook of Proverbs*, 296.
[17] *Under the Greenwood Tree*, Part IV, Chap. II.
[18] *Tess*, Chap. IV; *The Mayor of Casterbridge*, Chap. V.
[19] Bohn's *Handbook of Proverbs*, 431.
[20] *A Changed Man*, "The Waiting Supper"; cf. Ray, 363; Kelly, 79.

"The world's a very sensible feller on things in jineral, Dick; a very sensible party indeed." [21]

We feel an instant loss in vividness and force when we consider the commonplace proverbs whose familiarity has worn them thin. The frothy novel, *A Laodicean,* is particularly full of these rather colorless sayings. It is here we meet the following: "Diamond cut diamond"; [22] "Beggars mustn't be choosers"; [23] "You mustn't look a gift-horse in the mouth," [24] a proverb which still wears remarkably well; "Any port in a storm"; [25] "It's never too late to mend"; [26] "There's many a slip 'twixt cup and lip," [27] an adage as familiar to the Greeks as to ourselves,[28] and put most strikingly by the Weatherbury rustics in their comment on Bathsheba's marriage to Troy, " 'Twill be a gallant life, but may bring some trouble between the mirth . . ."; [29] "Every dog has his day," or as the Warwickshire folk add, "and a cat two afternoons!"; [30] "Cat will after kind," [31] spoken of charming Rosalind; "When the cat's away . . ."; [32] and others too numerous to name. Elsewhere rather formal proverbs occur: for instance, "Blood is thicker than water"; [33] "Marry in haste and repent at leisure"; [34] "What's done cannot be undone"; [35] "All's fair in love . . ."; [36]

[21] *Under the Greenwood Tree,* Part II, Chap. VIII; Ray, 236.
[22] Book II, Chap. V; cf. Bohn, 343.
[23] Book V, Chap. III; Ray, 99.
[24] Book V, Chap. V; *Folk-Lore,* XII, 279; Ray, 146.
[25] Book I, Chap. IV; York-Powell's ed. *Saxo-Grammaticus,* Intro. lxxxvii.
[26] Book VI, Chap. III; *Desperate Remedies,* Chap. XVII; Ray, 165.
[27] Book V, Chap. XI; cf. Ray, 121; V. S. Lean, *Collectanea,* IV, 143.
[28] Ray, 121.
[29] *Far from the Madding Crowd,* Chap. XXX.
[30] *A Laodicean,* Book III, Chap. VI; G. F. Northall, *English Dialect Society,* Vol. 73, page 13; Ray, 126.
[31] *A Laodicean,* Book VI, Chap. IV; *As You Like It,* III, 2; *Romeo and Juliet,* IV, 4, 11; Ray, 255.
[32] *A Laodicean,* Book II, Chapter II; *A Group of Noble Dames:* "The First Countess of Wessex"; Ray, 109; Kelly, 107.
[33] *A Group of Noble Dames:* "Anna, Lady Baxby"; Bohn, 332.
[34] *Jude,* Part V, Chap. IV; *A Changed Man,* "The Waiting Supper"; Ray 56, 403.
[35] *A Group of Noble Dames:* "The First Countess of Wessex"; Ray, 121.
[36] *A Pair of Blue Eyes,* Chap. IX.

"All's well that ends well"; [37] "It never rains but it pours"; [38] "One fool makes many"; [39] "Honesty's the best policy"; [40] "Give a dog a bad name, and hang him"; [41] "Still waters run deep," spoken by Hardy of the deceptively demure heroine of "A Mere Interlude"; [42] "New lords, new laws"; [43] and so on. It would be tiresome to enumerate all the familiar proverbs used by Hardy, and would serve no useful purpose; some, however, are interesting in and of themselves. The saying, "It's an ill wind that blows nobody good," for instance, has a special version in Cornwall, where the rocky coast is strewn with wrecks to be salvaged! [44] The sentinel at Salamanca, incredulous of Mrs. Prescott's protestations that she is an officer's wife, and yet does not know the countersign, remarks sourly,

"Where there's war there's women, and where there's women there's trouble!" [45]

The origin of the proverb is attributed to St. Columba, who is said to have forbidden both cows and women on the island of Iona, saying, "Where there's a cow, there is a woman, and where there is a woman, there's mischief." [46] In his disgust at the discovery of Stephen Smith's plebeian origin, the Reverend Mr. Swancourt exclaimed bitterly, "Let a beast be lord of beasts, and his crib shall stand at the king's mess," [47] an adage which is often put with humorous force, "Every ass thinks himself worthy to stand with the king's horses," or in still more homely phrase, "A humble-bee in a cowturd thinks himself a king." [48] But these proverbs

[37] *A Changed Man:* "The Romantic Adventures of a Milkmaid"; "The Waiting Supper"; Ray, 132.
[38] *The Dynasts,* Part Second, Act V, Scene II; Kelly, 56.
[39] *The Dynasts,* Part First, Act II, Scene IV; Ray, 10.
[40] *Desperate Remedies,* Chap. XVII; Bohn, 408.
[41] *The Dynasts,* Part Second, Act VI, Scene VII; Kelly, 162; Ray, 126, 180.
[42] *A Changed Man;* Ray, 206, 255; *2 Henry VI,* III, I, 53.
[43] *Far from the Madding Crowd,* Chap. VIII; Ray, 281.
[44] *The Dynasts,* Part First, Act I, Scene V; Ray, p. 1.
[45] *The Dynasts,* Part Third, Act I, Scene II; Ray, 60, 355.
[46] Lean's *Collectanea,* I, 475.
[47] *A Pair of Blue Eyes,* Chap. IX; *Hamlet,* V, II, 87.
[48] Ray, 95, 14.

which smack of field and soil are not for Elfride's dainty ears; they are like the delightfully wicked stories which the rector is always on the verge of telling but dare not tell! More in character is Swancourt's appeal to Catullus's epigram on women, " 'Mulier cupido quod dicit amanti, in vento' . . . what a memory mine is!" [49]

It is a relief to turn from these formal proverbs to sayings in which actual folklore is embedded; many sayings reflect the belief in omens, witchcraft, fairies, and ghosts; many bring to light a more primitive order of society—a simpler social order, outmoded laws, quaint punishments, half-hidden references to legend and "far-off, unhappy things." The superstitions of our ancestors live on in these proverbs; we lip them, and scarcely stop to think what startling things we are saying!

The proverbial dilatoriness of the "watched pot" [50] calls to mind the ill luck of watching any one out of sight, the penalty for which is never to see that person again.[51] It was the opinion of the rustics around the great bonfire on Egdon Heath that Eustacia Vye was as "deep as the North Star." [52] The expression perhaps comes from the saying, "Cold weather and knaves come out of the North," [53] yet fools are also said to hail from this point of the compass; witness Henchard's angry injunction to Elizabeth-Jane not to be "a no'thern simpleton!" [54] The North was the abode of giants, the Scandinavian Hell, and the northern side of the churchyard formerly was reserved for the burial of the reprobate and unbaptized! [55] Several proverbs on the good luck of dirt are familiar to us: "Dirt bodes luck," [56] "Every man must eat a peck of dirt before he dies," [56] and "The more muck, the more money." [56] It is likely that Matt

---

[49] *A Pair of Blue Eyes,* Chap. XXVII; Lean, Vol. II, Part II, 813, 887.
[50] *Wessex Tales:* "Interlopers at the Knap."
[51] Wm. Henderson, *Folk-Lore of the Northern Counties,* 117.
[52] *The Return of the Native,* Book I, Chap. V.
[53] Ray, 19; Lean's *Collectanea,* Vol. II, Part II, 822.
[54] *The Mayor of Casterbridge,* Chap. XXVII.
[55] Ellis's Brand, II, 295; Henderson, *Folklore of the Northern Counties,* 61; *Denham Tracts,* II, 38, 65; Grimm-Stallybrass, I, 34 and IV, 1297.
[56] Ray, 95; Lean, Vol. II, Part II, 39; Lean, Vol. III, 448.

Clark was alluding to this belief when he apologized to Oak for dropping his slice of bacon in the road, saying, "There, 'tis clane dirt, and we all know what that is . . . !" [57] Pennyways, the bailiff dismissed by Bathsheba, complained, ". . . And she've a few soft corners of her mind, though I've never been able to get into one, the devil's in it!" [58] The expression seems originally to have been a sort of formula, used to ward off some evil spell, and perhaps equivalent to, "I know you, witch!" We still say, "The devil you say," "Devil a bit," "what the devil," and the like, to express extreme incredulity.[59] In popular speech "hell" was at one time any dark hole or corner,[60] and our German cousins call the Devil the *Gott-sei-bei-uns!* invoking, as it were, a countercharm to his dreaded name! [61] Having sought shelter in the cottage of Elizabeth Endorfield, that "deep body," Fancy Day was rather startled to discover that the "white witch" knew all about her romance with Dick Dewy, and received the assurance, which we still humorously give to children, that a little bird had told her the secret.[62] Speaking birds are a familiar device in folklore; we remember the cranes of Ibycus, the Bird of Siegfried, and the numerous speaking birds in the English and Scottish ballads.[63] Perhaps the same bit of folklore will serve to explain the text in Ecclesiastes: "Curse not the king, no, not in thy thought; for a bird of the air shall carry the voice, and that which hath wings shall tell the matter."[64]

The elaborate folklore of "baby-bringers" is referred to in the following delightful conversation: Avice the Second is trying to explain to her daughter Jocelyn Pierston's long intimacy with their family:

---

[57] *Far from the Madding Crowd,* Chap. VIII.
[58] *Ibid.,* Chap. LII.
[59] Grimm-Stallybrass, II, 1015, Note I.
[60] *Ibid.,* IV, 1539.
[61] *Ibid.,* IV, 1606.
[62] *Under the Greenwood Tree,* Part IV, Chap. III; G. F. Northall, *E. D. S.* Vol. 73, page 20.
[63] Grimm-Stallybrass, III, 1045; James Napier, *Folk-Lore Record,* II, 107; Wimberly, *Folk-Lore in the English and Scottish Ballads,* 66–67.
[64] Eccles. X, 20.

"And you actually lived in Sylvania Castle yourself, Mr. Pierston," asked the daughter. "Was it long ago? . . . It must have been when I was away . . . or when I was very little."
"I don't think you were away." (Pierston.)
"But I don't think I could have been here."

.   .   .   .

"I think she was hiding herself in the parsley-bed," said Avice's mother, blandly.[65]

The cabbage-patch and the gooseberry-bush occur in similar euphemistic formulas.[66] Parsley is one of the funeral plants with an elaborate lore of its own; along with the widespread belief that to transplant parsley will cause a member of the family to die[67] runs a closely related belief that a too luxuriant lettuce-bed will stop a young wife's bearing.[68]

There are several proverbs which carry us back to an old-fashioned domestic economy. When the choice spirits of Mixen Lane had caught sight of Henchard's new wife, they jested rudely but Nance Mockridge thought even this poor wasted creature too good for Henchard, and commented, "She'll wish her cake dough afore she's done of him. There's a bluebeardy look about 'en; and 'twill out in time!"[69] Matthew Moon made the same prophecy as to Bathsheba's affair with Sergeant Troy.[70] Shakespeare uses it of an undertaking which is sure to fail,[71] and there is the phrase "half-baked" used to denote a person lacking some of his wits. When Joseph Poorgrass in dice-play lost to Wildeve the hundred guineas Mrs. Yeobright had entrusted to him, he was moved—apparently for the first and the last time in his history—to veritable anger; he called Wildeve a "regular sharper," and the latter retorted contemptu-

[65] *The Well-Beloved*, Part III, Chap. III.
[66] Thomas, *Folk-Lore*, XI, 235; Dyer, *Folklore of Plants*, 26–27.
[67] Dyer, *op. cit.*, 139–140; Mrs. Gutch, *Folklore of Yorkshire*, 63–64; Brand, III, 113.
[68] Dyer, 73.
[69] *The Mayor of Casterbridge*, Chap. XIII.
[70] *Far from the Madding Crowd*, Chap. XXXIII.
[71] *Taming of the Shrew*, I, I, 110; cf. Wright, *Rustic Speech*, 166.

ously, "Poor chips-in-porridge, you are very unmannerly." [72]
The chip in the porridge which did neither good nor harm
to the cooking itself is no doubt the "John-herb," or "John-
indifferent," the herb gathered for magical purposes on
Midsummer Eve, as were also the medicinal herbs mandrake, mugwort, and King Fern.[73] It was commonly used
to denote an absolutely insignificant person.[74] The expression, "You'll come to a bit o' bread," used of poor Cainy
Ball when he was seized with a choking fit and could not get
out the momentous story of Bathsheba's meeting with Troy
in Bath,[75] is much like the "chips-in-porridge." The phrase,
"a pretty kettle of fish," [76] meaning a sorry predicament, is
a direct relic of the great salmon-feasts in the Border counties, at which the freshly caught salmon were thrown into
the cauldron full of boiling water saturated with brine.[77]

Usage has dulled the significance of some of our most
fascinating proverbs. When Arabella confessed to Jude
she had married him because she had been "eating her head
off" at home,[78] she was unconsciously satirizing herself;
for the phrase was originally used of an animal, particularly
a horse, whose feed cost more than it would bring,[79] and
which, therefore, was doomed. The brutality of fact often
becomes the humor of paradox. The saying, "Murder will
out" [80] looks innocent enough at first sight, but if we place
ourselves in imagination back in the sixteenth century, its
once terrible significance becomes apparent. Tradition had
it that the body of one murdered, especially of one done to
death by witchcraft, would bleed afresh and even cry out at

---

[72] *The Return of the Native,* Book III, Chap. VII; Ray, 234.
[73] Lean's *Collectanea,* Vol. II, Part II, 761, and IV, 199; Rendel Harris,
Ascent of Olympus, 67, 73, 89–90; Grimm-Stallybrass, I, 61; Ray, 234.
[74] E. M. Wright, *Rustic Speech and Folklore,* 161; *Folk-Lore Record,* IV,
166.
[75] *Far from the Madding Crowd,* Chap. XXXIII; Lean's *Collectanea,*
Vol. II, Part II, 840.
[76] *Wessex Tales:* "The Three Strangers"; *Under the Greenwood Tree,*
Part II, Chap. VIII; *Two on a Tower,* Chap. IX.
[77] Joseph Wright, *English Dialect Dictionary,* III, 427; Scott, *St. Ronan's
Well* (1824), Chap. XII.
[78] *Jude the Obscure,* Part I, Chap. IX.
[79] *Oxford Dictionary,* Vol. III, Part 1, page 21.
[80] *A Laodicean,* Book VI, Chap. III; Ray, 179, 343.

the approach of the guilty one.[81] Up to the eighteenth century it was unwise to confess to finding a dead body, as the finder was held for murder unless he could prove himself innocent! [82] There are proverbs which contain references to ancient criminal procedure and to forgotten punishments. The ignominious progress of the unfortunate offender from the whipping-post to the pillory is crystallized in our adage "from pillar to post"; [83] we have reversed the natural order (whipping-post to pillory) of this relic of hideous punishments. When Liddy asserted that she'd say it out "in black and white" [84] that her mistress could not possibly love a man like Troy, she was reflecting the medieval attitude of mind which had a superstitious faith in print, as in a miracle, an attitude which culminated in the notorious "benefit of clergy." According to this right, clerics, and later on, all who could read their neck-verse, thereby proving their learning, were branded in the hand and allowed to go free.[85] This amazing exemption, which lasted until 1827, could not have existed for centuries save for the fact that the great mass of the English people, of course, not knowing Latin, could not claim it. This is the idea back of Sammy Blore's comment on his friend Haymoss's learning: ". . . Well, the Lord save good scholars—and take just a bit o' care of them that bain't . . ." [86] Back to the days of feudalism also goes the saying, "Neck or nothing," [87] the most expressive part of which we have forgotten . . .

---

[81] Brand, *Popular Antiquities of Great Britain,* Ellis's ed., III, 229–231; *Richard III,* Act I, Scene II, 1, 55; Lean's *Collectanea,* Vol. II, Part II, 646; Webster, *Westward Ho,* IV, 4; Chaucer, *Prioress's Tale,* 122, etc.; Dalyell, *Darker Superstitions of Scotland,* 36–43; Rev. James Napier, *Folk-Lore, or Superstitious Beliefs in West of Scotland,* 85–86.
[82] *Folk-Lore,* XXVII, 249.
[83] *Far from the Madding Crowd,* Chap. XV; Lean's *Collectanea,* Vol. II, Part II, 925.
[84] *Far from the Madding Crowd,* Chap. XXX; J. Wright, *Provincial Dict.,* I, 216.
[85] Poland, *A Century of Reform,* 60; Pike, *History of Crime in England,* I, 314; *Denham Tracts,* I, 147; Brand, III, 382–383; Lean, Vol. II, Part II, 924.
[86] *Two on a Tower,* Chap. XIII; Cf. Poland, 60.
[87] *The Trumpet-Major,* Chap. XXXII; *The Dynasts,* Part Second, Act IV, Scene III.

"for the King loves no cripples." [88] In the days of feudal
military service the vassal had far better break his neck than
his legs or his back. This is one of the proverbs on the theme
of "Whole hog or none"; others are "In for a penny, in for
a pound," [89] "Nothing venture, nothing have," [90] and the
far more vivid saying of Troy's that he may as well be hung
for a sheep as for a lamb! [91] The latter carries us back a
full century, when the death-penalty for sheep-stealing had
just been with difficulty abolished.[92] Probably the most
curious relic of quaint punishments of olden times is the
adage "A rod in pickle" [93] for one. The Greek and Roman
proverbs to this effect may indicate that the rods used for
flogging were at one time salted in brine, or even in urine.[94]
Perhaps wives guilty of scolding or infidelity were "lapt in
wether's skin." [95] In "The Wife Lapped in Morel's Skin"
the skin of the horse in which the refractory wife was
wrapped after being flogged with rods, was salted; [96] it is
not a far cry to the old flogging with salted rods. In medieval
Holland, crops were sometimes fertilized with brine or
urine.[97]

Perhaps it is too fanciful to interpret the following
proverbs as echoes of medieval law and custom, but the
temptation to do so is exceedingly strong. Stephen Smith's
mother protested that her statements were true, "Or there's
no bread in nine loaves!" [98] a saying which brings to mind
the dishonest baker condemned to the pillory because he had

[88] Ray, 347; Bohn's *Handbook of Proverbs*, 457; *Denham Tracts*, II, 260–261.
[89] *The Mayor of Casterbridge*, Chap. XV; Kelly, 84.
[90] *A Changed Man:* "The Waiting Supper"; Ray, 214.
[91] *Far from the Madding Crowd*, Chap. XXVI; Ray, 350; Kelly, 85.
[92] Pike, II, 451.
[93] *A Changed Man:* "The Romantic Adventures of a Milkmaid"; Lean's *Collectanea*, II, Part II, 650; Carew Hazlitt, *Faiths and Folklore*, II, 607; Ray, 267; Barham's *Ingoldsby Legends;* cf. Swift, *Sid Hamet*.
[94] Wright, *English Dialect Dictionary*, V, 139; Lean, Vol. II, Part II, 650.
[95] Child's *English and Scottish Popular Ballads*, ed. 1888, Vol. V, No. 277, pages 104–107.
[96] Lean's *Collectanea*, Vol. II, Part II, 650.
[97] Carew Hazlitt, *Faiths and Folklore*, II, 607, quoting Hartlieb, 1651, *Legacie.*
[98] *A Pair of Blue Eyes*, Chap. X

filled his loaves with huge stones.[99] There seems to be a relic of the "right of sanctuary," too, in the jest at the expense of homely women, "The plain ones be as safe as churches. . . ."[100]

The strangest echoes of ancient religions and superstitions survive in certain proverbs. When Arabella called any who might doubt Jude's paternity of Little Father Time "brimstone liars,"[101] she was, without knowing it, swearing a tremendous oath. It has become a phrase of coarse abuse, for we hear of "brimstone hussies," "a brimstone bitch," and the like.[102] But the brimstone oath was to the Romans an oath by all that they held most sacred; Roman houses were anciently hallowed against evil spirits with brimstone.[103] Far more primitive is Farmer Bawtree's comparison of the changeable couple who would one hour be throwing things at each other, and the next be singing "The Spotted Cow" . . . together "as peaceable as two holy twins. . . ."[104] The sacredness, with therefore, of course, the taboo of twins is the distinguishing mark of the most primitive savage religions today, and is one of the most fascinating problems of comparative folklore.[105] There are references to nursery rhymes ringing modern changes upon the stuff of folklore: when Jude, for instance, had recited the Nicene and the Apostles' Creeds in Latin for the crowd in the tavern, and been applauded for it, he turned angrily upon them:

"You pack of fools!" he cried. "Which one of you knows whether I have said it or no? It might have been the Ratcatcher's Daughter in double Dutch for all that your besotted heads can tell!"[106]

Verses like this or "The House that Jack Built" and other cumulative pieces seem to hark back to primitive times, when

[99] Pike, *History of Crime in England*, I, 239.
[100] *Tess*, Chap. XIV.
[101] *Jude the Obscure*, Part V, Chap. III.
[102] Wright, *English Dialect Dictionary*, I, 403.
[103] Ellis's Brand, III, 83–84.
[104] *The Woodlanders*, Chap. XLVIII.
[105] Rendel Harris, *Boanerges*, 103.
[106] *Jude*, Part II, Chap. VII.

charms were uttered, each time with repetition of all that
had gone before, as if the spell which had fallen on some object which the speaker wished to use had to be removed or
averted step by step, conciliating, as it were, a sequence of
powers.[107] To talk Dutch is to use high-flown language, and to
talk double Dutch, it may be gathered, is to talk completely
over one's head! [108] In another proverb Van Amburgh,[109] a
famous American menagerie exhibitor who visited English
fairs, seems to have replaced our old friend Humpty Dumpty,
who, in his turn, is a humorous personification of the egg, the
primitive symbol of the world and the mystery of life.[110]
Audrey Satchel's apprehensive bride-to-be would not let
him leave the church when the parson thought him too drunk
to be married; she realized that once he left there unmarried, "all Van Amburgh's horses won't drag him back
again!" [111]

The countryman likes a picture-making phrase: Fancy
Day was described as that "figure of fun" who is "just
husband-high." [112] But a little later, the Mellstock string
band and choir justly attributed their fall to Fancy, "the
bitter weed." [113] The phrase is applied to the bark of the
poplar, and also to a mischief-maker or mar-all.[114] When
Stephen Smith reproached his mother for her respectful
curtsy to the vicar, she retorted with righteous indignation, "What else could I do with the man to get rid of
him, banging it into me and your father by side and by seam
about his greatness? . . ." [115] A "tongue-banging" is a
scolding,[116] and we have the old proverb "to bang compliments backwards and forwards like two asses scrubbing one

[107] Lina B. Eckenstein, *Comparative Studies in Nursery Rhymes*, 114–122;
E. B. Tylor, *Primitive Culture*, II, 86.
[108] E. M. Wright, *Rustic Speech* . . . , 159; Lean's *Collectanea*, Vol. II,
Part II, 799, 907.
[109] Frost, *The Old Showman and the London Fairs*, 260, 368.
[110] Eckenstein, 104–114.
[111] *Life's Little Ironies:* "Andrey Satchel and the Parson and the Clerk."
[112] *Under the Greenwood Tree*, Part I, Chap. III.
[113] *Ibid.*, Part II, Chap. II.
[114] Dyer, *Folklore of Plants*, 174.
[115] *A Pair of Blue Eyes*, Chap. X.
[116] G. F. Northall, *Folk-Phrases of Four Counties*, E.D.S., Vol. 73, p. 7.

another!" [117] To have one's banns called is to be "called home," [118] a phrase which suggests the lovely rustic phrase used of dead flowers, "They've gone home." [119] Life is, indeed, as Stephen's mother says, a "strange picter"; [120] and is it not true that "all the world's of a piece," [121] and ". . . one thread runs through the same piece"? [122]

The countryman, like the poet, takes pleasure in pairs of words, and particularly delights in alliteration. He has "other fish to fry," [123] he is "out of the frying-pan into the fire," [124] a saying which loses the fine Elizabethan flavor of "Out of God's blessing into the sun"; [125] he says "My inside begins to cry cupboard" [126] and "to say sniff when another says snaff": [127] that is, to jump at an offer. Henchard quizzed Elizabeth-Jane, fearing she might have engaged herself to Farfrae, as to whether she had gone the least bit beyond "sniff and snaff." [128] "To hob and nob" may have meant originally to have one for a friend, Habban, Naeban, that is, for weal or woe; or, "hot or cold," the hob, or back of chimney place, being where the innkeeper warmed the drink for his guests.[129] When it seems probable that Bathsheba and Farmer Boldwood are to make a match of it, Laban Tall remarks sagely, "Better wed over the mixen than over the moor." [130] The rustic likes puns, as we see from Clerk Crickett's advice to young men in search of a wife: "Choose your wife as you choose your pig—a small ear and a small tale. . . ." [131] He also enjoys the com-

[117] Lean's *Collectanea,* Vol. II, Part II, 774.
[118] *Tess,* Chap. XXXII.
[119] E. M. Wright, *Rustic Speech,* 176.
[120] *A Pair of Blue Eyes,* Chap. XXIII.
[121] *Ibid.,* Chap. XXXVIII.
[122] *The Return of the Native,* Book III, Chap. VII.
[123] *A Pair of Blue Eyes,* Chap. IX; Ray, 245.
[124] *A Changed Man:* "Romantic Adventures of a Milkmaid"; Ray, 246.
[125] Lean, II, Part II, 155; *Hamlet,* I, 2, 66; *Much Ado About Nothing,* II, 1, 286; Lean, II, Part II, 706–707.
[126] *The Dynasts,* Part Second, Act VI, Scene V; Ray, 66, 237; Lean, II, Part II, 290.
[127] Wright, *Rustic Speech,* 169.
[128] *The Mayor of Casterbridge,* Chap. XVII.
[129] *A Pair of Blue Eyes,* Chap. VII; Ellis's Brand, II, 348–351.
[130] *Far from the Madding Crowd,* Chap. XXII; Ray, 362.
[131] *Desperate Remedies,* Epilogue.

pact word, the balanced and pointed paradox; witness the milkman's delight in the adage he has picked up from John Hostler: "More know Tom Fool than Tom Fool knows . . . a good saying well spit out is a Christmas fire to my withered heart. . . ." [132]

Folk-humor often reveals a keen perception of the idiosyncrasies of temperament and the irony of circumstance. Thus Tranter Dewy sums up admirably the fact that once a man has grown daughters, he is all the more likely to be doubly henpecked, in the saying, "Chanticleer's comb is a-cut, 'a b'lieve." [133] On the other hand, the humor is sometimes unconscious, not deliberate, depending upon the exquisite incongruity of the speech and the speaker, as in Henery Fray's complaint as to Bathsheba's high-handed procedure in acting as her own bailiff: "Pride and vanity have ruined many a cobbler's dog. Dear, dear, when I think o' it, I sorrows like a man in travel!" [134] Mother Cuxsom, musing on the passing of Cuxsom and the high success of such an impostor as Henchard, waxed philosophical, and felt some satisfaction in the reflection that the greatest worldly fortune must pass away in time: "Ah, yes," (she said) "Cuxsom's gone, and so shall leather breeches!" [135] Only the fairly well-to-do could afford leather breeches, and lucky was accounted the boy who won a pair at a village match of shaking-into-breeches. [136] Nor does folk-humor balk at the coarse, but richly expressive phrase; witness the comment of the elderly boozers in the Pure Drop Inn when the Durbeyfields begin to assume airs; some one observes, "Tess is a fine figure of fun . . . but Joan Durbeyfield must mind that she don't get green malt in floor." [137] Green malt is light barley which, having been steeped in soft water for forty-eight hours, is drained, and begins to sprout; [138]

[132] *The Hand of Ethelberta,* Chap. I; Gurdon, *Folklore of Suffolk,* 148.
[133] *Under the Greenwood Tree,* Part V, Chap. II; Ray, 235.
[134] *Far from the Madding Crowd,* Chap. XV; cf. Kelly, 103.
[135] *The Mayor of Casterbridge,* Chap. XIII.
[136] W. Sherren, *The Wessex of Romance,* 148.
[137] *Tess,* Part I, Chap. IV.
[138] Wright, *Eng. Dial. Dict.,* II, 717–719.

and "to give a girl a green gown," in ballad lore is to de-
flower her.[139] Arabella vowed that Jude's drunken dignity
at their second wedding was enough to make a cat laugh,
and the reader is forced to laugh with her, although this is
laughter that wrings the heart.[140]

Some of the countryman's sayings are almost too good
to be true; such, for instance, is Crickett, the parish clerk's
comment on the institution of marriage, "Yes, matrimony
d' begin wi' 'Dearly beloved,' and ends wi' 'Amazement,'
as the prayer-book says." [141] Surely this is the last word
on this mooted subject! Apropos the same subject, we have
Geoffrey Day's memorable retort to Dick Dewy, who believed that "Hanging and wiving go by destiny!" [142]

"If we are doomed to marry, we marry; if we are doomed to remain single, we do," replied Dick.

    .   .   .   .

". . . That's not the case with some folk. . . . There's that wife
o' mine. It was her doom not to be nobody's wife at all in the wide
universe. But she made up her mind that she would, and did it twice
over. Doom? Doom is nothing beside a elderly woman—quite a chiel
in her hands." [143]

Small wonder after things as good as this through a lifetime, always thrown out carelessly as if from a vast store-
house of wit, that the Mellstock folk prized Geoffrey highly:

"You might live wi' that man, my sonnies, a hundred years, and
never know there was anything in him."

"Ay; one of these up-country London ink-bottle fellers would call
Geoffrey a fool."

". . . Silent? ah, he is silent! . . . That man's silence is wonderful to listen to."

[139] *Child Waters,* Child, II, 83–100. No. 63; *The Knight and the Shepherd's Daughter,* Child, II, No. 410; *Glasgerion,* Child, II. No. 67, 136–142;
Lamkin, Child, II, No. 93, p. 324 ff; etc.; F. E. Hardy, *The Later Years,*
34, 35.
[140] *Jude the Obscure,* Part VI, Chap. VII; Lean, II, Part II, 781, 852.
[141] *Desperate Remedies,* Chap. VIII.
[142] *Wessex Tales:* "Interlopers at the Knap"; *The Tempest,* I, 1, 54; etc.
[143] *Under the Greenwood Tree,* Part II, Chap. VI.

"There's so much sense to it. Every moment of it is brimming over with sound understanding." [144]

And surely they are able judges of wit and wisdom. It was Spink who, when complimented on his learning, remarked that ". . . by the time a man's head is finished, 'tis almost time for him to creep underground" [145]—a mournful fact that many a scholar can vouch for! And Tranter Dewy defended the coarseness of all true stories with more common sense than many a critic of life and literature can boast, when he urged, ". . . My sonnies, all true stories have a coarseness or a bad moral, depend on't. If the story-tellers could have got decency and good morals from true stories, who'd ha' troubled to invent parables?" [146]

This admirable good sense comes into play in all the matters of life. The mailman who had had too big a swig of Manston's liquor was yet sober enough to disdain his tempter's facile philosophy; he still knew what was what:

"We be crippled disciples, 'a believe," he said, with a sigh and a stagger.

"Not drunk, but market-merry," said Manston. . . .

.   .   .   .

". . . Trust in the Lord—he'll pay!"

"He pay, 'a believe! Why should he when he didn't drink the drink, and the devil's a friend o' them who did? He pay, 'a believe! D'ye think the man's a fool?" [147]

He is canny in his estimate of his Creator; witness Joseph Poorgrass's timid fear after yielding to a "wet" when he should have been carrying Fanny Robin's coffin home: "Well, I hope Providence won't be in a way with me for my doings. . . . Your next world is your next world, and not to be squandered offhand." [148] But there are limits to his fatalism, and above all, he is no sniveling weakling:

[144] *Ibid.*, Part II, Chap. V.
[145] *Ibid.*, Part II, Chap. V; Cf. Ray, 16.
[146] *Ibid.*, Part I, Chap. VII.
[147] *Desperate Remedies*, Chap. XVII, 1.
[148] *Far from the Madding Crowd*, Chap. XLII.

when Henery Fray complained of the hard lot of the righteous, Matt Clark was quick to reply:

". . . Your lot is your lot, and Scripture is nothing; for if you do good you don't get rewarded according to your works, but be cheated in some mean way out of your recompense."

"No, no; I don't agree with 'ee there," said Matt Clark. "God's a perfect gentleman in that respect." [149]

These Hardy rustics are a source of refreshment to the reader: here in the talk of dialect speakers is the vivid, unspoiled phrase, the gusto of an experience which communicates itself directly and without loss, and the supreme zest that is to be found in little, insignificant, simple things. It is saddening to reflect that folk who see character so keenly and appraise it so accurately, voicing their strong, original feeling for life in slow but vivid speech shall in the fullness of time come to take their ideas and the words wherewith to express them from the staled lingo of the daily newspapers and the jaded formulas of the schools.

[149] *Far from the Madding Crowd*, Chap. XV.

XI

FOLK-LAW

Many survivals of folk-law are to be found in Hardy. Particularly rich is the lore of betrothal and marriage: we have handfestings in the Isle of Slingers, the rustic idea that marriage is for seven years and is a contract which may, under certain circumstances, be voided by either party; actual wife-sale, as in *The Mayor,* and the satirical Skimmity for those flagrantly unfaithful to the marriage vow. There are such old-fashioned tenures of land as lifeholdings; sins against property, at one time punished by the lord with a very high hand—sheep-stealing, poaching of all sorts, and cutting of timber without permission, several of them capital offenses up to a century ago; smuggling on the Western Coast; and the impressment of sailors by gangs of informers and ruffians. There are relics of the infamous criminal code —the strangling and burning of unfaithful wives, public hangings, the exposure of the victim to public view, a horrible sight in its rusty chains on a windy height. Most picturesque are the old trade- and hiring-fairs, where each advertised his vocation by his chosen garb and symbol; and the Lady-Day movings which followed inevitably upon the twice-a-year hirings. There are quaint trades like the reddleman's and the itinerant cider-maker's, privileged trades like the medieval glazier's, rough-and-ready modes of doing business like Henchard's in the Casterbridge Corn Market or the peripatetic timber-merchant's in Hintock Woods.

It will be necessary to look back at the origins of our present marriage customs and laws if we are to understand

variations from true survivals of folk-custom. It is wise to
regard the old Teutonic "bride-price" as a compensation to
the bride's male relatives for the *mund,* or protectorship,
over her, and an attempt also to secure to her thereby certain reasonable married rights.[1] The Old English marriage
had two distinct parts, the Beweddung, or betrothal, which
was what we call a real contract in law, and which was completed by the bridegroom's handing over the Weotuma, or
bride-price to the bride's menfolk; and the Gyfta, or actual
handing over of the bride on the wedding day.[2] From early
times, instead of paying the Weotuma to the bride's menfolk at the time of the Beweddung, it was customary to pay
over a part of it only in the form of the Arrha, a sort of
"earnest money" or *Handgeld,* pledging faith and assuring
good luck to the match;[3] the remainder of the Weotuma
was paid at the Gyfta.

The next step in the evolution of marriage forms was the
substitution by the bride and groom of some solemn act in
place of the actual *Handgeld;* each might take a piece of
straw, or a glove, and later a ring, pledging faith as he did
so. Such a marriage was an actual Handfesting: the bride
and groom betrothed themselves by an oath and were regarded as married folk without further ceremony, clerical
or civil.[4] In this form of contract the Arrha was paid, not
to the guardians of the bride, but to the bride herself; it was
the betrothal ring.[5] In the late Middle Ages arose the custom of exchanging rings, of drinking a cup of wine together
and pledging vows, or the breaking and sharing of a ring
or gold piece, and soon all legal distinction between the old
Wed and the newer *Arrha* was lost, marriages being conducted with a ring and a penny, a ring and a glove, or with a

[1] G. E. Howard, *The History of Matrimonial Institutions,* I, 220–221, 260;
Pollock and Maitland, *History of English Law,* II, 362.
[2] Howard, I, 258–259; Luke Owen Pike, *History of Crime in England,* I,
90–91; Havelock Ellis, *Studies in the Psychology of Sex,* 1923 ed., VI, 471.
[3] Howard, I, 266.
[4] *Ibid.,* I, 268, 278, 280.
[5] *Ibid.,* I, 278.

ring, a glove, and a penny.[6] We preserve the name *Wedding*, but keep the custom of Arrha thinly veiled in the marriage ring. With self-betrothal came the freedom of the contracting parties to conduct the ceremony themselves, that is, *Self-gyfta*. They usually chose a *Fürsprecher* who could prompt them in the Latin responses of the church ceremony, and out of this *Fürsprecher* grew both the ecclesiastical and the civil control of marriage, which originally was a simple social contract.[7] In medieval England and Scotland only persons of the higher classes were married by both ecclesiastical ceremony and civil contract; and these nuptials were celebrated, not in the church, but at the church door, or "porch," up to the time of Edward IV.[8] Who of us but remembers the Wife of Bath with her "housbondes fyve at chyrche dore"? In vain did the Council of Trent pronounce private marriage a sin; [9] the people clung to their handfestings, to private marriages which were seldom followed by church-going and clerical ceremony.[10] The Esks of Scotland permitted divorce after a year's union to which no child was born, and recognized cohabitation for a year as a legal marriage.[11] From the Middle Ages up to the Civil War the offspring of such marriages were time and again recognized in English and Scottish courts as legitimate.[12] Henry VIII wisely ordered the registration of marriages, and Elizabeth's Interrogatory to her ministers enjoined them to see that handfestings were followed by ecclesiastical ceremony.[13] But nothing helped greatly until the church hit upon the publication of banns: Cromwell's Civil Marriage Act, an intensely modern document, required that the banns be

---

[6] Howard, I, 280, 281, 282; Brand's *Popular Antiquities,* Ellis ed., II, 94.
[7] Howard, I, 281–282.
[8] Howard, I, 348–349; Brand, II, 134; Herrick's *Hesperides,* "Porch Verse"; *Cant. Tales,* "The Wife of Bath's Tale."
[9] Ellis, *Studies in the Psychology of Sex,* VI, 434.
[10] Howard, I, 348–349; Brand, II, 87–89.
[11] Brand, II, 87, 88, quoting Sinclair's *Statistical Account of Scotland,* XII, 615.
[12] Brand, II, 87–89.
[13] Brand, II, 89, quot. Strype's *Annals of the Reformation,* I, *Appendix,* 57.

published before the civil ceremony, that such ceremony be obligatory, and that the marriage be recorded in the parish register.[14] The revoking of this measure set the state back many years, and not until 1836 did anything better take its place.[15] The present marriage service of the Church of England, derived as it is through liturgies of Edward VI and Elizabeth from the ancient manuals of Hereford, Durham, York, and Sarum, preserves both the betrothal and the actual gyfta: the formula, *Wilt thou have this man . . .* is a confession of betrothal; then follows the tradition, the handing over of bride to bridegroom, the latter saying, *Here I . . . take thee . . . to my wedded wife. . . .* The ring is a relic of the arrha.[16] The civil service is really more ancient in its forms: here the old private betrothal survives, with its *I do* and *I will,* and the ring used is the actual betrothal ring.[17]

The Hardy reader expects to find evidences of primitive custom in the Isle of Slingers. The Pierstons, like the Avice Caros, had been islanders for centuries. Pierston half expected to have Avice the First come to him for the island betrothal as he was leaving the island; had she come, the betrothal, which was regarded as actual marriage, would have taken place, and would have been followed sometime later by a church marriage; no islander had ever been known to break that contract.[18] But Avice did not come; she had learned convention from the few foreigners on the Isle. When Marcia Bencomb compromised herself by running away with Pierston, her father was not greatly worried, although opposed to the match, because he felt that Pierston held to the ancient island notions of the sexes, and could well be trusted.[19] Avice the Second finally confessed to Pierston her secret marriage:

14 Howard, I, 418.
15 *Ibid.,* 435.
16 *Ibid.,* 283–284.
17 *Ibid.,* 284–285.
18 *The Well-Beloved,* Part I, Chaps. II, IV; Part II, Chap. III.
19 *Ibid.,* Part I, Chap. VIII.

". . . I mean he courted me, and led me on to island custom, and then I went to chapel one morning and married him in secret, because mother didn't care about him; and I didn't either by that time. . . ."[20]

This amazing statement is the utterance of a true island girl; she had obeyed custom as naturally as she obeyed the laws of breathing. Brand, the antiquary, mentions these Portland Isle handfestings with great interest.[21] The infamous Gretna Green marriages, in which runaway couples were married clandestinely by the oddest succession of officiants imaginable, are survivals of the old custom of private, non-clerical marriage. Paisley, Gordon, and Laing—blacksmiths, fishermen, joiners, and whatnot—married couples by this "good old unregular mode" for about a century, and the marriages were upheld in Edinburgh and Dublin courts as legal.[22] They fell just outside the English Marriage Act. These lay parsons were in bad odor even among their own folk; only the lowest would associate with them.

Country courtship in Hardy's novels is always informal; Tess and Angel Clare enjoyed unreserved comradeship out-of-doors;[23] Arabella trapped Jude by the tacit intention to marry which was implied in their "walking together";[24] later on Jude instinctively sought this mode of renewing his acquaintance with his city cousin, and then feared she would despise him as a country bumpkin;[25] thus Wildeve conducted his courtship of Thomasin in spite of her aunt's opposition;[26] and because he had "walked the path" in his day, Tranter Dewy knew that Dick was a "lost man."[27] There is something refreshing in the straightforward simplicity and good faith of the custom. The banns themselves

[20] *The Well-Beloved*, Part II, Chap. XIII.
[21] Brand, II, 87–89.
[22] Hone's *Table Book*, Part I, 431–435, 536–538; Part II, 125–126.
[23] *Tess*, Chap. XXXI.
[24] *Jude*, Part I, Chaps. VII, IX.
[25] *Ibid.*, Part II, Chaps. II, IV.
[26] *The Return of the Native*, Book I, Chap. III.
[27] *Under the Greenwood Tree*, Part II, Chap. III.

play a large rôle in the Hardy stories and novels: Tess was not "called home," [28] as the phrase goes.

Sergeant Troy's mysterious disappearance was attributed to his death by drowning; Bathsheba was regarded as a widow, and was driven by Boldwood's importunate suit to promise him that she would marry him in seven years, if he still wished it at the end of that time.[29] There is a valid reason for her plea of seven years' grace. We have the story of a woman who, after seven years' waiting for her husband, had the bell tolled for him as dead, and was acknowledged by her village as a true widow.[30] In 1895 a man on trial for bigamy gave as his defense the fact that he had been away from home seven years, and felt therefore free to marry again! [31] A year and a day or seven full years are periods for which the popular mind holds marriage binding: Mrs. Gomme was told, "I was faithful to him for seven years and had more than my two children," as if two were the number traditionally expected of a marriage.[32] Much of our evidence comes from the ancient game of "Sally Waters": one version runs thus:

> Sally, Sally Water, Sprinkle in the pan;
> Rise Sally, rise, Sally, and choose a young man.
> Choose to the east, choose to the west,
> And choose the pretty girl that you love best.
> And now you're married, I wish you joy;
> First a girl and then a boy;
> Seven years after son and daughter;
> And now, young people, jump over the water! [33]

The marriage custom surviving in this game points back to a time when a marriage was not of necessity for life, and

---

[28] *Tess,* Chap. X. See the banns in *Wessex Poems:* "The Bride-Night Fire"; *Time's Laughingstocks:* "A Sunday Morning Tragedy"; E. M. Wright, *Rustic Speech,* 271.
[29] *Far from the Madding Crowd,* Chaps. LI.
[30] Gomme, *Traditional Games of England and Scotland,* II, 177–179; Lina B. Eckenstein, *Comparative Studies in Nursery Rhymes,* 68–70.
[31] Gomme, *Trad. Games,* II, 177–178.
[32] *Ibid.,* II, 178.
[33] *Ibid.,* 151; Cf. Symondsbury variant, *Folk-Lore Journal,* VII, 207.

its object was to have children; the evidences of water-worship in the rhyme point to a cult in which children are eagerly desired. It seems suggestive of an age when young people were thrown together at feast times, quite without ceremony and set purpose, with the hope that marriages might result from the resulting intimacy. In some primitive societies, a barren wife will recognize the children of her husband by another woman as his and her own jointly.[34] The rhyme, "First a girl and then a boy," seems to point to a popular belief that a man's cycle of life is not complete until he is the father of a daughter who, in her turn, may bear a son: a folklorist tells the story of a man who left his wife for this reason, only two sons having been born to them.[35] Some of this seems rather fanciful, yet undoubtedly contains the root of some primitive ideas of marriage which we are only beginning to discover. Had Bathsheba married, not a villager would have condemned her; the folk-belief was in her blood, an instinctive refuge in her difficulty.

Henchard's sale of his wife has a grim humor: the place and the manner of the deed are grotesque enough; it is Henchard himself, impulsive and wrong-headed, whether drunk or sober, who is tragic. It was the gypsies' sale of their old horses which put the devil into Henchard's heart; he had apparently jested rudely with Susan on this score more than once. The rough company greeted his first challenge with a coarse laugh:

"Will any Jack Rag or Tom Straw among ye buy my goods?"

.   .   .   .

"Mike, Mike," said she; "This is getting serious. Oh! too serious!"
"Will anybody buy her?" said the man.
"I wish somebody would," said she firmly. "Her present owner is not at all to her liking!"
"Nor you to mine," said he. "So we are agreed about that. Gentlemen, you hear? It's an agreement to part. She shall take the girl if she wants to, and go her ways. I'll take my tools and go my ways.

<hr>

[34] Gomme, *Trad. Games,* II, 178–179.
[35] *Ibid.,* II, 178, quoting Miss Hawkins Dempster.

'Tis simple as Scripture history. Now then, stand up, and show yourself." [36]

Susan stood up, and some one facetiously bid five shillings.
Henchard in pure bravado forced the auctioneer to begin
at five guineas, and vowed he would not sell his wife for
less. Even Henchard was startled when the voice of Newson
was heard bidding five guineas, and the whole company was
sobered when he counted out the money upon the table.
The laughter died away into an ominous silence; then
Susan spoke:

"Now . . . before you go further, Michael, listen to me. If you
touch that money, I and this girl go with the man. Mind, it is a joke
no longer."

"A joke? Of course it is not a joke!" shouted her husband. . . ."I
take the money; the sailor takes you. That's plain enough. It has been
done elsewhere—and why not here?" [37]

Thus the bargain was made; at the door of the tent Susan
paused, turned, and pulling off her wedding-ring, flung it
across the booth at Henchard's face:

"Mike," she said, "I've lived with thee a couple of years, and had
nothing but temper! Now I'm no more to 'ee; I'll try my luck elsewhere. 'Twill be better for me and Elizabeth-Jane, both. So good-
bye!"

Seizing the sailor's arm with her right, and mounting the little girl
upon her left, she went out of the tent sobbing bitterly.

A stolid look of concern filled the husband's face as if, after all,
he had not quite anticipated this ending; and some of the guests
laughed.

"Is she gone?" he said.

"Faith, ay; she's gone clane enough," said some rustics near the
door.[38]

It was characteristic of Henchard that, awaking next day
from his drunken stupor, he should bitterly blame Susan's
meekness rather than his own temper.[39] It is the cry of the

[36] *The Mayor of Casterbridge,* Chap. I.
[37] *Ibid.*
[38] *Ibid.*
[39] *Ibid.*

great egotist wounded in his tenderest spot. Henchard proceeded to take his tremendous oath, but almost too easily gave up the search for Susan and the child, and began a new life, apparently with little regret for his loss.

Wife-sale is not extinct even today; occasionally cases of it crop up in our newspapers in America. English folk-lorists are full of instances of this sort of thing: one gives us the testimony of an old man who saw a woman sold in market for five shillings.[40] The *Yorkshire Gazette* for May 11, 1889, carried a story of a woman sold for one shilling, and led away to her new husband's home with a halter around her neck! [41] Rev. J. Edward Vaux vouches for two stories, one of a woman who was sold in the open market-place for half-a-crown; another of a publican who bought another's wife for a two-gallon jar of gin! [42] Numerous other well authenticated cases might be cited.[43] Perhaps it was the knowledge of scenes like this, although more likely it was her own morbid psychology, that led Sue Bridehead to exclaim that the flowers in the hands of the bride were sadly like the garland used to deck the sacrifice in olden times,[44] as she had complained of her own wedding that some one must give her to Phillotson like a she-ass, a she-goat, or any other domestic animal.[45]

When Mrs. Dornell betrothed her thirteen-year-old daughter Betty to Stephen Reynard, sixteen years her senior, she had the child propose to him in a jeweler's shop in the presence of the footman and the jeweler. The affair reminds us of a medieval betrothal, but we realize we are in modern times when Squire Dornell refuses to allow Reynard to claim Betty until she has reached eighteen.[46]

The tale of "Master John Horseleigh, Knight" takes

---

[40] A. Parker, "Oxfordshire Folklore," *Folk-Lore*, XXIV, 76.
[41] *Folk-Lore Journal*, VII, 318, quoting *Yorkshire Gazette*.
[42] Havelock Ellis, *Studies in the Psychology of Sex*, VI, 403, quoting Rev. J. Edward Vaux, *Church Folk-Lore*, 2nd ed., 146.
[43] M. Burne, *Folk-Lore*, XXII, 237; Brand, II, 107; Ellis, *Studies in the Psychology of Sex*, VI, 403, quoting *The Annual Register*, 1767.
[44] *Jude*, Part V, Chap. IV.
[45] *Ibid.*, Part III, Chap. VII.
[46] *A Group of Noble Dames:* "Betty, the First Countess of Wessex."

us back to the days when King Henry VIII had newly assumed the headship of the Church. In the earliest volume of the Havenpool marriage registers stands the entry:

"Mastr John Horseleigh, Knyght, of the p'ysshe of Clyffton was maryed to Edith the wyffe late of John Stocker, M'chawnte of Havenpool the Xiiii daie of December be p'vylegge gevyn by our sup'me hedd of the chyrche of Ingelonde Kynge Henry viii th 1539." [47]

The ancient family pedigree of the Clyffton Horseleighs does not mention this marriage, but an earlier one to the daughter and heiress of Richard Phelipson, of Montislope, Nether Wessex, who bore him two daughters and a son who succeeded to the estate. Sir John had indeed two contemporaneous wives, Edith, the second, his only legal one. The lady who passed in Sherton Abbas for his wife had thought herself free to marry; Sir John learned that her husband was alive and on the Continent, but kept the news from her. Wishing, however, to have legitimate issue, he appealed to his sovereign and received this curious dispensation. Edith's jealous brother, thinking his sister wronged, killed Sir John. Her little son died, and the clergyman who had married her did not help her to secure her rightful position. Thus it came about that the illegitimate son of Sir John founded a family. No doubt the King's headship of the church for a time led men to practise similar but more malicious devices than this.

Those who had incurred the suspicion of scandal, particularly those who were rumored to be guilty of flagrant violation of the marriage vow, were punished in Wessex by the terrible skimmington ride. "The Fire at Tranter Sweatley's," [48] published as early as 1875 in *The Gentleman's Magazine,* but written in 1866, shows Hardy's early interest in this theme. When because of an error in the license, Wildeve had been unable to marry Thomasin, the girl was terrified when she heard the rustics coming to serenade, as they thought, the newly married couple; she

[47] *A Changed Man:* "Master John Horseleigh, Knight."
[48] *Wessex Poems:* "The Bride-Night Fire."

feared it might be a skimmity, and probably only Thomasin's superior position protected her from this supreme indignity.[49] *The Mayor* is the *locus classicus* for a skimmity ride; here the reader may watch one in the making. Henchard had unwisely given the letters Lucetta had written him to Jopp to return to her; Jopp had read them to the rabble of Mixen Lane at Peter's Finger. A skimmity was planned, and Farfrae's men engaged to get Farfrae out of town. Thus it chanced that Lucetta, sitting, as was her custom, in the dusk one evening, heard a hubbub which grew louder every moment, and above it the voices of two maid-servants describing the procession:

"What—two of 'em—are there two figures?"

"Yes. Two images on a donkey, back to back, their elbows tied to one another's. She's facing the head, and he's facing the tail."

"Is it meant for anybody particular?"

"Well—it mid be. The man has got on a blue coat and kerseymere leggings; he has black whiskers, and a reddish face. 'Tis a stuffed figure with a mask."

.   .   .   .

"What's the woman like? Just say, and I can tell in a moment if it is meant for the one I've in mind."

"My—why—'tis just as she was dressed when she sat in the front seat at the time the play actors came to the Town Hall." [50]

As Lucetta started to her feet, Elizabeth-Jane came softly into the room, and eagerly attempted to close the shutters. Lucetta would not let her, and the words of the maids came up to them with hideous clearness:

"Her neck is uncovered, and her hair in bands, and her back-comb in place; she's got on a puce silk, and white stockings, and coloured shoes."

Again Elizabeth-Jane attempted to close the window, but Lucetta held her by main force.

" 'Tis me!" she said, with face pale as death. "A procession—a scandal—an effigy of me, and him!"

.   .   .   .

[49] *The Return of the Native*, Book I, Chaps. V and VI.
[50] *The Mayor of Casterbridge*, Chap. XXXIX.

"Let us shut it out," coaxed Elizabeth-Jane . . . "Let us shut it out!"

"It is of no use!" she shrieked out. "He will see it, won't he? Donald will see it! He is just coming home—and it will break his heart—he will never love me any more—and O, it will kill me, kill me!"

Elizabeth-Jane was frantic now. "O, can't something be done to stop it?" she cried. "Is there nobody to do it—not one?"

She relinquished Lucetta's hands and ran to the door. Lucetta herself, saying recklessly, "I will see it!" turned to the window, threw up the sash, and went out upon the balcony.

. . . The numerous lights around the two effigies threw them up into lurid distinctness; it was impossible to mistake the pair for other than the intended victims.

"Come in, come in," implored Elizabeth-Jane; "and let me shut the window!"

"She's me—she's me—even to the parosol—my green parasol!" cried Lucetta with a wild laugh as she stepped in. She stood motionless for one second—then fell heavily to the floor.

Almost at the instant of her fall the rude music of the skimmington ride ceased. The roars of sarcastic laughter went off in ripples, and the trampling died out like the rustle of a spent wind. . . .[51]

Grower, a burgess, hearing the din of the cleavers, tongs, tambourines, kits, crowds, humstrums, serpents, ram's-horns, and other "historical" music, came out to learn the cause and found the town constables, two shriveled men, hiding up an alley. Blowbody, a borough magistrate, then came up and led the party up to Corn Street. Charl and Jopp professed a childlike innocence of the affair; effigies, donkey, lanterns, band, and crowd had disappeared "like the crew of Comus." [52] Henchard, in an agony of remorse, had gone for Farfrae; but it was too late—Lucetta was dying.

The effigies, the "rough music," and the swift, mysterious dispersal all are characteristic of a skimmington. Hardy always has a definite artistic purpose in his use of folk-custom, and the artistic pattern of this chapter is seen work-

---

[51] *Ibid.*, Chap. XXXIX.
[52] *Ibid.*

ing itself out with magnificent effect. The naturalness with
which the skimmity is planned, the neatness with which it
is carried out, the grotesquerie of the spectacle—all mark it
as a page from life. Beneath it all is the pity of it, the cruel
certainty that this is the inevitable close to Lucetta's idyl.
The mayor, Lucetta, Farfrae, and Elizabeth-Jane could not
have gone on living in Casterbridge as before. Something
was sure to happen—something is always sure to happen.
The man who was fool enough to trust a woman's letters
to Jopp was a man with a genius for doing the wrong thing,
a man doomed to destroy himself. The skimmity ride is
but one step in the slow decay of Henchard's nature; here,
if ever, is a man who was born damned. Henchard is perhaps the greatest tragic spectacle of all modern fiction.

In 1917 a skimmington riding was broken up by the police
in a Dorset village.[53] The skimmity is still ridden in the state
of New York. As late as 1884 skimmingtons were a common
occurrence in many Dorset towns, although court decisions
of 1882 had declared such demonstrations a violation of
the Highway Act punishable by fine and imprisonment.[54]
In Warwickshire the procession was called "loo-belling"; [55]
in the northern counties, "riding the stang"; [56] and at Tor-
rington a picturesque variation of it was termed "Riding
the Black Lad." [57] Hogarth has immortalized a skimmity
in his illustration to an episode of *Hudibras*.[58]

The Goths were wont to erect the *Nidstaeng*, the pole
or stake of infamy, with solemn imprecations against one
whose oath from that time forth was held absolutely *nidung*,
or worthless and who was, as a result, an utter outcast.[59]

[53] Samuel Chew, *Thomas Hardy, Poet and Novelist*, 113; *Bridport News*,
1884.
[54] Chew, *op. cit.*, 113; Ernest Brennecke, Jr., *The Life of Thomas Hardy*,
72; W. Sherren, *The Wessex of Romance*, 21–22; *Folk-Lore Journal*, I, 298–299;
Folk-Lore Record, V, 166.
[55] *Folk-Lore*, XXIV, 240.
[56] Wm. Henderson, *Folklore of the Northern Counties*, 29–30; *Denham
Tracts*, II, 4–6.
[57] *Folk-Lore*, XIX, 90.
[58] Ellis's Brand, II, 182, 191.
[59] *Folk-Lore Journal*, I, 330–331; Henderson, *op. cit.*, 28–33; Ellis's Brand,
II, 189, Note: Vol. Lex. Run. V. nijd.

We do not know quite how this evolved into a form of ostracism in which social offenses, such as marked licentiousness or flagrant infidelity, were punished by making the guilty pair ride the pole; we possess no transitional form of the custom, but interpret the effigies as a relic of it. The ancient jest about the cuckold's horns, which seems to have been as great a favorite in the Greek theater as in the Elizabethan pit, figures in some of these processions; in some of them the man's effigy was adorned with a pair of ram's horns, and many of the verses that were sung to them rehearse the old jest, usually beginning "ran-a-dan-dan, ran-a-dan-dan!"[60] Sometimes the satire was directed against a common scold,[61] a henpecked husband,[62] an old man who had married a very young girl,[63] or a wife-beater.[64] During the Napoleonic Wars the "crimps" who informed as to the whereabouts of sailors in hiding, were treated to this rough ride.[65] But in the Northumbrian pit villages and in certain regiments the comrade who was newly married was ridden on a pole as a playful honor, and then made to stand treat to the company![66] But the most common occasion of a skimmity was in satire of marital infidelity.

In Hardy's writings there are relics of the ferocious English criminal code still in effect at the beginning of the nineteenth century, and only modified by the efforts of Peel, Romilly, Mackintosh, and Lord John Russell. We have glimpses of days when sheep-stealing was one of two hundred capital offenses; when wives who had murdered their husbands were first strangled and then burned; when the corpse was left hanging on its gibbet, the chains creaking horribly in the wind; when the lord of the manor could

[60] C. S. Burne, *Folk-Lore Journal*, IV, 261–262; Gomme, *Folk-Lore Journal*, I, 365; *Folk-Lore Journal*, I, 330–331; I, 394–395; Ellis's Brand, II, 194–195; Henderson, 29–30.

[61] *Denham Tracts*, II, 4–6; Ellis's Brand, II, 190.

[62] Ellis's Brand, II, 190; *Folk-Lore*, XXII, 237.

[63] G. H. Kinahan, *Folk-Lore Record*, IV, 99.

[64] Henderson, 32; *Folk-Lore Journal*, II, 187; Lady C. Gurdon, *Folklore of Suffolk*, 103; etc.

[65] Henderson, 30.

[66] Ellis's Brand, II, 195–196; N. Thomas, *Folklore of Northumberland*, 130; *Denham Tracts*, II, 5–6.

throw into his own dungeon, flog, or leave to starve the rogue caught poaching on his lands; when deadly man-traps infested woods and fields; when impressment of soldiers and sailors was a high-handed governmental kidnaping; when the stocks and pillory were still familiar sights.

Hardy apparently was fascinated by tales of Jack White's gibbet at Wincanton, its great iron arm attached to a strong oak-post, and even a portion of the cage in which the criminal had hung still standing until 1835.[67] The body of a murderer was either dissected or, with the head tarred to preserve it from the weather, hung as close to the scene of the crime as possible, pirates on the river-bank, bandits by the coaching-road.[68] Dissection of bodies was not abolished until 1832, and hanging in chains until 1834.[69] The gibbet itself was familiar to the boy Hardy, and he had tales of the solitary corpse which used to hang there from his grandmother, tales which he preserves in "One We Knew" [70] and in many tales and poems.[71] Above the hill on one side of the river in the Casterbridge of Henchard's day stood the gibbet and its ghastly burden.[72]

In the poem, "The Mock Wife," [73] Hardy draws upon a Dorchester tradition: in 1705 ten thousand people gathered in Maumbury Rings to see Mary Channing, who had poisoned her husband, strangled and then burnt to death.[73] On the western circuit alone there were two such cases between 1782 and 1784.[74] The horrible penalty was not abolished until the thirtieth year of the reign of George III.[75] Hanging was a public spectacle up to 1868; executions used to take place over the gateway of the county jail, and formed

---

[67] F. E. Hardy, *The Early Life of Thomas Hardy,* 199.
[68] H. B. Poland, *A Century of Law Reform:* Criminal Law Since 1800, p. 44.
[69] Poland, 44.
[70] *Time's Laughingstocks.*
[71] *A Group of Noble Dames:* "The First Countess of Wessex"; *Winter Words,* "No Bell-Ringing"; *Poems of the Past and the Present,* "The Tree"; *Wessex Poems,* "The Burghers"; etc.
[72] *The Mayor of Casterbridge,* Chap. XIX.
[73] *Human Shows;* Hopkins, *Thomas Hardy's Dorset,* 74.
[74] Luke Owen Pike, *Hist. of Crime in England,* II, 379–380.
[75] Pike, II, 380; Poland, 344.

the excuse for a general holiday. The rich paid for choice
seats; the tradesmen, farmers, and rustics ate, drank and
made merry with a callousness it is difficult to understand
today.[76] Dickens has described for us the terrible press at
the execution of Mr. and Mrs. Manning in 1849, when
several persons in the crowd were crushed to death.[77] The
memory of these things lingered in the memory of Old
Creedle—"ancient days, when there was battles and famines
and hang-fairs and other pomps . . ."[78] The almost universal contempt for the hangman was as great in Hardy's
Wessex as ever it was in Elizabethan times, when to call
a man a hangman was a fighting offense; the story and the
play of "The Three Strangers" reveal this plainly.[79] The
entire company at the christening party were relieved to
learn that the sheep-thief had made his escape.

Sheep-stealing was only one of many capital offenses;
others were horse-stealing, cattle-stealing, robbing rabbit
warrens or fish preserves, cutting timber without permission, forgery and counterfeiting, picking pockets, and stealing a few shillings from a shop.[80] It is to Peel's everlasting
honor that he modified this barbarous penal code, but the
death penalty for horse- or sheep-stealing was not abolished
until 1832.[81] Hardy introduces us to the notorious "Blue
Jemmy," who was said to have stolen a hundred horses,
and who was finally hanged at Ivel-Chester Jail.[82] The
gypsies were clever horse thieves; the reader will recall
that Oak's first thought was of them when he found Bathsheba's mare missing from her stall.[83]

The stocks were still to be seen in the Casterbridge of

---

[76] Pike, II, 451–452; Poland, 49–50.
[77] W. Sherren, *The Wessex of Romance*, 130–131.
[78] *The Woodlanders*, Chap. X.
[79] *Wessex Tales:* "The Three Wayfarers" (a dramatization of "The Three
Strangers").
[80] Sir Spencer Walpole, *History of England since* 1815, III, 55–56; *Ibid.*,
II, 58; Pike, II, 451; Poland, 81.
[81] Walpole, *op. cit.*, III, 56; Pike, II, 451.
[82] *Time's Laughingstocks:* "A Trampwoman's Tragedy," and Hardy's note.
[83] *Far from the Madding Crowd*, Chap. XXXII.

Henchard's day,[84] the Weatherbury of Oak's,[85] and many other Wessex places. Late in life Hardy himself recalled with horror the glimpse he had as a boy of a man set in the stocks, the sun scorching him and the flies crawling over him.[86] Customs change slowly in Dorchester: the last recorded case of this punishment is in 1872.[87]

Poaching and the unauthorized cutting of timber were capital offenses in the early nineteenth century; up to 1827 landowners were permitted to set out spring-guns and man-traps, and even after that date they continued to take the law in their own hands.[88] Poaching, however, was the countryman's instinctive assertion of a traditional privilege, a relic of the primitive days when the land and all the game on it were the property of the tribe,[89] and an offense which the tactful landlord often shut his eyes to. The medieval lord could throw into his dungeon and leave there to starve any "hand-having" or "back-bearing" thieves; he could have them flogged to death or hung aloft on some tree as a warning to others.[90] Young Somerset in de Stancy Castle, fell into one of these deep dungeons, out of which it was impossible to climb, and which was fitted with great rings for the prisoner's hands and feet.[91] The countryman's respect for timber rights is admirably shown in Giles Winterborne's refusal to cut down the elm which was the cause of Old South's illness before securing Mrs. Charmond's permission.[92] The poachers of Mixen Lane, Casterbridge, were a contemptible lot who made their living by petty professional theft.[93] Man-traps play a part in several of Hardy's stories, particularly in *The Woodlanders*. Mrs. Charmond's hus-

[84] *The Mayor of Casterbridge,* Chap. XXVII.
[85] *Far from the Madding Crowd,* Chap. XLIV; *Winter Words:* "In Weatherbury Stocks."
[86] F. E. Hardy, *Early Life,* 27; F. E. Hardy, *The Later Years . . .* , 144.
[87] Poland, 47–48.
[88] Walpole, II, 58; Poland, 57.
[89] Pike, II, 383–384.
[90] Aubrey's *Remaines,* Britten ed., 47, 58, 135; Pike, I, 217.
[91] *A Laodicean,* Chap. IX.
[92] *The Woodlanders,* Chap. XIV.
[93] *The Mayor of Casterbridge,* Chap. XXXVI.

band had a collection of man-traps which would have glad-
dened the heart of the sternest landlord, and he had a habit
of reciting the history of each of them.[94] Hardy seems to
endow these terrible gins with actual malice in a tense scene
in *The Woodlanders*.[95] Timothy Tangs had at last discovered the intrigue between Fitzpiers and his wife and,
before going away, he was determined to punish his enemy.
In his ignorant, half-crazed brain was the picture of this
enemy, caught in the teeth of the giant trap, as his great-
uncle had been caught in it years before, and had come out
maimed for life. He could see it set its teeth into Fitzpiers as
it had many times set them into small billets of wood fed
to it. So he set the trap. We watch Grace's swift approach
to the deadly thing with unmixed fear. Tim and Sue hear
one long cry, penetrating and indescribable, followed by
long silence. It is a moment of sheer horror, one of the
moments of fear imaginatively realized which stamp themselves more indelibly upon the brain than the terrifying experiences of actual life. In a moment assuagement comes,
but the shadow of the fear is in the background. In this
wonderful novel Hardy does for the woodlands what he
does for the heath in *The Return of the Native:* he paints
them in every mood—now soft, idyllic, and tender; now
dark, sinister, and full of dreadful mystery.

"The Distracted Preacher" is a delightful love story set
against the background of the West Coast smuggling trade.
The smuggling of wine and brandy from France was carried
on in just the way here described: the casks were sunk near
the seashore and were picked up later by boats; the great
stone jars which were shipped to France ostensibly as bal-
last, were usually returned full.[96] The nation as a whole
thought the high duties impolitic, and sympathized with
the smugglers, who used this moral support in some high-
handed and violent treatment of captured customs officials.

---

[94] *The Woodlanders*, Chaps. VIII, XLVII; cf. *Under the Greenwood Tree,*
Part V, Chap. I.
[95] Chap. XLVII.
[96] Pike, II, 398–400.

Lizzy's plea when asked to give up smuggling is typical of all the "trade"; she was, she says, born to it, it is in her blood, she needs the money for her mother, and owes nothing to a King she has never seen; moreover, she has a right to her own:

". . . I and Mr. Owlett and the others paid thirty shillings for every one of the tubs before they were put aboard at Cherbourg, and if a king who is nothing to us sends his people to steal our property, we have a right to steal it back again." [97]

By a delightful turn of circumstance the preacher finds himself one of the smugglers, an unconscious admirer of the clever device by which the casks were hidden in boxes containing newly set trees and sunk into the earth. The adage "Hampshire and Wiltshire moonrakers" refers to the peasants' practice of fishing up contraband goods at night.[98]

The procedure followed by press-gangs is vividly described in *The Trumpet-Major;* the informing, the chase, and the violent search made for Bob Loveday, are hardly exaggerations of actual fact.[99] "Crimps," or informers, were universally despised, and were sometimes ridden skimmity.[100] During the Napoleonic Wars, convicts were pressed into the military and naval service, and a century or more earlier, it was probably men who had been forced into the navy in this way who felt justified in turning pirates and harassing the government.[101]

Several poems treat the theme of the gypsy. "The Sacrilege: A Ballad Tragedy (*circa* 1820–)" [102] is a tale of an honest country boy who has taken to the gypsy life; he is infatuated with a gypsy girl whom he has taken from her lover, Cornish Wrestler Joe. He is constantly thieving to get her pretty things, and at last is caught stealing golden vessels from a cathedral and hanged. The fickle gypsy goes

[97] *Wessex Tales:* "The Distracted Preacher."
[98] Vincent Stuckey Lean, *Collectanea,* I, 94.
[99] Chaps. XXX, XXXI, XXXII.
[100] Henderson, *Folklore of the Northern Counties,* 30.
[101] Pike, II, 372–374.
[102] *Satires of Circumstance.*

back to Cornish Wrestler Joe, who has fitted up her van
in apple-green with gay curtains and a bright brass knocker.
It is not long, however, till the brother of the boy she
has destroyed has evened the score. "A Trampwoman's
Tragedy" is an admirable picture of gypsy life: the love of
the road, of lonely inns, and a horse taken in hour of need,
the gypsy girl's caprice, and the gypsy morality as a whole
—all are in this poignant tale.[103] In jest the gypsy girl tells
her lover that the child soon to be born is not his, but John's,
and laughingly advises him to console himself with Mother
Lee. He kills John, and hangs for it, but his ghost returns
to learn the truth; she is left alone to wander on the western
moor. These gypsies are not characteristic of the British
gypsies as they exist today. The latter preserve some primitive customs, among them physical proof of the bride's
virginity, a ceremony of marriage in which bride and groom
partake of confarreation-cakes, and adoption of the groom
into the woman's clan. They bury their dead, and with
them what they have most prized, often a violin or trinkets,
but they burn their clothes, bedding, and tent. Unfaithful-
ness in marriage is extremely rare, and is severely punished.[104] There is a Scottish tradition of Johnny Faw, Lord
of Little Egypt, who seems to have held some degree of
political power in Scotland under James IV and Mary,
Queen of Scots, possibly because the Scotch were at the time
too much embroiled in civil quarrels to risk a clash with the
powerful gypsy clan.[105] In the early nineteenth century it
was a statute offense to harbor gypsies,[106] perhaps because
they were notorious horse thieves, and occasionally stole
children. There was a superstition that their visits were
extremely unlucky.[107] In spite of this mass of prejudice, the

---

[103] *Time's Laughingstocks:* "A Trampwoman's Tragedy."
[104] T. W. Thompson, "The Ceremonial Customs of British Gypsies,"
Folk-Lore, XXIV, 321–340; E. M. Leather, *Folk-Lore,* XXIV, 239.
[105] *Denham Tracts,* II, 86; Ellis's Brand, III, 99–100; Child, IV, "Gypsy
Laddie," 61–64.
[106] Pike, II, 76.
[107] E. Wright, *Folk-Lore,* XXXVII, 367.

English rustic felt the fascination of the gypsy life and has caught it in one of his favorite folk-songs, "The Wraggle-Taggle Gypsies, O!" [108]

Hardy's rustics have a certain tenderness for the weak-witted which would do credit to people of finer understanding. Mad Judy, who sighed at a christening, and muttered discontentedly at a wedding, was kindly dealt with by the folk of her village.[109] Christian Cantle and Joseph Poorgrass are innocent butts; Leaf, who doesn't in the least mind having "no head," is humored in every possible way; he accompanied the Mellstock choir on their momentous visit to the rector; [110] and he is made welcome at Dick's wedding, although he comes uninvited.[111] Hardy may have taken the name from the phrase, "to have a leaf out," used of a half-witted person.[112] The common superstition is that the visit of such a person brings luck to one's house,[113] that "fool's handsel is lucky," [113] that a dog will not bite an idiot,[113] and that the parents of a half-witted child will always have a sufficiency of the good things of life.[114] The deep desire of the rustic for a modicum of respectability in death, if not in life, is revealed in old Creedle's lament at Giles Winterborne's death that now he is left alone, to be nailed up in parish boards, with no one to "glutch" down a sigh for him! [115] The village witch was formerly buried at a charge of a sixpence for the grave and the parish coffin; it was indeed a dreadful fate.[116]

The countryman's superstitious feeling for oaths comes out in several passages in Hardy: Cainy Ball, when questioned as to whether his tale of Bathsheba was true, burst

---

[108] Cecil Sharp, *English Folk-Song: Some Conclusions,* 99.
[109] *Poems of the Past and the Present:* "Mad Judy."
[110] *Under the Greenwood Tree,* Part II, Chap. III.
[111] *Ibid.,* Part V, Chap. I.
[112] E. M. Wright, *Rustic Speech and Folklore,* 175.
[113] Lean's *Collectanea,* II, Part I, p. 18; Jonson's *Bartholomew Fair,* II, I; Lawson, *Modern Greek Folklore and Ancient Greek Religion,* 307; Gregor, 27, 128.
[114] Lean's *Collectanea,* II, Part I, p. 18.
[115] *The Woodlanders,* Chap. XLIII.
[116] Denham, II, 338–339.

out crying; he did not mind saying it was true, but he didn't
like to say it was "damn true"! [117] Small wonder he was
afraid, because Joseph Poorgrass had demanded that he
swear a great oath, and seal it with his "blood-stone," which,
if he lies, will fall and crush him to powder.[117] This is in
Joseph's most sepulchral voice and sternest Old Testament
manner. Henery Fray was shocked to think that the former
bailiff would as soon tell a lie on Sundays as on working-
days—double perjury! [118] This superstitious view of oaths
takes us back to medieval courts when the contestants at
law had first to be searched to make sure that neither bore
about him anywhere any charm or magic herb to influence
the court's decision.[119] The countryman also had an almost
superstitious respect for the symbols of law; witness the
constable in "The Three Strangers" who would not pursue
the escaped sheep-thief without his staff, for fear the thief,
with full justice on his side, should take up the constable
himself; [120] or the two Casterbridge constables, "shrivelled
men," who had thrust their staves in terror up the water-
pipe at the time of the skimmity, thereby renouncing all
responsibility in the matter.[121]

The system of "lifeholding" had a curious interest for
Hardy; his mother's grandfather owned many such lifeholdings and was induced by his crafty solicitor to make
frequent wills with the result that three-fourths of his estate
was willed away to the lawyer himself.[122] There are many
"liviers" in Hardy: the "tenant-for-life" in the poem of that
title; [123] Edward Springrove's father; [124] Netty Sargent's
father; [125] the poachers and drunkards of Mixen Lane,
who had formerly been "liviers"; [126] the Durbeyfields, who

[117] *Far from the Madding Crowd,* Chap. XXXIII.
[118] *Ibid.,* Chap. VIII.
[119] Aubrey's *Remaines,* 77.
[120] *Wessex Tales.*
[121] *The Mayor of Casterbridge,* Chap. XXXIX.
[122] F. E. Hardy, *The Early Life of Thomas Hardy,* 182–183.
[123] *Poems of the Past and the Present:* "The Tenant-for-Life."
[124] *Desperate Remedies,* Chap. X, 6.
[125] *Life's Little Ironies:* "Netty Sargent's Copyhold."
[126] *The Mayor of Casterbridge,* Chap. XXXVI.

lost their home upon the father's death;[127] and Giles Winterborne, who lost all his holdings upon the death of Old South and Mrs. Charmond's failure to renew his leases.[128] Netty Sargent was faced with a difficult problem: the house built by her great-grandfather, with its little garden and field, had been granted upon lives; her dying uncle's life was the last life upon the property so that, if no new lives were admitted, at his death all would revert to the lord of the manor. The payment of a fine would entitle her uncle to a new deed of grant, by the custom of the manor. The story goes on to tell us how Netty Sargent, feigning that her uncle was too ill and nervous to make his signature in the presence of the agent, and that his arm was a trifle paralyzed, guided his hand in writing the necessary application for the "fine" which would renew the life-lease. The next day the old man was found dead in bed. The Squire's son was no fool, but good-naturedly let her keep her copyhold; and undoubtedly village sentiment approved his generosity and Netty's ruse.[129] The folk-belief that the signature of a person not yet cold in death, is valid in law may be a relic of sympathetic magic.[130]

The case of Giles Winterborne is, of course, most poignant. Old South's was the last of a group of lives at the end of which the homestead occupied by South himself, Winterborne's cottage, and half a dozen homes in the possession of various Hintock families for several centuries, would lapse and become part of the manor estate. Giles's ancestors had very unwisely fifty years before exchanged their original copyholds for life-leases in return for certain repairs to be made by the lord upon their somewhat dilapidated houses. Winterborne's father had neglected to avail himself of a privilege granted him to add his own and his son's life to the then existing lives on payment of a merely nominal sum, and had neglected to insure Old South's life.

[127] *Tess*, Chap. L.
[128] *The Woodlanders*, Chaps. V, XIII, XIV.
[129] *Life's Little Ironies*: "Netty Sargent's Copyhold."
[130] Ellis's Brand, II, 234.

On South's death, Mrs. Charmond's refusal to renew Winterborne's lease made him a landless man and plunged half a dozen Hintock families into poverty. Yet Winterborne reproached himself bitterly for thinking of land when Old South lay dying.[131] How much happier the people of Vindilia Isle with their sixteenth-century little stone freehold houses, for which they "covenanted" by "church gift," according to the custom of the isle! Instead of "conveying" property by legal formalities, the deed was presented to the person to whom it was to belong in church in the presence of a clergyman and witnesses.[132] These passed secure from generation to generation.

Perhaps the most picturesque reminders of the past in all Hardy's writings are the pages which bring before us the great trade- and hiring-fairs, outmoded ways of barter and commerce, quaint trades, medieval in origin, and the fine old-fashioned pride in one's vocation that distinguishes alike the shepherd, the corn-merchant, the cobbler, the farmer, and the cider-maker. Hardy refers in passing to the "privileged trades" of the Middle Ages; Baptista Heddegen's persecutor made it his boast that he could remain in Giant's Town because he was a glazier, and therefore "privileged." [133] Barbara, of the house of Grebe, spoiled her parents' dream of an ambitious match by running away with Edmond Willowes, whose father or grandfather had been the very last of the old glass-painters of Shottsford-Forum, carrying on a trade which had died out in every other part of England.[134] The old-fashioned tradesman's scorn of newfangled modes of advertising is shown in William Penny's case. Outside his shop hung the upper leather of a Wellington boot, pegged to a board as if to dry; in the spirit of ancient banking and mercantile houses he magnificently dispensed with a sign.[135]

[131] *The Woodlanders*, Chaps. V, XIII, XIV.
[132] *The Well-Beloved*, Preface; Sherren, *The Wessex of Romance,* 100.
[133] *A Changed Man:* "A Mere Interlude."
[134] *A Group of Noble Dames:* "Barbara, of the House of Grebe"; Aubrey's *Remaines,* 48.
[135] *Under the Greenwood Tree*, Part II, Chap. II.

One of the quaintest of trades is the reddleman's. Reddle has been known in Britain from very early times, and was no doubt originally used for many purposes other than marking sheep.[136] The reddleman's van and his person were painted a brownish-red, and perhaps it was this that gave him his unenviable social isolation, and gave rise to the otherwise absurd idea that reddlemen were often criminals who disguised themselves to escape detection.[137] He lived like a gypsy, though he would have scorned to be thought one, for he knew how welcome and indispensable he was at sheep-shearing time. Diggory Venn's appearance frightened Christian Cantle so much that he couldn't comb his hair for two days;[138] and little Johnny Nunsuch was so terrified that he dropped his lucky sixpence.[139] Even Thomasin failed to appreciate the reddleman until she noticed how good-looking he was once the red had all worn off.[140] Wessex mothers used to threaten naughty children with the saying, "The reddleman is coming for you,"[141] a saying which Johnny Nunsuch must have recalled when he met Diggory Venn on the heath at night:

"How I wish 'twas only a gipsy!"
"You are rather afraid of me. Do you know what I be?"
"Yes. The reddleman."
"You little children think there's only one cuckoo, one fox, one devil, and one reddleman, when there's lots of us all."
"Is there? You won't carry me off in your bags, will ye, master?"
"Nonsense! All that reddlemen do is to sell reddle. . . ."[142]

The Corn Market at Casterbridge was the scene of many a well-driven bargain. Thither went Bathsheba, resolved to act in the most approved manner. Here were tree-

---

[136] Bertram Windle, *Remains of the Prehistoric Age in Britain*, 148; Lean's *Collectanea*, III, 207, quoting Fitzherbert's *Book of Husbandry*, 1534, p. 35.
[137] *The Return of the Native*, Book I, Chap. IX.
[138] *Ibid.*, Book V, Chap. II.
[139] *Ibid.*, Book I, Chaps. VIII, IX.
[140] *Ibid.*, Book I, Chap. IX.
[141] *Ibid.*
[142] *Ibid.*

merchants, carrying saplings which they used partly as walking-sticks and partly to poke up pigs, sheep, and neighbors with their backs turned. As each talked, he would play with his sapling, bending it around his back, making an arch of it between his two hands, or tucking it under his arm as he reached in his pocket for a sample of grain. Bathsheba was careful to pour and exhibit her corn in a highly professional manner.[143] Our sympathies are all with Henchard when Farfrae's neat systems of bookkeeping have supplanted the mayor's rough-and-ready ways. We are angered to hear Farfrae praised thus:

". . . 'Twas verily fortune sent him to Henchard. His accounts were like a bramblewood when Mr. Farfrae came. He used to reckon his sacks by chalk strokes all in a row like garden-palings, measure his ricks by stretching with his arms, weigh his trusses by a lift, judge his hay by a chaw, and settle the price with a curse." [144]

No reader of *The Woodlanders* can forget Winterborne's embarrassment when meeting Grace Melbury on her return from school. Her first glimpse of him was as he stood, almost retiringly, in the market-place, holding a ten-foot apple tree with towering boughs. The timber-sale in the woods is one of the loveliest scenes in Hardy; the auctioneer walked about

. . . like some philosopher of the Peripatetic School delivering his lectures in the shady groves of the Lyceum. His companions were timber-dealers, yeomen, farmers, villagers and others; mostly woodland-men, who . . . could afford to be curious in their walking-sticks . . . corkscrew shapes in black and white thorn. . . . Two women wearing men's jackets on their gowns, conducted in the rear of the halting procession a pony-cart containing a tapped barrel of beer, from which they drew and replenished horns that were handed round, with bread-and-cheese from a basket.

The auctioneer adjusted himself to circumstances by using his walking-stick as a hammer, and knocked down the lot on any convenient object that took his fancy, such as the crown of a little boy's

---

143 *Far from the Madding Crowd,* Chap. XII.
144 *The Mayor of Casterbridge,* Chap. XVI.

head, or the shoulders of a by-stander who had no business there except to taste the brew; a proceeding that would have been deemed humorous but for the air of stern rigidity which that auctioneer preserved. . . .

. . . A few flakes of snow descended, at the sight of which a robin, alarmed at these signs of imminent winter, and seeing that no harm was meant by the human invasion, came and perched on the tip of the fagots that were being sold, and looked into the auctioneer's face, while waiting for some chance crumbs from the bread-basket. . . ." [145]

It is a charming scene, fresh and cool, with just a hint of bleakness. A scene which is in admirable contrast, wonderfully rich and warm with the tang of autumn in the air, is Winterborne's visit to the outlying districts of the woodlands with his apple-mill and cider-press. We see him at the wring-house, and watch him build up the pomace into molds, or "cheeses." Giles "looked and smelt Autumn's very brother." [146] Scenes like this are, alas, now quite rare!

Hardy describes for us both the hiring-fairs and the great trade-fairs of Wessex. Of the twice-a-year hiring-fairs, the most picturesque was that held at Candlemas, at which agreements were entered into to begin work on April 6, Lady Day, Old Style, and which necessitated the migrations of workfolk in the way described in *Tess*.[147] Gabriel Oak stood for hours at the Casterbridge Candlemas hiring-fair; finding that bailiffs were not in demand, he went to a smith's and had a shepherd's crook made, and to a shop, where he donned the shepherd's regulation smockfrock. In the square stood the carters and wagoners, a bit of whipcord twisted in their hands, thatchers holding cords of woven straw, shepherds, bailiffs, and others. Every farmer who questioned him was suspicious the moment he heard that Oak had had bad luck with a farm of his own. Finally he took out his flute and began to pipe "Jockey to the Fair" with Arcadian sweetness; a crowd soon gathered and in half an hour he had earned a pocketful of pence, enough to take him on

[145] *The Woodlanders*, Chap. VII.
[146] *Ibid.*, Chap. XXV.
[147] *Tess*, Chaps. LI, LII.

to Shottsford, the next hiring-fair.[148] Even more memorable is the great hiring-fair upon which Lucetta looked out from her windows in High Place Hall:

The fair without the windows was now raging thick and loud. It was the chief hiring fair of the year, and differed quite from the market of a few days earlier. In substance it was a whitey-brown crowd flecked with white—this being the body of labourers waiting for places. The long bonnets of the women, like waggon-tilts, their cotton gowns and checked shawls, mixed with the carters' smock-frocks. . . . Among the rest, at the corner of the pavement, stood an old shepherd, who attracted the eyes of Lucetta and Farfrae by his stillness. He was evidently a chastened man. The battle of life had been a sharp one with him, for, to begin with, he was a man of small frame. He was now so bowed by hard work and years that, approaching from behind, a person could hardly see his head. He had planted the stem of his crook in the gutter and was resting upon the bow, which was polished to silver brightness by the long friction of his hands. He had quite forgotten where he was, and what he had come for, his eyes being bent on the ground. A little way off negotiations were proceeding which had reference to him; but he did not hear them, and there seemed to be passing through his mind pleasant visions of the hiring successes of his prime, when his skill laid open to him any farm for the asking.

The negotiations were between a farmer from a distant country and the old man's son. In these there was a difficulty. The farmer would not take the crust without the crumb of the bargain, in other words, the old man without the younger; and the son had a sweetheart on his present farm, who stood by, waiting the issue with pale lips.

"I'm sorry to leave ye, Nelly," said the young man with emotion. "But, you see, I can't starve father, and he's out o' work at Lady-Day. 'Tis only thirty-five mile."

The girl's lips quivered. "Thirty-five mile!" she murmured. "Ah, 'tis enough! I shall never see 'ee again!"

. . . .

"Oh! no, no—I never shall," she insisted, when he pressed her hand; and she turned her face to Lucetta's wall to hide her weeping. . . .

[148] *Far from the Madding Crowd,* Chap. VI.

Lucetta's eyes, full of tears, met Farfrae's. His, too, to her surprise, were moist at the scene.

"It is very hard," she said with strong feeling. "Lovers ought not to be parted like that! . . ."

"Maybe I can manage that they'll not be parted. . . . I want a young carter, and perhaps I'll take the old man, too—yes, he'll not be very expensive, and doubtless he'll answer my pairrpose somehow." [149]

Thus the little tragedy was averted. The reader will recall how Tess hired out from Lady-Day to Lady-Day; and how she met Alec d'Urberville, now turned evangelist, on his way to the Candlemas fair at Casterbridge.[150] Martinmas Fair at Casterbridge or at Portland Bill was almost as brilliant as Candlemas; Avice the Second found the London streets at night for all the world like the Street of Wells at Martinmas fair. There comes to mind the charming picture of the long, steep pass lined on both sides with young girls bearing pitchers, waiting their turn to fill them from the fountains which rise bubbling there.[151] One of Hardy's idyls gives us a touching picture of the market girl who could not sell her wares, but won for herself a lover by her lonely, wistful air.[152] These hiring-fairs were often the occasion for youthful gayety, for village "hoppings," or dances, were popular with those who had little at stake, or who could lightly throw off the cares of the day.[153]

For centuries there were hiring-fairs, called Mops, probably after the servant-girl's badge of office, at which domestics sought new places in the households of the gentry.[154] The Stratford-on-Avon fair goes back to the days of King John.[155] At these fairs certain rhyming formulas, doggerel verses, were sung giving inside information as to the various

---

[149] *The Mayor of Casterbridge,* Chap. XXIII.
[150] *Tess,* Chap. XLIV.
[151] *The Well-Beloved,* Part II, Chaps. IX, XII.
[152] *Time's Laughingstocks:* "At Casterbridge Fair: IV. The Market-Girl."
[153] *Time's Laughingstocks:* "At Casterbridge Fair: III, After the Club-Dance: VI, After the Fair."
[154] N. Thomas, *Folklore of Northumberland,* 123; E. M. Wright, *Rustic Speech and Folklore,* 305–306.
[155] Wright, *Ibid.,* 306.

employers and households seeking servants; these probably
originated in the Middle Ages when servants could not
read, and still survive in the children's game, The Lady of
the Land.[156] An employer gave anything from a shilling
to a pound as "earnest money"; if the servant returned
the "God's penny," he might renounce the bargain, but
if the master changed his mind, the latter forfeited the
fee.[157] A few weeks after the regular hiring-fair, a Runaway
Mop was often held for the benefit of servants who had
run away from their situations; if they failed to keep this
second agreement, it is said they could be imprisoned.[158]
Interesting as these Mops are, Hardy's fairs have a larger
air. His shepherds, for instance, have a pride in their craft;
they go for a year or more. There is humility, but no
servility in the smockfrock and the polished crook. Oak's
failure to secure a place spelt discouragement; to the old
shepherd whom Farfrae befriended, it meant despair. Hardy
was keenly alive to the tragedy of the old, the faithful but
unwanted ones left in the wake of the surging years.

These hiring-fairs were followed inevitably by the Lady-
Day flittings on April 6, migrations which saddened Hardy
greatly, because they reduced the countryman to a mere
hireling, took from him the long and intimate associations
with one farm, and robbed him of precious old traditions
and the incentive to found new ones.[159] He gives us a gloomy
picture of one of these movings; we see the Durbeyfields
perched high on the furniture and bedding, Joan clutching
the clock, which now and then struck one or one-and-a-half
in mournful tones, make their way out of the village that
has been their only home. The meeting with Marian and Izz,
who had thrown in their lot with a prosperous ploughman's
family, emphasizes the relative misery of the homeless
Durbeyfields. After the driver had unloaded their goods

---

[156] *Ibid.*, 306; Gomme, *Traditional Games*, I, 319.
[157] Wright, 306; Gurdon, *Folklore of Suffolk*, 104.
[158] Wright, 306; J. B. Partridge, *Folk-Lore*, XXVI, 95.
[159] E. Brennecke, Jr., ed., *Life and Art*—Hardy's Collected Essays, "The
Dorsetshire Labourer."

by the church-wall at Kingsbere, and gone off with almost their last penny, the helpless family looked about the church for some place to sleep.[160] It is a picture that is drawn perhaps in too strong a light and shade, but back of it were similar scenes that impressed the novelist with the tragedy of these flittings everywhere.

Of all the fairs described by Hardy, the Greenhill, or Woodbury Hill, Fair is most memorable. The place itself is fascinating; tradition has it that it was once the site of an ancient British earthwork,[161] or perhaps of a British temple [162] which the Church with admirable wisdom converted to other uses. In 1296 the manor of Bere Regis passed to the Abbess of Trent, and with it a fair, a market, a free warren, and the forest of Bere; and at the dissolution of monastic houses, it was acquired by the d'Urbervilles, who secured a charter for a fair under Henry III, and derived a considerable income from it.[163] In medieval times it lasted five days, Wholesale Day, Gentlefolks' Day, All Folks' Day, Sheep-Fair Day, and Pack-and-Penny Day.[164] Hardy thus describes the sheep-fair in modern times:

Greenhill was the Nijni Novgorod of South Wessex; and the busiest, merriest, noisiest day of the whole statute number was the day of the sheep fair. This yearly gathering was upon the summit of a hill which retained in good preservation the remains of an earthwork, consisting of a huge rampart and entrenchment, of an oval form encircling the top of the hill. . . . To each of the two chief openings on opposite sides a winding road ascended, and the level green space of ten or fifteen acres enclosed by the bank was the site of the fair. . . .[165]

The novelist describes the shepherds' long journey, sometimes lasting three days or a week, taking care to drive the sheep not over twelve miles a day, resting in hired

160 *Tess,* Chaps. LI, LII.
161 Gomme, *Folk-Lore as a Historical Science,* 45.
162 Aubrey's *Remaines,* Britten ed., 108.
163 Sherren, *The Wessex of Romance,* 148.
164 *Ibid.*
165 *Far from the Madding Crowd,* Chap. L.

folds at night, after the day's march and fasting. Shepherds carried a kit, for sheep often went lame, and were provided with a pony and wagon for the lambings which might occur on the way. It is a scene of wonderful beauty:

> . . . the flocks became individually visible, climbing the serpentine ways which led to the top. Thus, in a slow procession, they entered the opening to which the roads tended, multitude after multitude, horned and hornless—blue flocks and red flocks, buff flocks and brown flocks, even green and salmon-tinted flocks, according to the fancy of the colourist and the custom of the farm. Men were shouting, dogs were barking with the greatest animation, but the thronging travellers in so long a journey had grown nearly indifferent to such terrors, though they bleated piteously at the unwontedness of their experiences, a tall shepherd rising here and there in the midst of them, like a gigantic idol amid a crowd of prostrate devotees. . . .[166]

It is a scene which some painter might readily wish to do. As we look back over the mass of folk-law, we are surprised to note its scope and variety. Little of it occurs for its own sake; most of it has a definite artistic purpose. It strengthens and deepens character; it makes incident after incident plausible, even inevitable; it crystallizes the subtle spirit of place. What would Giles Winterborne be without his love of trees and his way of giving life to them in their first sigh, or without his cider-mill? A noble, simple-hearted man, with unassuming acceptance of whatever work came his way, capable of great devotion—but not the Winterborne we know. What would Casterbridge be without its hiring-fair, its Mixen Lane, its skimmity rides, its long traditions of "battles and famines and hang-fairs and other pomps"?[167] The romance of place is strong in Hardy. Here are places steeped in the lives of those who have lived and died there, places as rich and ghoulish as churchyard soil, places that, like the battered mask at High Place, hint that

166 *Ibid.*, Chap. L.
167 *The Woodlanders*, Chap. X.

life is an ironic jest. And for assuagement of the insistent ironic note, there are pictures as fresh and beautiful as the sheep-fair at Greenhill or the woodlands filled with drifting snowflakes and little birds quite unafraid of man.

XII

PREHISTORY AND SURVIVALS OF
ANCIENT RELIGIONS

The recent discovery of the Piltdown skull is proof that England possessed a type of man as primitive as the famous Neanderthal Man, and that southern England has been inhabited from the very earliest times.[1] Moreover, palæolithic man in England comprised two widely different types of longheads from early times, the dark southern and fair northern, both occurring in western Britain from the beginning, and continuing pretty steadily with minor modifications up to modern times.[2] Still more amazing was the discovery in Aveline's Hole in 1922 of the remains of roundheaded individuals of Aurignacian type, showing that roundheads were actually living in the west of England as early as 8000 or even 10,000 B. C.[3] This presence of roundheads at so early a time helps to explain the modifications in the dominant long-headed physical type of the English race, but we must be careful not to confuse them with the more notable roundheads who were the chief civilizers of Europe, and later of England, and if not the authors of the Bronze Age, were at least the carriers of its tremendous advance in civilization. Geologists tell us that in the early Quaternary period there was a great land-bridge between the south of England and the north of France. From Quaternary times onward England became gradually populated further to the north, and civilizations identical

[1] Eugene Pittard, *Race and History*, 1926, 184–185.
[2] John Beddoe, *Anthropological History of Europe*, 175.
[3] Pittard, *op. cit.*, 194, Translator's note 2.

with those flourishing in France, for instance, must have
bloomed on English soil, the Chellean folk flaking their
hand-axes, the Mousterian, their cutters and points, in England just as on the Continent.[4] This continuity of civilization was broken when the land-bridge subsided, postponing
for England the peaceful invasion of the civilizing round-
headed folk who revolutionized Europe.

These roundheads are the puzzle of the anthropologist.
One wave of this folk came into France from the south,
probably from Asia via the shores of the Black Sea and
the Danube Valley, bringing with them the art of metallurgy
from a yellow race to which they did not, however, belong;
and the Swiss lake-dwellers are an important wave of this
roundheaded people, to whom we owe the cultivation of
cereals, the introduction of domesticated animals, and the
art of navigation.[5] In France, these roundheaded, bronze-
using folk produced no profound changes in racial type; in
England, which they reached later, they profoundly modified
the already mixed long-headed stock, not, however, wiping
it out, as an anthropological type once in possession of a
country is never completely extirpated, but becoming pre-
dominant in southwestern England, in Hardy's Wessex,
that is to say, as well as part of Wales.[6]

What we dare not assert, much as we should like to, is
that these brachycephalic folk, the people of the round barrows, are the people who brought in the Bronze Age; with
their coming, however, the distinguishing marks of Bronze
Age culture became increasingly evident.[7] Agriculture was
introduced with domesticated animals; flints were beautifully worked and pottery ornamented. Finally monumental
sepulture in megalithic tombs was introduced, probably from
a Paris area of the same cult, and by a similar folk; this
was shortly afterwards followed by those we call the East-

---

[4] *Ibid.*, 184–87.
[5] *Ibid.*, 122–125, 147.
[6] *Ibid.*, 126, 131, 184, 188; Beddoe, *Anthropological History of Europe*, 53;
Donald Mackenzie, *Ancient Man in Britain*, 109..
[7] Pittard, 125; Stanley Casson, *Folk-Lore*, XXXVIII, 267–268.

ern Beaker-folk from the Rhineland, who introduced the earliest metal.[8]

There seem to have been several waves of these round-headed folk; certain anthropologists say that the advance guard was Brythonic, and would place it near the close of the Hallstadt period.[9] When we speak of *Celt* in matters of race, we mean, not the Celts of Cæsar or Tacitus, who are properly Nordic folk, but the Celt of Broca, the so-called Alpine, or Ligurian man.[10] Recent finds at Hengist-bury Head near Southhampton, of pottery similar to the keeled or globular vases found in Pyrenean tumuli, and usually dated near the close of the Hallstadt period, seem to hint that these importers of Celtic pottery, or at least, of pottery from Celticized lands, were in England at a very early day.[11] What has been learned from the study of port-hole architecture in stone sepulchral monuments ties up with this theory; it seems probable that the English long barrows are contemporaneous with the final megalithic period of northern Europe, and of Scandinavia, in particular, and the late period in France, where passage-graves were being made, and therefore may be no older than 2000 B. C.[12] These peculiar cist-tombs with portholes seem to have come to England from a Paris area, where they were developed independently of other forms, via Brittany and the Channel Islands.[13] The roundheaded folk remain a good deal of a mystery.

The English racial type has remained essentially long-headed, with its original variations of the darker southern longheads and the fairer northern longheads all the more emphasized by the Scandinavian settlements in the north, and the people who have left Celtic place-names in the south

---

[8] T. D. Kendrick, *The Axe Age: A Study in Keltic Prehistory,* 172. The entire book throws light on recent anthropological and archæological findings.
[9] Pittard, 191–192, Note 1; 194.
[10] *Ibid.,* 82, Note 1; 82–83; 192, Note 2.
[11] *Ibid.,* 192, Note 2; Stanley Casson, *Folk-Lore,* XXXVIII, 267–268.
[12] Kendrick, *The Axe Age,* 52; 105–106; 120.
[13] *Ibid.,* 120.

and west of England. But there are also modifications due to the broadheads—the broad face and rather stocky build of the typical John Bull. The variations in Dorset are surprising to the tourist: in one village he finds a tall, fair people; in another, only a few miles distant, short, dark folk, with the broad face that is not characteristic of the Nordic type. In other words, Hardy's country contains a great diversity of physical types, and with them a complex prehistory. In the present stage of our knowledge, it is impossible to unstratify the successive layers of folklore in Wessex; the land has been too constantly inhabited from the earliest times for that. We may expect to find folklore survivals that hark back to the Old Stone Age, and are strikingly similar to the folklore of savages just emerging today from their Stone Age. We cannot label this bit of folklore Aryan and that non-Aryan; we cannot call this belief Teutonic, and that Celtic. Language is no criterion of race. The geologist, the archæologist, and the anthropologist must go on excavating, classifying remains of primitive man, animals, implements, pottery, and sepulchral monuments. But the folklorist, unable to reach any definite conclusions as to Wessex prehistory, may assist the scientist in building up the complete picture of the past of England. All over Dorset we find the sepulchral monuments built by prehistoric man—round barrows and long barrows, stone circles (which are not sepulchral, and are peculiarly characteristic of England), the upstanding stones which we hesitate to call true dolmens, finely chipped flints, tipped arrows, cinerary urns, and so on. We shall find survivals of primitive religious beliefs and customs: traces of sun- and moon-worship, relics of the worship of a goddess of fertility who goes by many names, but who is wonderfully like the Phœnician Astarte; the belief in giants, phallic worship reflected in the inexplicable Cerne Giant, and the ever-fascinating problem of Druidism.

Hardy assures us that Egdon is not one heath, but a composite of several heaths. It is mere impertinence to seek

to identify every barrow and to list every archæological
find on this or any other fictitious site. Hardy wishes to
convey the impression of the great age of the heath. At
the dawn of written history England is a vast palimpsest
on which prehistoric man has written his record in a script
we cannot decipher. Egdon is a primeval place, "a Face
on which Time makes but little impression." [14] We can
piece together a fragmentary view of the long-headed neolithic folk who built the long barrows, orienting them always
east to west, and, it would appear, first bleaching and then
burying the bones.[15] We know less about the folk of the
round barrows, whom we dare not as yet identify with the
civilizing folk of the Bronze Age. But round barrows and
long barrows continued to be made simultaneously. The
barrows of Egdon, like those of Dorset in general, contain
Stone Age implements of various periods.

Clym Yeobright as a boy was constantly finding flint
knives and arrowheads and wondering how stones could
grow into such odd forms.[16] Wildeve and Eustacia Vye were
accustomed to meet in a little ditch encircling Rainbarrow
which was part of an excavation made by prehistoric folk.[17]
A large barrow was opened on Egdon Heath, containing
large cinerary urns with bones in them; [18] these urns are
characteristic of Dorset, and carry us back to the days of
early Christianity when inverted pots were built into church-
walls, as it were, to conciliate the very gods whom the folk
had rejected.[19] On many of the great flat stones at Stonehenge are the cup-markings which have, perhaps too fancifully, been interpreted as "food-vases" and "drinking-cups"
for the dead.[20]

[14] *The Return of the Native,* Book I, Chap. I.
[15] Kendrick, *The Axe Age,* 26; O. G. S. Crawford, *The Long Barrows of the Cotswolds,* 13–14.
[16] *The Return of the Native,* Book III, Chap. II.
[17] *Ibid.,* Book I, Chap. IX.
[18] *Ibid.,* Book III, Chap. III.
[19] Bertram C. Windle, *Remains of the Prehistoric Age in England,* 152; Grimm-Stallybrass, IV, 1320.
[20] Rev. Walter Gregor, *Notes on the Folk-Lore of the North-East of Scotland,* 213; cf. Sabine Baring-Gould, *Strange Survivals,* 273–274, 280.

Egdon is recorded in the Domesday Book as a heathy, furzy stretch of country, which was apparently as Ishmael-itish then as now.[21] Southern England seems to have impressed Cæsar with its sinister gloom, for he was careful to get away from it before the dismal autumn weather descended each year.[22] The solitary figure of Eustacia Vye on Rainbarrow seemed indeed one of the folk who had built the barrows, "a sort of last man among them, musing for a moment before dropping into night with the rest of his race." [23] The bonfires on the heath seemed not so much a relic of Woden-worship as of something far older, prehistoric man's "instinctive and resistant act," the indication of "a spontaneous, Promethean rebelliousness against the fiat that this recurrent season shall bring foul times, cold, darkness, misery, and death." [24] On his lonely walks, Clym Yeobright peopled the heath in fancy with forgotten Celtic tribes who were more real to his disordered brain than the actual Egdon folk to whom he preached on Rainbarrow.[25]

Hardy indulges the ironic fancy that an ancient Briton, gleefully watching the moth-signal, notes that now, as in his day, it summons lovers to their rendezvous; [26] the pagan mounds seem to bide their time, waiting for the day when the vast churches shall vanish as completely as the temples of the heathen cults they have superseded.[27]

All over Egdon are the "Druidical stones," as the Wessex folk call them, and the reader of *The Return of the Native* will recall how completely Clym failed to interest Eustacia in one of them: she remembered, she said, only that there were boulevards in Paris.[28] In "Two Who Became a Story," two lovers met by a Runic Stone, happily unconscious of how their story would be bruited about in days to come.[29]

[21] *The Return of the Native,* Book I, Chap. VI.
[22] *Ibid.,* Book I, Chap. VI.
[23] *Ibid.,* Book I, Chap. III.
[24] *Ibid.,* Book I, Chap. I.
[25] *Ibid.,* Book VI, Chap. I.
[26] *Satires of Circumstance:* "The Moth-Signal."
[27] *Winter Words:* "Evening Shadows."
[28] Book III, Chap. III.
[29] *Moments of Vision.*

It was by the "Druid Stone" that another felt the presence
of his dead beloved, but feared to turn and look lest it
should prove to be only the shadow cast by the rhythmically
swaying tree-tops.[30] In Hardy's garden at Max Gate stood
a Druid Stone;[31] and not far from Max Gate were found
two skeletons, clasped in each other's arms, in a barrow
pronounced at least as old as 1800 B. C.[32] Corvsgate Castle,
whither Ethelberta went on her donkey, was a huge cemetery
of barrows.[33] Weydon Priors Fair overlooked valleys which
sloped up to downs, and were everywhere dotted with barrows and prehistoric forts.[34]

In the tale, "What the Shepherd Saw," the unfortunate
sheep-boy who saw the Duchess's cousin murdered was
forced to kneel at the Druidical trilithon on Marlbury Down
and swear to keep his gruesome secret.[35] The peasant calls
any great upstanding stones "Druidical"; they cannot be
proved to have any historical connection with the mysterious
religion—perhaps Babylonian, or even Persian, in origin—
which we call Druidism.[36] It is a poetical fancy to call this
great trilithon, its three stones forming a doorway, the altar
of a pagan temple. Archæologists are coming to believe
more and more that such sepulchral monuments were once
covered with earth; the true dolmen is not characteristic of
England, and most of the so-called English "dolmens" can
be shown to bear traces of an original mound.[37] Such famous
stones as Enstone, The Whispering Knights, and Arthur's
Stone are probably the remains of long barrows, originally
erected by megalithic builders whose beliefs and rituals are
still a mystery to science.[38] When, however, we find a definite
bit of folklore connected with a stone or group of stones, as

---

[30] Moments of Vision: "The Shadow on the Stone."
[31] F. E. Hardy, The Early Life of Thomas Hardy, 306.
[32] Winter Words: "The Clasped Skeletons."
[33] The Hand of Ethelberta, Chap. XXXI.
[34] The Mayor of Casterbridge, Chap. II.
[35] A Changed Man.
[36] Louis Siret, L'Anthropologie, 1921, 268 ff.; Donald Mackenzie, Ancient Man in Britian, 143; W. Bonser, Folk-Lore, XXXVII, 274–275.
[37] O. G. S. Crawford, The Long Barrows of the Cotswolds, Intro., 21.
[38] Ibid.

with the Long Stone at Minchinhampton, with its "midnight
flittings," or the King-Stone and his Knights at Rollright,
we have evidence of prime historical value.[39] The trilithon
on Marlbury Down which figures in "What the Shepherd
Saw" is not distinctive in name or legend; it is but one of
many "Devil-stones" whose names point to half-forgotten
giant-lore and a neolithic people who had not yet learned
the use of fire.[40] All "Druid Stones," of course, are favorite
haunts of ghosts; and the trilithon on Marlbury Down is no
exception.[41] All devil-names applied to places do not invariably imply some old giant-legend; rather they indicate merely
some particularly lonely and forbidding place. This is true
of the dell between Dogbury Hill and High Stoy, which
Tess had to cross, called "The Devil's Kitchen"; [42] and of
the nine gaunt, ghastly trees at "The Devil's Bellows" outside the home of Clym Yeobright and Eustacia.[43] "The
Devil's Door" in Wroxhall Abbey and elsewhere is a name
applied to a northern entrance seldom used, reminding us of
the burial of the unregenerate and unbaptized in the north
side of the churchyard.[44]

Hardy mentions other stone monuments too numerous to
list; the "nine-pillared cromlech" is a familiar part of many
Hardy scenes; [45] Sarsen Stones are almost equally well
known to Hardy readers.[45] Sarsen, a corruption of "Saracen," or foreign, is the rustic's name for any unusual stone
he cannot account for; a Sarsen Stone is a heathen stone.[46]

Stonehenge, where Tess spent her last night, is a fascinating problem to the student of prehistory. Stone circles
are not a part of megalithic art as a whole, but a specialty
in England.[47] Many of the stones at Stonehenge have been

[39] *Ibid.*, Intro. 26–27; Arthur Evans, *Folk-Lore*, VI, 18–33.
[40] Crawford, Intro., 30; Grimm-Stallybrass, IV, 1436, 1462.
[41] *A Changed Man:* "What the Shepherd Saw."
[42] *Tess*, Chap. XLIV.
[43] *The Return of the Native*, Book IV, Chap. V.
[44] C. S. Burne, *Folk-Lore*, XIX, 458–459; John Brand, *Popular Antiquities of Great Britain*, Sir Henry Ellis's ed., II, 292.
[45] *Wessex Poems*, "My Cicely"; *Time's Laughingstocks:* "The Revisita-
tion."
[46] E. Herbert Stone, *The Stones of Stonehenge*, 44–45.
[47] Kendrick, *The Axe Age*, 115–116.

brought from Wales, from the Prescelly Mountains, to which they are native, and from which they were hewn. The men who took the pains to shift this stone circle such a great distance and re-erect it at Stonehenge must have felt a reverence for the stones as part of an older circle sacred in the religious life of their ancestors.[48] The glamour around them grew with time, and with it a mass of legends. Among the latter is the peasant story of how Merlin transported the stones from Ireland by a wave of his wand: the real reason why the stones were moved once forgotten, the folk invented one from such legendary materials as lay at hand, and Arthur, to whom many large stones were ascribed as "Seats of Justice," was their most natural choice.[49] Giraldus Cambriensis called Stonehenge "Choirgaur," that is, *chorea gigantum,* a carol or dance of giants.[50] Among the many famous stones likened to dancers are the Nine Maidens of Bakewell, Derbyshire. Such stones were said to be witches turned into stone for dancing on the Sabbath; the myth is far older than its application to witchcraft.[51]

Colonel Waddell holds that Stonehenge was a Phœnician solar observatory, and translates a supposed Catti-Phœnician script on the markings of certain stones as showing the exact line for observations; and although the Phœnician script is fanciful, there is possible truth in interpreting Stonehenge as a place where such observations were taken.[52] We cannot prove that it was ever a Druid temple, or that human beings were sacrificed on any of the large, flat stones, some of which, the so-called Slaughter Stone, for instance, were still upstanding in old Aubrey's day, and others of which, such as the Altar Stone, may each have been used as a dais or platform of some sort.[53] Another authority will have it that

---

[48] *Ibid.,* 71, 102; *The Antiquaries' Journal,* III, 255 seq.

[49] *Ibid.,* Stanley Casson, *Folk-Lore,* XXXVIII, 206; *Denham Tracts,* II, 131.

[50] Grimm-Stallybrass, II, 552, Note 1; Gir. Camb. cap. 18.

[51] M. A. Murray, *The Witch Cult in Western Europe,* 108–109.

[52] Col. L. A. Waddell, *The Phœnician Origin of Britons, Scots, and Anglo-Saxons,* 226–232.

[53] E. Herbert Stone, F. S. A.: *The Stones of Stonehenge,* 118–119; 19–20.

Stonehenge is merely an unusually large stone circle; and
that like other stone circles, it was the site of a folk-moot of
the Iron Age.[54] Although this is the most recent expert opinion on Stonehenge, archæologists are far from unanimous
in it: Stone urges that it is not a true circle, and no one
doubts the original religious significance of the stones themselves.[55] In support of the theory, there is the practice, both
Irish and Anglo-Saxon, of holding moots or courts of justice out-of-doors, to counteract any harmful magic which
might be exercised within four walls;[56] and the use of natural stone for coronations may indicate the earlier use of
such stones as seats of justice, primitive courts, and sites of
folk-moots.[57]

A poet need follow no hard outline of fact. The stone on
which Tess flings herself is indeed a Stone of Sacrifice. In
this heathen temple she felt strangely at home; the wind
playing upon the great pillars, sounded like a gigantic harp.

In the far north-east sky he could see between the pillars a level
streak of light. The uniform concavity of black cloud was lifting
bodily like the lid of a pot, letting in at the earth's edge the coming
day, against which the towering monoliths and trilithons began to be
blackly defined.
"Did they sacrifice to God here?" asked she.
"No," said he.
"Who to?"
"I believe to the sun. That lofty stone set away by itself is in the
direction of the sun which will presently rise behind it." [58]

After a time the steady booming of the wind lulled Tess
to sleep, and Angel Clare watched the dawn break:

. . . the whole enormous landscape bore that impress of reserve,
taciturnity, and hesitation which is usual just before day. The east-

---

[54] A. Hadrian Allcroft, *The Archæological Journal,* LXXVIII, (1921),
299 ff.
[55] E. H. Stone, *The Stones of Stonehenge,* 34 ff.
[56] G. L. Gomme, *Folklore as a Historical Science,* 51; Bede, *Eccles. Hist.,*
Lib. 1, cap. 25.
[57] *Denham Tracts,* II, 130–131.
[58] *Tess,* Chap. LVIII.

ward pillars and their architraves stood up blackly against the light,
and the great flame-shaped Sun-stone beyond them; and the Stone of
Sacrifice midway. Presently the night wind died out, and the quiver-
ing little pools in the cup-like hollows of the stones lay still. At the
same time something seemed to move on the verge of the dip eastward
—a mere dot. It was the head of a man approaching them from the
hollow beyond the Sun-stone. . . .[59]

In one sketch, "A Tryst at an Ancient Earthwork," Hardy
describes Mai-Dun, the finest prehistoric earthwork in all
England.[60] This great contour fort [61] fascinated Hardy; he
asked himself who planned it, whether one of the Belgæ or
of the Durotriges, or some travelling engineer of Britain's
united tribes.[62] It is said to have been the Dunium of Ptol-
emy, the capital of the Durotriges, which, falling into
Roman hands, was fortified and greatly expanded on its already grand plan. Mai-Dun is huge and amazingly complex
in design. It was probably a large and permanently walled
city of the Bronze Age. The Romans developed Durnovaria,
our modern Dorchester, as a dwelling-place, and turned
Mai-Dun into a fort, which was abandoned after their with-
drawal. It must have taken the men of the Bronze Age, or
earlier, many years to erect these five miles of valla; its
situation and plan are magnificent even today.[63] We know
nothing definite of its history. The aged archæologist in the
tale unearths an exquisite mosaic proving Roman occupation, an iridescent bottle, a skeleton almost intact, and
finally, a golden statuette of Mercury. With a pang of regret, he is persuaded to replace these "finds," but several
years later the friend who had accompanied him to Mai-
Dun finds the gilt statuette among the deceased antiquary's
effects. He had labeled it "Debased Roman." [64] So much for
antiquarian zeal! Hardy refers to the old earthwork fre-

[59] *Ibid.*
[60] *A Changed Man.*
[61] A. Hadrian Allcroft, *Earthwork of England,* 99–104.
[62] *A Changed Man:* "A Tryst at an Ancient Earthwork."
[63] A. Hadrian Allcroft, *Earthwork of England,* 99–100, has fine maps and
illustrations of Maiden Castle.
[64] *A Changed Man:* "A Tryst at an Ancient Earthwork."

quently.[65] The archæological finds at Mai-Dun remind us of the queer assortment of Pompeian-like pottery which kept turning up in Jim Hayward's lime-kiln, once the site of an ancient earthwork.[66] The earliest known emblem of the Christian faith in England was found in Frampton, a Wessex village, bearing the first two Greek letters of the name of Christ, and an inscription to Neptune, with a head spouting dolphins! [67]

Second in interest only to Mai-Dun is Ring's-Hill Speer, a hilltop variously interpreted as a Roman camp, an old British castle, or a Saxon field of Witenagemote; it bore the remains of an outer and inner vallum.[68] Here flourished the romance of Lady Constantine and the young astronomer, St. Cleeve.

Peasants in "outstep" places still regard the sun and moon as endowed with sentience and life, and occasionally reveal the impulse to worship them. Tess, like all country-women who live most of their lives out-of-doors, in close touch with the forces of Nature, had this primitive capacity for nature-worship. This myth-making faculty is something very close to anthropomorphism. One glorious morning in the Froom Valley, in sheer exultation at the beauty of the day, she chanted to the sun a Christian psalm in pagan adoration.[69] To the Marlott harvesters, the sun, half-hidden by the mist, looked like a golden-haired, mild-faced godlike creature, gazing down at their earth with intensely eager curiosity.[70]

There is a scene that particularly endears the reader to the youthful Jude: Jude, in his wagon, had been reading the *Carmen Sæculare;* suddenly became aware of the soft, pervasive light of the moon, he stopped, and glancing around to make sure that no one could see, he knelt, book in hand, and chanted softly, "Phœbe, silvarumque potens Diana!" [71]

[65] *The Mayor of Casterbridge,* Chap. XLIII; *Jude,* Part I, Chap. VIII; *Wessex Poems:* "My Cicely."
[66] *A Changed Man:* "The Romantic Adventures of a Milkmaid."
[67] W. Sherren, *The Wessex of Romance,* 231–232.
[68] *Two on a Tower,* Chap. I.
[69] *Tess,* Chap. XVI.
[70] *Ibid.,* Chap. XIV.
[71] *Jude the Obscure,* Part I, Chap. V.

Another scene reveals the peasants' instinctive feeling for the moon, the strange spell which moonlight casts over them: at the moonlight gypsying on Egdon, all the dancers felt the powerful symptoms, and they danced like people in an ecstatic dream.[72]

In some parts of England and in Denmark, it was long believed that the sun dances on Easter Day.[73] Moon-worship lingered until recent times along the banks of the Ribble, in Lancashire, where moon-cakes were made and eaten, just as they are in modern China.[74] Astarte, whose worship was a moon-cult as well as a fertility-cult, has her tradition even today in the Isle of Slingers.[75] The English and Irish used to curtsy to the moon, invoking it with a prayer for health and good luck.[76] Moon-worship, however, is not characteristically Teutonic, for our heathen ancestors conceived the sun as a female deity, and worshiped her as a giver of life.[77]

The peasant's belief in a god of the weather finds striking illustration in Henchard's visit to the weather-caster, "Wide-O." Hardy tells us that in times of drought or tempests the peasants' impulse was to prostrate themselves in fear, as if at the mercy of incalculable and capricious powers.[78] The day Sue Bridehead went for a walk and bought her Venus and Apollo of the image-vender in sheer delight at the day, seemed to her a day sent by a passing caprice of the weather-god.[79] When Knight clung desperately to the Cliff-Without-a-Name, the very beauty of the day seemed a cruel indifference to his fate. He felt, as had felt many West Country folk before him, that "Nature seems to have certain moods, predilections for certain deeds at certain times,

---

[72] *The Return of the Native*, Book IV, Chap. III.
[73] Wm. Henderson, *Folkore of the Northern Counties*, 83; E. M. Wright, *Rustic Speech and Folklore*, 295; G. Schutte, *Folk-Lore*, XXXV, 367.
[74] Harland and Wilkinson, *Lancashire Folklore*, 3; J. J. Jevons, *Folk-Lore*, II, 229 ff.; N. B. Dennys, *Folk-Lore of China*, 28; Napier, *Folk-Lore; or Superstitious Beliefs in the West of Scotland*, 97.
[75] *The Well-Beloved*, Part I, Chap. II; Part II, Chaps. III, VI, XIII.
[76] Aubrey's *Remaines*, 36–37; 83–84; 95, 142, 180, etc.
[77] Grimm-Stallybrass, I, 103.
[78] *The Mayor of Casterbridge*, Chap. XXVI.
[79] *Jude the Obscure*, Part II, Chap. III.

without any apparent law to govern . . . them. She is read
as a person of a curious temper: as one who does not scatter
kindnesses and cruelties alternately, impartially, and in
order, but heartless severities, or overwhelming generosities
in lawless caprice. . . . In her unfriendly moments there
seems a feline fun in her tricks, begotten by a foretaste of
her pleasure in swallowing her victim." [80]

The rustics in *Two on a Tower* feel the caprice of a
thunder-god: they interpret St. Cleeves' death by lightning
as the punishment of a jealous god; [81] and when Grammer
Oliver, asleep by her hearth, is almost killed by lightning,
they are indignant at the unreasonableness of the elements,
which seem to be bent on murdering an innocent old
woman! [82] There is an old superstition that one must not
point at the rainbow or the stars; [83] and well up into the
last century English peasants could be found who would tell
you that if you counted the stars, you would surely be struck
blind.[84] The primitive mind ascribed thunder to an angry
and avenging god long before poetic fancy attributed the
echoing roll to the gods' game of bowls.[85]

The spirit of place is strong in simple country folk; they
feel that certain places have a friendly personality, and that
others are sinister and forbidding. Tess shares this spirit;
she seems at times a part of soil and wind and weather. On
her way to Talbothays, that richly beautiful country in which
she was to know exquisite happiness, Tess felt that some unknown good might come to her in her ancestral land.[86] The
bleakness of Flintcomb Ash communicated itself to Tess's
spirit; it seemed to her that the gaunt, spectral birds which
came from the North Pole spoke to her with their tragic eyes
of scenes of horror which they had witnessed,[87] and even
stolid Marian remarked that the birds had foreseen the

[80] *A Pair of Blue Eyes,* Chap. XXII.
[81] Chap. I.
[82] *Two on a Tower,* Chap. XVI.
[83] Grimm-Stallybrass, I, 146; Note 1; II, 732.
[84] L. Salmon, *Folk-lore,* XIII, 419; *Folk-Lore,* XII, 162-67.
[85] Grimm-Stallybrass, I, 167; IV, 1339; *Folk-Lore,* XXVI, 460.
[86] *Tess,* Chap. XV.

coming of the snow and sleet, keeping always just a bit in front of it.[87] Elfride had shuddered at the face of the Cliff-Without-a-Name,[88] as Mrs. Yeobright had at the nine ghastly trees that formed the Devil's Bellows.[89] But it is Egdon, of course, which has the most striking personality. Its lonely face looked tragic, Ishmaelitish. It seemed a Titan waiting for the last crisis—the end of all things. It seemed listening for something. It was most terrible when it spoke: the wind, moving through an infinity of tiny, bell-like flowers, shriveled to mere shells, spoke in a vaguely troubled voice, a murmur that complained perhaps that but few had known it, and none loved it. In its blackest mood, the heath destroyed its enemy, the Queen of Night; yet it was infinitely tender to Clym, for was not he a little mad?[90]

In *The Dynasts* time and time again Nature manifests a sympathy for man's little drama. The same idea is magnificently expressed in *The Queen of Cornwall*: Tristram is dead, and Iseult, and at last, the body of Mark is found. Brangwain exclaims:

> "Here's more of this same stuff of death. Look down—
> What see I lying there? King Mark, too, slain?
> The sea's dark noise last night, the sky's vast yawn
> Of copper-coloured cloud, meant murder, then,
> As I divined!"[91]

It was long believed that "Earth bears not on her breast the man of blood."[92] In German and English folklore, when a hanging, whether a suicide or an execution, takes place, a furious storm was thought to spring up: perhaps earth is conceived as resenting the pollution of the dead body, or, as is more probable, the wind is but the passing of Odin,

---

[87] *Tess*, Chap. XLIII.
[88] *A Pair of Blue Eyes*, Chap. XXI.
[89] *The Return of the Native*, Book IV, Chap. V.
[90] *Ibid.*, Book I, Chaps. I, VI; Book V, Chaps. VII, VIII, IX; Book VI, Chap. IV.
[91] *The Famous Tragedy of the Queen of Cornwall at Tintagel, in Lyonesse*, Scene XX.
[92] Grimm-Stallybrass, IV, 1475.

god of the gallows and leader of the Furious Host, come to welcome into his ghostly rout the latest horseman.[93]

There is considerable fetishistic belief in Hardy's folk; there are people to whom trees are live creatures, weeds have souls, and the most ordinary objects instinct with personality and feeling if placed in accidental associations of time and place. The tree in "The Tree: An Old Man's Story" [94] seems a live creature, as does also the tree whose life is mysteriously bound up with the life of its mistress in "The Tree and the Lady." [95] "The Felled Elm and She" tells the same tale more exquisitely: neither the great elm nor the lovely lady was aware that the life of each was dependent upon the other.[96] The most striking case in point, however, is the tale of Old South, who sat day after day, watching the tall elm rocking in the wind, singing its sad Gregorian melodies, and seeming to threaten to fall and crush him, its ancient enemy.[97] South has every reason to fear the tree; he feels a fatal bond between the tree and himself:

"Ah, when it was quite a small tree, and I was a little boy, I thought one day of chopping it off with my hook to make a clothes-line with. But I put off doing it, and then again thought that I would; but I forgot it, and didn't. And at last it got too big, and now 'tis my enemy, and will be the death o' me. Little did I think, when I let that sapling stay, that a time would come when it would torment me, and dash me into my grave." [98]

It is small wonder that Dr. Fitzpiers, puzzled by this curious fixed illusion, is anxious to get to the bottom of it:

"How long has he complained of the tree?"
"Weeks and weeks, sir. The shape of it seems to haunt him like an

[93] Grimm-Stallybrass, II, 635, III, 947–48; Mabel Peacock, *Folk-Lore*, XII, 165–166; Baring-Gould, *Strange Survivals*, 239–240, 251; Odin's Song in the *Havamal, Elder Edda*, Bellows' trans. 28–67; Frazer, *The Golden Bough*, one vol. ed., 355.
[94] *Poems of the Past and the Present.*
[95] *Moments of Vision.*
[96] *Winter Words.*
[97] *The Woodlanders*, Chaps. II, XIII.
[98] *Ibid.*, Chap. XIII.

evil spirit. He says that it is exactly his own age, that it has got human sense, and sprouted up when he was born on purpose to rule him, and keep him as its slave. Others have been like it afore in Hintock." [99]

They cut the tree at night; and the old man, seeing the mysterious enemy gone, was more frightened than ever; all day he lingered, but at sundown he followed the elm.[100] Among the many tales of trees which were a sort of life-index to the families that owned them, the most familiar is that of the old oaks at Bradgate Hall, near Loughborough, which are said to have lost their tops when Lady Jane Grey, their mistress, was beheaded! [101]

As Marty South watched Winterborne plant the saplings, setting them up with fingers that seemed to make them suddenly alive, sighing and swaying, she was moved to reflect,

"It seems to me as if they sigh because they are very sorry to begin life in earnest—just as we be." [102]

The idea is again expressed in the poem "The Pine-Planters." [103] The boy Jude could not bear to see trees cut down or lopped, from a fancy that it hurt them, or to see them pruned when the sap was up.[104] Jude, it may be objected, was a poet; but he was none the less a rustic. The very beauty of the world was a pain to Tess, as to Jude. One would think she might feel perfect happiness in the presence of Angel Clare, but she is too keenly aware of the sadness of the spring:

"What makes you draw off in that way, Tess? Are you afraid?" . . .

"Oh no, sir. . . . That is, not of outdoor things, especially when the apple-blooth is falling, and everything is so green."

. . . .

[99] *Ibid.*, Chap. XIII.
[100] *Ibid.*, Chap. XIV.
[101] G. H. Skipworth, *Folk-Lore*, V, 169.
[102] *The Woodlanders*, Chap. VIII.
[103] *Time's Laughingstocks.*
[104] *Jude the Obscure*, Part I, Chap. II.

"The trees have inquisitive eyes, haven't they? . . . And the river says, 'Why do ye trouble me with your looks. . . .'" [105]

Sometimes the countryman's fetishism has an amusing side. Mrs. Smith, in despair at the hopeless task of uprooting certain flowers to make room for others, exclaimed in despair, " 'Tis my belief that in the sacred souls of 'em, Jacob's ladders are weeds, and not flowers at all. . . ." [106] There used to be a common belief that weeds were natural to the ground, the result of God's curse, and that to attempt to clear the earth of them entirely was the mark of a rebellious spirit; the same was held true of large upstanding stones, which, no matter how often moved, would always find their way back to their original site! [107] The humor of the word "Christian" applied alike to plants and animals is self-evident.[108]

There is a tremendous oath in *The Mayor* which recalls the oath of Glasgerion, "by oake, and ashe, and thorne," recalls forgotten relics of primitive nature-worship, and the belief in tree-souls, bird-souls, stone-souls, and the like; it is the oath the weathercaster swears as he gives his prophecy of the weather, a strange mixture of herbal magic, witchcraft, and folk-medicine:

"By the sun, moon, and stars, by the clouds, the winds, the trees; likewise by the cats' eyes, the ravens, the leeches, the spiders, and the dung-mixen, the last fortnight in August will be rain and tempest." [109]

Cytherea Graye's attention to her attire on the day of her wedding to Manston has something fetishistic about it,[110] as has Elfride's nervousness when she perceives the earrings Knight has given her lying side by side with Stephen Smith's check on her bureau.[111] It is Henchard, however, who is

[105] *Tess,* Chap. XIX.
[106] *A Pair of Blue Eyes,* Chap. XXIII.
[107] Gurdon, 1–2; O. G. S. Crawford, *The Long Barrows of the Cotswolds,* 26–27.
[108] *A Pair of Blue Eyes,* Chap. XXIII.
[109] *The Mayor of Casterbridge,* Chap. XXVI; see also C. L. Wimberly, *Folklore in the English and Scottish Ballads,* 92, 362: Child, II, No. 67, "Glasgerion"; Wm. Henderson, *Folklore of the Northern Counties,* 198.
[110] *Desperate Remedies,* Chap. XIII.
[111] *A Pair of Blue Eyes,* Chap. XX.

the true *homo superstitiosus:* about to swear a momentous oath, he felt that he required some solemn place, some ritual to make it more binding; therefore, he entered the village church, and placing his hand upon the clamped Bible on the Communion-table, he swore:

"I, Michael Henchard, on this morning of the sixteenth of September, do take oath here in this solemn place that I will avoid all strong liquors for the space of twenty years to come, being a year for every year that I have lived. And this I swear upon the book before me; and may I be strook dumb, blind, and helpless, if I break this my oath." [112]

Hardy refers several times to the Cerne Giant, a huge figure carved in the chalky cliffs above Abbot's Cernel; he towers 180 feet into the air, holding a club in one hand, and about to lift the other.[113] Dorset folk take him pretty much for granted: they do not interest themselves in the theories about him. One of the latter is that he is of Phœnician origin, being a carving of the god Baal himself; [114] another that he was hewed out of the rock by medieval monks.[115] Still another story runs that he was a real giant, caught in his usual pastime of stealing and eating sheep on Blackdown one night, and there pinioned, killed, and his figure cut in the cliff as a warning to future marauders.[116] But the most interesting theory is that the Cerne Giant is a phallic symbol; we know that in Scandinavia, and elsewhere, ithyphallic divinities were frequently carved on rock surfaces in the Bronze Age; and to this age the Giant probably belongs.[117] The Maypole used to be set up on a steep hill immediately above the Cerne giant, in the center of a camp which seems to belong to the Bronze Age,[118] and General Pitt-Rivers found

---

[112] *The Mayor of Casterbridge,* Chap. II.
[113] *Life's Little Ironies:* "A Few Crusted Characters," "Old Andrey's Experiences as a Musician"; *Tess,* Chap. XLVIII; *The Dynasts,* Part First, Act II, Scene V.
[114] T. Hopkins, *Thomas Hardy's Dorset,* 97.
[115] Sherren, *The Wessex of Romance,* 165.
[116] Hopkins, *op. cit.,* 97.
[117] H. Colley March, *Folk-Lore,* X, 482.
[118] *Ibid.*

many worked flints of neolithic type, cores, speartips, scrapers, and one rude fabricator in the ploughed fields below Trendle Hill.[119] The Cerne Giant is assuredly not the work of medieval monks!

Tales of giants represent primitive man's instinct to deify great natural forces which are, at the time, beyond his power to explain; tales of giants hark back to the days when man did not yet know fire, nor the art of metallurgy; or, to be exact, they represent first a myth of observation, upon which, in the light of greater knowledge, are grafted folk-tales which liken the great, stupid, untamed forces of nature to good-natured, dull giants.[120] Giant-lore runs on into devil-legends by a curious transformation; great stones, once held to be the work of giants, are called "The Devil's Door," "The Hell-Stone," and so on; ancient buildings are attributed to the Devil; we have Devil's Dykes too numerous to mention, and so it goes.[121] From half-divine creatures, on the whole friendly to man, the giants were transformed by the medieval monks into our malicious Christian devil—if the paradox may pass.[122]

It has been thought that the huge wicker giants which well into the sixteenth century used to be carried in the Mid-summer procession of the Tailor's Company in London, and are still a familiar sight on the Continent, are a relic of the wicker giants of the Druids; but this is begging the question, for we have no proof that the belief in giants is peculiar to the Druids—whoever they may, on further research, appear to be—whereas we know the belief to be common to all primitive and savage folk today.[123] With this vexed question, we approach the mystery of the Druids, their race, their cult, and their possible identity with the so-called Iberic people who once inhabited southern Britain. It is too soon to risk any complete theory of Druidism. To call Druidism

---

[119] *Ibid.*, X, 478–479.
[120] Grimm-Stallybrass, II, 528–30, 532, 534, 552, 555; IV, 1436, 1462.
[121] *Ibid.*, II, 534; III, 1022, Note 2; IV, 1612.
[122] *Ibid.*, III, 1014.
[123] Ellis's Brand, I, 322–326; Frazer, *Golden Bough*, 654–56.

"Celtic" is an anthropological misnomer; yet it certainly is a totally different religion from the Teutonic one held by the Angles, Jutes, Frisians, and Saxons who invaded England in the fifth and sixth centuries; and, unlike them, it bears a certain similarity to Oriental religions. All we can assert is that this was the dominant religion of Britain and of Ireland, probably brought there by immigrants from the west of England, at the time of the Saxon invasions. We cannot postulate any intimate connection between the fires of the Druids in which, according to Tacitus, human sacrifices were offered in huge wicker cages, and the hideous sacrifices to Moloch, or Bel; nor with any Oriental sun-worship, Babylonian or Persian; nor with moon-worship, as practised by the seafaring Phœnicians in their worship of Astarte. Nor can we accept the fascinating theory that the Scottish witches derived their whole cult from the Druids,[124] and that the witches were priestesses of the same cult which was curiously observed by Cæsar and Pliny! We cannot connect so-called Druid Stones with Druidism proper; they are the product of rustic ignorance, at the bottom of which, however, lies some folk-tradition of great age. Mistletoe we now know to be an all-heal common to all primitive peoples, as sacred to the Greeks as to the Scandinavians, as prized by the modern Aino of Japan as by the most devout Druid.[125] The Chase, the oldest wood in England, the scene of Tess's betrayal, was well chosen for a dark setting; and in it were the aged oaks, bearing "Druidical mistletoe," and yews not planted by men.[126]

Hardy makes passing reference in a fragment of a proverb to one of the most primitive of all human fears, a fear which, in its day, and even at the present time, among certain savage tribes, has given rise to an elaborate taboo, the cult of the Boanerges, the ancient fear and worship of twin children. It is amazing to reflect that in a commonplace folk-saying we have preserved one of the oldest of all religious

[124] Gomme, *Ethnology in Folk-Lore,* 59 ff., 142.
[125] Rendel Harris, *The Ascent of Olympus,* 45 ff.
[126] *Tess,* Part I, Chap. V.

cults; it is Farmer Bawtree who speaks the phrase, in his uproarious story of the couple who would one hour be hurling the tongs and poker at each other, and in the next hour be singing "The Spotted Cow" together "As peaceable as two holy twins." [127]

The most fascinating survival of an ancient religion in Britain is the tradition of Astarte-worship in the Isle of Slingers. The sculptor Pierston searched all his life for the perfect woman—one who should be the epitome of all that is lovely and desirable in woman. At times he believed that his futile search was a punishment sent by Aphrodite herself for his sins against her in his art, and was seized by a Sapphic terror of love. The Island people were of Roman stock grafted on to the original Balearic folk; it is barely possible that Phœnician traders brought Astarte-worship to the Island in their trading for tin, but it is more probable that the Romans brought in the cult of a love-goddess—for their Venus was an Oriental goddess—and devoutly raised a temple to her.[128]

Portland is thought to be the original Vindilia Isle. Slings are deadly weapons in the hands of Portlanders, who hurl stones with the precision of marksmen.[129] There are but few surnames in the peninsula: Avice Caro's family received the name of the "roan-Caros" to distinguish it from others of the Caro name.[130] There is marked racial isolation in the Isle of Slingers, and a strong, rough pride in this isolation, mixed with a certain aloofness from "kimberlins," or foreigners. The Purbeck marble-quarriers, for instance, kept their industry in their own hands: a primitive corporation of about a dozen families, they did not intermarry with other families, or permit a "kimberlin" to enter their business.[131] In days remembered by the aged, Weymouth, only

---

[127] *The Woodlanders,* Chap. XLVIII. For the whole subject of twins, see Rendel Harris, *Boanerges.*
[128] *The Well-Beloved,* Chap. II, Part I; Chaps. III, VI, XIII, Part II.
[129] W. Sherren, *The Wessex of Romance,* 78.
[130] *The Well-Beloved,* Part I, Chap. I.
[131] Hopkins, *Thomas Hardy's Dorset,* 170–172; W. Page, *History of Dorset,* II, 336–337.

three miles from Portland, was held quite a foreign place;
and if visitors chanced to die on the Island, they were buried
in the Strangers' Burying-Ground.[132] The Island folk clung
until recently to many old customs: the handfestings, the
primitive betrothals which were really marriages, have long
since died out, of course; but within the present century the
freehold houses were passed from one Islander to another
by simple "church-gift." [133]

It is easy enough on this strange neck of land, to fancy, as
did Pierston, that one sees the shadowy shapes of the Slingers, and to hear their stones whizzing past on the wind.[134]
Hardy remarks upon the fine physical type in the Islands,
traces of Italian blood in features and coloring which are
the result of the marriage of Romans with the aborigines.[135]
The people of the Isle of Slingers are proud of their race,
their history, and the tradition of Phœnician trade with the
peninsula.

The love-goddess of the Island is a fascinating problem.
We know that the Phœnicians had a tin-trade at Cornwall,
but we are unable to fix upon the *Cassiterides* of Pytheas
with certainty. It is quite possible that the Phœnicians carried an Oriental cult to the Isle of Slingers, but it is at present impossible of proof. It is difficult to find the Phœnician
racial type even in Sicily and Sardinia, where, of all places,
we should expect most certainly to find it, but the type is
said to crop up occasionally in Cornwall.[136] The Isle of
Wight may have been the *Mictis* of Pytheas's lost diary, but
even this is hypothesis.[137] A well-established tradition, however, is always worthy of respect, if not of credence, and
such a tradition we find in the Isle of Slingers. Admitting the
possibility of visits of Phœnician traders to the Isle, there
are other evidences of Oriental cults in distant parts of
England which can hardly be accounted for as brought by

132 Sherren, *The Wessex of Romance,* 85.
133 *Ibid.,* 100.
134 *The Well-Beloved,* Part II, Chap. VIII.
135 *Ibid.,* Part II, Chap. III.
136 John Beddoe, *The Anthropological History of Europe,* 50.
137 W. Ridgeway, "*Greek Trade-Routes to Britain,*" *Folk-Lore,* I, 107.

the Phœnicians. In Lancashire, for instance, on the banks of the Ribble within the last century, cakes in honor of "The Queen of Heaven," the moon, were still made and eaten— a custom which parallels exactly the Chinese custom of "congratulating the moon." [138] Wherever we find moon-worship, we know that we have to do with an Oriental cult; the Teutonic mythology conceives the sun as a female deity, and worships her as a giver of life.[139] It is impossible to interpret this moon-cult in Lancashire and the tradition of a Phœnician love-goddess in the Isle of Slingers in the light of a single historical invasion, unless it be the Roman invasion. The Lancashire moon-cakes may well be a survival of the worship of Minerva Belisama, and this goddess, like Sul at Bath, and Venus at Portland, may, after all, be none other than the Oriental Astarte. She is a goddess of fertility, and the eating of the cakes, which is really an eating of the god, is a simple fertility rite which would quite naturally be associated with the cult of a goddess of this sort.[140] The Romans borrowed all their gods; the temple to Venus may well have been raised on the site of an earlier shrine to some Oriental love-deity.

The survivals of Oriental cults in England are intimately associated with the almost insoluble problem of Druidism, and Druidism, on its part, is inextricably bound up with the races which inhabited England before the Anglo-Saxon invasion. The West of England has been inhabited from the earliest times.[141] The roundheaded folk, who appear to have learned the art of making bronze from the Orient, were certainly in England as early as 2000 B. C., although the Bronze Age in Britain did not begin until much later.[142] These roundheads may have brought with them, as their native, or as is more likely, their adoptive, religion a great many of the beliefs we today label as non-Aryan. Druidism

[138] Harland and Wilkinson, 3; Dennys, *Folklore of China,* 28: *Folk-Lore,* II, 229.
[139] Grimm-Stallybrass, I, 103.
[140] Harland and Wilkinson, 3–4.
[141] Pittard, *Race and History,* 194, Translator's Note.
[142] Kendrick, *The Axe Age,* 52, 105–106, 120.

itself may be of Oriental origin.[143] When we meet it flourishing as an elaborately organized priestly cult among the
Celtæ of Cæsar's *Commentaries,* we must remember that
these people are not racially Celts, but of Nordic stock, and
that they may have adopted a religion that is not native to
them. Druidism may be, in fact, an Oriental religion, or an
amalgamation of several non-Teutonic cults. There are such
marked likenesses in the cults of a goddess of fertility in
practically all ancient religions that one is tempted to regard
them as older than any organized religion, as survivals of
prehistoric rites. The goddess of love—who is a fertility
goddess among the Egyptians, the Phœnicians, the Greeks,
the Romans, and even the Scandinavians, had two modes of
manifestation—two forms, a black and a white.[144] Everywhere we find her with a magic girdle or necklace, perhaps
originally composed of medicinal herbs.[145] She seems very
early to have become associated with death, and to have
taken in charge young girls, mothers, and children who
died.[146] She seems also to have had some connection with
phallic worship, being a female counterpart in Scandinavian
mythology to Freyr, the god of the boar; Saxo's tale of King
Frô gives us a picture of markedly Oriental rites at Upsala
—wild dances, orgies culminating in the ceremonial prosti-
tution of women and a sacrificial drama in which a prisoner
playing the rôle of Freyr was killed to solemn dances and
wild threnodies.[147] The rites of this boar-god are very similar to those of the Egyptian Apis. The Phœnicians who set-
tled in Cyprus instituted there the rites of Adonis and Aphrodite, or as they called her, Astarte; and at Cyprus, as at
Byblus, these rites resembled the worship of Osiris.[148] The

[143] Mackenzie, *Ancient Man in Britain,* 143; *Folk-Lore,* XXXVII, 274–275.
[144] Grimm-Stallybrass, I, 312–313, and 313, Note 1; I, 315; Mackenzie,
Ancient Man in Britain, 150–164.
[145] Grimm-Stallybrass, I, 306–307; Rendel Harris, *The Ascent of Olympus,*
110–112, 131–132.
[146] Grimm-Stallybrass, I, 305.
[147] Gudmund Schütte, "Danish Paganism," Folk-Lore, XXXV, 367–68;
York-Powell's ed. *Saxo-Grammaticus,* Intro., lxii.
[148] Frazer, *The Golden Bough,* 329 ff.

idolatrous Hebrews followed this worship of Astarte in Babylon, learning from their conquerors to burn incense to the "Queen of Heaven." [149] The giving or withholding of fertility to her devotees was an attribute of Astarte, and some scholars believe that the name Aphrodite is nothing more than a Græcized form of "love-apple," from some primitive Semitic stem now lost to us.[150]

There is still another striking likeness in comparative mythology to be noted: Demeter, a far older goddess than any Olympian deity, a goddess of fertility with orgiastic rites an integral part of her sublime "mysteries," had a black form as well as a white. It is her rites at Eleusis, a fertility cult in origin, though raised in time to a highly spiritual religion, which most closely resembled Astarte's.[151] The black Diana of the Ephesians comes also to mind, and the old tradition goes over into Christianity; there is a medieval conception of a black Madonna, a sorrowing Mother of Men.[152] All these resemblances may seem, on first thought, to have little to do with our problem as to who was the love-goddess of the Isle of Slingers; but they help to show the complexity of the problem, and to suggest a possible interpretation. The goddess may have been Venus, the Roman goddess, who was, after all, an Oriental goddess; or the temple cherished in local tradition may have been raised on the site of an earlier one to Astarte, whose worship was brought there by Phœnician traders, or by far older inhabitants of the peninsula, a roundheaded folk, not Oriental, but enriched by an Oriental culture, and devotees of an Oriental cult.

In the tale, "A Mere Interlude," the heroine, unable to get a boat out of Pen-Zephyr, found herself wandering about the quaint town; the picturesque streets, the Pier and the Harbor, seemed to her unchanged by time; she looked down

[149] Frazer, *Ibid.,* 337.
[150] Rendel Harris, *The Ascent of Olympus,* 131–132.
[151] Grimm-Stallybrass, I, 313.
[152] *Ibid.*

upon men loading and unloading there, just as in the time of the Phœnicians.[153]

"Aquæ Sulis" treats the tradition of the goddess Sul at Bath; on the site of Sul's temple at Bath was reared a cathedral. The delightfully ironic poem presents the goddess as a bit of a flirt, first reproaching her rival for his discourtesy, and then inviting him to kiss and be friends, for are they not both relics of lost causes, a mere Jumping Jack and Jumping Jill?[154] Sul was the goddess of the healing waters at Bath, and her maidens, the Sulevæ, were deities of the fountains and rivers in the vicinity of Bath.[155] Strabo —who like Timæus, and Pliny, is only quoting of course from the lost diary of Pytheas, describes Pytheas's visit to Britain, and particularly notes a deity at Bath in whose temple the fires never go out, but where the fire turns into little lumps like stone: in other words, in Sul's temple—for Sul is Pytheas's Minerva—coal was used![156]

Wessex speaks sonorously of imperial Rome. Hardy refers constantly to the great Roman roads which traverse Wessex like huge ribbons, particularly Icknield Street and Long-Ash Lane.[157] The Icenway, running due east and west from London to Land's End, has a particularly interesting folklore; it is the old Watling Street, the road the peasants call the "Milky Way," or "the London Road," using the terms synonymously.[158] They also say that it leads to the end of the world, and that if one follows it, he will return to the place from which he set out.[159] They regard it as a path of souls, as do many savages today. We should like to

---

[153] *A Changed Man.*
[154] *Satires of Circumstance.*
[155] Lina B. Eckenstein, *Comparative Studies in Nursery Rhymes,* 76–77.
[156] Mackenzie, *Ancient Man in Britain,* 115.
[157] *Wessex Poems:* "My Cicely"; *Late Lyrics:* "By Henstridge Cross at the Year's End"; *Jude the Obscure,* Part I, Chap. III; *A Changed Man,* "The Grave by the Handpost"; *A Group of Noble Dames,* "Dame the First, Betty, the First Countess of Wessex"; *The Return of the Native,* Book I, Chap. I; etc.
[158] Anglo-Saxon Chron., Ingr. 190; Grimm-Stallybrass, I, 356–62; *Folk-Lore,* XXVI, 158; *Folk-Lore,* XXXVIII, 158–59; Gurdon, 166.
[159] Gurdon, 166.

know who the Watlings were, and how it came about that
they gave their name to a street and to the Milky Way, a
mystery which Chaucer might have solved for us.[160] Perhaps they are to be correlated with simple herm-worship,
with the Athelstan and Hermes pillars set up at crossroads.[161]

Dorchester reminds one of Roman occupation at every
turn. Maumbury Rings, the Cirque of the Gladiators, must
have rivaled the Colosseum itself in its day. Here Henchard
met Susan, his wronged wife; here boxing and wrestling
bouts were long held, on the very site where the town-
gallows once flourished, and where in 1605 a murderess was
strangled and then burnt till her heart leaped from her body;
here an imaginative person in broad daylight might well
fancy he saw the slopes lined with Hadrian's soldiery watching the gladiatorial combat.[162] Some workmen at Max Gate
unearthed a whole platoon of Hadrian's, and a Roman lady
of evident nobility and her spouse, an event which Hardy
commemorates in "The Clasped Skeletons." [163] In Fiesole
Hardy saw Roman coins which reminded him of an ancient
coin unearthed at Max Gate bearing the image of Constantine.[164] But, as a rule, the old Roman road suggested
to Hardy, not the legionaries who proudly reared "The
Eagle," but his mother leading him down the road as a
small boy.[165] At Dorchester, too, was the Roman burying-
ground in which the dust of Mrs. Henchard mingled with
the dust of women of whom all that remained was the glass
hairpins and amber necklaces they had worn, and of men
who had been buried with the coins of Hadrian, Posthumus,
and the Constantines in their mouths.[166] It was to these

---

[160] *The Hous of Fame*, 2, 427.
[161] Grimm-Stallybrass, I, 355–365; I, 394; I, 118.
[162] *The Mayor of Casterbridge*, Chap. XI.
[163] Ernest Brennecke, Jr., *The Life of Thomas Hardy*, 162; *Winter Words:*
"The Clasped Skeletons."
[164] *Poems of the Past and the Present:* "In the Old Theatre, Fiesole."
[165] *Time's Laughingstocks:* "The Roman Road."
[166] *The Mayor of Casterbridge*, Chap. XX; *Wessex Poems*, "Her Death
and After."

mounds that a sorrowing man came, not to meditate, not to search for solemn relics, but to bury his little white cat.[167] The pageant of history fascinated even phelgmatic Phillotson, with whose unavailing efforts to finish a work on Roman-Brittanic antiquities the reader sympathizes.[168]

The English peasant is a bit of a heathen at heart. Jan Coggan had a hearty contempt for the fellow who would change his ancient doctrine for the sake of getting to heaven; to turn chapel-member was almost like turning King's-evidence! [169] Nat Chapman lamented the passing of the good old-fashioned religion, an hour a week with God Almighty, and the rest with the devil.[170] The rustic was prone to believe that God might be omnipotent and omniscient according to the Service, but not in daily life. There is the sad case of William Worm, who had suffered for years from the frying of fish in his poor head, and who could only continue piously to hope that God would find it out some day and relieve him! [171] Nor was Providence always viewed as a beneficent power: at the close of Donald Farfrae's plaintive song, "My Ain Countree," Christopher Coney commented:

"What did ye come away from yer own country for, young master, if ye be so wownded about it? . . . Faith, it wasn't worth while on our account, for as Master Billy Wills says, we be bruckle folk here —the best o' us hardly honest, what with hard winters, and so many mouths to fill, and God A'mighty sending his little taties so terrible small to fill 'em with. . . ." [172]

No one realized the power of the parson—for good or for ill—in the rural community more keenly than Hardy, but he was also aware of the peasant's point of view; he could understand the latter's feeling that the parson in village disputes usually sided with the powers-that-be, espe-

---

[167] *Satires of Circumstance,* "The Roman Gravemounds."
[168] *Jude the Obscure,* Part III, Chap. VI; Part IV, Chap. IV; etc.
[169] *Far From the Madding Crowd,* Chap. XLII.
[170] *Two on a Tower,* Chap. XIII.
[171] *A Pair of Blue Eyes,* Chap. IV.
[172] *The Mayor of Casterbridge,* Chap. VIII.

cially with the squire.[173] Moreover, the rustic, simple and devout at heart, is endowed with too much shrewd common sense to be over-orthodox; he perceives humorous incongruities between theological precept and practice. Perhaps he views the future with the tacit hope that the Creator is, after all, an Englishman, and knows the code.

[173] Brennecke, *The Life of Thomas Hardy,* 57–58.

XIII

MEDIEVAL LEGENDS AND
NAPOLEONANA

~~~~~~~~~~~~~~~~~~~~

Hardy makes use of medieval legends, some of which have their roots in folklore far older than the Middle Ages. Most striking are the tales of Famous Sleepers—of Tannhaüser [1] and Friedrich Barbarossa,[2] Dietrich of Bern, Charlemagne, Siegfried, among Teutonic heroes; of Arthur, Brian Boroimhe, the Fianna of Ireland, and Thomas the Rhymer among Celtic heroes. The root of the Venusberg story and the fascinating Tannhaüser fiction is extremely ancient: it is the story of a mortal man who has been enticed into an underground world, wedded to a goddess or elfin queen, but, seized by an irresistible longing for the earth, has escaped, sought forgiveness and reconciliation, only to return disillusioned to his underground life. This is the root of folk-tales in every branch of Aryan folklore—modern Greek, Albanian, Swedish, Danish, Norwegian, Icelandic, Scotch, Welsh, Irish, German, and English.[3] It would appear that Dame Venus of the legend was substituted about the fifteenth or sixteenth century for some far older goddess, one of the great female deities who in Teutonic folklore are the counterpart of Wotan and his Furious Host, who ride through the air in midsummer and midwinter with great trains of souls, souls of dead women and children in their wake. Venus originally was Holle (Holda), Frikka, or Bertha.[4] The legend is, in one sense, a rework-

---

[1] *The Woodlanders*, Chap. XXVIII.
[2] *The Dynasts*, Part Second, Act I, Scene III.
[3] Sabine Baring-Gould, *Curious Myths of the Middle Ages*, 216–217.
[4] Grimm-Stallybrass, *Teutonic Mythology*, II, 455; III, 932, 935, 937; IV, 1368.

ing of the old belief in Wotan and his Furious Host.[5] Siegfried and other heroes dwelt in the old mountain castle of
Geroldseck awaiting the summons of their people in time of
need; Friedrich Barbarossa's red beard twined three times
about the legs of the great table at Kifhaüser, and then the
hero woke, crying out in a mighty voice, and was with difficulty persuaded to sit down and go to sleep until the hour of
Germany's need should strike.[6] The Emperor's red beard
in itself harks back to the Donar cult.[7] Charlemagne was
said to have awaked as early as the First Crusade![8] Of
Ogier the Dane, Tam Lane, Thomas the Rhymer, Oisin,
and even Herne the Hunter much the same tale is told, now
with one variation, now with another. The sleeper legends,
which may have originated in the primitive belief that the
dead return, persists in modern folklore: the French peasants say that Napoleon will return when France summons
him,[9] and similar tales are told of English and Russian
military heroes. Tannhaüser is, of course, the loveliest of
these legends; it shows us the hankering of the medieval
man after the old heathenism, his return to it, his heartfelt
repentance, the harshness of the clergy, and his disillusion
and despair as he returns to his old way of life.

Equally beautiful is the tale of Ahasuerus, the Wandering Jew, immortalized in the etchings of Doré. The tale
dates back to the chronicle of the Abbey of St. Albans, which
was copied and continued by Matthew Paris. The Jew was
said to have visited the abbey, and told his marvelous story
to the wondering monks. Another version of the legend
was told by Paul von Eitzen, Bishop of Schleswig, according to which Ahasuerus appeared to a great crowd at Ham-
burg in 1547 and related his melancholy history. The story
sprang into sudden popularity in the sixteenth century,[10] has

[5] *Ibid.*, III, 937, 942, 961.
[6] *Ibid.*, 955.
[7] *Ibid.*, 959.
[8] *Ibid.*, IV, 1590.
[9] Donald Mackenzie, *Ancient Man in Britain*, 29–30.
[10] Baring-Gould, *Curious Myths of the Middle Ages*, 1–30.

been a favorite with poets and novelists, and evidently was
a favorite with Hardy; [11] the wanderer weighted with this
strange curse seemed to Hardy a fitting type of the unful-
filled artist, of the man who follows some elusive goal.
There were many medieval legends of wicked Jews, the most
beautiful of which is Chaucer's *Prioress's Tale*. Even today
there are folk-tales of this character: in Cornwall, where
after the Conquest the tin mines were farmed by Jews,
legends still persist of the restless Jews who haunt the mines,
and such mining terms as "Jew's bowels" for small pieces
of smelted tin, and "Jew's leavings" for mine refuse, are
familiar to all.[12] The boy Jude read in an old tract one of
these modern folk-tales: One man prayed for money wherewith to build the church, and the money came; another
prayed just as earnestly, but to no avail; for, as he later
learned, the breeches in which he knelt had been made by a
wicked Jew! [13]

Some of the medieval tales of wicked Jews remind us
much of familiar stories of devil-pacts. *Faust,* the supreme
version of such a pact, takes on new meaning when viewed
down the long vista of Germanic folklore. Tales of devil-
pacts linger down to our own day. Tess questioned a shepherd about the Cross-in-hand, the old stone pillar at which
Alec had forced her to swear an oath never to tempt him
again; and the reply was:

" 'Tis a thing of ill-omen, miss. It was put up by the relations of a
malefactor who was tortured there by nailing his hand to a post, and
afterwards hung. His bones lie underneath. They say he sold his
soul to the devil, and that he walks at times." [14]

This version of the Cross-in-hand story is in striking contrast to the lovely legend of "The Lost Pyx," [15] in which

---

[11] *The Well-Beloved,* Part II, Chap. II; Part III, Chap. II; *The Return
of the Native,* Book II, Chap. VII.
[12] E. M. Wright, *Rustic Speech and Folklore,* 199–200.
[13] *Jude the Obscure,* Part I, Chap. III.
[14] *Tess,* Chap. XLV.
[15] *Poems of the Past and the Present.*

the priest, returning in haste to find the lost pyx, finds the oxen, sheep, does, and even the conies and badgers reverently gathered to worship. It was at this Christ-Cross Stone that the lover saw transfigured in the woman of his choice all the fleeting loves of the past, and realized that she was indeed "the Chosen." [16]

In Batcombe churchyard, near the north wall of the church, lies the tomb of the Wessex conjuror Mynterne, whose request to be buried "neither in the church nor out of it" was followed to the letter, though later the tomb was moved just within the church wall. [17] Small wonder that the conjuror quarreled with his vicar, if the tales told of him be true! Certainly he was hardly entitled to burial in consecrated ground; for the tale goes that as Mynterne rode away one day, he suddenly recollected that he had left his books of magic open; as he hastened back, one of his horse's hoofs knocked off a pinnacle of Batcombe Church Tower, and to this day the pinnacle leans markedly and bears the imprint of that wild ride! [18]

Stories of devil-pacts, in their turn, are related to tales of sacrilege in general. We have such a legend in "No Bell-Ringing Tonight: A Ballad of Durnover"; [19] after lying drunk for a week at the Hit or Miss, the bell-ringers had rashly swilled the sacramental wine; but when they essayed to ring the bells, not a solitary peal was to be heard. They realized the curse that had fallen upon them, and never tried to ring the bells again. A richly humorous story of sacrilege occurs in *Jude:* the text-painters were forced to work late Saturday night repainting the Ten Commandments in the church at Gaymead; to speed them up the vicar had unwisely allowed them a portion of drink:

"As evening drawed on they sent for some more themselves, rum, by all account. It got later and later, and they got more and more fuddled, till at last they went a-putting their rum-bottle and rummers

[16] *Late Lyrics:* "The Chosen."
[17] R. Thurston Hopkins, *Thomas Hardy's Dorset,* 233–235.
[18] *Folk-Lore,* X, 481.
[19] *Winter Words.*

upon the Communion-table, and drawed up a trestle or two, and sat round comfortable, and poured out again right hearty bumpers. No sooner had they tossed off their glasses than, so the story goes, they fell down senseless, one and all. How long they bode so they didn't know, but when they came to themselves there was a terrific thunderstorm a-raging, and they seemed to see in the gloom a dark figure with very thin legs and a curious voot, a-standing on the ladder and finishing their work. When it got daylight they could see that the work was really finished, and couldn't at all mind finishing it themselves. They went home, and the next thing they heard was that a great scandal had been caused in the church that Sunday morning, for when the people came and service began, all saw that the Ten Commandments wez painted with the 'Nots' left out. . . ." [20]

This was the story that was directed at Jude and Sue as they sat painting the two tables in the little church near Aldbrickham, and shortly afterwards they were told that their services were no longer desired.

Hardy refers to several other legends: to the story of the orange tree which saved virgins from the poisonous breath of the dragon in the days of Saint George, a story which is to be found in the *Legenda Aurea;* [21] to the Philosopher's stone,[22] the medieval alchemist's dream; to Prester Chan [23] of mighty renown; to the heroine of "The Mistletoe Bough," the bride of Lord Lovel in the English ballad, and Ginevra of Modena in another version of the story, who in a mad game of hide-and-seek on her wedding night locked herself into an oaken chest and perished there; [24] to the strange and philosophical stork, who is said to live only in free states,[25] and to bring luck to the inmates of the house whereon he perches, provided always they lead upright and chaste lives; [26] to the fable of the man who could not cross

[20] *Jude the Obscure,* Part V, Chap. VI.
[21] Baring-Gould, *Curious Myths* . . . 295–299; *A Pair of Blue Eyes,* Chap. XII.
[22] *The Dynasts,* Part First, Act II, Scene I.
[23] Baring-Gould, *Curious Myths,* 32–54; *The Mayor of Casterbridge,* Chap. XIX.
[24] *A Laodicean,* Chaps. IX, X.
[25] Sir Thomas Browne, *Vulgar Errors,* Book III, Chap. XXVII.
[26] Grimm-Stallybrass, III, 1134; Vincent S. Lean's *Collectanea,* II, Part I, 16.

the stream with any one of his charges at a time, leaving the other two alone on the bank—the fable of the fox, the goose, and the corn;[27] and to the delightful fable, related by Selden in his *Table Talk,* of the wise fox, who having seen his silly friend the sheep lose her head for having told the lion the truth, and his enemy the wolf torn to pieces for speaking flattery, replied cannily that he had a cold and could not smell when asked if the lion's breath smelt.[28] "Panthera"[29] employs a second-century legend which makes Christ the son of Mary by a Roman general once stationed in Judea: Hardy invests the tale with a simple dignity. Its source is to be found in certain fragments of lost Apocryphal books, he tells us, in Origen's *Contra Celsum,* and in some of the Talmudic writings.[29] When Tess donned her wedding gown, she gazed into the glass as if expecting it to change hue, or rend in two, as did the magic mantle donned by Guinevere and the ladies of Arthur's court.[30] The magic mantle as a test of chastity and a magic beaker as a test of cuckoldom runs through romance all the way from Chrestien of Troyes to Malory; a particularly interesting version of the story is found in the ballad of "The Boy and the Mantle."[31]

Hardy was always fond of a curious story: In "Ralph Blossom Soliloquizes," he uses the odd record of a seventeenth-century Budmouth Register; it is the tale of one Ralph Blossom, a lovable rogue, who had betrayed seven women and brought them upon the town rates, but against whom, as he lay dying, no one would bring an order.[32] "The Children and Sir Nameless," based probably upon some oral tradition, is the story of the lord of Athelhall, a cold man who rejoiced that he had no children, and drove out any who strayed into his park; on his death, a great seven-foot figure

---

[27] *The Hand of Ethelberta,* Chap. XXXV.
[28] *A Pair of Blue Eyes,* Chap. X.
[29] *Time's Laughingstocks:* "Panthera."
[30] *Tess,* Chap. XXXII.
[31] W. H. Schofield, *English Literature from the Norman Conquest to Chaucer,* 197–199.
[32] *Late Lyrics.*

of him carved in alabaster was placed in the church. Three hundred years passed; the figure was placed upon the floor, and the little children, who sat restlessly waiting for the close of the service, often wondered who was the old man beneath their feet.[33] The d'Urberville family history is to found mainly in county records.[34] Hardy was finally admitted to Wool House to view the d'Urberville portraits, and copies were subsequently painted for him by John Everett.[35]

The Monmouth tradition which Hardy celebrates in "At Shag's Heath" [36] and in "The Duke's Reappearance" [37] is based upon a family reminiscence of the Sweatmans, Hardy's mother's family. In June, 1685, at the time of Monmouth's rebellion, the old Sweatman house at Melbury Osmond was occupied by Christopher Sweatman and his daughters. The story goes that after his defeat, Sweatman gave Monmouth shelter there; but, finding him later making love to his daughter in the garden, ordered him away. Several days later came the news that Monmouth had been captured and executed; but, according to this version of the story, Sweatman vowed that he had seen a mysterious figure removing the hidden ducal trappings from the cupboard.[38] The more fully accepted version is that Sweatman was visited by one of Monmouth's highest officers.[39] It is small wonder that the memory of this rebellion still lingers in folk-tradition: 328 men of Wilts, Somerset, Devon, Hants, and Dorset were executed as Monmouth sympathizers; and 894 were sent to plantations; one was a relative of Hardy on his mother's side.[40] The memory of Judge Jeffreys' Bloody Assizes, in which Dorchester folk suffered sentence of death, lingered until recent times; as far west as Lydford's Castle Jeffreys'

[33] *Late Lyrics.*
[34] Hopkins, *Thomas Hardy's Dorset,* 60, 129–133.
[35] Ernest Brennecke, Jr., *Life of Thomas Hardy,* 161.
[36] *Human Shows.*
[37] *A Changed Man.*
[38] Brennecke, *Life of Thomas Hardy,* 39–40.
[39] F. E. Hardy, *The Early Life of Thomas Hardy,* 7–8.
[40] W. Sherren, *The Wessex of Romance,* 253; F. E. Hardy, *The Later Years of Thomas Hardy,* 126; *The Early Life . . ,* page 7.

ghost is said to frighten women and children.[41] It was of Jeffreys old Buzzford was thinking when he thus described Casterbridge:

"True, Casterbridge is a old, hoary place o' wickedness, by all accounts. 'Tis recorded in history that we rebelled against the King one or two hundred years ago, in the time of the Romans, and that lots of us was hanged on Gallows' Hill, and quartered, and our different jints sent about the country like butcher's meat; and for my part I can well believe it." [42]

The reader must not be unduly troubled over Buzzford's "in the time of the Romans"; the rustic's chronological ignorance is often highly diverting. Robert Lickpan insisted that the Luxellians had their title from Charles the Third or the Fourth, although Stephen Smith drew the line at a Charles the Fourth! [43] The carter sadly discouraged the boy Jude in his dreams of going to Christminster by telling him that up there folk spoke only foreign tongues, tongues used "before the Flood," and the expression is still used to denote a far distant time.[44]

It is, however, in the legends of the Napoleonic era that folk-tradition lives most indubitably. Hardy based poems and tales of a Napoleonic invasion upon traditions related to him as a boy by old folk who had been themselves eyewitnesses of or had known those who had seen the Rainbarrow Beacon burning year after year, folk who had known many false alarms and had felt the intense fear of "Boney," the Corsican ogre.[45] For these legends, which he uses with fine effect in "The Alarm," [46] "A Tradition of 1804," [47] *The Trumpet-Major*,[48] and the rustic scenes in *The Dynasts*,[49] he was largely indebted to his grandmother, who died when

---

[41] W. S. Lach-Syrma, "Folk-Lore Tradition of Historical Events," *Folk-Lore Record*, III, Part II, 157–158.
[42] *The Mayor of Casterbridge*, Chap. VIII.
[43] *A Pair of Blue Eyes*, Chap. II.
[44] *Jude the Obscure*, Part I, Chap. III; L. Salmon, *Folk-Lore*, XIII, 427.
[45] *The Trumpet-Major*, Preface.
[46] *Wessex Poems*.
[47] *Life's Little Ironies*.
[48] Particularly Chaps. XI, XXV, XXVI.
[49] Part First, Act II, Scene V.

he was seventeen, and to whom he pays tribute in "One We Knew." [50] It is true that the boy Hardy devoured Gifford's *Wars of the French Revolution,* to which his grandfather, an ardent volunteer, had subscribed. But his sources were mainly oral tradition.[51]

In 1883 Hardy met the son or grandson of one of the men who kept the Rainbarrow Beacon from 1800 to 1815; [52] from him no doubt he had ancedotes a-plenty, the description of the two ricks of fuel kept always on hand—one of furze and heather for quick ignition; the other of wood for slow burning. From him he must have heard many a conversation that passed around the great fire full of the expectancy, now solemn, now funny, of an attack from the French tyrant. These anecdotes and conversations we find heightened to art in *The Dynasts.*[53] From oral tradition Hardy had the description of the gorgeous "Bang-up Locals," nicknamed "The Green Linnets"; [54] and from the local museum the record of a green sergeant and his first attempt at drilling these raw recruits which is the basis of the uproarious scene in *The Trumpet-Major.*[55] The life of "Farmer George" at Weymouth had been brilliantly pictured by Thackeray, but was doubtless supplemented by stories of eyewitnesses; [56] the riotous joy which attended the reception of the news of Nelson's victory at the Mouth of the Nile, and the Celebration of Peace in 1815, are matters of history rather than folk-legend.[57] Hardy confessed that he invented Selby's tale that Napoleon actually

[50] *Time's Laughingstocks;* Brennecke, 40–41.
[51] Preface note to Chap. XXIII, *The Trumpet-Major:* F. E. Hardy, *The Early Life,* 21, 14.
[52] F. E. Hardy, *The Early Life,* 211–212.
[53] Part First, Act II, Scene V.
[54] *The Dynasts,* Part First, Act II, Scene V; *The Return of The Native,* Book II, Chap. VI.
[55] Chap. XXIII, and Preface Note; Sherren, 119.
[56] *Winter Words:* "The Ballad of Love's Skeleton"; *The Trumpet-Major,* Chaps. XI, XXX; Sherren, 114–115, 260–262; Hopkins, 149–150; *The Early Life . . . ,* 275; Thackeray, *George the Third.*
[57] *The Dynasts,* Part First, Act V, Scene VII; Sherren, 118; *The Dynasts,* Part Third, Act V, Scene VI; Wm. Hone's *Year Book,* William Barnes, pp. 1176–1177.

landed one night at Lulworth Cove, and he was surprised to learn that his reading public believed it founded upon a folk-tradition.[58] No such tradition existed.

Hardy was devoted to the old campaigners, paying yearly visits to Chelsea, where one year he met a delightful old fellow named Bentley.[59] Other Wessex folk brought into *The Dynasts* are Samuel Clark [60] and a Mr. Leigh,[60] not to forget Captain Hardy, in charge of Nelson's flagship, with whom the poet was proud to claim blood relationship.[61] "The Alarm" was written "In Memory of One of the Writer's Family who was a Volunteer during the War with Napoleon," and may well refer to Hardy's father's father.[62]

Of actual Napoleonic folklore, there is remarkably little. The universal hatred and terror of Bonaparte led to the burning of countless effigies; terrific cartoons were everywhere to be seen, some of which are still in existence; he was the favorite villain of dumbshows, and puppet-shows.[63] He was more than "Boney," the "Corsican Ogre"; he was feared as a new Antichrist, second only to the devil himself.[64] It was thought that he was well-nigh immortal, not to be killed as other men were. The phrase, "marrow to Boney," that is, a match for Bonaparte, is still used of one who is bad beyond redemption or who has done a particularly bad action.[65] He was held to be a most "charnel-minded villain towards womenfolk," [66] and a grisly monster, who, like the Cerne Giant of old, lived upon human flesh, having "rashers o' baby" every morning for breakfast.[67]

---

[58] F. E. Hardy, *The Later Years of Thomas Hardy,* 195.
[59] F. E. Hardy, *The Early Life . . .,* 140; *The Dynasts,* Part Third, Act VII, Scene VIII.
[60] *The Dynasts,* Part Third, Act VII, Scene V.
[61] *The Trumpet-Major,* Chap. XXXIII; F. E. Hardy, *The Early Life,* 177; F. E. Hardy, *The Later Years,* 112, 114.
[62] *Wessex Poems;* F. E. Hardy, *The Early Life,* page 14.
[63] *The Dynasts,* Part Third, Act V, Scene VI; *The Trumpet-Major,* Chap. XXV, XXVI, and Preface Note.
[64] *The Dynasts,* Part Third, Act V, Scene III; *The Trumpet-Major,* Chap. I.
[65] E. M. Wright, *Rustic Speech and Folklore,* 183.
[66] *The Dynasts,* Part Third, Act V, Scene VI.
[67] *The Dynasts,* Part First, Act II, Scene V.

One of Hardy's early outlines for *The Dynasts* involved the conception of Napoleon as haunted by a Familiar; another as a conjuror enabled by magic to read his opponents' thoughts! [68]

It is worth note, however, that except in times of the greatest panic, the even flow of rural life was not nearly so much disturbed by the tumults of war as we are prone to conceive. Foreign affairs were real—and invisible—like ogres, witches, and all the paraphernalia of magic. It is likely that the mass of the folk—ploughmen, shepherds, haycutters, pine-planters, cidermakers, and reddlemen— went about their daily tasks very much as in time of peace. The old ballads and tales were still told and sung, and the old dances danced; the waits still went their holy rounds; christenings, weddings, buryings, and randies of all sorts were a present thing. In the midst of war, despite the sharp agony of loss, there must, we think, have been moments in the life of the English folk when the great dramas that were being played out in Spain and France and Egypt seemed no more than "unhappy, far-off things." And it was perhaps largely this very devotion to habit, this dogged persistence, this capacity for laughter in tragic and disastrous days that brought Napoleon's career to a close. Certainly he feared England and the English as he feared no one else. It was in this spirit that the English relished the famous anecdote of Nelson, according to which the great admiral's body on its way home was robbed of its preservative liquor to furnish drink for the fighting crew. The first boatman tells the story:

"But what happened was this. They were a long time coming, owing to contrary winds, and the 'Victory' being little more than a wreck. And grog ran short, because they'd used near all they had to peckle his body in. So—they broached the Adm'l! . . . Well; the plain calendar of it is, that when he came to be unhooped, it was found that the crew had drunk him dry. What was the men to do? Broke down by the battle, and hardly able to keep afloat, 'twas a most

[68] F. E. Hardy, *The Early Life of Thomas Hardy,* page 266.

defendable thing, and it fairly saved their lives. So he was their salvation after death as he had been in the fight. If he could have knowed it, 'twould have pleased him down to the ground! How 'a would have laughed down the spigot-hole: 'Draw on, my hearties! Better I shrivel than you famish.' Ha-ha!" [69]

[69] *The Dynasts,* Part First, Act V, Scene VII.

XIV

HARDY'S USE OF FOLKLORE AND FOLK-CUSTOM

As a folklorist Thomas Hardy has complete mastery of his material: the highest praise has been accorded him by the London Folk-Lore Society for his accurate, vivid, unadulterated recording of Wessex folklore.[1] He is, however, so much more than the folklorist that our chief interest lies in the use he makes of this material. Hardy has been thought unduly somber and ironic. This profound melancholy and deep-seated irony, like Browning's obscurity, lies partly in the poet's temperament, and partly in the heart of his subject. Let us grant, to begin with, that Hardy, like Æschylus, had a temperamental leaning towards the use of premonitions, omens, ghosts, and prophecies. He was born and spent the impressionable years of boyhood and young manhood among a people who still thought in a primitive way, upon whose lips an ancient dialect still lived, and in whose hearts lingered the dark, inexplicable fears of prehistoric man. Hardy grew up in this atmosphere; though always above it by reason of a cultivated mother, the forces of a formal education, and a widening acquaintance with the world outside of Wessex, he was none the less a part of his own community, and gloried in the fact. Hardy's intimate knowledge of folklore and folk-custom had an almost incalculable influence upon his art. It deepened a temperament already melancholy; it profoundly affected his philosophy of life; it fed his imagination with rich and varied

[1] *Folk-Lore*, VI, 59; W. Crooke, *Folk-Lore*, XXIII, 32.

stuff; and it gave us his most precious quality—a brooding pity for all living things.

Hardy found food for curious study, for contemplation and musing upon the ultimate realities, in many folk-beliefs. It was evident to him that magic, which is only a rude and undeveloped science, sees the world from a point of view exactly opposite to that of religion; in this respect it is like legitimate science. In both magic and science the element of caprice is eliminated from the workings of natural laws; religion, on the other hand, conceives nature as variable, elastic, and subject to a conscious personal power who may be conciliated. Even when magic employs spirits, personal agents of the kind assumed by religion on a far greater scale, the believer in magic treats these agents as impersonal, inanimate, absolute forces, coercing and constraining them by setting them to work out some given effect from a fixed sequence of given causes. Magic fails, not because of its logic—which is admirable—but because it misconceives the natural laws it seeks to use, and, like all primitive science, reasons on too narrow a set of facts. Modern science, however, owes to magic the fundamental assumption that there are certain invariable and necessary sequences of cause and effect, independent of personal will or caprice. Alchemy, for instance, prepared the way for chemistry, not by its faulty methods of investigation, but by its insistence upon the possibility of chemical changes. To the truly devout, the forces that govern the world are conscious and personal, and may be invoked and conciliated so as to render at least some of the evil that all admit, innocuous to the chosen people. To the scientists—and in a much lesser way, to the *homo superstitiosus*—no supreme Will manifests itself as in control of the general scheme of things; there are only tremendous, inexplicable forces; the duality of the world and the existence of disease, hatred, and death are insoluble problems.

Hardy must have viewed the long vista of witchcraft and magic with fascination. The present writer has seemed to overhear in certain poems of Hardy the ironic suggestion that the fruition of human effort is an actual miracle and that faith is a sublime magic in a "God-forgotten world." The poet deals so constantly with the chance happening, the coincidence apparently trifling, yet in reality fraught with momentous consequences, that he seems to imply the realization of the difficulty with which the human will ever gets it own way, lost as it is in a world of vast forces, working with machine-like precision, careless of man's happiness, but with superb irony, occasionally allowing the line of natural forces to coincide with the bent of human desires. It has been said that the proud motto of the Roman Catholic Church might with more truth be applied to this underground faith in magic, this deep-seated superstition, of which few of us have rid ourselves completely: *Quod semper, quod ubique, quod ab omnibus.* Hardy's sympathy with folk deeply imbued with folklore undoubtedly profoundly affected his philosophy of life and gave him a finer tolerance.

Equally important is the consideration that much of Hardy's material owes it most distinctive quality—picturesque, dramatic, or epic—to folklore and folk-custom. His people are what they are because of their environment and ancestry. Hardy was a firm believer in the effect of climate upon character; he felt that America was a tragic country,[2] its tragedy reflected in the countenances and in the manners of American visitors to England, and he consistently refused to visit our country.[3] Most of us will admit that in *Tess* and *Jude* he has overstressed the note of tragic irony, he has made his people too completely the victims of an unjust destiny, and has violated the laws of artistic probability. This objection cannot be made to the tragic action of the great books—*The Woodlanders, The Mayor,* and *The Return of the Native.* We need to understand the little obscure things of daily life which exert so powerful an influence on character. Is not superstition one of them?

[2] Ernest Brennecke, Jr., *The Life of Thomas Hardy,* 4.
[3] *Poems of the Past and the Present:* "On an Invitation to the United States"; F. E. Hardy, *The Later Years.. . ,* 120, 134, 185–6.

These believers in charms and spells, in witchcraft and magic, in omens, premonitions, and fatality are the sort of people to whom the most commonplace happening seems fraught with hidden significance. We may expect to see them do unusual things, and to accept extraordinary events, on the other hand, as quite in the order of things. Superstition is one of the subtle, obscure things that reach the secret springs of emotion. A study of the folk-beliefs of Hardy's peasants serves to convince the reader that the tragic irony which pursues a man like Henchard or Giles Winterborne is an irony that the peasant himself would be the first to accept. It is possible to look too long at this somber side of Hardy's work, but it will not do to ignore nor deny it.

The stuff of folklore and folk-custom also enormously enlarges the narrative field, permitting the use of highly striking, yet natural, situations, and widening the epic sweep of story. This dangerous liberty Hardy uses like a master. He is seldom melodramatic; his effects, though striking, are not cheap nor easy. He carries his story along quietly enough for many chapters, then, much in the technic of Thackeray, suddenly throws a great scene, for which he has been making careful preparation, into high relief. How much must happen before Susan Nunsuch melts the ghastly image and Eustacia Vye is lost in the weir! But when the time for the scene comes, the poet does it full justice, and it stands out forever in our imaginations as does a brilliantly lighted room viewed from an outer darkness. Without the stuff of witchcraft we should not have the material for this subtle story and this somberly splendid scene. The most casual reader will admit the rôle played by superstition in Henchard's downfall; not all at once, however, does he sink, but slowly and inevitably. How much must take place before the scene of the skimmity is opened before us; yet all that happens leads up to this catastrophe with a naturalness which has been the admiration and despair of Hardy's brother novelists. Moreover, the conception of places as full of mysterious sentience, of the heath as a

great protagonist, gives *The Return of the Native* an epic
sweep that is altogether lacking in most modern fiction. The
peasant's almost fetishistic, pantheistic feeling for Nature
and inanimate things serves to intensify this atmosphere.

Hardy uses folklore in two distinct ways, each of them
founded on a long, fine literary tradition. One is the way
of Peele in *The Old Wives' Tale,* of Greene in *Friar Bacon
and Friar Bungay,* and of Shakespeare in *A Midsummer
Night's Dream;* the other is the way of Marlowe in *Dr.
Faustus* and of Shakespeare in *Macbeth.* The former is the
way of fancy, full of an incidental charm, a somewhat
decorative, scenic, and atmospheric use of folklore. The
latter goes to the heart of the matter in hand, seeks to interpret it through deep and strong imaginative insight, and
aims at nothing less than conviction. Willing suspension
of unbelief may do for fancy; it will not serve the purposes
of this higher poetry. The Senecan convention had a foundation of folklore upon which to build. The Elizabethan ghosts
were convincing to the Elizabethan audience, let us not
doubt that. In his treatment of character Hardy uses folk-
lore motifs in this deeply imaginative way; he aims at and
he secures absolute conviction. We shudder at Susan's dreadful image, but we believe her capable of it, and we half
believe that she is conspiring with Eustacia's ancient enemy,
Egdon Heath, to witch the Queen of Night to death. The
very weather seems hostile to Henchard; things go dam-
nably wrong with him, until we sympathize with his superstitious fear that some one may be mixing some evil brew or
wasting away some image to confound him. When we assist
at the Hintock maidens' love rites, we almost expect to see
their lovers come out of the misty woods.

The poet also uses folklore and folk-custom to paint
scenes of pastoral beauty; he paints canvas after canvas
of rustic gayety. Now it is a "picture of the Dutch School,"
now the many-mooded Hintock woods, now the fairs with
their characteristic sports and pastimes, now a farmhouse

kitchen overflowing with dancing folk. He paints the life of a whole countryside in every aspect; he gives us the line and color, the sounds and movement of the scene. And, best of all, he shows us the other side of the picture, shows us the vast zest these Wessex folk have for life. They are not too melancholy a folk; though they may brood and muse, and seem at times too stolid and patient, they have a deep-veined characteristic English gayety, a gusto which takes the grave with the gay. Hardy knows his province supremely well, and through it, the whole world. It is because his roots go so deep in the soil that one cannot conceive his falling into serious neglect. Manners change; human nature remains essentially unchanged. These Wessex people are people we have known, people we seek instinctively to identify with actual places, and to assign a niche in time. Like the de Stancy portraits, they seem ever about to step out of their frames as if eager to walk and talk with us. Much of their reality lies, not only in Hardy's skill in characterization, but in the vividness and naturalness of the background, in this elusive spirit of place which he has caught and preserved.

To speak of lesser matters seems almost unnecessary; yet it may be remarked in passing that much of Hardy's phraseology is borrowed directly from folklore and folkcustom. The phrase "to work like Diggory" means to work with dogged persistence; [4] the name is highly appropriate to Thomasin's devoted knight. When the poet describes Marshal Ney's horse magnificently decked in bright blue, red, and green, he instantly recalls that it was only a lingering on into modern times of the old barbaric trick to strike terror to the heart of the foe.[5] A mist across the moon, casting a weird green light upon the earth, is like a witch's incantation scene.[6] Life is a play, a harlequinade, a puppetry

[4] E. M. Wright, *Rustic Speech and Folklore,* 16.
[5] *The Dynasts,* Part Third, Act VII, Scene IV.
[6] *Human Shows:* "Once at Swanage."

in which the Showman Years unveils scene after scene.[7] A chance mishap is like an uncovered play at chess.[8] The wile-weaving daughter of high Zeus, who seemed to be punishing Pierston, the sculptor, for his sins against her in his art, is for every man the Unattainable—all things to all men, and no man's to possess. The poet says it thus:

> She, proudly, thinning in the gloom:
> "Though, since troth-plight began,
> I have ever stood as bride to groom,
> I wed no mortal man!" [9]

Hardy said of himself that he was quick to bloom, slow to ripen.[10] I know no modern poet whose heart is so ripe as Hardy's: he grew slowly, but he grew to the day of his death. There are some who may think that the stuff of folklore is essentially ugly, but from this stuff he weaves a pattern of wonderful beauty. There are some who find him unduly somber. There are some who are offended at his hard sayings—and for these there is always another poet. We have heard much of the satanic Hardy, but I confess I have been unable to find him. This man has not set his wits against the gods to cast them from their seats. There is not an iota of intellectual arrogance in him. He is on the side of the angels. Whatever he thought of the world and its systems, he loved his fellow men. He had not fiddled and danced at village randies for nothing; he had not listened to numberless good things at the inn so soon to forget them. He had not mused upon the melancholy mystery of life alone. He had heard it voiced time and again by country folk, and voiced with sweetness, patience, and the saving grace of humor. It is not the Olympian of *The Dynasts* that we honor most; it is the modest, almost shrinking man who would fain be remembered thus:

---

[7] *The Dynasts:* Forescene; Part First, Act I, Scene VI; Act V, Scene V; Part Second, Act I, Scene III; Act V, Scene VII; Act VI, Scene VIII; Part Third, Act I, Scene X; Act VI, Scene VIII; Act VII, Scene VIII; Afterscene; etc.

[8] *The Dynasts,* Part Second, Act I, Scene II.

[9] *Poems of the Past and the Present:* "The Well-Beloved."

[10] F. E. Hardy, *The Later Years of Thomas Hardy,* 178.

When the Present has latched its postern behind my tremulous stay,
   And the May month flaps its glad green leaves like wings,
Delicate-filmed as new-spun silk, will the neighbours say,
   "He was a man who used to notice such things"?

If it be in the dusk when, like an eyelid's soundless blink,
   The dewfall-hawk comes crossing the shades to alight
Upon the wind-warped upland thorn, a gazer may think,
   "To him this must have been a familiar sight."

If I pass during some nocturnal blackness, mothy and warm,
   When the hedgehog travels furtively over the lawn,
One may say, "He strove that such innocent creatures should come to
     no harm,
   But he could do little for them; and now he is gone."

If, when hearing that I have been stilled at last, they stand at the door,
   Watching the full-starred heavens that winter sees,
Will this thought rise on those who will meet my face no more,
   "He was one who had an eye for such mysteries"?

And will any say when my bell of quittance is heard in the gloom,
   And a crossing breeze cuts a pause in its outrollings,
Till they rise again, as they were a new bell's boom,
   "He hears it not now, but used to notice such things"? [11]

[11] *Moments of Vision:* "Afterwards." (By permission of The Macmillan Company.)

BIBLIOGRAPHY

Abercrombie, Lascelles, *Thomas Hardy: A Critical Study,* New York: Mitchell Kennerley, 1922.

—— Nation-Athenæum (London), Dec. 29, 1923, XXXIV, 491, Review of the *Famous Tragedy of the Queen of Cornwall at Tintagel in Lyonesse.*

Adams, Joseph Quincy, *Shakesperean Playhouses,* Boston: Houghton Mifflin Company, 1917.

Allcroft, A. Hadrian, *Earthwork of England,* Macmillan and Co., 1917.

—— *Archæological Journal,* LXXVIII, 1921, pp. 299 ff.

Antiquaries' Journal, The, vol. III, pp. 255 et seq.

Archer, William, *Real Conversations,* London: Wm. Heinemann, 1904.

Armstrong, Martin, *The Spectator* (London), Dec. 8, 1923, CXXXI, 904: Review of the *Famous Tragedy of the Queen of Cornwall.*

Aubrey, John, Antiquary, *Remaines of Gentilisme and Judaisme* (1686), ed. James Britten, F.L.S., vol. 3, 1881.

—— *Miscellanies,* London, Bohn ed.

Bantock, Granville, *One Hundred Songs of England,* Boston: Oliver Ditson, 1914.

Barnes, William, Dorset poet, *Poems of Rural Life in the Dorset Dialect,* London: Kegan Paul & Trench, 1888.

—— "Glossary of the Dorset Dialect," *Transactions of the Philological Society,* 1864.

—— Signed articles in Hone's *Year Book.*

Barrett, William Alexander, *English Folk-Songs,* London: Novello and Co., Ltd., no date.

Baskervill, Charles Read, *The Elizabethan Jig,* University of Chicago Press, 1929.

—— "Mummers' Wooing Dialogues," *Modern Philology*, XXI, 241–72.

—— *Studies in Philology*, University of North Carolina, XVII, 19–87.

Beddoe, John, *Anthropological History of England*, Paisley, England: 1912, new ed.

Bell, Elizabeth Turner, *Music for Fifty Figure and Character Dances for Schools*, London: George G. Harrap and Co., Ltd., 1921.

Bellows, Henry Adams, *The Poetic Edda*, New York, 1923; London: Oxford University Press, 1926, "American Scandinavian Series."

Billson, C. J., *Folk-Lore of Leicestershire and Rutland, County Folklore*, vol. I, London, 1895.

Black, William George, *Folk-Medicine: A Chapter in the History of Culture*, London: F.L.S., vol. 12, 1883.

Blakeborough, Richard, *Wit, Character, Folklore and Customs of the North Riding of Yorkshire . . .* London, 1898.

Bohn, Henry George, *A Handbook of Proverbs*, London, 1860, 1901; Contains Ray's collections complete, Bohn's Reference Library.

—— *A Handbook of Games*, London, 1850: Bohn's Scientific Library.

—— *A Polyglot of Foreign Proverbs*, London: Bell, 1884.

Book of English Songs from the Sixteenth to the Nineteenth Century, London: Office of the National Illustrated Library.

Brand, John, F.S.A., *Observations on the Popular Antiquities of Great Britain . . .* ed. Sir Henry Ellis, 1841, 1882–1888: London: George Bell and Sons; Reprint in Bohn's Antiquarian Library, 3 vols., 1908.   *p. 134-39*

—— "ed. with very Voluminous Corrections and Additions," W. Carew Hazlitt, London: Reeves, 1905, 2 vols. cf. *Faiths and Folklore*.

Brennecke, Ernest, Jr., *The Life of Thomas Hardy*, New York: Greenberg, 1925.

—— *Thomas Hardy's Universe: A Study of a Poet's Mind*, Boston: Small, Maynard, 1924; London: T. Fisher, Unwin, Ltd., 1923.

—— *Life and Art*, ed. miscellaneous essays of Thomas Hardy, New York: Greenberg, 1925.

Brown, Ivor, *Saturday Review* (London), CXXXVI, 613–614; Reviews of the *Queen of Cornwall* and *O Jan! O Jan! O Jan!*

Browne, Sir Thomas, Complete Works of, London: Pickering, 1838: *Pseudodoxia Epidemica, or, Vulgar Errors*
Religio Medici
Urn Burial

Burchenal, Elizabeth, *American Country-Dances,* G. Schirmer, 1918, 2 vols.

Burton, Robert, *The Anatomy of Melancholy,* London: Bell, 1893.

Campbell, J. G., *Superstitions of the Highlands and Islands of Scotland,* Glasgow, 1900.
—— *Witchcraft and Second Sight in the Highlands and Islands of Scotland,* Glasgow, 1902.

Chambers, E. K., *The Mediæval Stage,* 2 vols., Oxford: Clarendon Press.

Chappell, Wm. and Wooldridge, K. E., *Old English Popular Music,* London: Chappell, 1893, 2 vols.

Chew, Samuel C., *Thomas Hardy, Poet and Novelist,* New York: Alfred A. Knopf, 1928.
—— *New Republic,* Feb. 27, 1924, XXXVIII, 23–24: Review of the *Queen of Cornwall.*

Child, Francis James, *The English and Scottish Popular Ballads,* Boston: Houghton Mifflin, 1888–1898, 5 vols., 10 parts. The 1904 Sargent-Kittredge ed., 8 vols., is best.

Clodd, Edward, *Magic in Names,* London: Chapman, 1920.

Cockayne, Rev. Oswald, *Leechdoms, Wortcunnings, and Starcraft of Early England,* 2 vols., London: Longmans, 1864–65: in *Chronicles and Memorials of Great Britain and Ireland,* v. 35.

Crawford, O. G. S., *The Long Barrows of the Cotswolds,* Gloucester, 1925.

Dalyell, John Graham, *The Darker Superstitions of Scotland,* Glasgow: Griffin, 1835.

Davis, F. Hadland, *Drama,* August and September, 1923, XIII, 359–60: "The Hardy Players."

De Lee, Joseph B., M.D., *Hygiene of Pregnancy,* Saunders Co., Section IV, Chap. XV, 238, 241–45: "Prenatal Care."

Denham, N. A., *Denham Tracts,* ed. Dr. James Hardy, F.L.S., vols. 29, 35, 1892, 1895, London.

Dennys, N. B., *The Folk-Lore of China,* London: Truebner, 1876.

Ditchfield, P. H., Rev., *Old English Customs Extant at the Present Time,* London: Methuen, 1901.

Dyer, T. F. T., *The Folk-Lore of Plants,* New York: Appleton, 1889.

Eckenstein, Lina B., *Comparative Studies in Nursery Rhymes,* London: Duckworth and Co., 1906.

Ellis, Havelock, *Studies in the Psychology of Sex,* 5th ed. 6 vols., Philadelphia: F. A. Davis Company, 1923.

Fogel, Edwin M., *Beliefs and Superstitions of the Pennsylvania Germans,* Philadelphia: America Germanica Press, 1915, No. 18, America Germanica Monograph Series.

Folk-Lore Society (London) *Publications:* 88 vols., 1878–
    Folk-Lore Record, London: 1878–1882, continuing the Archæological Review.
    Folk-Lore Journal, London: 1883–1889.
    Folk-Lore, 1890   , including *County Folk-Lore,* 5 vols.

Frazer, Sir James, *The Golden Bough,* abridged in one volume, New York: The Macmillan Company, 1922.

Freud, Sigmund, *The Interpretation of Dreams,* 3rd ed. Authorized English translation with introduction by A. A. Brill, London: Allen, 1919.

Frost, Thomas, *The Old Showmen and the London Fairs,* London: Chatto and Windus, 1881.

Garrod, D. A. E., *The Upper Palæolithic Age in Britain,* Oxford: The Clarendon Press.

Gomme, Alice B., Mrs., *The Traditional Games of England, Scotland, and Ireland,* London: Nutt, 1894, vol. I; 1898, vol. II.

Gomme, Sir Laurence, *Ethnology in Folklore,* London: Kegan Paul, Trench, Truebner, and Co., 1892.

—— *Folklore as a Historical Science,* London: Methuen, 1908.

—— *The Village Community,* London: 1890; New York: Scribners', 1890.

Gould, Rev. Sabine Baring-, *Curiosities of Olden Times,* Edinburgh: Grant, 1896.

—— *Curious Myths of the Middle Ages,* London: Rivington's, 1873.

—— *Strange Survivals,* London: Methuen, 1892.

Gregor, Rev. Walter, *Notes on the Folk-Lore of the North-East of Scotland,* London: F.L.S., vol. 7.

Grimm, Jacob, *Deutsche Mythologie,* vierte Ausgabe, trans. James Steven Stallybrass: London: Swan, Sonnenschein, and Allen, 1880–1888.

Grimshaw, Arthur E., *Old English Tunes, Ballad Tunes, and Dances of the Sixteenth and Seventeenth Centuries,* Breitkopf & Härtel.

Gurdon, Lady Camilla, *The Folk-Lore of Suffolk,* County Folk-Lore, vol. I, F.L.S., vol. 37.

Gutch, Mrs. E., *Folk-Lore of the North Riding of Yorkshire,* County Folk-Lore, vol. II, F.L.S., vol. 45.

Halliday, William R., *Greek and Roman Folklore,* New York: Longmans, Green, 1927.

Hardy, Florence Emily, *The Early Life of Thomas Hardy,* London and New York: Macmillan, 1928.

—— *The Later Years of Thomas Hardy,* London, 1929; New York, 1930, Macmillan.

Hardy, Thomas:

Works, *Wessex Edition,* 21 volumes, Macmillan. Complete.

American Edition of Novels and Tales, New York: Harper and Brothers, 1912–1913.

Order of Novels and Tales by publication date:

Desperate Remedies, 1871.

Under the Greenwood Tree, 1872.

A Pair of Blue Eyes, 1873.

Far from the Madding Crowd, 1874.

The Hand of Ethelberta, 1875–1876.

The Return of the Native, 1878.

The Trumpet-Major, 1880.

A Laodicean, 1880–1881.

Two on a Tower, 1882.

The Mayor of Casterbridge, 1886.

The Woodlanders, 1887.

Wessex Tales, 1888.

A Group of Noble Dames, 1891.

Tess of the d'Urbervilles, 1891.

Life's Little Ironies, 1894.

Jude the Obscure, 1896.

The Well-Beloved, 1897.

A Changed Man, and Other Stories, 1913.

Quotations in the text are from the edition of Harper and Brothers by their generous permission.

Order of Poetical Works by publication date:

Wessex Poems, 1898.

Poems of the Past and the Present, 1901.

The Dynasts, Three Parts, 1903–1908.

Time's Laughingstocks, 1909.

Satires of Circumstance, 1914.

Moments of Vision, 1917.

Collected Poems, including with slight revisions all previous works except *The Dynasts,* 1919.

Late Lyrics, and Earlier, 1922.

The Famous Tragedy of the Queen of Cornwall in Lyonesse, 1923.

Human Shows, Far Phantasies, 1925.

Winter Words, 1928.

Quotations in text of thesis are from the *Collected Poems* (1925), *The Queen of Cornwall,* and *The Dynasts,* by permission of The Macmillan Company.

For bibliography of Thomas Hardy, see John Lane's Bibliography of First Editions, in Lionel Johnson's *Art of Thomas Hardy,* Dodd, Mead & Co., revised ed. 1925, 1928. Also see Arundell Esdaile's *Short Bibliography of Thomas Hardy's Principal Works,* in Harold Child's *Thomas Hardy,* Holt, 1916.

Harland, John and Wilkinson, T. T., *Lancashire Folk-Lore,* London: Frederick Warne and Company, 1867.

Harris, J. Rendel, *The Ascent of Olympus,* Manchester: University Press, 1917; Longmans.

—— *Boanerges,*

—— *Picus Who is Also Zeus,* Cambridge: The University Press, 1916; New York: G. P. Putnam's Sons.

Hartland, Dr. Edwin Sidney, *Folklore of Gloucestershire, County Folk-Lore,* vol. I, F.L.S., vol. 37.

—— *Ritual and Belief,* London: Williams, 1914.

—— *The Science of Fairy Tales: An Inquiry into Fairy Mythology,* London, 1891; New York, Scribners', 1891.

Hazlitt, W. Carew, *Faiths and Folklore,* new ed. of Brand's *Popular Antiquities,* London: Reeves, 1905.

Henderson, William, *Notes on the Folk-Lore of the Northern Counties of England and the Border,* London: F.L.S., vol. 2, 1878.
Hone, William, *Every-Day Book and Table Book,* 3 vols., London: Tegg, 1838.
—— *Year Book,* London: Tegg, 1839.
—— ed. J. Strutt's *Sports and Pastimes of the British People,* London: Tegg, 1831.
Hopkins, R. Thurston, *Thomas Hardy's Dorset,* London: C. Palmer, 1922; New York: Appleton, 1922.
Howard, George Elliott, *The History of Matrimonial Institutions,* Chicago: The University of Chicago Press, 1904, 3 vols.
Hull, Eleanor, *The Cuchullin Saga,* London: David Nutt, 1898.
Hyde, Dr. Douglas, *The Literary History of Ireland,* London, 1899.

Inwards, Richard, *Weather Lore,* London: Stock, 1893.

Johnson, Lionel, *The Art of Thomas Hardy:* London: Elkin Matthews and John Lane, 1894; Dodd, Mead & Co., new ed., 1923; revised and reprinted, 1928. Appendix contains exhaustive bibliography of first editions of Hardy's works (1865–1922) by John Lane.
Journal of American Folklore, The, Boston: 1888–
Jubainville, H. d'Arbois, *L'Épopée celtique en Irlande,* Paris, A. Fontemoing, 1883–1902 (12 vols.) vol. V.

Keightley, Thomas, *The Fairy Mythology:* London: Bohn's Antiquarian Library, 1900.
Kelly, Walter Keating, *Proverbs of All Nations,* London: Kent, 1870.
Kendrick, T. D., *The Axe Age: A Study in Keltic Prehistory,* London: Methuen, 1927.
Kidson, Frank, and Neal, Mary, *English Folk-Song and Dance,* Cambridge University Press, 1915.
—— and Martin Shaw, *Songs of Britain,* London and New York: Boosey, 1913.

Lane, John, "Bibliography of First Editions of Thomas Hardy," in Lionel Johnson's *Art of Thomas Hardy,* 1928 reprint, rev. ed.
Lawson, J. C., *Modern Greek Folklore and Ancient Greek Religion,* Cambridge University Press, 1910.
Lea, Hermann, *A Handbook of the Wessex Country of Mr. Hardy's*

Novels and Poems, London: Kegan Paul, Trench, Truebner, and Co., 1906.

—— *Thomas Hardy's Wessex,* London: Macmillan, 1913.

Lean, Vincent Stuckey, *Collectanea: Collections of Proverbs, Folk-Lore, and Superstitions, also Compilations towards Dictionaries of Proverbial Phrases and Words Old and Disused,* Bristol, Eng.: Arrowsmith, 1902–1904, 4 vols., 5 parts.

MacAfee, Helen, *Yale Review,* New Series, Jan., 1925, XIV, 385 ff: Review of *The Queen of Cornwall.*

Mackenzie, Donald A., *Ancient Man in Britain,* Blackie and Son, Ltd., 1923.

Mackenzie, W. Roy, *The Quest of the Ballad,* Princeton: Princeton University Press, 1919.

Marvin, Dwight E., *Curiosities in Proverbs,* New York: Knicker-bocker Press, 1916.

Modern Philology, Chicago, 1903—

Murray, M. A., *The Witch Cult in Western Europe,* Oxford: The Clarendon Press, 1921. '

Napier, James, *Folk-Lore: or Superstitious Beliefs in the West of Scotland within this Century,* Paisley, 1879.

Nares, Robert, *Glossary of Words, Phrases, and Allusions,* London: Routledge, 1905, new ed. by J. O. Halliwell and Thomas Wright.

Northall, G. F., *Folk-Phrases of Four Counties,* Eng. Dialect Soc., vol. 73, 1894.

Oxford Song Book, The, ed. Percy Buck and Thomas Wood, 1916–1927.

Page, William, F.S.A., *The History of Dorset,* London: Constable, Ltd., 1908, 2 vols., vols. X and XI, *The Victoria History of the Counties of England.*

Payne, Joseph Frank, M.D., *English Medicine in Anglo-Saxon Times,* Oxford: The Clarendon Press, 1904.

Peacock, Mabel, *Folk-Lore of Lincolnshire, County Folk-Lore,* vol. V, F.L.S., vol. 63.

Pettigrew, Thomas J., F.R.S., F.S.A., *On Superstitions connected with the History and Practice of Medicine and Surgery,* London: Churchill, 1844.

Pike, Luke Owen, *The History of Crime in England,* London: Smith, Elder, and Co., 1876, 2 vols.

Pittard, Eugéne, *Race and History,* trans. V. V. C. Collum, New York: Alfred A. Knopf, 1926, *History of Civilization* Series.

Playford, John, *An Introduction to the Skill of Musick, London, Printed by J. Godbid for J. Playford at his Shop in the Temple near the Church, 1672.*

—— *The Musical Companion, in Two Books* . . . , *printed by W. Godbid, 1673.*

Poland, Henry Bodkin, "Changes in Criminal Law and Procedure," in *A Century of Law Reform,* London and New York: Macmillan, 1901.

Pollock, Sir Frederick, and Maitland, Frederic William, *The History of English Law,* Cambridge University Press, 1895, 2 vols.

Powell, F. York, ed., Saxo-Grammaticus, *Danish History,* London, 1894.

Puckett, N. M., *Folk-Beliefs of the Southern Negro,* Chapel Hill: University of North Carolina Press, 1925.

Ray, F., *Collection of Proverbs,* Cambridge: Hayes, 1678.

Richards, John Morgan, *A Chronology of Medicine, Ancient, Medieval, and Modern,* London: Ballière, 1880.

Schofield, W. H., *English Literature from the Norman Conquest to Chaucer,* New York: Macmillan, 1925.

Sharp, Cecil J., *English Folk-Song: Some Conclusions:* London: Novello and Co., Ltd., 1907.

—— *English Folk-Songs from the Southern Appalachians,* New York: Putnam, 1917.

—— *Folk-Songs of England,* London: Novello, no date, 5 vols.

—— *Folk-Songs from Somerset,* London: Simpkin, 1910.

—— *The Morris Book,* London: Novello, 1909–1912, 3 vols.

—— *One Hundred English Folk-Songs,* Boston: Oliver Ditson, c. 1916, Musicians' Library.

—— *Sword Dances of Northern England,* London: Novello, 1913.

Sherren, Wilkinson, *The Wessex of Romance,* new ed., London: Griffiths, 1908.

Squire, J. C., *London Times Supplement,* Nov. 15, 1923: Review of *The Queen of Cornwall,* "Tristram and the Mummers."

——— *London Mercury,* Dec., 1923, IX, 202–203: *The Queen of Cornwall.*

——— *Saturday Review* (London), CXXXVI, 704–705, Dec., 1923: Review of *The Queen of Cornwall.*

Stone, E. Herbert, F.S.A., *The Stones of Stonehenge,* London: Robert Scott, 1924.

Strutt, Joseph, *Sports and Pastimes of the People of England,* ed. William Hone, London: Tegg, 1831.

Swainson, Rev. Charles, *Folk-Lore and Provincial Names of British Birds,* London: F.L.S., vol. 17, 1886.

Thomas, Northcote, *Folk-Lore of Northumberland, County Folk-Lore,* vol. IV, F.L.S., vol. 53.

Tiddy, Reginald J. E., *The Mummers' Play,* Oxford: The Clarendon Press, 1923.

Timbs, John, F.S.A., *The Romance of London,* London: F. Warne, Ltd., no date.

Tylor, Edward B., *Primitive Culture,* 4th ed., London, 1903, 2 vols.

Victoria History of the Counties of England, London: Archibald Constable and Co., Ltd., 1908.

Waddell, Laurence A., *The Phœnician Origin of Britons, Scots, and Anglo-Saxons,* London: Williams and Norgate, Ltd., 1924.

Walpole, Sir Spencer, *History of England from the Conclusion of the War of 1815,* 2nd ed., London: Longmans, 1879–1886.

Walsh, James J., *Mediæval Medicine,* London: Black, 1920.

Wilson, Thomas, Teacher of Dancing, *The Complete System of English Country Dances,* London: Sherwood, Needy, and Jones, 1815.

Wimberly, Charles Lowry, *Folklore in the English and Scottish Ballads,* Chicago: University of Chicago Press, 1928.

Windle, Bertram C., *Remains of the Prehistoric Age in Britain,* London: Methuen, 1904.

——— *Life in Early Britain,* London: Nutt, 1897; New York: Putnam, 1897.

——— *The Romans in Britain,* London: Methuen, 1923.

Wright, Elizabeth Mary, *Rustic Speech and Folklore,* Oxford University Press, 1913.

Wright, Joseph, *English Dialect Dictionary,* London: Henry Frowde, 1905; New York: Putnam's, 1905, 6 vols.

—— *Dictionary of Obsolete and Provincial English,* London: Bohn, 1857, 2nd ed., 2 vols.

Wright, Thomas, *Essays on Subjects connected with Literature, Popular Superstitions, and History of England in the Middle Ages,* London: John Russell Smith, 1848.

INDEX